COO

Cooking for Regeneration

Macrobiotic Relief from Cancer, AIDS, and Degenerative Disease

By Cecile Tovah Levin

Japan Publications, Inc.

Cover design—A stylized lotus: root rising up out of the mud and murky waters, blossoming into the Golden Lotus of Enlightenment, radiating the Light of endless blessings. This symbolizes the regeneration of man out of the depths of degeneration, chaos and misery, and into the realm of paradise, characterized by health, love, harmony, and peace.

Note to the reader: The purpose of this book is for reorientation and education of the reader toward the natural way of life according to the laws of nature. It is not meant to be a substitute for medical advice. If you are suffering from illness, it is suggested that you seek the guidance of a reputable physician and qualified macrobiotic counselor before implementing the approach to health presented in this book.

Published by JAPAN PUBLICATIONS, INC., Tokyo and New York

Distributors:
UNITED STATES: *Kodansha International/USA, Ltd., through Harper & Row, Publishers, Inc., 599 Lexington Avenue, Suite 2300, New York, N. Y. 10022.* SOUTH AMERICA: *Harper & Row, Publishers, Inc., International Department.* CANADA: *Fitzhenry & Whiteside Ltd., 195 Allstate Parkway, Markham, Ontario, L3R 4T8.* MEXICO AND CENTRAL AMERICA: *HARLA S. A. de C. V., Apartado 30–546, Mexico 4, D. F.* BRITISH ISLES: *Premier Book Marketing Ltd., 1 Gower Street, London WC1E 6HA.* EUROPEAN CONTINENT: *European Book Service PBD, Strijkviertel 63, 3454 PK De Meern, The Netherlands.* AUSTRALIA AND NEW ZEALAND: *Book Wise International, 1 Jeanes Street, Beverley, South Australia 5007.* THE FAR EAST AND JAPAN: *Japan Publications Trading Co., Ltd., 1–2–1, Sarugaku-cho, Chiyoda-ku, Tokyo 101.*

First edition: December 1988

LCCC No. 87–80496
ISBN 0–87040–692–2

Printed in U.S.A.

Dedication

To George and Lima Ohsawa
and to all those who can grasp
the depth of their spirit and message;

To all my teachers, especially
Michio and Aveline Kushi, Hideo Omori,
Noboru Muramoto, Herman and Cornellia Aihara
and others who have shared their wisdom
and shown me the Way over the years;

To all my brothers and sisters, past, present, and future,
Who are seeking true happiness, enlightenment and liberation;

To my beloved Mother and Father, may they rest in peace,
Who showed me the way to go
and the way not to go—

And to my children, Hana and Asa,
Who are full of love,

I am infinitely grateful.

Acknowledgments

This book could not have come into being were it not for the inspiration and brilliant teachings of George and Lima Ohsawa and their disciples: Michio and Aveline Kushi, Hideo Omori, Noboru Muramoto, Herman and Cornellia Aihara and others who have led the way for me. My heartfelt gratitude to them is endless.

For the physical preparation of the manuscript, I am indebted to Alice Burnett, Genevieve Genin and Hillary Teixeira for typing with devotion and love.

I offer sincere thanks to Elaine Gyorke, Mary Cordaro and Scott Jones for their sensitive and astute editing and encouragement.

My thanks to the photographer, Lois Frank, whose pictures of the food added life to the book.

And for their fine work in publishing Macrobiotic literature, together with their patience and faith in me to complete this book, I am indebted and grateful to Iwao Yoshizaki and Yoshiro Fujiwara of Japan Publications, Inc.

Illustrations are by the author.

Spring

Summer

Autumn

Winter

Foreword

Since mankind began to appear on this planet two major biological revolutions have taken place: (1) the cultivation of grains and agricultural products, especially cereal grains, and (2) the discovery and utilization of fire in the preparation of food.

The first revolution realized humanity as the most developed species on the planet, with vertical spinal column and expanded consciousness. The second revolution secured for the human species the freedom of managing its destiny by changing its physical, mental, psychological, and spiritual qualities.

All issues relating to humanity, such as civilized and primitive mentality, health and sickness, prosperity and poverty, peace and war, arise as symptoms stemming from a biological cause: food and its preparation.

In this century we are experiencing extensive degeneration prevailing upon the earth: physical, psychological, and spiritual. We are also experiencing chaos, confusion, and disorder in daily living, in spite of the developed technologies of modern, material civilization.

This degeneration is now leading the destiny of the modern species toward possible extinction. The survival of the human race on this planet is the most serious problem confronting us today.

The solution to this global issue exists only through the recovery of proper quality of food and the management of proper cooking.

The human race is a social and intellectual species. Its fundamental status is biological, psychological, and spiritual. This foundation of humanity can be secured and developed by proper food and proper cooking.

In the name of the Macrobiotic natural-food movement, international education has been conducted for over half a century. Ways of eating practiced by traditional cultures have been rediscovered, namely, the use of whole grains, beans and legumes, fresh vegetables prepared in various ways, sea vegetables, fish and seafood, and seasonal fruits. The use of organic, natural-quality food, natural pure water, sea salt, and non-stimulant beverages has been emphasized.

Millions of people have gained their health, well-being, and peace of mind through daily practice of macrobiotic dietary patterns and cooking techniques.

Teachings and publications have been presented in many countries.

Macrobiotic way of life suggestions include:

- Live together with the natural order of the changing environment, seasons, and climate.
- Respect parental and ancestral biological, cultural, and spiritual traditions.
- Love and care for children, offspring, and younger generations.
- Treat every person as your brother and sister.
- Contribute to the development of one healthy, peaceful world.

Lifestyle

1. Shift to a more orderly lifestyle from chaotic living.
2. Maintain an orderly environment avoiding disorderly, dark, and depressing surroundings.
3. Engage in active exercise and maintain energetic daily living.

4. Regulate sexual behavior avoiding multiple partners.
5. Cultivate more positive, ambitious wishes toward life.
6. Be grateful to parents, ancestors, people, society, nature, and the universe.
7. Develop the spirit of mutual assistance to brotherhood and sisterhood to extend to society at large.

The macrobiotic way of eating includes the following guidelines:

General Dietary and Way of Life Recommendations

1. Increase the consumption of complex carbohydrates and reduce the intake of simple sugars.
2. Increase the intake of high-fiber foods and reduce those with no fiber.
3. Emphasize unsaturated fat and decrease saturated fats.
4. Change from refined salt to more traditionally processed salt which contains trace minerals.
5. Emphasize natural vitamins and minerals, those contained within foods, and reduce artificial vitamins and enzymes in supplemental form unless they are required temporarily.
6. Increase the consumption of natural, organically cultivated foods and reduce heavily chemicalized items.
7. Increase whole, unrefined foods and reduce heavily artificialized foods.
8. Increase vegetable-quality protein and reduce animal-quality protein.
9. Shift to more nutritionally balanced food from unbalanced food.
10. Shift to more economically affordable food from uneconomical and expensive foods.
11. Shift to more energy-saving food from food requiring a larger investment of energy, comparing the energy output from the food.
12. Shift to food more naturally processed from food artificially produced for commercial purposes.
13. Select food prepared and cooked using more traditional methods rather than fast foods prepared for quick turnover.

Daily Practice

1. Approximately 50 percent of the volume of food consumed daily is to be whole cereal grains such as brown rice, barley, millet, whole wheat, whole oats, corn, buckwheat, rye, and cereal-grain products including sourdough bread, pasta, whole wheat noodles and others.
2. Approximately 5 to 10 percent of the volume of food consumed daily is to be soup consisting of a variety of vegetables, sea vegetables, grains, beans, and occasionally fish.
3. Approximately 20 to 30 percent of the volume of food consumed daily is to be vegetables prepared using various cooking styles, such as steaming, boiling, sautéing, frying, pickling and, occasionally, raw salad.
4. Approximately 5 to 10 percent of the volume of daily food consumed is to be beans of various kinds and bean products as well as sea vegetables prepared using various cooking methods.

5. Occasional consumption of fish and seafood, mainly less fatty kinds and those containing less cholesterol.
6. Occasional consumption of seasonal fruits—raw, dried, and cooked.
7. Occasional consumption of a small amount of roasted nuts and seeds.
8. Daily consumption of a small volume of condiments and traditionally prepared seasonings.
9. Daily consumption of an adequate amount of non-stimulating beverages.

Preparation and Eating

1. The processing, preparation, and cooking techniques of foods are to be traditional methods avoiding application of microwaves and irradiation.
2. Chewing very well is essential; preferably more than fifty times per mouthful is recommended.
3. The use of variety in terms of selection of grains, beans, vegetables, sea vegetables, and other food substances is recommended.
4. Refrain from overeating and eating before sleeping.

Cecile Tovah Levin, the author of *Cooking for Regeneration*, has presented macrobiotic philosophies, views, lifestyles, and the art of cooking through this book. For over twenty-eight years she has studied macrobiotic philosophy and culture in the United States, Japan, and other parts of the world. She has experienced various lifestyles and developed deep insights into human life. She has developed her art of cooking with many excellent and unique women, namely Mme. Lima Ohsawa, by whom she is certified in cooking for healing and spiritual development; Mme. Michi Ogawa, long-time personal secretary to George Ohsawa and reknowned cooking teacher in Japan; Mme. Kazue Omori, wife of Hideo Omori, the great macrobiotic teacher and healer in Japan; Mme. Darbin Yamaguchi, highly respected macrobiotic cooking teacher in Japan; Aveline Kushi, world-reknowned macrobiotic cooking teacher; Cornellia Aihara, famous cooking teacher in the United States, and others. Over the years, she has been inspiring, teaching, and guiding thousands of people to help them achieve their health, well-being, mental, and spiritual development.

What makes this book unique is not only the complete menus, beautifully and tastefully arranged, but also the thoughtful guidance in food preparation according to the seasons, climatic conditions, environmental differences, and personal needs.

This unique presentation is appropriate for everyone who wishes to develop physical, psychological, and spiritual well-being. With the help of this book, I hope all people, brothers and sisters who are sharing this planet at this time, may develop health and happiness as well as freedom from sickness, crime, and social chaos. Let us work together toward the achievement of one, healthy, peaceful world.

Michio Kushi
Brookline, Massachusetts
January 1988

Preface

When the degeneration of the human race reaches the epidemic proportions that it has reached today in the twentieth century, it would seem obvious that the path we have chosen as a species, as a nation, and as individuals must be questioned and thoroughly investigated. If we are really honest with ourselves we will see that the basic cause of all our illnesses and misfortunes lies within us, within our ignorance and lack of respect for the laws of life. Our difficulties are only reflections of the pursuit of illusions, motivated by disorderly and self-centered desires. They are not due to the attack of enemies from the outside, whether political or viral, as much as to our own unclear thinking and unbalanced blood quality.

Cancer and AIDS are the epitome of degenerative disease. They are also the turning point upon which people can change the direction of their lives. The tragedy and glory of cancer, AIDS, and other physical and emotional illnesses are not only the sorrow of the deterioration and unhappiness of the human species, but also the awakening of mankind to the transgression of his ways and the conscious search for Truth.

All created things are a reflection of Heaven's energy in material form. During the course of its existence, the essence of each thing returns, more or less, back to Heaven through its expression and activity, culminating in its dematerialization and transformation.

Human beings represent the ultimate creation in the centripetal spiral of transmutation and evolution of Heaven's force. As human beings, we have the capacity to experience the highest levels of consciousness and cognizance of this movement. We are conscious catalysts in the materialization of Heaven's energy into Earth and its subsequent transformation back into the primordial spiritual energy. Through us the cycle is complete.

It is essential to understand that food is a synthesis of the forces of Heaven and Earth. The quality of the food we eat determines the coarseness or refinement of our body, mind, and consciousness. Through the right selection and preparation of our daily food, we develop a heightened awareness of, and refined sensitivity to, the origin of all life and of our relationship to it. We can then see that, because the primordial energy permeates everything, the fruits of the vegetable kingdom are transmuted through us as the fruits of our labor and creative expressions. Thus, if we are constipated or stagnated, physically or mentally, Heaven's energy is also constipated and stagnated. As a result, "as above so below" will take place and God's Will will not be manifest on Earth. Therefore, until we change our destructive patterns, we will continue to see and experience only the egocentric deviations of man's will.

Once we understand our relationship with nature and the universe, our true custodianship of the earth will begin, as our ancestors exemplified, and all species, as well as nature herself, will be revived and resurrected in all their glory. Only then will true peace reign upon the earth.

Once we understand the way of healing cancer and AIDS through the power of our daily food, the pattern of the way of healing all other diseases will fall into place.

Changing the eating habits of the world, of a nation, even of a family is a process of gradual evolution. It is also a process of great joy, since it is a method of uplifting the whole human condition out of the lower levels of consciousness. It is necessary to grow out of the pattern of destruction of oneself, of others, and of the environment, all of which is motivated by the glorification and edification of the ego, and into a level of consciousness which preserves life, out of respect for, and gratitude toward, the universal powers which created us. It is through the processes of purification of the body and mind that we can finally begin to directly and tangibly experience our oneness with those universal creative powers which we call God. In this way, we can begin to realize our innate Godliness and, through this realization, create the harmony and peace for which the whole world longs and yearns.

It is the purpose of this book to present a practical guide to the self-healing of cancer, AIDS, and other degenerative diseases, as well as a way of maintaining health for daily life and self-purification, leading to a peaceful and happy world. The macrobiotic way of life, which includes, but is not limited to, the way of eating, provides a sound foundation for all those practices engaged in the "upliftment" of mankind and the establishment of world peace through world health.

The book is divided into four seasons, showing the continuous change of energy month by month. Although it was written in Southern California, modifications are indicated for adaptations to other climates. Rather than offering only recipes, complete menus are presented to show the way of creating well-balanced meals, as well as variety from day to day, changing with the season as the seasonal energies change around us. For those who cannot come for personal study, it will benefit not only the beginning students who are involved with healing their own illnesses, but will also strengthen the practice of long-time practitioners and those who are cooking for others. However, a book is never a complete substitute for direct experience with a teacher. For a well-rounded education, one should study with many teachers.

The foods presented, and their way of preparation, are for the purpose of cleansing, strengthening, and balancing. The dishes are uncomplicated, with a clear indication within themselves of the direction and quality of energy they are meant to contribute to the balance of the meal and to the needs of the individual. They are presented with an air of simple elegance, so as to stimulate the aesthetic senses as well as the appetite.

Many friends have expressed the need for a book of menus showing the way to create complete meals which are balanced within themselves and harmonious with the changing seasons and cycles of life, whether from summer to winter, morning to evening, or childhood to old age (sagehood). I sincerely hope that this book fulfills that need. The menus and recipes should be read as a study in the dynamic balance of Yin and Yang.

The menus are further supported by essays on the meaning of macrobiotics, the Five Transformations, inspirational sayings, and nutritional charts substantiating the wholeness of the macrobiotic way of eating.

All the information presented here is based on more than twenty-five years of study and practice, both in the West and in the Orient, with particular emphasis on the teachings of George and Lima Ohsawa, Michio and Aveline Kushi, Hideo Omori, Herman Aihara, and Noboru Muramoto. It is recommended that *Cooking for Regeneration* be used in conjunction with the various and brilliant books written in English by the above teachers/authors, with the exception of Hideo Omori, whose writings have not yet been translated.

I hope you enjoy the menus presented here with the spirit of joy in regeneration in which they are given.

Contents

List of Tables and Diagrams

Introduction

Food is Spirit. It has come to us through the divine intercourse of Heaven and Earth. The infinite and eternal cosmic vibrations of Light-Fire have coalesced and crystallized to form the air, water, earth, plants, all creatures and us—they are the very heart and soul of us. And we radiate this Light back into the cosmos in our laughter and song and dancing eyes, in our inspiration and creativity.

We are permeated by the food of Light, vibrations, air, and water. We are nourished by the food of plants. We are sustained by the food of love, by the endless love of our Heavenly Father and Earthly Mother. We are inspired by the interpretation of that love through music, art, and the beauty of nature.

When we take this food into ourselves, let us first consider whether or not we are worthy of it. Let us then receive it in gratitude and offer it back to the Spirit from whence it came. In receiving and returning this offering of food, let us be certain that it is worthy of us, that it is pure and carrying the life-force it is meant to carry. Let us consider whether the food we eat is worthy of the Great Spirit of the Universe and of the same Great Spirit, or God, which we carry within.

Food is Life. Life is Food. That which does not sustain life, health, integrity, joy, and peace is not the best food for mankind.

Since food creates us, food can also heal us. Right food creates healing and balance; wrong food creates degeneration and decay. Wrong food can destroy us. It can destroy our lives. Wrong food can destroy mankind through biological degeneration. We are now in a time of devastating and catastrophic biological degeneration. Now is the greatest opportunity to recover the Way of Life and to rediscover the Way of the Spirit according to the infinite and eternal natural Order of the Universe.

George Ohsawa said, "If you are not happy it is your own fault."* If we think we have sinned, it is only to the degree that we have made ourselves, or others, sick and unhappy. Sin means separation from God. Separation from God is the true cause of sickness and loneliness. In practical daily life, separation from God means separation from the way of life according to the order of the universe, not following the laws of nature, not flowing with the seasons, transgressing the harmony of Heaven and Earth.

We do not need to look upon illness, or any degenerative disease, as an enemy entering from the outside to victimize us. It is simply the natural way of the body to adjust itself to circumstances in order to maintain life as much, and as long as possible. We should see any difficulty as a gift of learning and use it to reorient our way of thinking from ignorance to an awakened consciousness of the laws of nature and the way of life. Our self-healing is the pivotal point upon which our mental and spiritual growth turns. It is the vortex on which we can change our whole life from ignorance and suffering toward understanding, happiness, and peace.

That which distinguishes the macrobiotic way of life and approach to healing from all other approaches is its foundation upon the principles of yin and yang, the bipolar forces of energy in the universe which result in the manifestation and move-

* From the teaching of Epictetus.

ment of all phenomena. It can be said that yin and yang are the two hands of God, the Alpha and Omega, the creative and receptive, masculine and feminine elements which permeate and govern all life.

The specific application of these principles to food forms a fundamental base from which all other activities spring, since our very perceptions of the universe, our environment, ourselves, and our purpose in life are influenced by our food.

With an understanding of the yin and yang energies in our daily food, we can more consciously prepare those foods with more control over their affect on us. In this way, we become the masters of our human quality, our evolution, and our destiny.

Part 1

Macrobiotics — Universal Order in Everyday Life

The Principles of Macrobiotics

Albert Einstein came close to discovering the blueprint of the universe when he wrote: "One might arrive ultimately at the concept of a self-perpetuating pulsating universe, renewing its cycles of formation and dissolution, light and darkness, order and disorder, heat and cold, expansion and contraction, through never-ending eons of time."[1]

We find similarities to this description throughout the philosophical teachings and writings of the East, in the *Rig-Veda*, the *Upanishads*, the *I-Ching*, and other classical tomes, as well as among the teachings and writings of sages and scholars East and West since antiquity. Throughout the ages, three-quarters of the peoples of the world have seen life as cyclical. The linear view of life is as short-sighted as the old concept in the West that the Earth was flat.

The earth is indeed round and the cycle of life is spiralic, just as the solar system portrays. This same pattern is seen in every atom, with its proton at the center, as the sun, and the electrons arranged spiralically around it, as the planets.

It is the very movement of this spiral, condensing and expanding, between materialization and pure undifferentiated energy, that is the pulsation of the universe, the dance of life, the inhalation and exhalation of God. It is the very breath that enlivens us and the spark that vitalizes every creature.

All primitive and traditional people have known this force and depicted it in their sacred art as well as in their everyday decorative crafts, in architectural design, paintings, pottery, weavings, clothing and jewelry.

The spiral of life governs creation, evolution, nature, history and the daily life of mankind. It describes the changes between youth and old age, happiness and unhappiness, sickness and health, fortune and misfortune.

When the spiral is centripetal in direction, causing tension, heat and density, it is referred to as *yang*. When it is centrifugal in direction, causing looseness, coolness and emptiness, it is referred to as *yin*. Everything fluctuates between, and is delineated by, various stages between the two points at the extremes of the spiral. And everything is relative to each other. Nothing has a fixed identity. Everything is changing. Water is warm to a cold hand, cool to a hot hand. Meanwhile, the temperature of the water itself is changing, due to the warmth or coolness of the hand, the quality of movement it made in the water, the length of time it stayed in the water, as well as the passage of time itself.

So, a country undergoing the yang tension of war suffers and withers; it is going through political and economic winter. While a country enjoying the yin comfort of peace, blossoms and creates great works of art and economic prosperity; it is going through the spring of cultural renaissance.

As we recognize the forces of yin and yang in our daily lives and become aware of their mechanism, function, and influence on us, we can begin to use them, with sensitive awareness, to guide our lives more consciously. We no longer have to be victims of circumstances, disease, or events previously beyond our control. With an understanding of yin and yang, of how life works, we have the tools with which we

---

1 Lincoln Barnett, *The Universe and Dr. Einstein* (New York: Harper and Brothers, 1948), p. 104.

can control and guide our destiny. This is the practical road to true freedom and justice. This is the royal road to lasting and unconditional happiness.

In the spiralic process of the formation of a solar system, the undifferentiated energy of the infinite universe condenses into gases, vapors, moisture, liquid, and matter, forming the planets in their various stages of evolution from the periphery of the spiral toward the center. This explains why outer planets tend to be so large and covered with clouds of gases and why inner planets, such as those between the earth and the sun, tend to be smaller and stark.

At the very center of the spiral is the sun. Since the center point of the spiral is receiving the most concentration of energy, and is under great pressure, intense fusion and heat are created, which explode into continual fire. In the course of spiraling in toward the center, each planet passes through every phase from the outside to the inside, gradually and inevitably entering and becoming fuel for the sun. The sun then radiates this energy back into the universe as sunshine, returning the energy it has collected over billions of light-years of creation.

At the point of balance between the periphery and center of the spiral, between the infinite expansion of the universe and the infinite concentration of the sun, there is just enough liquid and just enough heat to support life. The planet Earth is presently in this position.

As the earth turns on its axis and travels in its spiralic orbit around the sun, it receives varying influences from its surroundings and positions, creating the change in seasons, summer and winter, day and night. More subtle influences are also received as the earth passes through different parts of the heavens, in the form of cosmic rays and different qualities of energy from the Milky Way and other constellations and celestial bodies. We carry all these influences within us. This is the origin of astrological divination.

The natural result on Earth of the combining of water from the heavens and heat from the sun is the creation of chlorophyll. Since water is a condensation of moisture from infinity, it dominates the earth and its influence precedes that of the sun. Thus, chlorophyll, though it is necessarily influenced by the sun, is dominated by water. Where there is water, chlorophyll is abundant. Therefore, its nature is predominantly yin. This chlorophyll forms the basis for the development of all vegetation.

When we eat vegetables, we are eating chlorophyll. We are transmuting chlorophyll, through the process of digestion in the small intestine, into hemoglobin. We are changing the energy of infinity, in the form of water, into the energy of the sun, in the form of fire.

In the process of evolution, the planets are spiraling toward the sun. In the process of man's evolution, we are also spiraling toward the sun. The sun's Light is everywhere, both around us and within us. It is at the center of every cell, as the proton (sun) radiating energy (shining) toward the periphery. We see this Light as our aura, our laughter, the sparkle in our eyes, our love.

In order to strengthen the transmutation of chlorophyll to hemoglobin, in order to speed its evolution into the sun of our cells, and in order to speed our human evolution toward the Light, we purposely influence it with fire. This is called *cooking*.

Through cooking our food, with varying amounts and degrees of water and fire, representing yin elements and energy and yang elements and energy, we can control our physical and mental condition and quality. The addition of sea salt, pressure, and time, further facilitates this process. This is kitchen alchemy.

The control of universal energy to create our life, using the tools of yin and yang, is the key to our health and freedom.

According to our judgment, we create our life. By our judgment we select, prepare, and eat food. At the same time, the selection, preparation, and ingestion of the food we eat determines the quality of our judgment. It is an interdependent cycle of mutual cause and effect. As we think, we eat. As we eat, we think.

We can describe our judgment, way of eating, stages of health, development of consciousness, and course of sickness in seven levels, though there are no hard and rigid boundaries of demarcation. Everyone experiences different degrees of development within themselves at any one time, and these are in a state of constant flux and change. But, we can describe general periods of growth and evolution. As we mature and practice, the lower qualities become less dominant while the higher qualities become more developed. It takes a certain degree of self-discipline to make progress.

The following can serve as a general guide to help you discern where you are and why, the direction to go, and the result.

Kingdom of Human Evolution	*Level of Judgment*	*Way of Eating*	*Development of Consciousness*
7	Supreme	Predominantly whole grains. Eating what is appropriate to foster adaptability to the environment. Cooking for Freedom and Enlightenment.	Unconditional acceptance and love. Eternal happiness. Nirvana, Satori, Seventh Heaven.
6	Ideological	Soup, mostly whole grains, vegetables, little liquid. Cooking for refinement of thinking, intuition, and consciousness.	Concepts of righteousness/unrighteousness, justice/injustice, dictated by religions, doctrines and disciplines.
5	Social	Soup, infrequent animal food, more grains, vegetables, infrequent salads or fruit, no desserts, little liquids. Cooking for goal.	Concepts of good/bad, proper/improper, right/wrong, dictated by morals, ethics, economics and politics.
4	Intellectual	Soup, less animal food, more grains, vegetables, little salads or fruit, little desserts and liquids. Cooking for health and understanding.	Reliance on logic, what can be proved or disproved by reason.
3	Sentimental	Soup, some animal food, whole grains, vegetables, salads and fruits, desserts, liquids. Cooking for emotional pleasure.	Conditional love/hate, like/dislike, preference/aversion, happiness/unhappiness.
2	Sensory	Soup, animal food, some grains, some vegetables, salads and fruits, desserts, liquids. Cooking for physical pleasure.	Seeking comfort and pleasure.
1	Mechanical	Soup, animal food, some vegetables, little grain, salads, fruits, desserts, plenty of liquid. Indiscriminate cooking and eating.	Automatic and spontaneous response.

Levels	The Stages of Health	The Course of Sickness
7	No lying—absolute honesty. Unconditional gratitude.	Sickness unto death, or awakening. Arrogance—the ultimate cause and result.
6	Smartness in thinking and doing. Quick and right action. Flexibility, adaptability, and harmony.	Nervous disorders—physical paralysis, paranoia, schizophrenia, catatonia, destructive and suicidal tendencies.
5	Good humor, even disposition, cheerfulness and joy. No anger, impatience, or depression.	Organ disease; narrow-mindedness, blind conceptual and illusory thinking. Rigid stubbornness.
4	Good memory: the older you get the more you remember.	Emotional disorders—anger, frustration, hate, depression, fear, despair.
3	Deep and good sleep. Little to no movement. No dreams, except true dreams. Refreshed after 4 to 6 hours.	Blood disease; nervousness, anxiety, suspicion; lack of confidence and courage.
2	Good appetite—enthusiasm for simple food, work, friends, adventure of life, growth, big dream.	Aches and pains; worry, uncertainty, insecurity.
1	No fatigue. No complaining.	Fatigue; unclear thinking, confusion, indecisiveness.

The Seven Levels of the Way of Eating are slightly adjusted from the standard levels presented by George Ohsawa in *Zen Macrobiotics* in order to take into consideration present day life-styles and eating practices, as well as traditional eating patterns in cold mountainous regions and other parts of the world.

For strict healing purposes, the original teaching should be adhered to and is herein included, with a note by Michio Kushi taken from *The Book of Macrobiotics.*

Diet No.	*Cereals*	*Vegetables Sautéed*	*Soup*	*Animal*	*Salads Fruits*	*Dessert*	*Beverages*
7	100%	—	—	—	—	—	As little as
6	90%	10%	—	—	—	—	possible, but comfortable
5	80%	20%	—	—	—	—	”
4	70%	20%	10%	—	—	—	”
3	60%	30%	10%	—	—	—	”
2	50%	30%	10%	10%	—	—	”
1	40%	30%	10%	20%	—	—	”
−1	30%	30%	10%	20%	10%	—	”
−2	20%	30%	10%	25%	10%	5%	”
−3	10%	30%	10%	30%	15%	5%	”

It has been common practice in Oriental countries and in ancient societies throughout the world, that the majority of food was cereal grains and their products: brown rice in Oriental countries; corn in the American continents; wheat, oats, millet, barley and rye as well as brown rice in European countries; buckwheat in northeastern Europe. Often, these grains and their products were eaten with almost no side dishes for a period of up to ten days, in order to re-orient people's physical and mental conditions. A small volume of seasonings and condiments, and a reasonable volume of beverages, were used as a part of such practices. At that time, these whole cereal grains and their products were prepared in various ways, in the form of gruel, pancakes, bread, noodles, chapati, and other forms. However, the practice of such a diet consisting of 100 percent whole grains should not continue longer than two weeks unless under experienced supervision. In normal daily life, the principle food can fluctuate between 30 percent and 70 percent of each meal, and supplemental food can be adjusted accordingly, depending upon our daily activities and social environment. However, the greater the proportion of principle food, the more balance is achieved among physical, mental, and spiritual capacities.—Michio Kushi.

Unless we make a clear decision and take decisive steps to change our ways, the biological deterioration of human life will continue to increase, as the following charts, showing the epidemic course of cancer, indicate. The second chart is an assessment of the rate of cancer cures over the past thirty-two years. The *New York Times* article, from which it was taken, expressed disappointment at the lack of greater improvement. Perhaps, if we work togethèr, we can turn this misfortune to benefit and change the course of history toward harmony and health, according to the universal natural order.

For a more comprehensive discussion of yin/yang and its specific applications to physiological and psychological health, as well as to spiritual development, please read the works of George Ohsawa, Michio Kushi, Herman Aihara, Noboru Muramoto, and other teachers of the Oriental healing arts and way-of-life philosophies.

Probability at Birth of Eventually Developing
Cancer of Major Sites (Including Carcinoma in Situ)
By Race and Sex, US, 1975, 1980, and 1985

Site	White Males			Black Males			White Females			Black Females		
	1975	1980	1985	1975	1980	1985	1975	1980	1985	1975	1980	1985
All Cancer	30.3	33.6	36.9	28.0	31.6	35.2	33.9	35.0	36.1	29.9	30.7	31.5
Buccal Cavity and Pharynx	1.5	1.6	1.6	1.3	1.7	2.1	0.7	0.8	0.9	0.6	0.7	0.9
Esophagus	0.5	0.5	0.5	1.1	1.3	1.5	0.2	0.2	0.3	0.4	0.6	0.7
Stomach	1.2	1.2	1.2	1.6	1.6	1.6	0.9	0.8	0.8	1.1	1.0	0.8
Colon-Rectum	5.3	5.9	6.5	3.6	4.3	5.1	5.8	6.4	6.9	4.6	5.5	6.3
Pancreas	1.2	1.2	1.2	1.2	1.2	1.2	1.1	1.2	1.3	1.3	1.3	1.4
Larynx	0.8	0.8	0.9	0.9	1.0	1.1	0.1	0.2	0.2	0.2	0.2	0.2
Lung	6.9	7.8	8.7	7.4	8.5	9.6	2.5	3.3	4.2	2.3	3.0	3.8
Female Breast	—	—	—	—	—	—	9.6	9.9	10.2	6.9	7.2	7.5
Uterus	—	—	—	—	—	—	7.0	6.0	5.0	8.3	6.7	5.1
Cervix	—	—	—	—	—	—	3.7	3.2	2.7	6.8	5.3	3.8
Corpus and Unspecified	—	—	—	—	—	—	3.5	2.9	2.4	1.7	1.5	1.4
Ovary	—	—	—	—	—	—	1.5	1.5	1.5	0.9	1.0	1.0
Prostate	6.1	7.4	8.7	7.2	8.3	9.4	—	—	—	—	—	—
Testis	0.2	0.3	0.4	0.1	0.1	0.1	—	—	—	—	—	—
Kidney	0.8	1.1	1.3	0.6	0.7	0.8	0.5	0.6	0.7	0.4	0.5	0.6
Bladder	2.5	2.9	3.2	1.0	1.0	1.1	1.0	1.1	1.2	0.6	0.7	0.7
Melanoma	0.6	0.9	1.3	0.1	0.1	0.1	0.6	0.9	1.1	0.1	0.1	0.1
Thyroid	0.2	0.2	0.2	0.1	0.1	0.1	0.5	0.5	0.5	0.3	0.3	0.2
Leukemia	1.2	1.2	1.2	0.8	0.8	0.8	1.0	0.9	0.9	0.7	0.7	0.8
Lymphomas and Multiple Myeloma	1.6	1.8	2.0	1.4	1.6	1.8	1.6	1.8	2.0	1.3	1.3	1.4

Note: Exclusive of epidermoid skin cancer.
Source: *CA-A Cancer Journal for Clinicians*, Vol. 35, No. 1, 1985.

The War on Cancer: A Critical Assessment

Studying changes in patient survival and other factors, the General Accounting Office has made these assessments of improvements in the treatment of 12 cancers. Survival data for some cancers reflect earlier detection and other factors as well as changes in treatment.

	Reported 5-year survival rate*			
Cancer Type	1950	1982	Changes in Treatment	G. A. O. Conclusion
Bladder	53%	77%	Improved surgery, detection and use of radiation; new chemotherapy too recent to affect data.	**Moderate improvement.**
Breast	60	75	New chemotherapy and hormone treatments, used with surgery, are too recent to affect data.	**Slight improvement.**
Cervical	59	67	Earlier detection; improved surgical procedure has helped small proportion of patients.	**Slight improvement.**
Colon	41	53	No changes in technique, but surgery can be performed on more patients because of other medical advances.	**Slight improvement.**
Rectal	40	50	Increased use of radiation and chemotherapy with surgery is too recent to affect data.	**Slight improvement.**
Endometrial	72	87	Combined surgery and radiation, but extent of adoption is unknown; earlier detection benefits a small proportion of patients.	**Moderate improvement where new combined therapy was used.**
Head and neck	45**	54	Improvements in surgical procedures.	**Slight improvement.**
Leukemias	10	33	Chemotherapy for acute leukemias.	**Dramatic improvement for acute leukemias,**

* Rates for whites only; reporting on other races was inconsistent over study period.

** Rates for 1960.

				slight or no improvement for chronic leukemias.
Lung	6	12	Chemotherapy for small-cell lung cancer.	**Slight improvement for small-cell carcinoma patients, no change for other lung cancers.**
Non-Hodgkin's lymphoma	31[2]	48	Chemotherapy and radiation.	**Dramatic improvement.**
Prostate	43	71	Improved selection of therapies and use of radiation.	**Moderate improvement.**
Stomach	12	16	None.	**No improvement.**

Source: The New York Times (Thursday, April 16, 1987)

In order to change the conditions indicated on the previous charts, the following guidelines should be considered.

The Seven Principles of the Order of the Universe describe the absolute nature of infinity

1. All phenomena are differentiated manifestations of One Infinity.
2. Everything changes.
3. There is nothing identical.
4. All antagonisms are complementary.
5. What has a front has a back.
6. The bigger the front, the bigger the back.
7. What has a beginning has an end.

The Twelve Theorems of the Unifying Principle complete the Seven Principles and describe the nature and function of the relative world

1. One Infinity differentiates itself into Yin and Yang, which are manifest when the infinite expansion polarizes itself at the point of bifurcation.
2. Yin and yang are continuously produced by the pure infinite expansion.
3. Yin is centrifugal. Yang is centripetal. Yin and yang together produce energy and all phenomena.
4. Yin attracts yang. Yang attracts yin.
5. Yin repels yin. Yang repels yang.
6. Yin and yang, combined in varying proportions, produce all phenomena.
7. The force of attraction and repulsion is proportional to the difference of the components of yin and yang.
8. All phenomena are ephemeral, constantly changing their qualities of yin and yang. Everything is restless.
9. Nothing is completely yin or completely yang. Everything involves polarity and is relative.
10. Nothing is neuter. Either yin or yang are always in excess.

11. Yin produces yang and yang produces yin at the extremes.
12. Everything is yang at the center and yin at the surface.

Classification of Yin (▽) and Yang (△) (1)

	Yin	*Yang*
Tendency	Expansion	Contraction
Direction	Ascent	Descent
Structure	Space	Time
Position	Outward	Inward
Construction	Surface	Inside
Light	Dark	Bright
Weight	Light	Heavy
Vibration	Short Wave	Long Wave
Color	Purple	Red
Temperature	Cold	Hot
Catalyst	Water	Fire
Atomic	Electron	Proton
Elements	K, O, P, Ca, N . . .	H, As, Cl, Na, C . . .
Country of Origin	Tropical	Cold
Seasonal Influence	Summer	Winter
Agricultural	Salad	Cereal
Vitamins	C	K, D
Biological	Vegetable	Animal
Birth	Cold Season	Hot Season
Nerves	Orthosympathetic	Parasympathetic
Sex	Female	Male
Attitude	Gentle, Negative	Active, Positive
Work	Psychological	Physical
Taste	Hot (spicy), Sour, Sweet	Salty, Bitter

(From the teachings of George Ohsawa.)

Yin and Yang and the Five Transformations

In this beginningless and endless infinite and eternal universe, all life is one. All life is a simultaneous whole. What appear as time and space, past, present, and future, are only apparent points on a shifting scale, from which we can make reference, for convenience.

Life is characterized by movement and change, a constant ebb and flow, an expansion and contraction, a coming in and a going out, a rising up and a lying down. This flux is the mother of all opposites; yet they are born of each other and exist only because of each other. In this way, one bears two and two give rise to all phenomena, by virtue of their interaction. These two apparently opposing forces are called yin and yang.

All phenomena in the finite world can be described in terms of yin or yang in relation to other phenomena. Summer is hot and at the peak of growth. It is filled with the yin efflorescence of nature, the culmination of winter's potential. By contrast, winter is cold and barren; it concentrates and stores yang energy for summer.

The characteristics of summer and winter seem sharply opposed, but they gradually shift, one into the other, through the transitions of autumn and spring. Spring and autumn both have warm balmy days and cool evenings, yet spring energy is rising and more yin, while autumn energy is declining and more yang.

Thus, summer is dominated by Fire and expansion, winter is dominated by Water and floating; spring is dominated by Wood which is rising, autumn is dominated by Metal, concentrating and storing. At the center is Earth, which is dominated by Soil. It unifies and gathers and gives in its season.

If we follow the seasons within each day, we find morning is equal to spring in its way; noontime carries the heat of the summer; afternoon declines with the coolness of autumn; night is dark and cold like the winter, but soon it gives rise to the morning, like spring.

Since summer and winter, morning and evening carry distinctly varying charges, the food that we eat must vary accordingly, if we are to harmonize with the energies they bring.

In the morning when we awake we are full of the excess yin accumulated overnight during the body repair process. The first thing we do is to eliminate this excess in the form of urine and bowel movement. Then, to make balance with the rising yin of the day, as well as the revitalizing yin we have accumulated from sleep, the first food of the day should be slightly yang. Since everyday we awake as if reborn, it is appropriate to recreate our emergence from the sea, replenishing ourselves with its life-giving waters. Thus, the best first food of the day is the slightly salty taste of *miso* soup. Prepared with plants of the ocean together with plants of the earth, and representing our transition from water to land, miso soup helps us adjust smoothly from night to day.

Furthermore, the fermentation of miso nourishes us with the first forms of life, enhancing the growth of digestive bacteria and our ability to live on the land. Taken together with soft, whole brown rice, barley, millet, or other whole grains, complete proteins are formed which sustain us all day with high level energy which is clean and strong.

As we work through the day, feeling good and at ease, we gradually yangize and absorb the sun's yang. By the end of the day we are drained of the yin we stored during sleep, and we seek something fresh and possibly sweet.

This is the time for the elaboration of vegetable side dishes at dinner. The tastes should be varied from salty to sweet and pungent to sour. In this way, all the parts of our body are nourished and stimulated. We feel satisfied and do not suffer cravings and hidden hunger.

Each season and time has its dominant taste to nourish the organ corresponding to the energy active at that time of the year and day.

In this way, we can harmonize our eating with the changing energies in the near and more distant environment around us.

The Five Transformations
  are stages of change
Through which all phenomena
  move and arrange
What appears to be fixed,
  but which never is so,
For what seems to be high
  is transmuted to low.
What ends up being low
  starts to rise and expand
And, without much ado,
  becomes high again.
There is little distinction
  between spirit and form
As matter diffuses
  and then is reborn.

CTL

The Five Transformations are cyclic in movement. The following diagrams can be plotted to portray any pattern of change.

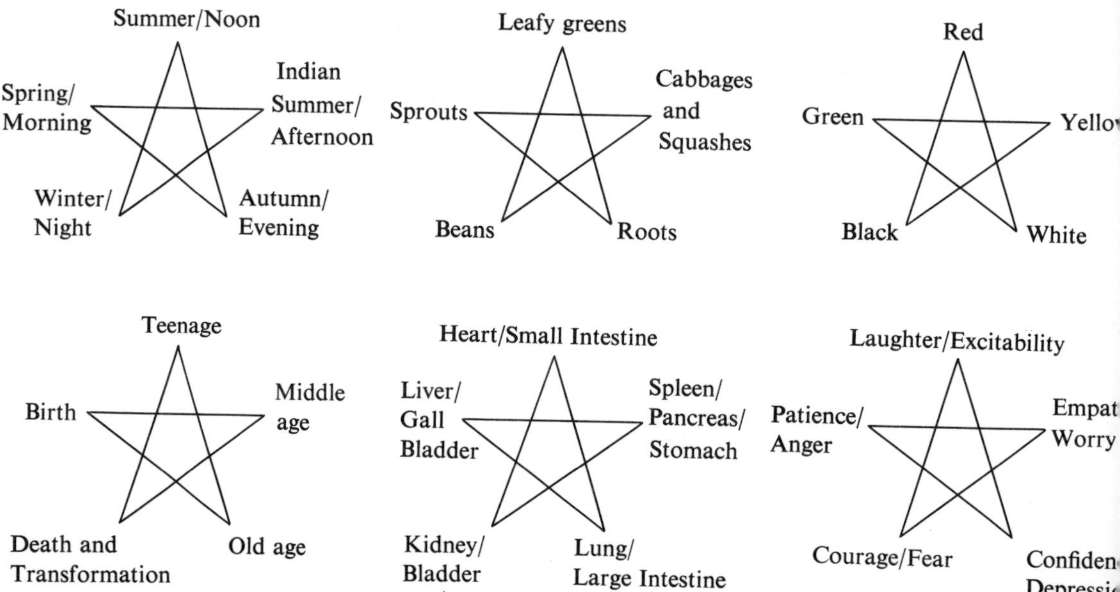

For a more comprehensive discussion of the Five Transformations regarding healing, please read *Healing Ourselves* by Noboru Muramoto.

The Five Transformations of Energy

	Wood	*Fire*	*Earth*	*Metal*	*Water*
Number	3, 4	9	2, 5, 8	6, 7	1
Planet	Jupiter	Mars	Earth	Venus	Mercury
Direction	East	South	Center	West	North
Season	Spring	Summer	Indian Summer	Autumn	Winter
Adverse Climate	wind	heat	moisture	dryness	cold
Temperature	warming	hot	cooling	cool	cold
Time of Day	morning	noon	afternoon	evening	night
Color	green	red	yellow	white	black
Solid Organ	liver	heart	spleen/pancreas	lung	kidney
Empty Organ	gallbladder	small intestine	stomach	large intestine	bladder
Tissue	muscles	blood vessels	flesh	skin	bones
Body Fluid	tears	sweat	saliva	mucus	urine
Indicator	toe nails	complexion	lips	body hair	hair
Gland	pituitary	thymus	pancreas	thyroid	adrenals, sexual organs
Sense Organ	eyes	tongue	mouth	nose	ears
Sense	sight	speech	taste	smell	hearing
Age	birth and childhood	teenage	middle age	old age	death and transformation
Emotion	patience/ anger	laughter/ excitability	empathy/ worry	confidence/ depression	courage/fear
Expression	shout	laugh	sing	weep	groan
Reaction under Stress	control	sadness/grief	stubborn, belch	cough	tremble
Faculty	spiritual	inspirational	intellectual	vital	will
Taste	sour	bitter	sweet	pungent	salty
Grain	wheat	red millet/corn	yellow millet	rice	beans
Vegetable	leeks	scallions	mallows	onions	greens
Fruit	plum	apricot	date	peach	chestnut

By studying and observing the Five Transformations, we gradually become aware of, and profoundly impressed by, the magical movement of yin and yang. We begin to see life dancing before our eyes, in a masterful choreography. We hear the endless movement of the universe as a great symphony orchestrated to perfection. And we begin to feel and to know that we are an integral part of this magnificent performance. Our thoughts, words and actions affect everything, near and far, as we are affected by everything, throughout time and space. Our sense of oneness with life grows until we Know we are One with All.

The language of yin and yang is subtle and bold. We can see it in color, size and shape, direction, texture and temperature, sound, season and time, elements, odor and taste. These are the sounds and the colors of life's song.

Classification of Yin (▽) and Yang (△) (2)

	Yin (▽) *Centrifugal*	*Yang* (△) *Centripetal*
Tendency:	Expansive	Contractive
Framework:	Space	Time
Environment:	Polar	Tropical
Season:	Autumn, Winter	Spring, Summer
Nature:	Water	Fire
Temperature:	Cold	Hot
Soil:	Sedimentary, wet	Volcanic, dry
Direction of Growth:	Vertical above ground; horizontal underground	Vertical below ground; horizontal above ground
Speed of Growth:	Faster	Slower
Size:	Larger, taller	Smaller, shorter
Position:	Outward	Inward
Structure:	More expanded and hollow	More compacted and solid
Sex:	Female, feminine	Male, masculine
Weight:	Lighter	Heavier
Water Content:	Watery	Dry
Texture:	Softer	Harder
Color:	White—black—purple—blue—green	Yellow—orange—red—brown—black—white
Odor:	Strong, effusive	Mild, mellow
Taste:	Spicy—pungent—sour—sweet (simple sugars)	Sweet (complex sugars)—salty—bitter
Atomic Factor:	Electron	Proton
Elements:	Potassium (K), Oxygen (O), Nitrogen (N), Phosphorus (P), Calcium (Ca)	Sodium (Na), Hydrogen (H), Arsenic (As), Carbon (C), Iodine (I), Magnesium (Mg)
Biology:	Vegetal	Animal
Nervous System:	Orthosympathetic	Parasympathetic
Nutriments:	Fat — protein — carbohydrate —	Mineral
Vitamins:	B, C	A, D, K
Cooking Methods:	Fermentation—quick pickling—steaming—boiling	Water-sautéing—oil-sautéing—deep-frying—pressure-cooking—baking—long pickling

Food for Spirit—Cooking for Purification

It has been my experience that food is the best medicine.

For example, seeds, grains, cereals, beans, and corn nourish the whole body, since they incorporate the whole plant within them, from root to stalk, leaf, flower, fruit, and seed. Seeds have the ability to nourish the whole body.

Roots have the ability to nourish our roots, our digestive organs, since they both function with the same purpose in the total organism. Stalks nourish our skeletal structure and nervous system, in the same way as they function in the plant. Leaves nourish our lungs, since they are the respirators of the plant kingdom. Flowers produce the seeds, as the flowers of our reproductive organs produce our seeds—ovaries producing eggs and testes producing sperm. We do not eat flowers, however, to create strong reproductive organs; we eat roots, which strengthen the transmutation of food into blood in the small intestine. And we eat seeds which create strong blood and strengthen our seeds. Without strong blood, strong eggs and sperm cannot be produced.

If we take foods in their season, they will be in harmony with the rising or falling energy of that season and with the rising or falling energy of the organs related to that season. For instance, it is appropriate to take more green leafy vegetables in the summer than in the winter. In the winter it is appropriate to take more roots, which store well. In the same way, it is appropriate to take more fruits in summer than in winter, although, even in summer, their use should not be in excess.

There is summer food and winter food, autumn food and spring food, following the cycles of nature itself. By extension, there is morning food, afternoon food and evening food. And there is a time to rest from food, to abstain altogether, especially at night. The night-time energy is going down, everything becomes quiet, the body seeks rest and tends to lie down. Eating, which stimulates rising energy, at this time is totally inappropriate. Especially when the body is tired, the digestive organs are also tired and want to rest.

As we learn how to read nature, we will be able to carry on an intimate communication with the foods we prepare to nourish our bodies. Foods speak to us with a very clear and distinct language of their own, through color, shape, size, hardness or softness, water content, taste, smell, direction of growth, speed of growth, origin of growth, texture, alkalinity or acidity, and chemical properties. All grains and vegetables have north and south, or yin and yang, poles, meridians, or energy lines, between these poles, and chakra centers of energy, just as our own bodies have. They should be prepared with an eye toward maintaining the integrity of these meridians and chakras. In this way, they will impart their natural innate balance to us when we eat them. This calls for skill and awareness in the art of cutting. It is also very important to use the whole plant, or the whole vegetable, as much as is edible, when cooking. Different parts of the plant have different medicinal properties which should not be lost or ignored. Also, eating the skin, roots, and leaves of a plant maintains its wholeness in us.

The harmonious combination of foods is also necessary to make a dish balanced and delicious. This is an art that can range from simple basic dishes to the subtle nuances of more complex dishes. Not only do foods need to be balanced in a harmonious way within each dish, but also between dishes in each meal and between meals in a day. If we begin by including a variety of vegetables representing every part of the plant, as well as a variety of colors, we have a better chance of receiving complete nourishment.

The art of cooking, of using fire, water, and salt, is the art of alchemy in the kitchen. Fire, water, salt, pressure, and time have the ability to change the quality of food to make it more digestible, more easily assimilated, and more compatible with our human body and needs. For instance, all animals below the human level eat their food raw, without any special preparation. It was only when man began to use fire and salt that he was able to stand erect, develop his nervous system and brain, and create language and civilization. Until that time, man had not yet evolved into true human structure and consciousness. It is through his ability to change the nature and quality of his food that man became capable of changing and directing his own nature and quality. Through the art of cooking, man has learned how to adapt to his environment, to the changing seasons, and to his changing needs, physically, mentally and spiritually. This is the key to mankind's ultimate freedom.

Food cannot be taken arbitrarily, since every mouthful affects the quality of our blood, the function of our organs, the sensitivity of our nervous system, our emotional feelings, our mental awareness, and our expression. What we eat affects our whole vibrational field, as well as our social interactions.

Food is energy. It can be considered from a purely nutritional point of view, but that is not enough. For example, there are yin and yang sources of vitamin C, such as fruits and roots. Some of their qualities are diametrically opposed. Fruits combine vitamin C with sugar, whereas roots combine vitamin C with minerals. Vitamin C with sugar will weaken the blood and make it sticky, whereas vitamin C with minerals will strengthen the blood and make it clean.

Food selection, preparation, balancing, and combining changes subtly from season to season. For example, in winter we can take three parts roots to one part greens, whereas in summer we can take three parts greens to one part roots. Lighter cooking is appropriate for summer; heavier, longer cooking is appropriate for winter. Nevertheless, if we take too much raw vegetables or fruits in summer, we will make ourselves weak and spoil our ability to adapt spontaneously to cold weather without getting sick. People who take too many fruits in summer, or other strong yin food, easily "catch cold" in winter when the cold weather causes the body to yangize and discharge excess yin, in the form of water, mucus, sneezing, coughing and loose bowels.

Fruits and milk are strong sources of sugar, in the forms of fructose and lactose. Most people do not consider these foods as forms of sugar. However, both of them decay or spoil quickly, even with refrigeration. Whatever spoils quickly will surely make us spoiled, too. Everyone knows how sugar "eats through" the minerals in teeth, causing cavities. Acid foods dissolve minerals, too. If they have such a devastating effect on hard substances such as teeth, you can imagine what they do to the bones, tissues, and blood. All the minerals of the body are diminished.

Acid dissolves minerals in teeth, bones, tissues, and blood, and leads to decay, anemia, and mental disorders. Acid foods are protein, vinegar, citrus, sweets, alcohol, and acid fermentation, such as sugar, fruits[2], alcohol, vinegar, and yogurt (as opposed to alkaline fermentation as in miso and soy sauce). Acid dissolves minerals, weakens blood by dissolving iron, leading to anemia, often showing as white spots on the skin or white membranes under the eyelids. Taking an iron supplement is not as important as stopping acid foods. Stopping acid foods is as important as taking iron-rich foods, or foods that build blood. Potassium also creates iron deficiency when it is taken in excess, as in bananas, potatoes, green peas, and eggplant. These yin elements dissolve the minerals in the blood and tissues and their holding/connecting power is lost. Concentrative power and clear decisive thinking are also weakened.

A sense of subtlety is necessary to develop when preparing foods for healing. The food should be whole, simple, clean in the specific charge of energy it carries. The purpose of each dish should be clearly understood and stated in its preparation. For example, according to the Law of Correspondences, roots are used to strengthen the lower organs. Beans strengthen the kidneys and reproductive system. Stalk vegetables strengthen the legs, back, and skeletal structure. Leafy vegetables nourish the lungs.

---

[2] Most fruits are acid in themselves and tend to be alkaline-forming in the body. However, the high sugar content in fruits is still acid-forming. For a detailed explanation of acid and alkaline, see *Acid and Alkaline*, Herman Aihara (GOMF, Oroville, CA., 1971).

If these foods are prepared improperly, or with strong vinegar or sweetener, their strengthening qualities will be lost and the opposite effect will result.

Foods need to be combined with awareness of their yin or yang properties. A dish made of all yang foods will be as imbalanced as a dish with all yin foods. Yang foods can be complemented with yin foods or sauces, whereas yin foods can be complemented with yang foods or sauces.

The selection of organically grown foods over non-organically grown ones is always preferable, when possible. Foods grown inorganically are yinnized, swollen, full of water, and chemicalized. For marketing purposes, they are forced artificially to grow faster than normal, so they do not stay in the soil long enough to absorb sufficient nutrients from the earth, rain, and sun. They lack essence, which is revealed in their bland, indistinctive taste. They also lack staying power and spoil easily and more quickly than naturally grown foods full of minerals. As a result, they lack strong healing power.

When we eat, it is important to eat consistently, regarding both the quality of our intake, the quantity, and the time of eating. This enhances the rhythmical function of the organs and harmonious function of the nervous system.

It is important to eat some kind of fermented food everyday. This nourishes the digestive bacteria and maintains a symbiotic relationship of active enzymes within the fertile soil of our intestines. This activity maintains healthy digestion and transmutation of food into blood.

Menus and recipes are to be used as guides to help the reader develop a more intimate understanding of food and how to work with food for healing. For this purpose, I have resorted to using measurements and instructions for the sake of clarity. Definitely, certain preparations need specific instructions. However, in time, with study, understanding, and skill, one should be able to cook intuitively—with knowledge of what to prepare for what condition, how to balance food for the day, the weather, the season, and the climate—and using body sense to measure and balance through the use of hands, fingers, sight, sound, smell, and taste.

There are no spices, sugar, or artificial flavorings used in these recipes. The foods are combined with concern for a balance of complete nourishment within each meal and within each day. Balanced sea salt, miso, and *tamari* soy-sauce are used for basic seasonings, to bring out the natural flavors of the foods themselves, with an eye toward enhancing their natural healing power.

In many cases, I have indicated the specific application of certain foods, dishes, or menus, for certain conditions or situations. When followed properly and consistently, eating and living macrobiotically, according to the laws of nature, will have the same cleansing, clarifying, balancing, and healing effects mentally and spiritually as it will have physically and emotionally.

Chewing is as important to daily life as prayer or meditation. Chewing is the conscious act of filtering and transmuting the outer world into the inner world of our body within which we live. It is important to not swallow pieces when you eat. Chew until everything in your mouth is liquified. The best way is to take small bites. Then you can chew until the amount of saliva becomes greater than the liquified food in your mouth. When saliva predominates, whatever poison or acid is in the food will have a better chance of being neutralized.

When we eat grains and vegetables and chew them until they are liquid, we are reducing them to the consistency of milk. We are, in fact, then taking the milk of our Mother Earth. In this way we can rejuvenate our cells and tissues and keep our whole body young.

Simple food, natural environment, and physical exercise, together with self-reflection, meditation, breathing and spiritual exercises, make one whole and establish peace and harmony within oneself and within one's extended world family. In this way, we can flow comfortably with the seasons of life, from youth to adulthood to old age and on.

In this way the cycle of life completes itself in harmony and mankind can achieve the real happiness it seeks.

The Esoteric Significance of Fruit, Grains, and Vegetables

What is fruit? Fruit is delicious, it is craved, sought after, insatiably devoured and luxuriated in. Fruit is the harvest of one's labors, the epitome of one's life. It is the end result of all sowing and labor. It is the culmination of all production, of beingness itself.

The varieties of fruit are countless, the tastes are innumerable in their subtleness. The one taste that predominates among them all is their sweetness. We are happy if the fruit of our labors is sweet. It designates success and completion. To speak of bitter fruit means failure and the need to start again. When the fruit is sweet, the cycle is finished. Life has ripened to its fullest.

The fruits of the table all represent the completion of a cycle in the trees and plants which bore them. They are the end result of a whole process of growth and expansion, of coming to flower in the process of reproduction. Within the fruit is the seed, ready to begin new life. When the seed is mature, the fruit drops from the tree, protecting and nourishing the seed as a placenta nourishes the egg. The tree itself ovulates every spring. The fruit acts as a miniature womb until the seed is safely embedded in the larger womb of Mother Earth. Then the fruit, like the placenta, falls away in decay, no longer needed. Its purpose has been fulfilled, its function achieved. The fruit is the end of a cycle; the seed is the beginning.

Botanically, *fruit* means seed, with its surrounding structure, and refers to such foods as cereal grains, peas, and beans. It is the popular usage of the term which refers to apples, grapes, bananas, and so on.

Fruit energy is much more yin, more expansive, than grain energy. The tree which produces fruit is itself much larger, taller, more expansive than the plant which produces grain. It reaches up and out toward the heavens, while the grain plant remains comparatively closer to the earth. The fruit of the tree is very sweet, soft, and juicy, with a loose molecular structure. Fruit carries predominantly Earth's yin centrifugal energy. This promotes degeneration, disintegration, dematerialization, i.e., decay and death. The grain plant is small, compact, and dry. Grain itself is tiny, hard, concentrated and dry. It carries Heaven's yang centripetal consolidating energy, which promotes materialization, stability, endurance, and long life.

In the process of its maturation, fruit develops as an extension of the leaves, both in structure and chemistry. As it ripens, it exchanges its function of taking in carbon dioxide and giving off oxygen, as the leaves do, to taking in oxygen and giving off carbonic acid. The starch also undergoes transformation into sugar. Other insoluble substances, like *pectose*, change into soluble form, like *pectin.* With the continuation of *oxidation*, which is the causative agent of the above processes, the fruit gradually becomes overripe and falls into decay, thus releasing the seed. This is a similar process to the disintegration of the *endometrium* (uterine lining) when the overripe egg falls into decay after lack of fertilization at its peak by the sperm, resulting in menstruation. By extension, excessive eating of fruit during pregnancy often results in miscarriage. The fruit is simply following its own nature.

Before the coming of the white man, when daily life was governed by natural order, the Hawaiians traditionally considered the succulent tropical fruits of the islands as taboo, forbidden food reserved only for the Gods and the birds. It was commonly understood that if the women indulged in fruit, the family line would die.

In 1881, Dr. Pavy wrote in *A Treatise on Food and Dietetics Physiologically and Therapeutically Considered*[3]:

> Whilst advantageous when consumed in moderate quantity, fruit, on the other hand, proves injurious if eaten in excess. Of a highly succulent nature, and containing free acids and principles prone to undergo change, it is apt, when ingested out of due proportion to other food, to act as a disturbing element, and excite derangement of the alimentary canal. This is particularly likely to occur if eaten either in the unripe or over-ripe state: in the former case, from the quantity of acid present; in the latter, from its strong tendency to ferment and decompose within the digestive tract. The prevalence of stomach and bowel disorders, noticeable during the height of the fruit season, affords proof of the inconveniences that the too free use of fruit may give rise to.

In most parts of the world, the fruit-growing season and the life-span of the fruit are comparatively short. The potential life-force in a fully ripened fruit is very small, lasting only for a period of weeks, days, or even hours. Even in low temperatures, fruit decays quickly. On the other hand, seeds hold a life-force potential of a thousand years or more, when properly stored, whole, and unhusked. Seeds are the epitome of life itself, in the process of eternal self-renewal.

The flavor of seeds is also sweet, but a sweetness of deep character which harmonizes the relative bitterness of the roots, the pungency of the stalk, the saltiness of the leaves, the sourness of the unripe fruit, and the sweetness of the ripe fruit, all of which remain in potential form in the seed itself. The seed is a microcosm of infinite and eternal harmony.

Being the end result in the whole process of the growth of the tree or plant, the fruit is governed by Earth's yin centrifugal force, expanding and evaporating up into the heavens.

The seed, created at the yang center of the fruit, compacted by the spiral of creation, is dominated by Heaven's yang centripetal force, condensing downward into the crystallization of matter. The nature of the fruit is to lose form and evaporate. It is going toward "death." The nature of the seed is toward creation of form and consolidation. It is going toward "life."

---

[3] *A Treatise on Food and Dietetics Physiologically and Therapeutically Considered*, Dr. Pavy (William Wood and Company, New York, 1881).

In the case of the family of cereal grains, a miracle is achieved. It is the ultimate marriage of Heaven's and Earth's forces as they meet and merge in the grain that is both fruit and seed as one.[4] Over how many eons of evolution and through how many labors of death and rebirth, dissolution and crystallization of energies, did innumerable manifestations and descriptions take place before these two potent forces intermingled in a state matured and refined enough to marry in the form of grain, the seed of ten thousand rebirths? O Glorious Grain, the Seed of Life and Mother of a Thousand Blessings!

Eating grains, planting the seeds of life within the grounds of our bodily temple, these seeds which we sow anew day after day, produce an endless harvest of many fruits. These are the fruits of our labors: consciousness, love, work, children, language, music, art, health, long life, universal harmony, peace, happiness, and eternal freedom. These are the fruit of the seed. These are the fruit of the spirit encapsulated in the most yang form, crystallized, as if the seed were nature's microchip holding infinite wisdom.

Seeds, cereal grains, are the main form which carry us, as a ship, through life. Vegetables serve as the oars and rudder, maintaining balance and momentum. Each vegetable, whether it be root, tuber, stalk or stem, leaf, flower or fruit, is only a small part of the seed itself, which holds that part in the form of potential energy. When we eat grains, we eat the whole plant. When we eat vegetables, we eat only part of the plant. Therefore, it is necessary to take a full range of vegetables representing the whole plant in order to maintain balance. Grain and seeds have the ability and capacity to create strong blood and nourish the whole body. Vegetables are an extension of grain in their ability to nourish the particular part of the body that a particular part of the plant is related to. In this way, vegetables supplement grain. This is why grain is appropriate as primary food and provides the staple food for mankind, while vegetables are appropriate as secondary food and provide a variety of side dishes.

According to the Law of Correspondences, each part of the plant relates to a part of the body. Roots nourish the lower body—the roots of the body, the intestines. These roots draw nourishment from the environment, either the external earthly environment or the internal human environment. Stalks and stems nourish the skeletal system and carry within them the circulatory and nervous systems which circulate nourishment through the blood or chlorophyll, oxygen or carbon dioxide systems. Leaves do the work of the lungs, and the flowers represent the reproductive system. We choose that part of the plant or vegetable to influence the related organ or system in the body either to tonify or sedate, expand or contract, nourish or discharge excess, cleanse or rebuild. In this way, all vegetables, including beans and sea vegetables, prepared as side dishes, are used medicinally. To take green salad at the expense of the root is to nourish one part of the body at the expense and depletion of the other. To be whole and harmonious, one should take every part of the plant as an extension of the seed where the energy is held in undifferentiated form.

Since the seed holds the energy of the vegetable in its essence, it is akin to the spiritual energy of Heaven. It is dominated by Heaven's force. When it is planted, in its various stages of evolution, it is nourished by the earth and comes forth as the

[4] Cereal grains are the most compact of "fruits," where the germ is the seed and the rest of the kernel is the fruit.

various vegetables, fruits, nuts, and flowers, to which the earth gives birth. These are dominated by Earth's force. These are the offspring of Mother Earth.

To achieve balance, health, and clarity, our food should be balanced, whole, and pure. To achieve long life, those foods which are themselves long-lived may be emphasized, for if we eat that which decays quickly, our own flesh will also quickly decay. Thus, cereal grains are the ultimate food for mankind.

Of course, everything has some kind of benefit. Fruits are also beneficial in their place. In the summertime, when the weather is hot and fruit is plentiful, it is refreshing and relaxing to enjoy a snack or dessert of fresh or cooked fruit. For this, we choose the smaller, more yang, compact, red or yellow fruit, such as berries, apricots, strawberries, cherries, or watermelon, the only melon with a solid center. Nothing is more fun than picking wild berries and popping them into your mouth.

However, fruits are high in calories and may make us warmer in the summer heat. Compared to such sweet, initially warming food, green and white vegetables, either raw, lightly pickled, or blanched, such as cucumbers, cabbage, or romaine lettuce, are more cooling and refreshing, due to their chlorophyll content and lack of sugar.

In winter, apples are appropriate and can be stewed or baked in order to help the body maintain its warmth and ability to adapt to the cold weather. However, if we enjoy fruits too often, the sugar content will weaken our blood quality and cause us to feel ultimately cold, tired, weak, mentally scattered and depressed.

Since fruit is yin compared to vegetables and grains, it can be used to temporarily balance an over-yang condition, such as yang constipation, tight kidneys due to excess salt, or hypertension. Apples or apple juice can be used to reduce fever of a yang variety. In this way, fruits can be used medicinally. However, excessive use of fruits and juices will end up weakening the body—the blood, nervous system, and organs—to various degrees. Therefore, fruit should be taken with care.

On the other hand, the vegetable kingdom is much more vast than that of fruits and offers a greater variety of species and qualities of energies with which to work. There is probably no physiological adjustment that cannot be made with the right vegetables. There are over eight thousand different kinds in the West, forty thousand different kinds in the East.

For these reasons, grain is considered as "first food," vegetables are considered as "second food," and fruits are considered as "third food" and least in importance.

The cereal grains rank first in food value among all the foods of the vegetable kingdom due to their abundance as well as their high nutritive value. They have been the most widely consumed food throughout the history and prehistory of mankind. These farinaceous seeds—such as rice, wheat, millet, barley, sorghum, rye, oats, manna grass, buckwheat, quinoa, and corn—are derived from the *Cerealia*, a tribe of grasses considered throughout the world as sacred. Indeed, the Japanese call them *kusa* or "Sacred Grasses."

The farinaceous seeds next in importance are the *Leguminose*, the tribe of pulses made famous by Daniel in the Bible for nourishing his illumination. (See Daniel 1: 8–17.) These consist of peas, beans, and lentils.

Of the grains, wheat is the highest in nitrogenous material, such as *gluten*, which is the building block of protein. The next highest component is starch. The sugar content is approximately one-ninth the quantity of protein. Rice has the lowest level of protein of all the grains. It also has the lowest sugar content. Rice ranks the highest among all the grains in starch, which makes it the most easily digestible of all grains. It is certainly the most soothing and healing in disorders of the digestive tract, such as diarrhea or dysentery. Rice has been used as the principle food by one-third of the human race. It needs to be eaten together with other seeds, grains, or beans, to make a complete, protein-rich meal. It has also been shown that complete protein can be obtained when rice is eaten with sea vegetables and other vegetables. Unlike protein, starch does not make the body hard.

Rice (*Oryza sativa*) has been cultivated since ancient times in India, China, Japan, other countries of the Far East, Southern Europe, the West Indies, Central America, and the United States. There are more than one hundred varieties of rice known and cultivated. Rice and other cereal grains provide the most economical base for nourishing the majority of the population.

In an article on "Vegetarianism for a World of Plenty," printed in the March, 1979 issue of *Moneysworth*, Robin Hur, author of *Food Reform: Our Desperate Need*, clearly and undebatably illucidates the far-reaching problems resulting from a meat- and sugar-based national diet. These problems include, but are not limited to: the increase in mechanization of food production and the processing of food; the decrease of fossil fuel and ore resources; the increase in air, water, and land pollution; the decrease in arable land due to overgrazing; the lowering of the water tables and deforestation and creation of desert land, as in Texas and East Africa; as a result, the increase in the use of pesticides, chemical fertilizers, and preservatives on crops and in animal and dairy food products; the decrease in the health of the people, the increase in heart disease, cancer, immune-system-deficiency diseases, obesity, diabetes, multiple sclerosis, arthritis, mental disease, crime, and aging; the increase in environmental pollution-control expenditures, the increase in medical care expenses, medical insurance, disability insurance, and Social Security outlays; the decrease in family happiness and national peace; the increase in military and defense spending, and the decrease in the quality of the human being.

None of this would happen if the nation as a whole changed to a grain-and-vegetable diet. Food production, health care, environmental protection and military defense budgets would drop drastically. Since it takes only a quarter-acre of farm land to feed one person on a grain-and-vegetable diet, 95 percent of the nation's farm land could be converted to tree farming, export crops, spacious living, and recreation areas. The earnings from the export crops alone would be enough to balance the nation's budget. Ninety-five percent of the energy expended to produce food based on a meat-and-sugar diet would be saved and the earth could be restored to its natural balance. Thus, everyone would benefit. The earth, the environment, the people and the nation would be saved. The life expectancy would go up ten to thirty years, physical and emotional illness, pain, sorrow, and crime would all but disappear. Cooperation would take the place of competition. Peace, prosperity, and harmony would be restored.

The Kitchen—Inner Sanctum of Creation

The kitchen is the alchemical laboratory in which we create the life, health, strength and flexibility, happiness, harmony, and dynamic expression of ourselves, our family, loved ones, and friends. From our kitchen, the quality of our energy reverberates out into the world as the ripples of a pebble in a pond. Thus, our personal habits are never secret or hidden.

When we take responsibility in the kitchen for the quality of life, we take responsibility for the quality of society and for mankind as a whole. This responsibility lies mainly in the hands of the women of the world. The women create life, nurture life, and are the first educators. Thus the women can control the quality of the life that issues from them. If the women follow the universal order, the men will make order in the world.

First, the kitchen should be clean and arranged in an orderly and attractive fashion. The atmosphere should be peaceful, quiet, and cheerful. The food-storage area should be away from the fire, preferably in a dark, cool corner.

The cook should be clean and tidy, with a clear and calm mind focused on the task at hand. A basic understanding of yin and yang, the nature of foods and their affect on the body, and skill in the art of cooking are essential. In time, with sincere study and practice, this basic understanding will develop into a profound understanding of cooking, the nature and mechanism of health and disease, and the creative process of life.

The meal should be planned in advance, so that the order of cooking proceeds smoothly and efficiently and meals can be prepared in a balanced way. It is not necessary to spend undue time in preparations. With practice, skill increases.

All materials and foodstuffs used should be as natural as possible, including: deep-well, spring, or purified water; wood, coal, or gas cooking fire; pottery, glass, enamel, cast-iron or stainless-steel pots and pans; bamboo and wooden cooking utensils; organic (as much as possible) whole grains, vegetables, sea vegetables, beans, seeds, nuts, fruits, and seasonings. The use of aluminum, metals treated with non-stick coatings, plastics, electric "fire" or microwave ovens are preferably avoided.

Foods should be prepared fresh as often as necessary. The whole food should be used as much as possible and cut with the purpose of maintaining its yin and yang balance.

The most simple and basic seasonings and flavorings should be used to enhance the true flavors of the foods and to control and harmonize their energies with the seasons, as well as with the people eating the meal. These seasonings should be naturally processed and used in moderation. Recommended are unrefined mineral-balanced, clean sea salt; cold-pressed vegetable oil, such as sesame oil, corn oil, rape seed oil (palm oil, cottonseed oil, coconut oil, and soybean oil are toxic to human beings); natural macrobiotically processed miso and tamari soy sauce; whole-grain vinegars and naturally processed whole-grain sweeteners.

Vegetables should be selected from every part of the plant, representing every basic color, to ensure a wide range of balanced energies and nutrients.

The dishes should be prepared in a variety of styles to make the foods appetizing and delicious, and to provide the appropriate stimulation needed by the body.

The meal should be arranged and served with an artistic eye, appealing to the senses and aesthetic tastes as well as to the appetite.

In this way, the cook creates health and beauty, with a clear conscience, and engenders the love and respect of his or her family and friends.

Through proper cooking and eating, society prospers.

Food Selection

Grains and Seeds

In selecting grains, beans, and seeds, look for those that are organically grown. Grains or beans processed in any form—as pressed, rolled, cracked, or flaked—have lost some degree of life energy. If planted, they will not grow. When you plant them in your body, they will not give adequate energy to support strong daily life. However, they may be used occasionally.

Whole grains and beans should be well-formed, without blemishes, distortions or discolorations. Green grains are only immature kernels and should be used along with the others.

Grains and beans are best stored in a cool, dry place. Keeping them in paper sacks allows them to breathe.

Sea Vegetables

Sea vegetables come from many parts of the world, including America, Europe, and Asia. There are a variety of kinds available to us today, such as *kombu*, *wakame*, *hijiki*, *arame*, *nori*, dulse, sea palm, and *Alaria*. Before the Industrial Revolution, when people were living closer to nature in agricultural communities, over a hundred different varieties of sea vegetables were enjoyed.

In selecting sea vegetables, choose those from cold, unpolluted waters. They are usually dried for easy packaging. They should be sun-dried, fairly clean of sand, and natural. Avoid sea vegetables that may have been prepared with flavorings, colorings, or chemical additives.

The best way to store sea vegetables is in a cool, dry place. If the air is humid, keep them in a tightly closed tin. Damp sea vegetables tend to become moldy.

Vegetables

When faced with the wide range of foods and vegetables presented to us in the marketplace, which have come from all over the world, often crossing seasonal borders, we should keep in mind that our main purpose is to establish an intimate oneness with our immediate environment, in order to create within ourselves harmony, strength, endurance, adaptability, flexibility, and clarity. When we eat foods from other climates or seasons, our body loses adaptability to the climate or season we are living in.

If we eat tropical foods in a temperate zone, summer foods in wintertime, fruits and salads on rainy days, or afternoon foods in the morning, we will cause imbalance both within ourselves and between ourselves and our surroundings. This imbalance gradually, or immediately, manifests in a number and variety of symptoms. Then we have to spend time making adjustments to cure the symptoms. It is much easier and more sound to lay a foundation for our daily practice based on following the natural order of the progression of seasons through the days and the years.

Geographically, we can extend our limits latitudinally around the world, but keeping within a 500-mile limit from where we live longitudinally. The closer the origin of our food is to us, the better. Ideally, it would come straight from our garden just before preparation.

There are several ways to know which vegetables are in season. Generally, winter vegetables are hardy and store well, such as squashes, roots, and hardier greens. Winter vegetables grow close to and under the ground. Summer vegetables consist of green and white leafy varieties, which are fragile and do not store for long periods of time. Summer vegetables grow above and less close to the ground.

We can understand the seasonal cycle of vegetables more clearly if we observe the Five Transformations of Energy.

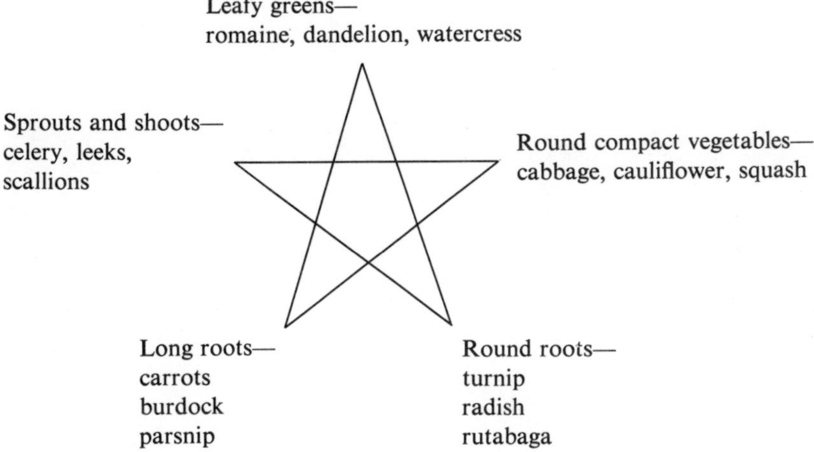

Just by observing nature, we can see that sprouts are abundant in spring, greens are abundant in summer, squashes and pumpkins are abundant in autumn, and roots are abundant in winter. A general rule is: in summer eat three parts greens to one part roots; in winter eat three parts roots to one part greens.

You can also ask the produce man which vegetables are local and which come from afar. Those that are imported are usually more expensive. Choosing local vegetables is more economical.

Select those vegetables which are the most symmetrical, are firm, with no bruises or blemishes, have true color, and are not waxed. Those with the smallest navels, hearts, or root centers are the most yang and have the best flavor. Choose smaller sizes, rather than larger, as the smaller size is more yang in quality and richer in taste. Bigger is not always better. Make sure the vegetables are whole and complete. Vegetables begin to lose their energy and nutrients after they are cut.

Whenever possible, choose organically grown, non-irradiated vegetables and foods. They have a higher percentage of nutrients, since the soil is improved with compost rather than depleted and chemicalized.

The following is the Firman E. Baer report from Rutgers University. It is an analysis of two lots of vegetables almost identical in appearance, one lot grown organically on soil rich in all needed plant requirements and another lot bought on the open market grown with commercial fertilizers. The difference in mineral content is very great in all minerals and trace elements, especially in cobalt, an ingredient of B_{12}, and in both copper and iron, necessary for blood hemoglobin.

The difference in mineral content shown in the chart substantiates the higher nutritional value, and thus healing quality, of organically grown vegetables.

Variation in Mineral Content in Vegetables

	Percentage of dry weight		Milli-equivalents per 100 grams dry weight				Trace elements parts per million dry matter				
	Total Ash or Mineral Matter	Phosphorus	Calcium	Magnesium	Potassium	Sodium	Boron	Manganese	Iron	Copper	Cobalt
Snap beans											
Organic	10.45	0.36	40.5	60.0	99.7	8.6	73	60	227	69	0.26
Inorganic	4.04	0.22	15.5	14.8	29.1	0.0	10	2	10	3	0.00
Cabbage											
Organic	10.38	0.38	60.0	43.6	148.3	20.4	42	13	94	48	0.15
Inorganic	6.12	0.18	17.5	15.6	53.7	0.8	7	2	20	0.4	0.00
Lettuce											
Organic	24.48	0.43	71.0	49.3	176.5	12.2	37	169	516	60	0.19
Inorganic	7.01	0.22	16.0	13.1	53.7	0.0	6	1	9	3	0.00
Tomatoes											
Organic	14.20	0.35	23.0	59.2	148.3	6.5	36	68	1,938	53	0.63
Inorganic	6.07	0.16	4.5	4.5	58.8	0.0	5	1	1	0	0.00
Spinach											
Organic	28.56	0.52	96.0	203.9	257.0	69.5	88	117	1,584	32	0.25
Inorganic	12.38	0.27	47.5	46.9	84.6	0.8	12	1	19	0.5	0.20

Most vegetables can be stored in the refrigerator before use. Squashes, onions, garlic, and ginger can be stored in a vegetable bin without refrigeration. Roots can be stored in a sand box or wrapped in paper and kept in the refrigerator. Lotus root stores well in the refrigerator if first wrapped in a brown paper bag. Greens keep best in the glass-covered refrigerator drawers.

It is not advisable to store cooked foods in plastic of any kind. Undesirable chemicals are absorbed from the plastic into the food. Also, plastic tends to create a positive ion field which changes the quality of the food and hastens spoilage.

Metal containers, or glass jars with metal lids, are also to be avoided for refrigerator storage. The salt in the cooked foods corrodes the metal and an undesirable chemical interchange takes place.

The best storage containers for cooked food are glass, Pyrex, Corning Ware, or porcelain or ceramic-covered dishes.

In preparing vegetables for cooking, they should be trimmed of all spoiled or inedible parts before washing in water. It is better not to soak vegetables during this process, as it leads to a loss of nutrients.

When trimming vegetables, take care to remove as little as possible of the root and navel as well as the shoot, especially in such vegetables as onions, turnips, *daikon*, radishes, carrots, and others. Removing too much of the top and bottom neuterizes the vegetable of its yin and yang poles, thus destroying its balance and healing power.

All water used for washing vegetables and other foods should be pure. If the quality of the tap water is questionable, it may be used for the first washings, if necessary, but should be followed by pure water for the final washings.

In proportioning vegetables for a dish, it is better to use a whole, small vegetable, if possible, than half, or part of, a larger vegetable, to prevent loss of energy and nutrients. Vegetables should be cut just before cooking. Ideally, they should come from the garden directly before preparation, cooking, and eating. In this way, the life-force is strongest.

Vegetables, as well as all foods, should be handled and treated with the greatest respect. They are the synthesis of the forces of Heaven and Earth giving themselves to us so that we can live. They are closer to us than our family and friends, actually transforming themselves into our very body and healing us of our sickness. This process is a miracle of miracles and borders on the sacred. All the more reason for blessing our food.

A Table ef Daily Foods

▽▽▽=Very yin
▽▽=More yin
▽=Yin
△=Yang
△△=More yang
△△△=Very yang

CEREALS
corn ▽
rye
barley
oats
wheat
quinoa
rice △
millet
amaranth
buckwheat △△

PEAS and BEANS
white soybeans ▽▽▽
fava beans
black soybeans
green peas—fresh
black-eyed peas
green peas—dried
broad beans
lima beans
mung beans
string (pole) beans
yellow split peas
small white beans
kidney beans ▽
pinto beans
red beans
black turtle beans
chick-peas (garbanzos)
lentils
azuki beans △△△

VEGETABLES
eggplant ▽▽▽
tomato
green pepper
okra
zuccini
sweet potato
white potato
mushroom
shiitake (dried Japanese mushroom)
asparagus
artichoke
spinach
bamboo shoots
purple cabbage
beets
red pepper
snow peas ▽▽
spaghetti squash
Tahitian squash
Mediterranean squash
cucumber
yellow crook-neck squash
coltsfoot
garlic
shiso (beefsteak plant)
cilantro
parsley
celery
scallions
mustard greens
turnip greens
bok choy
leeks
collards
romaine lettuce
rapini
broccoli
chicory
endive
cauliflower
green cabbage
red radish greens
daikon greens
jicama
turnip
black radish
red radish
daikon
onion
parsnip
carrot greens
dandelion leaves △
acorn squash
butternut squash
buttercup squash
Hokkaido pumpkin (*kabocha*) △△
watercress
lotus root
carrot
burdock
dandelion root
jinenjo △△△

FISH
oyster ▽
clam
octopus
carp
mussels
halibut
lobster
trout
sole
salmon △
shrimp
herring
sardine
red snapper
caviar △△

ANIMAL FOODS
snail ▽▽▽
frog
pork ▽▽
beef
horsemeat
hare
chicken ▽
pigeon △
duck
turkey
eggs △△
pheasant △△△

DAIRY PRODUCTS
yogurt ▽▽▽
kefir
sour cream
sweet cream
cream cheese
butter
buttermilk
cow's milk ▽▽
cottage cheese
Camembert
Gruyere
Roquefort △
Edam
goat's milk △△

FRUITS and NUTS
pineapple ▽▽▽
papaya
mango
guava
grapefruit
banana
fig

date
lemon
orange
lime
pear
peach
honeydew
cantaloupe
watermelon
Brazil nut
macadamia nut
pistachio
pine nut
cashew
hazelnut
peanut
almond
walnut
olive ▽
apricot
cherry
strawberry △
chestnut
apple

BEVERAGES
alcoholic drinks ▽▽▽
commercially dyed tea
coffee
artificially sweetened drinks
champagne
wine
fruit juice
beer
popular herbal teas
bancha leaf tea
carbonated water
spring water
mineral water
mugwort tea ▽
senna (*Habucha*)
lotus root tea
azuki tea
roasted *hatomugi* tea
roasted barley tea
twig tea (*bancha*) △
chicory coffee
grain coffee
burdock tea
dandelion coffee
Mu tea △△
ginseng tea △△△

MISCELLANEOUS
sugar ▽▽▽
honey
molasses
margarine
coconut oil ▽▽
palm kernel oil
peanut oil
olive oil
soy oil
sunflower oil ▽
safflower oil
corn oil
sesame oil △

Note: This list of foods and drinks from yin to yang is meant to be a general guide. Exceptions will always exist.

On Salt

Only in recent times has salt been so misunderstood, maligned, adulterated, and feared. Yet without salt, we cannot live. We are, after all, "the salt of the earth." Our blood is saline, resembling and reflecting the sea, the blood of the earth. We came from the ocean, over a long course of evolution and we carry a reflection of the ocean within us. The ocean is the mother of the earth and continues to nurture us from within as it did before from without. When it is in good health and balance, our blood maintains the 7:1 potassium to sodium ratio of the ocean. Not only our blood, but many of our body fluids are saline, such as saliva, tears, urine, and amniotic fluid, which is a miniature of the ocean in itself. Good health is based on a slightly alkaline system.

Many people have become afraid of salt for having the very qualities which give it virtue: the power to cause contraction. However, when the blood vessels and organs, especially the heart, are congested with animal fats and coated with cholesterol, plaque, and sludge, the passage through these vessels narrows, blocking the free flow of blood. If, in addition to this, an excessive amount of salt is eaten, as in commercially prepared foods, the vessels contract and narrow even more, aggravating the already-present high blood pressure. In extreme cases, a vessel closes completely, causing many complications, including organ malfunction and even heart attack.

In order to alleviate this problem, popular approaches to nutrition recommend a reduction in cholesterol and a cessation of salt. Instead of stopping the intake of fatty foods and other sticky, mucus- and sludge-forming foods—such as oils, sugars, honey, and sweet, sticky, oily, floury products—and taking steps to clean them out of the body through dietary adjustment, the secondary element of salt is given almost full responsibility and dismissed from the diet.

The next step is to administer the opposite of salt, potassium. The main virtue of potassium is its power to cause expansion. Potassium is taken in the forms of special drinks, soups, pills, and foods, such as potato (650 potassium: 1 sodium) and banana (850 potassium: 1 sodium). A banana a day, however, will not keep the doctor away. Imagine a balloon filled with oil or fat. The more it is filled the more it expands. The walls become more and more coated with sludge. If you try to blow air into the balloon, you find it will not take as much as an otherwise clean balloon would. The same is true with the lungs or any other oxygen-holding cell.

The potassium dilates the cell or vessel walls, expanding the passageway clogged by sludge. In the process of dilation, instead of becoming clean or stronger, the cell/vessel/organ walls become weak and flaccid, losing elasticity and contractive power, resulting in malfunction.

However, salt substitutes have become popular in the supermarkets and health food stores. These are typically made from such ingredients as *potassium chloride*, which is used as a fertilizer, having an yin expansive tendency; *glutamic acid*, an amino acid, which has an yin tendency; *potassium glutamate*, a compound combining potassium with *glutamine*, an amino acid, both having yin tendencies; and *tricalcium phosphate*, the combination of which is extremely yin. Calcium is itself yin as opposed to its counterpart, magnesium, which has a yang constrictive nature. The many salt substitutes, as well as commercially industrialized salts, even have sugar or dextrose added to them, both of which have extremely yin expansive tendencies, as well as a deleterious effect on the red blood cell.

The quantity of sodium included in these formulas is reduced to 0.0019 percent, as opposed to 83.0 percent potassium chloride. In other words, such formulas based on potassium chloride instead of sodium chloride, are totally opposite normal salt and the normal 7 potassium: 1 sodium balance in the blood. The result is a disastrous deterioration of the blood quality.

Even more widely used than salt substitutes is the industrially produced chemical compound sold as common table salt. This salt is produced in the cheapest way possible with no concern for the source or quality of the salt. Waters polluted with heavy metals and industrial wastes are often close and convenient sources of salt production. The salt is chemically treated, stripped of all the trace minerals essential to whole salt, bleached and refined to 99.99 percent pure sodium chloride. The toxic chemicals and additives used to treat and refine the salt are left in and add to the harmful effects. In this state, the altered salt damages the blood, body fluids, and organ functions, leading to a number of physiological and psychological imbalances and diseases. These include water imbalance, kidney malfunction and failure, overweight, hypertension, and heart trouble, among others.

Of all the essential minerals and trace elements that are stripped from the salt—including sulfur, phosphorus, potassium, calcium, magnesium, and iron—the most important to life is magnesium. Magnesium vitalizes all our cells. It is extracted from chlorophyll and transmuted into iron. Magnesium deficiency can lead to anemia, loss of calcium, overweight due to swelling; nerve, muscle, and skeletal weakness; dizziness, and nervousness.

Without proper salt, our body loses all vitality. The function of the nervous system breaks down, the blood cells deteriorate, contractive power is lost, and the body suffocates in an accumulation of toxic wastes.

True salt is mineral-balanced and whole. Natural sea salt is composed of 92 percent sodium chloride, 5 percent water, and 3 percent minerals. These minerals should include all 92 of the minerals of the earth, according to Noboru Muramoto, author of *Healing Ourselves*. Rainfall washes the minerals out of the earth, dissolves and carries them to the ocean. The ocean water evaporates in the sun and wind, concentrating the minerals left behind.

Since we came from the sea about 250 million years ago, the concentration of seawater has changed, but we still carry the same proportion of minerals in our blood as the ancient sea. At present the seawater has about 3.4 percent minerals in it (2.8 percent is NaCl). The body liquid has about 0.85 percent salt. This is why we cannot cook with seawater.

If we use natural sea salt, we will be eating all the elements of the earth and never need mineral supplementation. Supplements of vitamins and minerals became popular only after the industrial/commercial processing and refining of foods depleted them of their natural supply and balance. Even land salt has been leached of its minerals by the constant depletion of sun and rain. Up until the 1900s, foods were taken in their whole, organic form for thousands of years. There was seldom any need for supplementation.

> "The traditional way of production of sea salt with natural sunshine and cleaning with water is the best available method. Sea salt for daily use should contain 8 to 12 percent other mineral compounds besides 88 to 92 percent NaCl. Taste and quality of dishes and pickles seasoned or processed with such unrefined sea salt is greatly different in richness, and nutritional value is much higher than with refined salt."[5]

The best way to make sea salt, according to Noboru Muramoto, master salt-maker, is to first find an unpolluted coastal source of seawater which is clean and active. Form natural salt beds in which the salt can concentrate through evaporation by sun and wind. Let the lime sink undisturbed to the bottom. Then boil the concentrated seawater in a large enamel pot. Excess calcium will coagulate in clots and must be removed. The salt will crystallize and can be taken out at the right time to drain.

In this way the salt can also be cleaned of yin protein from the ocean, which tends to make skin rashes, and sand, which harms the kidneys and causes numbness in the muscles.

Thus, the salt is cleaned and still maintains its mineral balance. Made this natural way, it is always damp and never dry. Sea salt should always be taken in its whole, unadulterated form.

We should be as concerned with whole salt as we are with whole grains. It is the consistent taking in of partial foods, such as white flour, white rice, white sugar, demineralized salt, as well as any extracted and concentrated food, which causes the imbalances in our own bodies known as disease.

Alchemically, sodium and magnesium transmute into iron in our body. This is the iron that forms the hemoglobin in the red blood cell. As the blood passes through the

---

5 Michio Kushi, *The Book of Macrobiotics* (Tokyo: Japan Publications, Inc., 1977), p. 51.

lungs, the iron in the hemoglobin catches the oxygen brought in with the breath. This oxygen is the prime element in the process of combustion, which is essential in the digestion and metabolism of food. Without adequate salt, proper digestion cannot take place. With excess potassium, indigestion and fermentation is common, with the discomfort of gassiness. Not only is digestive combustion hampered, but the resulting spiritual brightness experienced through health and well-being is impeded.

Professor Chishima, previously of Nagoya Commercial University and President of the Society of Neo-Haematology, Gifu, Japan, made movies of the affect of a 5 percent saline solution on the blood. Before our eyes, the red blood cell became stronger and brighter, vivified by the small amount of salt. The blood became so bright that it virtually radiated on the screen. This is the same brightness that makes us feel emotionally happy, positive, optimistic, and cheerful. This iron-strong blood is magnetic to the higher vibrations of infinity itself, which is the source of our imagination, inspiration, revelation, and creativity. Without salt, or with an excessive potassium: sodium ratio in the blood, this attraction does not occur and our mentality becomes dark, pessimistic, fearful, defensive, and destructive.

The origin of the words *salt* (*sal*), and *sun*, or *solar* (*sol*) is similar. We cannot live without either of them. Surely salt, natural, mineral-balanced, sun-dried sea salt, is infinitely more valuable than gold.

The way of using sea salt is as important as the quality of the salt itself. Improper use, or excessive use, can disturb the balance of the body. There is no one who has not experienced thirst from the excessive intake of salt. Yet the amount that can be called excessive varies from person to person. Everyone's need for, and tolerance of, salt is different. Indeed, too much is as bad as none at all. Yet, it is an individual balance. Even our own balance changes from season to season, age to age, climate to climate and day to day. Excess salt can be balanced with a cup of tea, a vegetable or fruit, or with exercise or a hot bath.

The main point is not to make yourself thirsty. When we drink excessive liquid, we not only lose salt, we also lose many other essential minerals, just as a mountain becomes leached as the spring rains flow down its sides, leaving heavy deposits of mineral-rich silt at the bottom. Liquids, acid foods, such as citrus fruits and vinegar, wine and alcohol, dissolve the minerals in our body and displace them to various other parts of our body, causing the formation of spurs and stones. This mechanism is also influential in the creation of arthritis.

The secret of using salt properly is to cook it into the food, so that it enters the intestines with the food and is transmuted into blood along with the other nutrients absorbed from the digested food. If the salt is applied externally to the food, or added too late in the cooking, it is easily separated from the food in the mouth, dissolved in the saliva, and channeled to the kidneys, where it may cause the kidneys to contract, thus inhibiting the kidneys' ability to filter the body fluids efficiently. This causes a retention of fluids, along with those toxins and elements held within the fluid which are otherwise discharged. In this way, excessive salt or salt which is applied externally to the food, tends to hold yin elements in the body, whereas salt that is incorporated into the cooking tends to discharge yin elements from the body. Whereas one can hamper, the other can heal. Yet salt itself is not the culprit; it is the unskilled use of salt which is responsible.

In the history of mankind, wars have been fought over and men have died for, salt. Salt is the king of minerals and, in the course of evolution, has been a determining factor, along with the discovery and use of fire, in the achievement of upright stature and full development of man as *homo sapiens*. Through the use of fire and salt, man has been able to develop his nervous system, brain, language, and civilization. With proper natural sea salt he can continue to refine his higher human qualities in the course of evolution.

Jesus said, "Have salt in yourselves, and have peace one with another" (St. Mark 9: 50).

Average Concentration of Minerals Found in Sea Salt
(in parts per million parts of sea water by weights)

Chlorine	19,215.	Chromium	0.002
Sodium	10,685.	Mercury	0.0002
Oxygen	1,930. (also as gas)	Neon	0.00012
Magnesium	1,287.	Cadmium	0.00011
Sulfur	899.0	Selenium	0.00009
Calcium	410.	Germanium	0.00006
Potassium	396.	Xenon	0.00005
Bromine	66.8	Scandium	0.00004
Carbon	28. (also as gas)	Gallium	0.00003
Strontium	7.7	Zirconium	0.00003
Boron	4.4	Lead	0.00003
Silicon	3.0	Bismuth	0.00002
Hydrogen	2.7 (also in water)	Niobium	0.00002
Flourine	1.3	Gold	0.00001
Nitrogen	0.7 (also as gas)	Thalium	0.00001
Argon	0.45	Helium	0.000007
Lithium	0.17	Lanthanum	0.000003
Rubidium	0.12	Neodymium	0.000003
Phosphorus	0.09	Thorium	0.000002
Iodine	0.06	Cerium	0.000001
Copper	0.023	Cesium	0.000001
Barium	0.021	Terbium	0.000001
Indium	0.02	Yttrium	0.000001
Zinc	0.011	Dysprosium	0.0000009
Molybdenum	0.01	Erbium	0.0000009
Nickel	0.007	Ytterbium	0.0000008
Arsenic	0.003	Hafnium	0.0000008
Uranium	0.003	Gadolinium	0.0000007
Iron	0.002	Prasodymium	0.0000006
Manganese	0.002	Beryllium	0.0000006
Vanadium	0.002	Samarium	0.0000004
Aluminum	0.001	Holmium	0.0000002
Tin	0.0008	Lutecium	0.0000002
Cobalt	0.0004	Tantalum	0.0000002
Antimony	0.0003	Thulium	0.0000002
Silver	0.00028	Europium	0.0000001
Krypton	0.0002	Tungsten	0.0000001
		Protactinium	trace
		Radium	trace
		Radon	trace

Compiled by Turekian and Goldberg, Encyclopedia Britannica 1973.

On Dairy

Why do human beings drink animal milk?

No other animal in nature takes the milk of another species. All mammals give milk to their young until they have accumulated enough calcium to create teeth and grown enough to take the food of their species. Then they are weaned from their mother's milk and begin to establish their own independence. Only human beings continue to take milk and milk products, never weaning themselves from this infant stage.

It has been observed that people dependent on dairy products develop a general mentality of dependence—on authority figures, leaders, governors, guardian angels, liberators, and soothsayers. A real teacher or leader is one who shows us the way to take responsibility for our own lives. No one can live our life for us. "God helps those who help themselves." "For everyone that useth milk is unskillful in the word of righteousness: for he is a babe" (Hebrews 5: 13). Therefore, "As newborn babes, desire the sincere milk of the word, that ye may grow thereby" (1 Peter 2: 2).

Many Oriental people, Native American Indians, and others did not take milk for thousands of years until recently, under Western influence. They proved that milk and its products are not necessary for health or long life. Though it has been observed that the high calcium content of cow's milk makes bigger bodies, large body size does not necessarily mean physical strength or stronger bones. It has been shown in martial arts demonstrations that the bones of dairy-fed Westerners break much more easily than the bones of non-dairy, basically grain- and vegetable-eating Orientals.

The Recommended Daily Allowance of calcium for adults in America is one gram, more than twice as much as the 400 to 500 milligrams suggested as practical by the World Health Organization. Our human body does not need so much calcium. We are not making cows' bodies. We get all the nutrients we need, including protein and calcium, directly from the vegetable world, just as cows do. When we eat vegetable-quality food, and chew well, we are drinking the milk of our Earth Mother. "And it shall come to pass in that day, that the mountains shall drop down new wine [pure water], and the hills shall flow with milk [grains and vegetables—the milk of Mother Earth] . . ." (Joel 3: 18) ". . . although the fact that Canaan is a land flowing with milk and honey is so often mentioned [in the Bible] as one of its advantages, very little fuss is made about milk. Even in the nourishment which God gave to the people as a sign of His special Kindness are enumerated fine flour, oil and honey, but not milk."[6]

Dairy comes in many forms, though the source of all dairy products is milk: cow's milk, sheep's milk, goat's milk, yak's milk, horse's milk, and water-buffalo's milk. Biologically, animal milk is not suitable for human beings. It comes from a lower stage of evolution in the spiral of humanization. People probably started using animal milk when their own human milk failed, due to poor health, or when other food was lacking.

Milk is an yin transmutation of yang blood. It is white and sweet, while blood is red and salty. Since milk is so yin, it promotes expansion and growth—growth of babies as well as growth of bacteria from the air.

---

6 Julius Preuss, *Biblical and Talmudic Medicine* (New York: Hebrew Publishing Co., 1978), p. 562.

In nature, milk passes directly from the mother's body to the baby's body. It is never exposed to the air. As soon as raw milk hits the air, it begins to oxidize and spoil. It attracts bacteria which thrive in such an environment. This is why Louis Pasteur "pasteurized" milk by boiling, to kill the bacteria and any living organisms in it. However, this also kills many essential digestive enzymes and elements which give the baby immunity to disease. Dairy-fed infants do not get this immunity. Thus, the immune system begins to weaken in infancy. Many infants suffer from colic and rashes due to animal milk, and adults suffer indigestion or other types of intolerance to animal milk. They do not have the necessary enzymes to digest it, even if they drink raw milk. Human milk never causes such disturbances.

In order to preserve milk before pasteurization was developed, it was soured to make buttermilk, yogurt and sour cream, or it was salted and aged to make cheese.

All milk and milk products in their sweet and sour forms are more yin. All milk and milk products in their salted, aged, and compacted forms are more yang. Those yin products—milk, yogurt, cream, butter, and soft cheese—tend to rise up in the body, just as they do in a vessel. Those yang products—denser and heavier cheeses—tend to sink down in the body, just as they do in a vessel. Thus, various forms of dairy settle in corresponding parts of the body. There they may curdle, congest, create mucus, cysts, tumors, calcification, and, over time, stones.

Milk is already full of fat. This fat is concentrated to make butter and cheese. For example, it takes fifteen liters of milk to make one pound of butter. Imagine how much more fat is compressed into cheese. This concentration of heavy fat settles in all the organs of the body, especially in the lower body. The liver, involved in the digestion of fats, becomes overloaded. The gallbladder and bile ducts become blocked from the concentrations of fat and stones that accumulate. The pancreas becomes surrounded and impregnated with fat, impeding the efficient function of blood-sugar regulation, leading to hypoglycemia, anemia, diabetes, and leukemia. The villi in the small intestine become coated, which inhibits the smooth transmutation of food into blood, leading to anemia and fatigue. The heart and blood vessels become coated and plaqued with fat and cholesterol and the whole circulatory system suffers. Dairy is a major cause of sinus trouble, asthma, allergies, and psoriasis. Psoriasis itself is the body's desperate attempt to discharge through the skin the excess fat that the overloaded organs can no longer discharge through their normal channels.

Fat and cholesterol are not the only culprits. The hypercalcemia caused by the intake of excessive calcium, especially in the form of "vitamin D fortified" milk and dairy products, is often related to female breast cancer. Many diseases of the reproductive organs are directly related to dairy, which comes from the organs related to reproduction in the animal. Perhaps we should do as the Romans did and use butter only as a liniment for children.

For a thorough discussion of the negative biochemical effects of dairy food on human beings, please read *A Macrobiotic Explanation of Pathological Calcification* by J. Yogamundi Moon.

How to Check Your Daily Condition to Determine How to Eat

A broad variety of whole grains, beans, seeds, sea vegetables, roots, round ground vegetables and dark leafy greens, as well as occasional fruits, when appropriate, are recommended for daily food. However, specific adjustments may be necessary from day to day to balance your constantly changing condition, as well as to harmonize with the weather and season.

Your daily condition determines your daily nutritional needs. There are innumerable simple signs by which to check your health. These have traditionally been used by people all over the world to guide them in their personal self care. If any symptoms increase or continue, it is advisable to consult a certified macrobiotic consultant or medical doctor.

All conditions are categorized according to yin (▽), expansive nature, or yang (△), contractive nature. The following is a representative listing of some of these signs.

Feature	*Condition*	*Yin/Yang Nature*	*Cause*	*Adjustment*
Head	Frontal ache	Yin	Soft drinks, chemicals, sugar, fruit juice	Chew 1 to 2 teaspoons sesame salt (gomashio).
	Posterior ache	Yang	Excess salt, baked food, animal food	Take shiitake mushroom tea.
Brow	Vertical lines	Yang	Animal foods, baked flour products, excess salt	Reduce cause. Increase vegetables.
Hair	Curly	Yang	Extreme yin and yang food: meat and sugar	Take balanced grains and vegetables.
	Frontal loss	Yin	Excess liquids	Take less liquid, juice, alcohol.
	Posterior loss	Yang	Excess animal food and dairy	Reduce cause. Increase vegetables.
	Split ends	Yin	Excess liquids, juices	Reduce cause and increase sea salt.
Complexion	Red	Yang	Excess animal food	Reduce animal food. Increase vegetables.
	Pale	Yin	Excess sugar, fruits, potassium, drugs	Take grains and vegetables.
	Oily Pimples	Yang	Excess animal oils and fats	Reduce fats. Increase vegetables.
Eyes	Bloodshot	Yin	Excess alcohol, fruit juice, soft drinks, drugs; eyestrain	Reduce cause. Rest. Take well-cooked grains and vegetables.
Eyelids	Swollen	Yin	Excess liquid or oil	Reduce liquid and oil.
Under eyes	Swollen	Yang	Excess salt plus liquid	Take grated daikon drink, hot apple juice, hot bath.

Feature	*Condition*	*Yin/ Yang Nature*	*Cause*	*Adjustment*
Ears	Red	Yang	Excess animal food or salt	Reduce cause. Take tea, apple juice, vegetables, hot bath.
Nose	Swollen	Excess yin and yang	Liquids, fruits, animal fats, dairy	Reduce cause. Eat grains and vegetables.
	Indented	Yang	Excess salt, eggs, chips	Reduce cause. Increase vegetables.
Body	Odor	Yang	Animal foods, acidic foods	Reduce cause. Increase dark leafy greens.
Skin	Dry	Excess yin or yang	Animal fat clogging pores; sugar, citrus, vinegar, acid, alcohol	Reduce cause. Increase grains and vegetables. Brush skin.
Nails	White spots	Yin	Excess vitamin C, drugs and medications	Reduce cause. Eat balanced grains and vegetables.
	Split	Yin	Fruits, juices, sodas, sugar	Reduce cause. Eat balanced grains and vegetables.
Abdomen	Gas	Yin	Improper cooking, chewing and digestion; Raw vegetables and fruits; Carbonated liquids	Chew well. Cook vegetables. Drink kuzu tea.
Bowel movement	Constipation	Yang	Animal foods, hard dry baked foods	Reduce cause. Increase vegetables.
	Diarrhea	Yin	Fruits, juices, raw foods, oily food	Eat balanced grains and cooked vegetables. Take thick kuzu with tamari.
Urination	Frequent, full	Yin	Excess liquid	Reduce liquid and cause: excess salt, oily food, dry food.
	Frequent, sparse	Yang	Excess salt or dry food	Reduce cause. Take daikon drink or bancha tea with hot apple juice.
	Pale, clear	Yin	Excess salad, fruit, juice; insufficient minerals	Reduce cause. Take whole grains, cooked vegetables with appropriate salt seasoning.
Emotions	Anger	Yang	Animal food, excess salt or yang cooking	Reduce cause. Eat green and white vegetables, small salad.
	Depression	Yin	Fruits, juices, sugar or other sweets, insufficient whole foods and minerals	Reduce cause. Increase whole grains. Drink tamari bancha tea.
	Confusion and anxiety	Yin/yang imbalance	Inconsistent balance in daily food	Prepare whole grains and vegetables in well-balanced way. Eat less. Chew well.

Feature	Condition	Yin/Yang Nature	Cause	Adjustment
Weather/ season	Hot: irritable, impatient	Yang	Animal food, excess fire	Take quick-boiled or steamed green and white vegetables.
	Cold: inactive, pessimistic	Yin	Excess fruits, vegetables; insufficient fire and minerals	Take well-cooked, sautéed vegetables with delicious salty taste.

For a more comprehensive coverage of these conditions, please see the sections on Internal and External Remedies. Also consult *Macrobiotic Home Remedies* by Michio Kushi.

The Order of Cooking

Plan your menu according to the climate, season, weather and daily condition of the diners. Try to balance each recipe, each menu, the meals of the day, the meals of the week, the month and the seasons. By following nature, the moon and the sun, the years of your life should go smoothly.

Gather all ingredients necessary from the beginning. Clean and wash all the grains, beans, seeds, and vegetables at one time. Drain them and pat them dry, so that you do not work in a flood.

Prepare the soup stock to boil and simmer during the rest of the preparation. Then put up the beans and main grain to cook while preparing the side dishes. Soak any sea vegetables included in the menu.

Proceed to the cutting of vegetables. Start with those vegetables which need a longer time to cook. After cutting and starting their cooking, cut and start cooking the sea vegetables. Leave the fast-cooking vegetables for last, cutting them while everything else is cooking. Leafy greens are best cooked whole, rinsed in cold water, gently squeezed and then cut, to prevent loss of nutrients. Pickles can be made first, before anything else, or the night before, or on weekends.

To facilitate the order of preparation, and make efficient use of the stove, whole grains can be cooked on the right back burner, the most yang position (△△). Beans or soups can be cooked on the left back burner, the next yang position (▽△). These long-cooking foods, in larger pots, are then out of the way. Sea vegetables or longer-cooking root dishes can be cooked on the right front burner, the less yin position (△▽). Then boiled salads or greens can be cooked on the left front burner, the most yin position (▽▽). This practice enhances the smooth flow of cooking and moving in the kitchen.

Some general suggestions:

- A diluted salt-water glaze added to roasting nuts and seeds adds an alkaline balance to their protein and may be preferable to the addition of tamari soy sauce.

- Among beans, soybeans and their products are appropriate for soybean-based miso soup. Garbanzos may be added to chick-pea miso soup.
- When cooking beans or bean products, tamari soy sauce or miso may be added to soybeans. Otherwise, sea salt is recommended for other beans.
- It is not advisable to use tamari soy sauce on grain as a condiment, unless that grain has been fried in oil with vegetables. Otherwise, it is too yang and will stimulate thirst, hunger, and cravings.

There are many different kinds of miso. In the Orient, every year many families traditionally made their own miso. Hundreds of different varieties developed. We are enjoying a few of these at this time.

Hatcho miso is made only from soybeans and sea salt. It is aged for a minimum of three years and is the strongest of the misos.

Barley or mugi miso is made from barley, soybeans, sea salt and water. It is aged for a minimum of eighteen months and is recommended for daily use throughout the year.

Brown rice or *genmai* miso is made from brown rice, soybeans, sea salt and water. It has a higher percentage of sea salt than barley miso.

Red (*Aka*) miso is made from rice *koji*, soybeans, and sea salt. It is a more quickly fermented miso.

Miso can be made from almost any variety of grains and beans. For a more comprehensive overview of miso, please read *How to Cook with Miso* by Aveline Kushi.

Many people have expressed concern over the loss of vitamin C and essential enzymes due to the application of fire in cooking. However, there is no need for concern. One should understand the necessity of balancing water with fire. In raw vegetarian cuisines, Water energy dominates, Fire energy is lacking. This is why followers often become weak and seek some form of animal food such as cheese or eggs. Through the application of fire, we can change the yin qualities of foods to yang and thus provide our body and mind with the strength, staying power, and centering they need.

If green and white vegetables, high in vitamin C, are cooked quickly, vitamin C loss will be at a minimum.

The same is true for enzymes. Quick-cooking retains the more stable enzymes and controls the more volatile yeasts and molds which foster candida and other yeast infections.

The use of miso, tamari soy sauce, *natto*, *tempeh* and bran pickles, provides us daily with a full range of digestive enzymes. A variety of other pickles also provide us with adequate enzymes, as well as vitamin C.

With the conscious use of fire, water, fermentation, salt, pressure, and time, we have the best tools for creating the greatest flexibility and control in maintaining our health and adaptability.

Variations of quantity and time in the use of water, fire, salt, time, and pressure alter the energy in the food. These factors need to be carefully regulated when applied to healing, in order to change extreme yin or yang conditions and establish balance and normal function. These cannot easily be taught in, or learned from, any book. Therefore, it is highly recommended that one studies with a certified and/or qualified teacher.

The cooking techniques presented in this book have been kept simple for the purpose of cleansing and healing. For the healthy and active person, there are many more techniques and styles that can be used in more elaborate preparations.

The Way of Cutting (*Kirikata*)

Vegetables can teach us a lot about life. They speak to us in a language of their own. To most people, this language is secret, but to those who understand, it teaches the wisdom of the universe.

Vegetables speak to us in blatant silence, through their color, shape, size, structure, density, and taste, and through their direction and season of growth. Everything we need to know is there, if only we will see.

For instance, the onion is like a small Earth. It has two poles, north and south. The south pole is solid like the Antarctic continent. The north pole is open like the Arctic Ocean. The lines running north and south between the poles are energy lines, meridians, through which Heaven's force and Earth's force are channelled. All vegetables have similar meridians, analogous to the meridians in our own body. For this reason, we do not cut onion rings, severing the lines of energy. We cut along the meridians to preserve their yin/yang balance and the integrity of the whole.

The art of food preparation is inspired by the art in nature. Food that is as beautiful and delicious as it is nourishing appeals to the body, mind, and spirit, and heals the whole person.

One of the most important aspects of food preparation is the way of cutting. The integral harmony of yin and yang must be maintained in each slice of food in order to retain wholeness in the meal. The size of the pieces must relate to each other to unify the dish. The size of the main ingredient of a dish determines the size of the supporting ingredients. The vegetables may all be cut in the same style, as long as it is appropriate to each vegetable, or they may be cut in a variety of styles, as long as a similar size is maintained. This ensures evenness in the cooking and creates harmony in the dish. Interestingly, the size and shape of the cut alters the taste of the food.

Koguchigiri: *Ko* means "small," *Guchi* means "edge." *Koguchigiri* means "cutting into thin bite-size rounds."

Koguchigiri Hanagata: Cut into thin rounds; then carve into flowers or pinwheels by cutting small wedges from the edge.

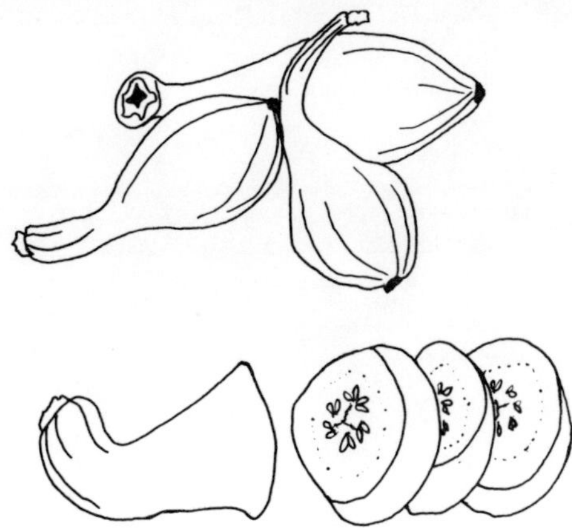

Wagiri: *Wa* means "circle." Cut into circles thicker than for Koguchigiri.

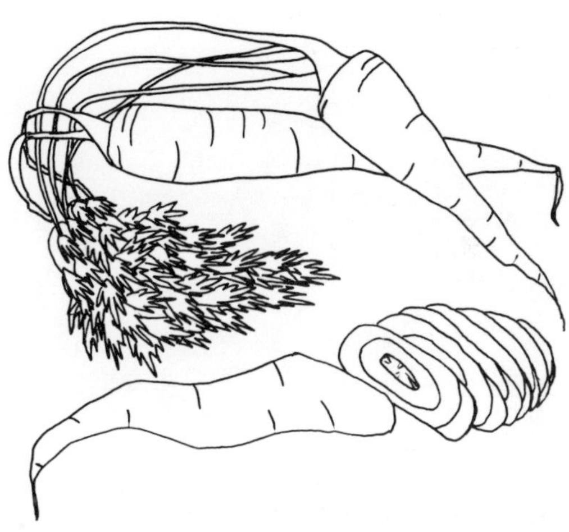

Hasugiri: *Hasu* means "diagonal." Any long vegetable can be cut in thin or thick diagonals. This way, each slice has both yin and yang tendencies and is balanced.

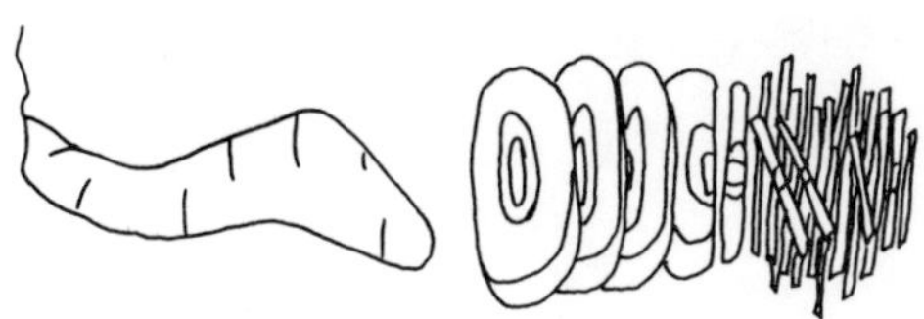

Sengiri: Two words have the sound of *Sen*. One means thousand and the other means line. The style of cutting in a thousand lines is also called matchsticks or "julienne." First cut Hasugiri in 1 1/2″ lengths. Then turn and cut along the length in thin or thicker lines.

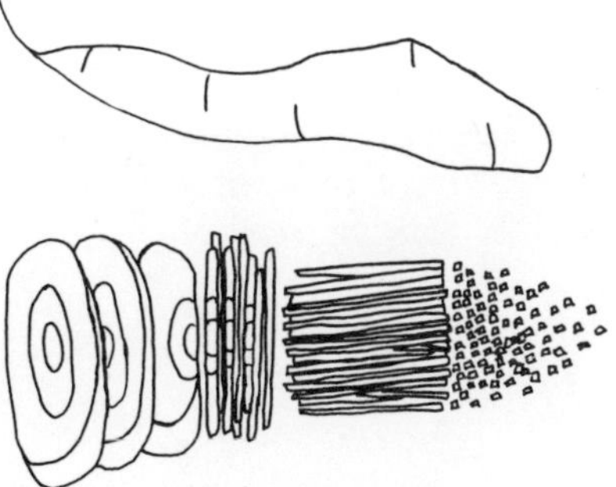

Mijingiri: *Mijin* is a particle of dust. It is a way of mincing vegetables in tiny pieces, sometimes as fine as powder.

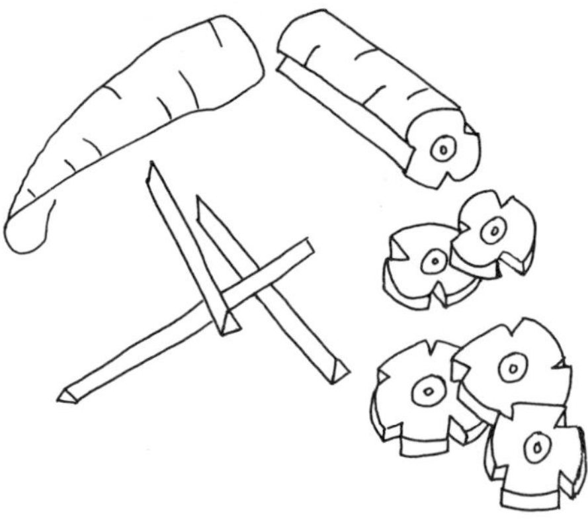

Hanagata: *Hana* means "flower." Carve three or five long thin wedges along the length of the vegetable. Then cut into rounds.

Hangetsugiri: *Han* means "half," *getsu* means "moon." Cut vegetable into half lengthwise. Then cut across, Koguchigiri, in half-moons.

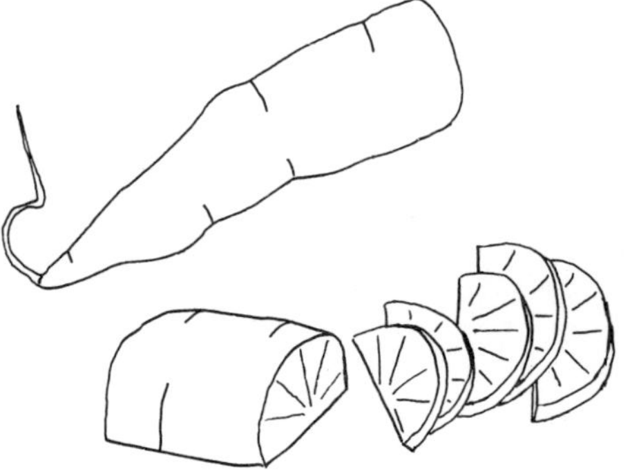

Ichogiri: *Icho* means "ginkgo tree" in Japanese. It has heart shaped leaves. Cut the vegetable into quarters lengthwise. Then cut across, Koguchigiri.

Sainome: *Sai* are "dice," *nome* is the face, or eyes, of the dice. Cut the vegetables in cubes, the size depending on the vegetable, style of cooking, and dish being prepared.

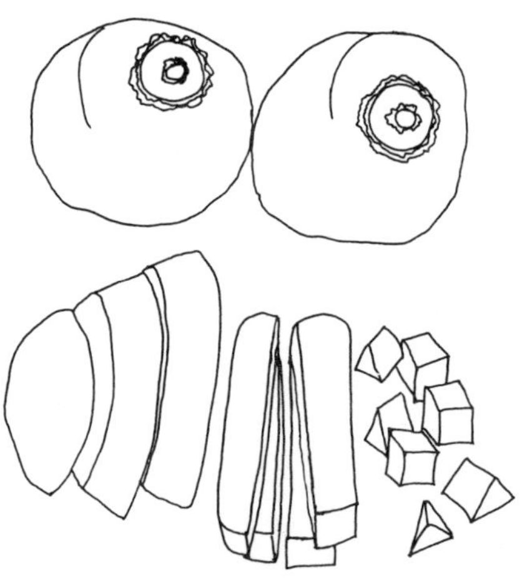

Kikukagiri: *Kikuka* are chrysanthemum flowers. Many vegetables can be cut like chrysanthemums, especially those used decoratively for salads, like red radish. Turnip, *daikon* or other large vegetable should be cut in 1″ to 2″ sections first. Then, place between a pair of chopsticks and slice crosswise in 1/16″ to 1/8″ widths down to the chopsticks. Turn the vegetable 90° and slice in the opposite direction. Soaking in ice water will open the vegetable "petals" like a flower.

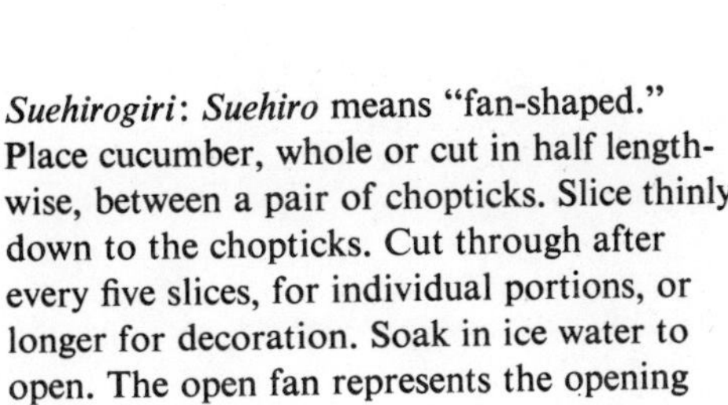

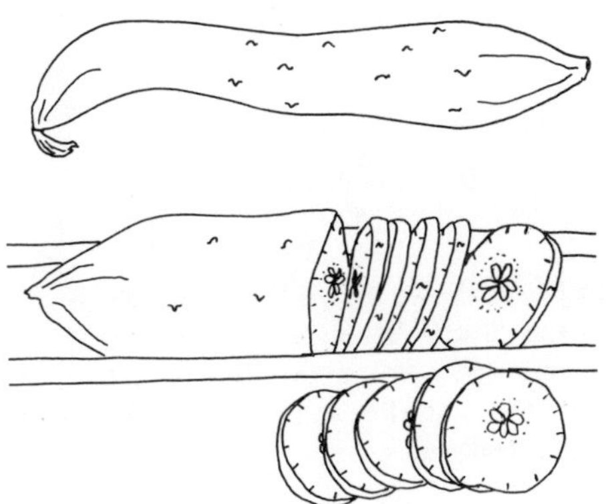

Suehirogiri: *Suehiro* means "fan-shaped." Place cucumber, whole or cut in half lengthwise, between a pair of chopticks. Slice thinly down to the chopticks. Cut through after every five slices, for individual portions, or longer for decoration. Soak in ice water to open. The open fan represents the opening of the future.

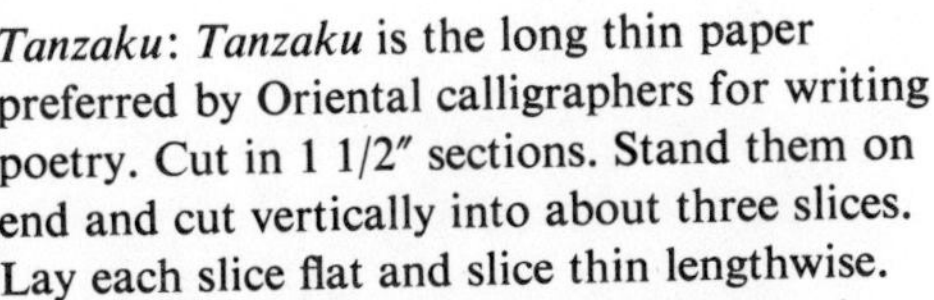

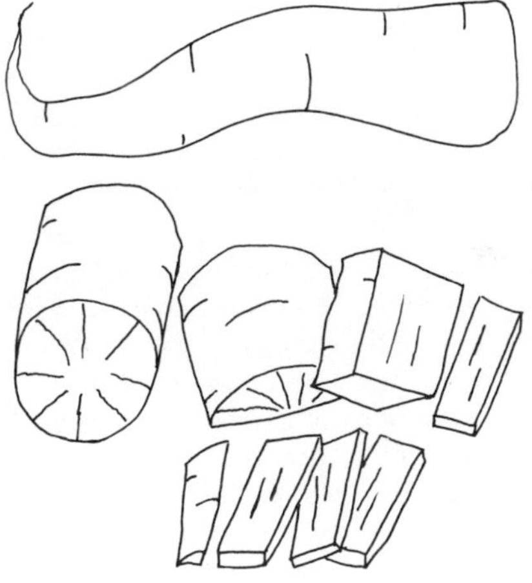

Tanzaku: *Tanzaku* is the long thin paper preferred by Oriental calligraphers for writing poetry. Cut in 1 1/2″ sections. Stand them on end and cut vertically into about three slices. Lay each slice flat and slice thin lengthwise.

For decorative cut, slice several pieces in opposite cuts lengthwise without cutting through the ends. Fold one side over the other.

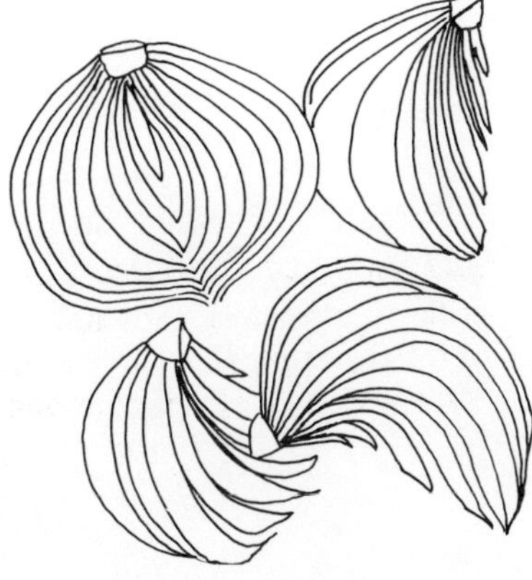

Mawashigiri: *Mawashi* means "turn." To cut round vegetables, cut in half from core to top. Turning on axis, slice in half-moons, or crescents, in desired thickness. Be sure to include part of the core in each slice.

Rangiri: *Ran* means "irregular." For large vegetables, slice in quarters or sixths lengthwise. Then cut the same as roots. Start at the thick end, or top of the root. Slice on 1″ diagonal, turn slightly and slice on similar diagonal. Continue to the end, lengthening angle of diagonal as vegetable becomes thinner. This is a rolling cut. Cut all pieces the same size.

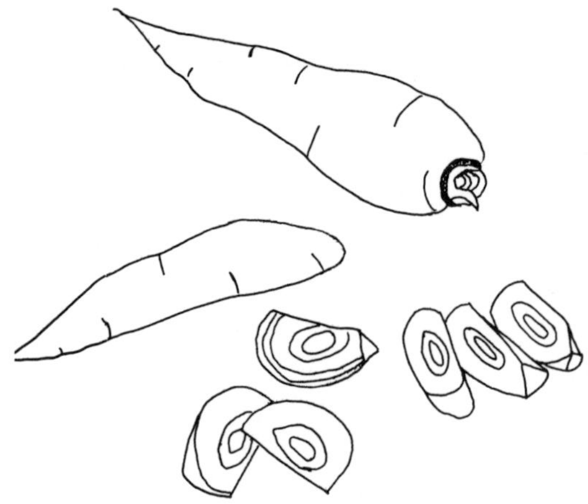

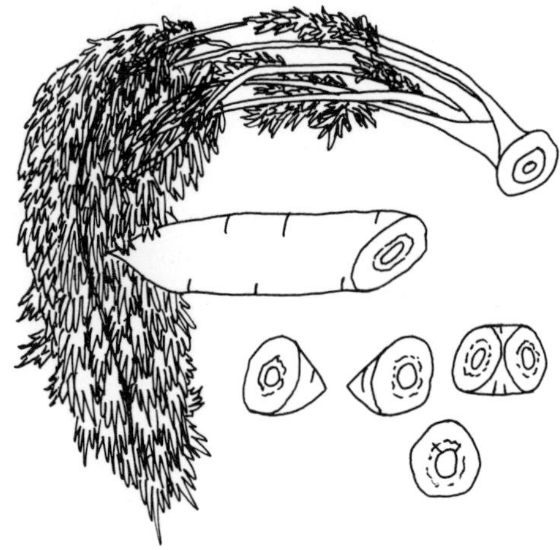

Shikagiri: *Shika* means "deer." *Shikagiri* means "deer's feet style." Cut vegetables in a similar way as Rangiri. This time, turn vegetable 180° and slice sharp angles. The result is like deers' feet.

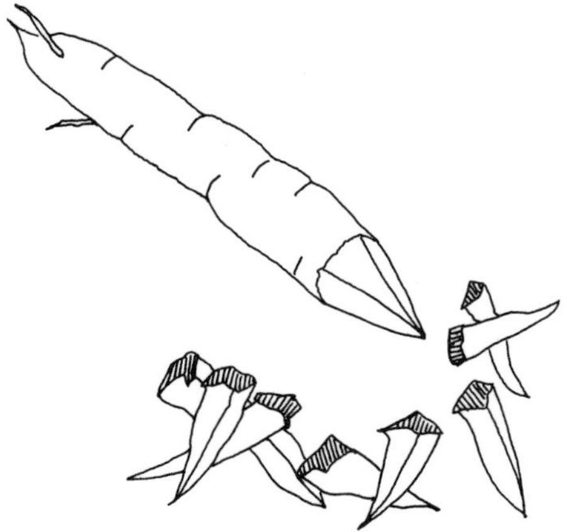

Sasagaki: *Sasa* is a small bamboo leaf, *gaki* means "to shave." This cut is like pencil shavings and is a traditional cut for burdock. Thicker roots should be sliced in "fingers" lengthwise through the thick half. Then, shave the root in about 1″ lengths catching part of the skin and a part of the core in each cut. Rotate the root as you cut. Then shavings may be thicker or thinner, depending on the vegetable and taste desired.

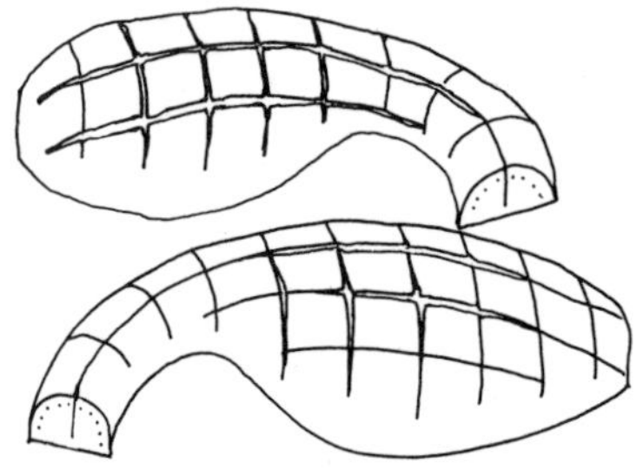

Kikkogiri: *Kikko* is tortoise shell. Cut a 1/2″ grille, or crosshatch pattern, through the skin of the vegetable, about 1/4″ to 1/2″ deep, without going all the way through.

Methods of Cooking

Various methods of cooking exist to give us flexibility in creating internal balance. Different methods of cooking contribute different qualities of energy to the food. Also, different methods of cooking are appropriate for different climates, seasons or weather conditions.

For example, boiling and quick water-sautéing are suitable for spring; boiling and steaming are suitable for summer; boiling and longer water-sautéing are suitable for Indian Summer; pressure-cooking and oil-sautéing are suitable for autumn; baking and deep-frying are suitable for winter.

Of course, all methods of cooking can be used all year round, but their frequency changes with the season. It is recommended to pressure-cook grains in cold weather and pot-cook them in hot weather, unless otherwise individually recommended.

We can see the shift of energy more clearly in the Five Transformations diagram.

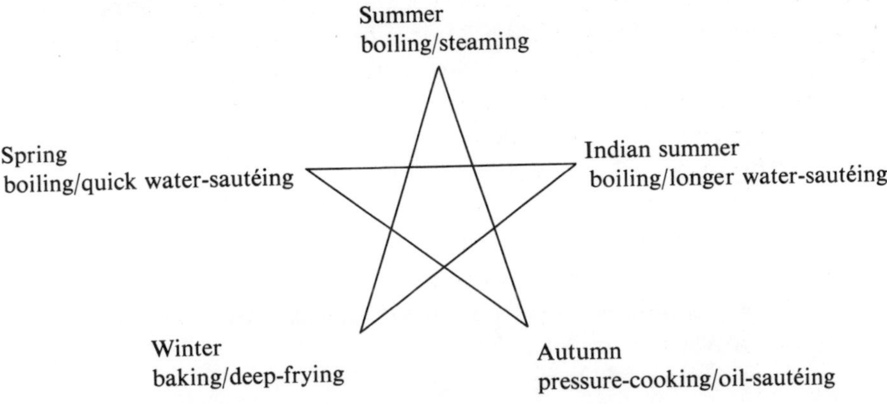

- *To steam* means to cook food in a double-layered pot. The bottom layer holds boiling water which sends steam up into the top layer through holes in its base. When steaming squash, bread, tofu, and other preparations, it is best to use a steaming cloth. A 2-foot square of white muslin, wrung out in pure, cold water, is used to line the top layer. The vegetables are placed on the cloth, which is then folded over the food. Then the pot is covered. The steaming cloth absorbs excess moisture and the vegetables are kept fairly dry.
- *To quick-boil* means to bring more or less water to a boil, depending on how much is needed, adding a pinch of sea salt, for yin ingredients, and boiling the vegetables quickly, uncovered, on a medium-high fire, until their color becomes bright. They may be removed while still slightly crunchy, or cooked a little longer until tender. Do not overcook or the vegetables will lose their color. Greens should be rinsed in cold water immediately after boiling in order to stop the cooking and preserve the color. This is especially appropriate for more light green and white vegetables.
- *To boil* is to follow the same procedure as for quick-boiling, except for covering and cooking the foods longer, until they are done. This is especially suitable for grains, beans, sea vegetables, and roots.
- *To water-sauté* is to substitute water for oil for the purpose of sautéing. Sautéing is a technique for discharging excessive yin elements from the food. To water-

sauté, bring to a boil a 1/4 inch of water. For more yin ingredients, add a pinch of sea salt after the water comes to a boil. Sauté vegetables on a medium high fire in order of yin to yang, until the color becomes bright or more mellow, depending on the vegetable, and the strong smell evaporates.

- *To oil-sauté* is to follow the same procedure as for water-sautéing, but using 1 or 2 tablespoons of sesame or corn oil instead. Since oil is more yin than water, it attracts that much more heat from the fire. Oil-sautéing is stronger and thus a more yangizing method of cooking.
- *To bake* is to cook the foods in the oven or Dutch-oven, a special heavy pot used on top of the stove.
- *To roast* is to toast grains, beans, seeds, or nuts in a dry cast-iron skillet on top of the stove, stirring them with a bamboo or wooden paddle or spoon. Use a medium to low fire.
- *To wash* grains and beans: Pick out stones, twigs, and poorly formed grains and beans. (Collect the latter to wash, roast, and boil for tea). Wash several times in a bowl of cold water, pouring off any debris that floats to the top. Add new water each time, repeating until the water runs clear. Never rub the grains, as this will polish them. Do the last wash in a fine-meshed strainer, rinsing out with pure water any dust that may have settled to the bottom.
- *To pressure-cook* brown rice, millet or barley:

  1 cup rice to 1 1/4 cups water
  2 cups rice to 2 1/2 cups water
  4 cups rice to 5 cups water
  5 cups rice to 6 1/4 cups water
  6 cups rice to 7 1/4 cups water
  (Water is reduced slightly as rice is increased over 5 cups.)
- *To pot-cook* brown rice, millet or barley:

  1 cup rice to 1 1/2 cups water
  2 cups rice to 3 cups water
  4 cups rice to 6 cups water
  5 cups rice to 7 1/4 cups water
  6 cups rice to 8 1/2 cups water
  (Water is reduced slightly as rice is increased over 5 cups.)

Note: These measurements may change at high altitudes. In a dry climate, 1 cup rice to 1 1/2 to 2 cups water may be pressure-cooked. Cook for 40 to 50 minutes.

To cook other grains, such as buckwheat, whole wheat, rye, oats, amaranth, quinoa, corn, bulgur and couscous, different procedures are necessary. Some of these are presented in the recipes that follow. Others will be presented in the forthcoming book, *Growing Up Macrobiotically*.

Way of Serving and Eating

Whole grain forms the basis and center of food for human beings. It has supported human development around the world for thousands of years. It is the most balanced food in the Vegetal Kingdom. It is also the most yang. Therefore, it is appropriately placed at the center, or to the right, on the dinner plate. Beans, generically close to grains, are placed in the next lower position. Sea vegetables, the first vegetables on Earth, needed for their alkaline minerals to balance the acid protein of beans, may be placed to the left of the beans. Then, in ascending order of natural growth, roots, round ground vegetables, and greens may be arranged. Pickles, to be eaten at the end of the meal to assist digestion, may be placed at the top of the plate.

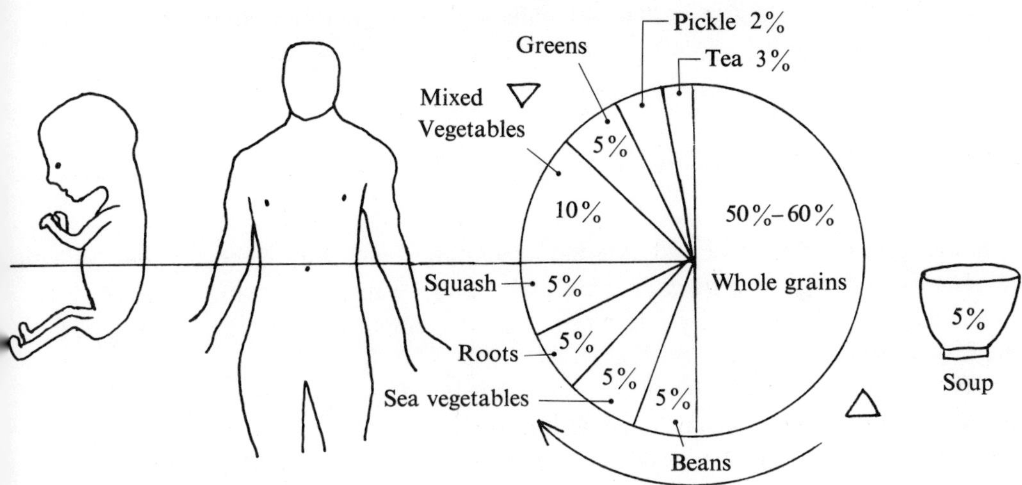

Eating in a clockwise direction, we follow the order of foods on the plate from yang to yin. This allows digestion to take place in an orderly fashion, from more-cooked food to less-cooked food, and the digestive organs can expand gradually.

This arrangement also draws our attention to the natural process of growth in nature. Out of the seed issue the roots, round vegetables, and shoots. The plate is designed like a fetus. The lower roots nourish our roots, the digestive organs. The middle round vegetables nourish the middle organs of our body, the stomach, pancreas, and liver. The upper greens nourish the upper respiratory organs of our body, the lungs. They also nourish the blood, heart, and circulatory system.

In this way, we can more clearly and directly see the relationship of various foods to the parts of our body and we can more knowingly eat to strengthen those parts that are weak.

For the purposes of healing, it is better to eat in calm and quiet surroundings. This way we can pay better attention to enjoying our meal and to chewing well. Chewing is the last step in the process of cooking, the transmutation of vegetal matter into human being. Chew each mouthful a minimum of fifty times. If you can chew two hundred times, healing will be hastened.

Saliva is one of the sacred fluids of the body. It is in the mouth that carbohydrates are digested. The work of the teeth cannot be done in any other place in the body. The food should be chewed until the quantity of saliva overcomes the quantity of food and all that is left is liquid. Do not swallow pieces of food. Gandhi said, "Chew your liquids and drink your foods."

One of the reasons most people do not chew very well is because of inappropriate methods of cooking. Many cooks add seasoning to the food toward or at the end of the cooking, so it only covers the outside of the food. When we eat this, we savor the seasoning, but swallow it quickly. The remaining food has so little taste that we swallow it just to get rid of it.

Instead, if the seasoning is cooked into the food, macrobiotically unifying flavor and substance, the delicious taste will not only last but improve as long as we chew. Then the pleasure of chewing increases.

There are three stages in the process of chewing. Stage one is to chew to break down the solid structure of the food. Stage two is to chew the pulp to extract the liquid. Stage three is to chew the liquid to release the universal energy which enlivens us.

This is the royal road to the Pearly Gates of Heaven. Do you know where they are?

Gratitude, Prayer, and Grace

All life is spiralic. It is described as a movement and rest. During the day we are busy at work; at night we sleep. We are active and we rest. We rest in order to become active again. The days and nights, our movement and rest, form the spiralic design of our life.

When we take our meals, we must also rest from all external activity, in order to relax and facilitate the internal movement of digestion. This period of separation and distinction between outer activity and inner activity was ritualized long ago into forms of prayer: the time for offering gratitude for the meal to be received and for receiving grace through the nourishment given from Heaven and Earth.

In giving thanks for the nourishment that sustains us, we should consider all the forces of heaven and earth, the rain and the sun, the farmers, the transporters, the market men and women, and the cooks who made it possible for it to be brought before us. We also give thanks for the company of those sharing the meal with us. We should sit with good posture and breathe deeply and calmly to facilitate digestion.

Having acknowledged its source and prepared our body and mind for receiving it, with calm and glad heart, we enjoy our meal and renew ourselves.

Zen Prayer Before Meals

Innumerable labors have brought us this food.
We should know how it comes to us.
In receiving this offering, we should consider
   whether our practice and virtue deserve it.
Desiring the natural order of mind, we should
   be free from hate, greed and, delusion.
We eat to support life and practice the way of God.

Part 2

Cooking for Regeneration According to the Cycle of Seasons

Spring Cooking

Spring is the renaissance of life. After a long winter of storing energy, the earth releases its concentrated life-force, stimulated by the expanding warmth of the sun. Seeds sprout from beneath the ground, animals emerge from hibernation, and people come forth from the shelter of their homes, to mingle together in the light. In a spasm of spring fever, semen rises like sap in the trees, and the Earth mates with the Gods. Thus, Wood symbolizes the rising energy of Spring.

The Spring Equinox brings the time for planting. Encouraged by the increasing heat of longer days, the earth expands and opens, its energy rising in a miraculous display of grasses, plants, and flowers of innumerable colors and designs. The vegetal kingdom is born again out of her womb, nourishing her children with this green placenta.

The young plants are nursed by spring rains, the morning dew of the dawn of the year. Grasses unfold with the fresh taste of water, as sprouts, wild onions, celery and scallions, mustard greens and mugwort, sourdock and other young leafy greens, wakame and *mekabu*, strawberries, green apples, and green tea. The young roots are small and immature. The cool, wet energy of green and white vegetables refreshes the body and dispels the heaviness of winter cooking. Wild herbs prod the body back into action and stimulate creative imagination.

Grains are also expanded, forming the double-lobes of barley, wheat and rye. They nourish the lobes of the liver and gallbladder. Fermented foods, such as sourdough steamed bread, brown rice and barley vinegars, tempeh and natto, sauerkraut and pickles, help to relieve any congestion in the liver due to the extra proteins and oils needed in winter to combat the cold. If the liver is well balanced, no anger will arise.

The cooking becomes lighter than the longer cooking of winter. Fresh and sour tastes enliven the meals. When used well, the sour taste is slightly astringent, and helps the energy flow evenly. In excess, the sour taste causes flightiness or hypertension and can lead to anemia. If deficient, the lack of sour taste can cause laziness and leukemia.

The sour flavor is used to help the liver discharge excess; to temper excess sweet, as parsnip greens do for parsnip roots. To counteract excess sour, use a hot, pungent, spicy taste, like mustard greens, scallions, and ginger.

As the weather gets warmer, we can gradually use more greens than roots. Less oil-sautéing, more water-sautéing, boiling, and occasional steaming on hot days is appropriate. Longer, stronger cooking can be temporarily interjected on days when winter lingers, with heartier meals to warm the body. As soon as the warmth returns, reduce the cooking fire and return to lighter fare.

In this way, spring cooking prepares the body to adapt to summer heat.

March

MENU I

Miso Soup with Turnip and *Shiitake*	*Kiriboshi Daikon* with Carrot
Pot-cooked Brown Rice	Tofu with Nori and Scallion
Hijiki with Carrot and Baked Tofu	Chinese Mustard Greens
	Bancha Twig Tea (Kukicha)

1. Miso Soup with Turnip and Shiitake

1 6″ strip kombu
3 shiitake mushrooms
2 6″ strips wakame
1 turnip
Barley miso (*mugi* miso)

Cook kombu and shiitake in a 2 quart pot for 1 hour. Soak, squeeze, and cut wakame. Wash and trim turnip, removing purple skin. Cut in 1/8-inch crescents from top to bottom. Remove kombu and shiitake from pot and set aside to dry. Add wakame and its soaking water. Simmer at least 15 minutes. Add turnip and cook until tender.

Put 1 to 2 tablespoons miso in a small bowl. Add soup broth, dilute, and pour back into pot. Mix well and taste. If a stronger taste is desired, add more miso. If the taste is too strong, add boiled water. Never boil miso. When adding more miso, never put a used spoon back into the miso container. Wash and dry it first. Simmer soup 2 to 3 minutes without boiling, so the miso can marry with the soup.

2. Pot-cooked Brown Rice

2 cups short grain organic brown rice
3 cups water
1 pinch sea salt

Sprinkle rice onto a plain plate and check for stones or black or deformed grains. Pour out a little at a time so that you can go fast, emptying clean rice into your cooking pot. Wash rice thoroughly several times in a cooking pot or separate bowl, swishing it gently with your hand. Do not rub the grain as this will polish it. Repeat several times until the water runs clean. For the last washing, pour all the rice into a strainer or colander and rinse under running water. I prefer to use purified water for the last wash. Pat the bottom of the colander vigorously with a sponge or dishcloth to drain out excess water. Squeeze out water and repeat until the rice is fairly dry.

Place the rice in the cooking pot and add 1 1/2 cups of water for each cup of rice. In this case, add 3 cups of water. As you make more rice, diminish water by 1/4 to 1/2 cup.

Bring the rice to a boil with the cover slightly ajar to prevent boiling over. Add salt and lower the fire as far as it will go without going out. Put cover on tightly and cook 1 hour. If you cannot adjust your fire easily, you may need to use a flame tamer.

When the rice is done and all the water has been absorbed, remove from fire, uncover, and let steam evaporate. With a wet bamboo rice paddle, turn the rice gently from bottom to top to distribute the light and heavy grains.

Break up any clumps with the edge of the paddle. Do not mash the rice. The rice should look unbroken and shiny. Cover the rice with a clean white cloth or a bamboo mat. Serve warm or at room temperature.

Note: If the weather is still cold, you can continue to pressure-cook the rice. As soon as the weather becomes warm, you can begin to pot-cook, unless you are weak.

3. Hijiki with Carrot and Baked Tofu

1 package hijiki
1 medium carrot
1 cake baked tofu
Tamari soy sauce

Soak hijiki until tender about 10 minutes. Squeeze out soaking water and cut in 1 1/2-inch pieces. Cut carrot in fine julienne (*sengiri*) style in 1 1/2-inch slivers. Cut tofu in half lengthwise and in thin rectangles widthwise.

Using 1/4 cup hijiki soaking water, sauté hijiki well until the strong smell evaporates. Add tofu and sauté 1 minute. Add carrot. Add hijiki soaking water minus the last tablespoon of sandy water. Bring to boil, lower fire, and simmer about 40 minutes, until 1-inch water remains. Add tamari lightly to taste and cook until dry.

4. Kiriboshi Daikon with Carrot

1 package kiriboshi daikon (dried daikon)
1 carrot
Tamari soy sauce

Soak dried daikon until tender, about 10 minutes. Squeeze and cut in a 11/2-inch grid. Cut carrot in julienne style to match daikon. Cook daikon and carrot in daikon soaking water until 1 inch of water remains. Add tamari lightly to taste and cook until dry.

5. Tofu with Nori and Scallions

1 6″ strip kombu
3 shiitake mushrooms
Tamari soy sauce
1 block firm-style tofu
1/2 bunch minced scallions
1 sheet roasted nori

Make a broth of the kombu and shiitake taken from the miso soup. Cut shiitake in julienne style. Add tamari to taste. Cook at least 1/2 hour. Slice tofu horizontally to form 1/4-inch slabs. Cut in 1-inch squares. Cut each square in half diagonally to form triangles. Cook the tofu for 10 minutes until firm. Add scallions. Turn off the fire.

Serve immediately, 5 pieces of tofu per serving with one piece of shiitake. Garnish with nori strips cut in 1/4-inch by 1 1/2-inch lengths.

6. Chinese Mustard Greens

1 small bunch Chinese mustard greens
1 pinch sea salt

Wash and dry mustard greens. Cut stems and leaves in 1-inch pieces on the diagonal. In 1/4 inch of boiling salted water, cook quickly first the greens then the stems, until bright green and tender. Sprinkle the stems lightly with a pinch of salt. This helps them steam in their own juice. Delete salt for milder flavor.

7. Bancha Twig Tea (Kukicha)

Kukicha is twig tea from the bancha bush. Rather than using the yin, rare green leaves from the top of the bush, the more yang branches and twigs that have been on the bush at least 3 years are used. They are rich in minerals and calcium and are less expensive than the leaves, which makes us happier all around.

These twigs should be lightly roasted and stored in a dark, cool place, preferably in a crock or can. Even if twigs come already roasted, you may want to roast them lightly once more.

To use, bring water to boil in a teapot and add 1 to 2 tablespoons of twigs. Return to a boil, lower the fire, and simmer 5 minutes for yang people, 15 to 20 minutes for yin people. Simmering 1/2 hour makes a very mellow brew. The same twigs can be used for two or three pots of tea.

> "The comprehension and application of our philosophy-medicine not only leads to physical health but also opens wide the gates to awareness of Eternal Happiness, Infinite Freedom and Absolute Justice."
>
> —George Ohsawa
> *Cancer and the Philosophy of the Far-East*

MENU II

Clear Soup with Tofu and Celery (Osumashi)	Cabbage Rolls
Pressure-cooked Brown Rice	Watercress Ohitashi
Barley-Lentil Stew	Takuan or Other Pickle
	Bancha Twig Tea (Kukicha)

1. Clear Soup with Tofu and Celery (Osumashi)

2 6″ strips wakame
Sea salt
Tamari soy sauce
Celery
Tofu

Soak and cut wakame in 1-inch pieces. Use soaking water for stock. Cook wakame at least 15 minutes. Add salt to half the taste. Add tamari to fulfill the second half of the flavor. Cut celery in 1/2-inch pieces and cook uncovered at a boil for 1 minute. Cut tofu in 1/3-inch cubes and simmer until it rises. The taste of this soup should be delicious and refreshing. The quantity of celery and tofu depends on the amount of soup you are making.

2. Pressure-cooked Brown Rice

4 cups brown rice
5 cups water
2 pinches sea salt

Wash rice as in Menu I. Place all ingredients in a 4 quart stainless-steel pressure cooker. After closing the lid and placing the pressure gauge, bring rice to a boil slowly on a medium fire for 20 minutes. After 20 minutes, bring up to pressure. Then lower the fire as far as it will go without going out, and cook for 40 minutes. You may need to use a metal flame tamer to control the fire and prevent scorching.

If you have an electric stove, bring rice up to a boil on the big coil and transfer it to the small coil, cooking it on warm so as not to scorch the rice. Whenever possible, gas is preferable to electricity for all cooking.

3. Barley-Lentil Stew

1/2 cup barley
1 cup lentils
2 cloves garlic
1 onion
1 stalk celery
1 carrot
3 cups water
1/2 tsp. sea salt

Clean, wash, and drain barley and lentils. Crush and mince garlic. Cut all vegetables in 1/4-inch dice. Water-sauté onion, garlic, celery, and carrot, in that order. Add lentils, barley, and water. Bring to a boil and add salt to taste. Cook on low fire for 1 1/2 hours.

4. Cabbage Rolls

3 leaves cabbage
1 onion

1 carrot
1/2 bunch scallion
Tamari soy sauce
1 6″ strip kombu
sea salt

Quick-boil cabbage leaves, one for each roll. Cut onion, carrot, and scallion julienne style. Water-sauté and steam vegetables in order given. Add tamari to taste, a little stronger than usual. Divide the vegetables into three equal portions and place them on the bottom of the cabbage leaves. Fold the leaves tight, folding in edges as you go. Secure with toothpicks.

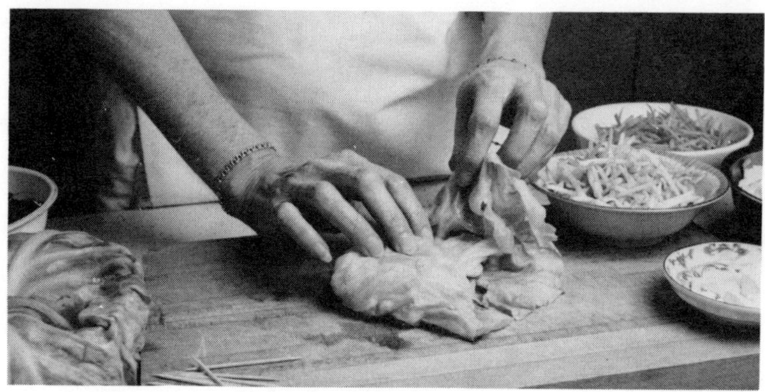

Put kombu in the bottom of the pot. Add 1/2 inch of water and bring to a boil. Add salt and tamari to taste. Arrange cabbage rolls in pot on top of kombu. Cover and cook 10 minutes. Serve one per person.

5. Watercress Ohitashi

1/2 bunch watercress
Sea salt

Dip watercress quickly in salted boiling water until bright green. Rinse in cold water. Squeeze out excess water. Serve two to three sprigs per person, arranging in a spiral.

6. Takuan or Other Pickle

Serve one or two 1/16-inch slices per person. Takuan pickle may be bought at many health food stores. It comes from China, Japan, Korea or Thailand. To make it at home, see the Special Foods section.

7. Bancha Twig Tea (Kukicha)

—Errors almost always come from false basic premises, assumed as self-evident and carelessly taken for granted.

—Unknown

—A man whose stomach proceeds beyond his nose is a fool.

—Japanese saying

—A man with a full stomach cannot see secret things.

—Zulu saying

MENU III

Bok Choy Soup	Chinese Cabbage and Daikon Pickles
Brown Rice with Kasha Croquettes	Takuan or Other Pickle
Vegetable Stew	Roasted Barley Tea (Mugicha)
Kale with String Beans	

1. Bok Choy Soup

1 6″ strip wakame
1 stalk bok choy
1 carrot
Sea salt
Tamari soy sauce

Soak and cut wakame in 1-inch pieces. Simmer in soaking water 15 to 20 minutes. Wash and dry vegetables. Cut bok choy in 1-inch pieces. Separate stems and leaves. Cut the carrot in thin diagonals. Add bok choy stems to soup. Boil uncovered 1 minute. Add carrot, cover and cook until tender. Add bok choy leaves and cook uncovered 1 minute, until bright green and tender. Add salt and tamari to taste.

2. Brown Rice with Kasha Croquettes

2 cups brown rice
1 cup kasha
2 pinches sea salt
3 3/4 cups water
1 onion
Tamari soy sauce
1/4 cup whole wheat flour

Pressure-cook brown rice and kasha in salted water. Cut onion in 1/4-inch dice. Water-sauté. Add tamari lightly to taste. When rice is done, let it cool. Mix in onions and flour. If necessary, add more flour, but use just enough to bind the croquettes. Form croquettes about 3 inches long by 2 1/2 inches wide. Bake in oven on oiled cookie sheet at 400°F. for 20 minutes.

3. Vegetable Stew

12″ strip kombu
4″ daikon
1 thick or 2 thin stalks broccoli
1 medium carrot
Sea salt
Tamari soy sauce

Soak kombu. When soft, cut in half lengthwise, then into rectangles 3 inches long by 1 1/2 inches wide. Slit lengthwise down the center leaving 1/2-inch borders at both ends. Pull one end through the slit to form a twist.

Cut the daikon in 1/4-inch triangles. Cut broccoli in 1/8-inch circles on the diagonal. Separate flowers and leaves from stalks. Cut the carrot in half lengthwise, then in 1/4-inch diagonals.

Bring 3 inches of water to a boil. Add kombu, daikon, broccoli stalks, and carrot. Cover and simmer 3 minutes. Add broccoli flowers and leaves. Sprinkle lightly with salt. Cover and simmer until vegetables are tender. Add tamari to taste.

4. Kale with String Beans

1 bunch kale
1 carrot
12–15 string beans
Tamari soy sauce

Wash, dry, and trim all vegetables. Cut the kale in 1/2-inch lengths on the diagonal. Cut the carrot in julienne style. Cut string beans in 1-inch diagonal strips. Quick-boil kale, string beans, and carrot in 1 to 2 inches of salted boiling water. Check kale stems for tenderness. As soon as they are done, remove with a slotted spoon, dot lightly with tamari, and toss together.

5. Chinese Cabbage and Daikon Pickles

1/2 Chinese cabbage
1/2 daikon
3 cloves of garlic
1/2″ ginger root
Water
Sea salt
1/4 cup brown rice vinegar (optional)

Cut the cabbage in 1-inch squares. Cut daikon in thin half-moons. Crush and mince garlic. Mince ginger root. Boil water. Add enough salt for a slightly salty taste. Place the vegetables in a glass jar. Then, pour the liquid over the vegetables and let cool before covering. Cover and allow to pickle in a cool place for 3 days before refrigerating. You may add brown rice vinegar at this point, if desired.

6. Takuan or Other Pickle

See the Special Foods section.

7. Roasted Barley Tea (Mugicha)

"Theory without practice is useless;
practice without theory is dangerous."
—George Ohsawa

"Depth of conviction outweighs height of logic."
—CTL

MENU IV

Miso Soup with Cabbage
Rice Stew (Ojiya)
Savoy Cabbage with Kasha
Baked Daikon with *Kuzu* Glaze
Nori Condiment (Nori Tsukudani)
Takuan or Other Pickle
Bancha Twig Tea (Kukicha)

1. Miso Soup with Cabbage

1 6″ strip wakame
3 leaves green cabbage
1/3 bunch watercress
Barley miso (mugi miso)

Soak, squeeze, and cut wakame. Simmer in soaking water 15 to 20 minutes. Cut cabbage into 1-inch squares. Cut watercress in 1 1/2-inch lengths. Cook cabbage several minutes until tender and bright green. Add miso. While miso is cooking into the soup, add watercress. Continue cooking, uncovered, 2 to 3 minutes. For details see Menu I.

2. Rice Stew (Ojiya)

3 cups brown rice
5 cups water
1 onion
3 shiitake mushrooms
1 3″ strip kombu
1 carrot
Watercress
Sea salt
Tamari soy sauce

Cut all vegetables in 1/4-inch dice. Pressure-cook the vegetables with the rice. Use 5 cups water, a pinch of salt, and 1 tablespoon tamari. Cook for 1 to 2 hours.

3. Savoy Cabbage with Kasha

1/4 cup buckwheat groats
2/3 cup water
Garlic
1/4 tsp. sea salt
3 large leaves Savoy cabbage

To make kasha, roast buckwheat groats lightly in a dry skillet. Then slowly add the kasha to boiling salted water, to which garlic has been added. Cover, lower fire, and simmer 20 minutes. Mix lightly when done.

Cut Savoy cabbage in 1-inch squares and steam in 1/4 inch of boiling salted water. Sprinkle with a pinch of salt while steaming. When done, mix together with kasha and serve as a side dish.

4. Baked Daikon with Kuzu Glaze

1 daikon
2 Tbsps. kuzu
1 cup water
Tamari soy sauce
Watercress

Wash, dry, and trim daikon. Cut in 1-inch-thick circles. Bake on an oiled cookie sheet covered with another cookie sheet. While baking, dilute kuzu in 1/3 cup of cold water. Add 2/3 cup of water and 1 1/2 tablespoons tamari. Bring to a boil, stirring until thickened and translucent. Wash and dry watercress and separate into 2-inch sprigs. When daikon is done, arrange in a serving platter. Garnish with watercress and glaze with kuzu sauce.

5. Nori Condiment (Nori Tsukudani)

1 package nori
Tamari soy sauce
1/2 tsp. ginger (optional)

If wild nori is used, wash it very well. Cut or break nori into small pieces. Cover with water and cook 30 to 60 minutes, until pasty. Add tamari lightly to taste, and cook several minutes more. Cool and store in a glass jar in the refrigerator. Serve 1/2 teaspoon per person on grain.

A stronger tamari taste lasts longer, and is good for winter. A lighter tamari taste is appropriate for summer, but the nori condiment will not store as long.

Nori condiment is useful for dissolving animal fats in the body. You may add a little grated ginger, about 1/2 teaspoon, if necessary for hard tumors.

6. Takuan or Other Pickle

See Special Foods section.

7. Bancha Twig Tea (Kukicha)

> "What is really going on all about us is a play of two forces. Call it positive and negative, call it attraction and repulsion, call it movement and rest—but by whatever name it goes, it is two opposites acting and interacting and counteracting and reacting one on the other through the whole universe . . ."
>
> —Luther Burbank

MENU V

Miso Soup with Butternut Squash	Cabbage with Chinese Cabbage Pickle
Brown Rice with Burdock	Daikon with Takuan
Azuki Kabocha	Bancha Twig Tea (Kukicha)
Endive with Carrot and Tempeh	

1. Miso Soup with Butternut Squash

2 6″ strips wakame
1/4 butternut squash
Barley miso (mugi miso)
3 minced scallions

Soak, squeeze, and cut wakame in 1/2-inch pieces. Simmer in soaking water 15 minutes while preparing vegetables. Wash and dry squash. Cut in half. Scoop seeds out and set aside. Using 1/4 of the squash, cut it in 1-inch crescents, then into 1-inch pieces. Add squash to soup stock and cook until tender, about 10 minutes. Add miso to taste as per Menu I. Add scallions and cook together 2 to 3 minutes, uncovered, without boiling.

2. Brown Rice with Burdock

3 cups brown rice
1 medium burdock root
3 3/4 cups water
2 pinches sea salt

Wash, dry, and trim burdock. Cut in fine julienne. Prepare rice for pressure-cooking as in Menu II. Pressure-cook rice and burdock together. Mix well before serving.

3. Azuki Kabocha

2 cups azuki beans
1/4 kabocha (Hokkaido pumpkin)
6 cups water
1 6″ strip kombu
1/2 tsp. sea salt
2 sheets nori

Remove stones from beans, wash and pat dry in a strainer. Wash, dry, and cut kabocha into 1-inch pieces. Cook beans in 5 cups of water in a ceramic bean pot on top of a flame tamer with kombu and kabocha added from the beginning. After the beans have come to a boil, add 1/2 cup cold water. Bring back to boil, and add 1/2 cup cold water again. This helps the inside of the beans to cook at the same speed as the outside. It also helps the beans to become soft faster, and makes the flavor more harmonious. When the beans are soft, after about 2 1/2 hours, add salt and nori torn into small pieces. Cook 1/2 hour more.

4. Endive with Carrot and Tempeh

1 head endive
1 carrot
1/2 package tempeh
Tamari soy sauce

Wash endive well to remove sand. Drain and pat dry. Wash, dry, and trim carrot. Trim the bottom of the endive and cut the leaves in half widthwise. Cut the carrot in a long julienne. Crumble the tempeh. In 1/4-inch of boiling water, add a little tamari to taste, and cook the tempeh until done. Add the carrots and cook until tender. Add the endive and cook several minutes until the stems are tender but the leaves are still bright green. Mix together.

5. Cabbage with Chinese Cabbage Pickle

1/2 head green cabbage
1/2 cup Chinese cabbage pickle

Wash, dry, and trim the cabbage. Cut in 1-inch squares. The Chinese cabbage pickle can be salt-pressed 1 week ahead of time. Cut the pickle into 1/4-inch pieces.

Water-sauté the cabbage in 1/4-inch of boiling water. Add the pickle and steam together until the cabbage is tender. Mix well so that the pickle flavors the cabbage.

6. Daikon with Takuan

1 small daikon
4″ takuan (pickled daikon)
Several leaves of takuan pickle, if available

Wash, dry, and trim the daikon. Cut in a coarse julienne, about 1/3-inch thick. Cut the takuan pickle into a fine julienne. Mince the leaves. Cook together in 1/4-inch of boiling water.

7. Bancha Twig Tea (Kukicha)

> "Doctors are men who prescribe medicines of which they know little, to cure diseases of which they know less, in human beings of which they know nothing."
>
> —Voltaire
>
> "Eventually, man will turn his eyes from the microscope to the macrocosm, and contemplate the limitless horizons of the Infinite Universe. Man will owe to the virus a new medicine—fundamental and divine, omnipotent and omniscient. It will deal with life and man, not analytically, not dualistically, but with Universal Understanding."
>
> —George Ohsawa
> *Cancer and the Philosophy of the Far-East*

April

MENU VI

Okayu with Dandelion	Mixed Vegetable Nishime
Brown Rice with Roasted Barley	Gomashio with Kombu
	Celery Miso Condiment
Carrot Nishime	Bancha Twig Tea (Kukicha)

1. Okayu with Dandelion

1 cup brown rice
7 cups water
1/2 tsp. sea salt

1 small bunch dandelion greens
Tamari soy sauce

Wash rice well as per Menu I. Bring to boil in a regular pot. Add salt and cook on a low fire for 1 hour. Wash and dry greens. Quick-boil in salted water until bright green. Rinse in cold water, squeeze out excess water, and cut into 1 1/2-inch lengths. Dot lightly with tamari. Garnish okayu with dandelion greens set off-center in the bowl.

2. Brown Rice with Roasted Barley

2 cups brown rice
1 cup barley
3 3/4 cups water
1 pinch sea salt

Clean and wash grains as per Menu I. Roast barley in dry skillet until golden. Combine all ingredients and pressure-cook as per Menu II.

3. Carrot Nishime

3 carrots
Carrot tops
Sesame oil to brush pot
Water
Sea salt
Roasted sesame seeds

Cut carrots in small deer's-feet (shikagiri) style. Mince carrot tops. Brush pot with oil. Quick-sauté the carrots. Add carrot tops and quickly sauté. Add 1/2 the amount of water, cover, and bring to a boil. Uncover and let off the first steam. Cover and cook until tender. When tender, sprinkle lightly with salt. Shake the pot and cook until dry. When dry, garnish lightly with roasted sesame seeds.

Note: Carrots prepared this way are usually seasoned with salt. Tamari soy sauce is rarely used as it makes the carrots too yang and gives them a heavy, muddy taste.

4. Mixed Vegetable Nishime

1 onion
3 leaves cabbage
1 turnip
1 carrot
1 pinch sea salt
2 snow peas per person
Tamari soy sauce

Wash, dry and trim all vegetables. Cut the onion in 1/4-inch crescents. Cut the cabbage in 1-inch squares. Cut the turnip in thin triangles. Cut the carrot in thin diagonals.

Water-sauté in 1/4-inch of boiling salted water, onions, turnips, cabbage and carrot. Add 1/2-inch of water, bring to a boil, and add a pinch of salt. Place the cover ajar, lower the fire, and simmer until tender. Add snow peas and cook uncovered until snow peas are bright green.

5. Gomashio with Kombu

14 Tbsps. brown sesame seeds
2 tsps. sea salt
4″ square kombu

See the Special Foods section for standard gomashio. This time, use 2 teaspoons sea salt. Slowly roast kombu in a dry skillet until it crumbles. In a *suribachi*, grind into powder enough kombu to make 1 tablespoon. Then grind together with sesame seeds and sea salt.

6. Celery Miso Condiment

2 stalks celery
Sesame oil to brush bottom of pan
2 tsps. mugi miso

Wash, dry, trim, and de-string celery. Mince fine. Brush saucepan with sesame oil and sauté celery. Add 1/4-inch water. Cover and steam until tender.

Dilute miso in remaining steaming water and mix with celery. Cook together 1 minute more without boiling. Serve 1/2 tsp. as garnish on grain.

7. Bancha Twig Tea (Kukicha)

> "[We] must not think that this world is meaningless and filled with confusion, while the world of Enlightenment is full of meaning and peace. Rather, [we] should taste the way of Enlightenment in all affairs of this world."
>
> —Buddha

MENU VII

Azuki Bean Potage
Millet with Watercress
Vegetable Tempeh
Broccoli with Sunflower Seeds
Romaine Lettuce with Watercress
Takuan or Other Pickle
Bancha Twig Tea (Kukicha)

1. Azuki Bean Potage

1 cup azuki beans
1 onion
1 stalk celery
3″ daikon
Kombu
5 cups water
1/2 tsp. sea salt

Pick through the azuki beans, wash well and pat dry. Wash and dry vegetables. Cut all vegetables in 1/4-inch dice. Water-sauté onion, celery and daikon. Then add azuki beans and kombu cut into 1/2-inch pieces. Add 5 cups of water and pressure-cook 1 hour or more. When beans are tender, add salt. Cook another 15 minutes.

Note: It is best to cook azuki beans in a ceramic bean pot on a flame tamer. They should be cooked 2 1/2 hours before adding salt. After adding salt, cook another 1/2 hour. The beans may be soaked overnight to shorten cooking time. If possible, it is best to avoid pressure-cooking azuki beans, as this makes them too yang and tends to create a bitter taste. Adding vegetables may counteract this.

2. Millet with Watercress

3 cups millet
4 cups water
1 pinch sea salt
1/2 bunch watercress

Pressure-cook millet as in Menu II. Wash and dry watercress. Mince and mix into cooked millet while still hot.

3. Vegetable Tempeh

1 onion
1 carrot
3 scallions
1 cake tempeh
Tamari soy sauce

Cut onion in thin crescents from core to top. Cut carrot in thin diagonal slices 1 1/4-inches long. Cut scallions the same length as carrot on the diagonal. Use 1 cake of tempeh. Cut in half lengthwise and in 1/8-inch thick rectangles widthwise.

Water-sauté onion, tempeh, and carrot. Be careful not to break tempeh. Cover and steam until carrot is tender. Add scallions and tamari lightly to taste. Steam 1 minute more.

4. Broccoli with Sunflower Seeds

1 large or 2 small stalks broccoli
Tamari soy sauce
Roasted sunflower seeds

Wash, dry, and trim broccoli. Cut broccoli in 1/4-inch strips lengthwise. Then cut in 1-inch lengths widthwise on the diagonal separating stems from leaves and flowers.

Steam broccoli in 1/4 inch of boiling salted water, first the flowers and leaves, then the stems. When bright green and tender, add tamari to taste. Cook until dry and garnish with roasted sunflower seeds.

5. Romaine Lettuce with Watercress

1 head romaine lettuce
1/2 bunch watercress
Sea salt
2–3 tsps. umeboshi juice

Cut the romaine lettuce in half lengthwise and wash well. Shake out water and pat dry. Wash watercress and drain. Cut the romaine hearts into quarters and pull the leaves apart.

Quick-boil in 1/2-inch of boiling salted water. Rinse in cold water, squeeze and cut in 1-inch lengths. Dip watercress quickly in boiling water, rinse in cold water, squeeze out excess water and cut into 1/4-inch pieces. Toss together with romaine lettuce and 2 to 3 teaspoons umeboshi juice.

6. Takuan or Other Pickle

See the Special Foods section.

7. Bancha Twig Tea (Kukicha)

"Let him who seeks, not cease seeking until he finds.

—*The Gospel According to Thomas*

MENU VIII

Cabbage Soup with Nori and Shiitake
Brown Rice with Kasha
Lentils with Burdock
Hijiki with Lotus Root
Country-style Daikon (Furofuki Daikon)
Takuan or Other Pickle
Bancha Twig Tea (Kukicha)

1. Cabbage Soup with Nori and Shiitake

1/4 head green cabbage
1 6″ strip kombu
3 shiitake mushrooms
1/2 bunch watercress
3 sheets nori
Sea salt
Tamari soy sauce

Soak kombu and shiitake overnight, or cook 1 hour, to make stock. Remove from liquid and set somewhere to dry. Cut cabbage into 3 wedges. Cut watercress into 2-inch lengths. Break up nori into small pieces and cook in stock. Add salt to make half the taste and tamari to make half the taste. Create a delicate taste for the soup. Add cabbage and cook until bright green and tender. Add watercress at end and simmer until it becomes bright green. Serve 1 wedge per bowl.

2. Brown Rice with Kasha

2 1/2 cups brown rice
1/2 cup buckwheat groats
3 3/4 cups water
2 pinches sea salt
1–2 minced scallions

Pressure-cook as per Menu II. Garnish with minced scallions.

3. Lentils with Burdock

2 cups lentils
1 onion

1 small or 1/2 medium burdock root
3 1/2 cups water
1/2 tsp. sea salt

Cut the vegetables in 1/4-inch dice. Water-sauté onion, then burdock, until the strong odors come off. Add lentils and water. Pot-cook for 40 minutes. Then add salt. Cook another 15 minutes. This stew has a hearty flavor.

4. Hijiki with Lotus Root

1 package hijiki
1 lotus root
Tamari soy sauce

Soak, squeeze, and cut the hijiki in a 1 1/2-inch grid. Wash, dry, and cut lotus root in half lengthwise and in thin, half-crescents on a slight diagonal.

Water-sauté hijiki in 1/4 inch of soaking water. Add more water if necessary to prolong sautéing until the strong smell goes off. Add the lotus root and sauté 1 or 2 minutes. Add hijiki soaking water minus the last sandy tablespoon. Bring to a boil, cover ajar, lower the flame, and simmer 40 minutes. When the water is down to 1 inch, add tamari lightly to taste and cook until dry.

5. Country-style Daikon (Furofuki Daikon)

1 daikon
2 6″ strips kombu
3 shiitake mushrooms
1/2 bunch scallions
Sea salt
Tamari soy sauce

Brush the kombu with your fingers to remove sand. Place in the bottom of a pot. Add 2 inches of water and shiitake mushrooms. Bring to a boil, lower the fire and simmer 1/2 hour. Meanwhile, cut the daikon in 1-inch thick circles. Cut the scallions into 1 1/2-inch lengths on the diagonal.

Season the broth half with salt and half with tamari. The flavor should be a little on the strong side. Arrange the daikon in the pot in a single layer. Cover and simmer until tender. Turn once and cook until translucent. Garnish with scallions at the end. Cook 1 minute or until bright green.

6. Takuan or Other Pickle

See the Special Foods section.

7. Bancha Twig Tea (Kukicha)

> "All sick [people] overeat, consciously or unconsciously. They should be eating less or even fasting, as Jesus, Buddha and other great spiritual leaders practiced and taught."
>
> —George Ohsawa
> *Practical Guide to Far-Eastern Macrobiotic Medicine*

"What I have eaten in late years would be considered starvation rations for most men, even those over seventy, but I have thrived on it."

—Luther Burbank

"There are persons who should not perform a fast. Fasting is dangerous for people who have low blood pressure and for those who are lacking in blood such as patients of cancer, tuberculosis and other diseases of yin nature, for no new blood is produced during fasting."

—Hideo Omori
Macrobiotic Notes
New Studies on Macrobiotics—

MENU IX

Daikon Rice Soup
Azuki Rice
Stuffed Turnips
Kombu (Kizami Kombu) with Carrot
Mustard Greens with Aburage
Takuan or Other Pickle
Bancha Twig Tea (Kukicha)

1. Daikon Rice Soup

1/2 medium daikon
1/2 bunch scallions plus roots
1/2 cup rice
5 cups water
Kombu—the same amount as scallions
1/2 tsp. sea salt
Tamari soy sauce

Cut daikon and scallions in julienne style. Wash and roast the rice until golden. Add water to the rice and bring to a boil. Add kombu, daikon, and scallion roots. Add salt. Lower fire, cover, and cook 1 hour. Add 1 tablespoon tamari or enough to make a mild taste. Add scallions just before serving.

2. Azuki Rice

2 1/2 cups brown rice
1/2 cup azuki beans
4 1/4 cups water
2 pinches sea salt

Pressure-cook as per Menu II. *Note:* Azuki beans may be pressure-cooked with rice.

3. Stuffed Turnips

5 turnips
1 onion
1 carrot
1/4 cup sesame seeds
1–2 Tbsps. miso
2 6″ strips kombu

Sea salt
Tamari soy sauce

Wash, trim, and dry the vegetables. Cut the turnip stems off 1/2 inch above turnip. Carefully wash out the sand between the stems. Trim any inedible portion at the base of the stems and around the top of the turnip. Cut off the little cap across the top of the turnip about 1 inch on either side of the stem. Scoop out and mince the inside of the turnip to within 1/4 inch from the bottom. Be careful not to go through the bottom. Mince the onion and carrot.

Wash and roast the sesame seeds. Be careful not to scorch them. Quickly water-sauté the onion, turnip, and carrot. Add miso diluted in the sautéing water. Steam together 1 minute. Add sesame seeds.

Stuff each turnip with this mixture. Meanwhile, place kombu in a shallow pot in 1/2 inch of water. Bring to a boil. Add salt and tamari to make a slightly strong broth. Place the stuffed turnips, with the caps on, into the broth. Cover and cook until turnips are tender, about 15 minutes. Serve in a dish with 2 tablespoons of broth and with the turnip caps a little ajar.

4. Kombu (Kizami Kombu) with Carrot

1/2 package shredded kombu (Kizami kombu)
1 onion
1 carrot
Tamari soy sauce

Soak kombu. Cut onion and carrot in julienne style in equal lengths. Squeeze and cut kombu to match lengths of the carrot. Water-sauté onion. Add kombu, carrot, and the kombu soaking water. Bring to a boil and simmer until the kombu is tender. Add tamari to make a mild taste. Cook until dry. Kombu strengthens the blood vessel walls.

5. Mustard Greens with Aburage

1 bunch mustard greens
4 pieces aburage (fried tofu pouches)
1 large carrot
Tamari soy sauce

Wash and dry mustard greens and carrot. Cut mustard greens in 1/2-inch strips. Quick-boil aburage to remove soybean oil. Cool. Squeeze out excess water. Cut in julienne style.

Cut the carrot in eighths lengthwise and in thin triangles at a slight diagonal. Water-sauté aburage, mustard greens, and carrot. With the cover ajar, steam several minutes until greens and carrot are tender. Cook dry on a high fire. Sprinkle lightly with tamari to taste.

6. Takuan or Other Pickle

See the Special Foods section.

7. Bancha Twig Tea (Kukicha)

"The art of cooking is the art of creating life. Our health and our resulting happiness, freedom and thinking ability depend on it."

—George Ohsawa

Practical Guide to Far-Eastern Macrobiotic Medicine

MENU X

Clear Soup (Osumashi) with Broccoli	Vegetable Sushi
Brown Rice with Azuki Beans	Watercress Ohitashi
Bulgur-stuffed Acorn Squash	Takuan or Other Pickle
	Bancha Twig Tea (Kukicha)

1. Clear Soup (Osumashi) with Broccoli

1 6″ strip kombu
1 1″ thick straight carrot
1 stalk broccoli
1 sheet nori
Sea salt
Tamari soy sauce

Brush kombu with fingers to remove any sand. Cook 1/2 hour in 1 1/2 quarts of water to build stock. Meanwhile, cut carrot into flowers. Separate broccoli flowers from stems. Set stems aside for other cooking. Quick-boil the carrots until tender. Take out with a slotted spoon and set aside. Quick-boil the broccoli flowers until bright green and the stem portion is tender. Set aside. Remove kombu and hang up to dry. Season the broth half with salt, half with tamari. Cut nori into thin strips 2 inches long. Arrange two carrot flowers and two broccoli flowers in each bowl. Pour hot soup over them and garnish with nori.

2. Brown Rice with Azuki Beans (Azuki Gohan)

3 cups brown rice
1/2 cup azuki beans
5 1/4 cups water
1/4 tsp. sea salt

Remove stones from rice and azuki beans, then wash and drain them separately. Soak the beans at least 1 hour. Mix the rice, beans, water, and salt, and pressure-cook as in Menu II. Mix before serving.

3. Bulgur-stuffed Acorn Squash

1 acorn squash
Sesame oil
3 pinches sea salt
1 1/2 cups water
1 onion
2 cloves garlic

1 cup bulgur
Watercress

Wash, dry, and trim acorn squash. Cut in half widthwise, scoop out the seeds and set aside. Cut each half in 1/2-inch circles. Rub each circle lightly with sesame oil and arrange on a cookie sheet. Sprinkle lightly with salt. Add water halfway up the squash, about 1/4 inch. Cover with another cookie sheet. (Use stainless-steel cookie sheets or an enamel or Pyrex baking tray.) Bake at 400°F. for 30 to 40 minutes, or until tender.

Meanwhile, carefully peel onion, removing only as little as possible. Cut into 1/4-inch mince. Crush and mince garlic. Water-sauté onion and garlic. Add bulgur and water. Bring to a boil, add 2 pinches salt, lower fire and cook, covered, 1/2 hour.

Mince watercress and mix into cooked bulgur. When squash is done, stuff each circle with bulgur, mounding attractively. Bake together, covered, 5 to 10 minutes more.

4. Vegetable Sushi

1 head green cabbage
2 carrots
Nori
Tamari soy sauce

Wash, dry, and trim cabbage and carrots. Remove the heart of the cabbage and submerge the cabbage completely in boiling water for several minutes to soften the leaves. Do not leave it in too long or the leaves will become too soft. Rinse in cold water and drain well. Peel off as many leaves as you need. Put the rest of the cabbage away for further use. Cut the carrots lengthwise in 1/2-inch wide strips. Quick-boil the carrot strips until tender.

Make two styles of sushi, one with cabbage on the outside, and one with nori on the outside. Shave the thick stem of the cabbage to half thickness to facilitate rolling. Lay a sheet of nori on top of one leaf of cabbage. Arrange three carrot strips along one edge and roll to the far side. Cut in 1 1/2-inch lengths. Next, do the same, but this time lay a leaf of cabbage on top of a sheet of unroasted nori. Cut to the same size. Arrange alternately on a platter, spiral side up, and dot each top lightly with tamari.

5. Watercress Ohitashi

1 bunch watercress

Remove any yellow leaves, wash and pat dry. Trim bottom of stems, if necessary, and boil in 1/2 inch of boiling water for 1/2 minute. Rinse in cold water and squeeze gently. Serve 2 to 3 sprigs per person according to size.

6. Takuan or Other Pickle

See the Special Foods section.

7. Bancha Twig Tea (Kukicha)

"If symptomatic medicine does not undergo reform, it will be the ruination of mankind."

—George Ohsawa
Cancer and the Philosophy of the Far East

May

MENU XI

Vegetable Barley (*Hatomugi*) Soup	Chinese Greens with Garlic
Brown Rice	Takuan or Other Pickle
Whole Lotus Root *Nitsuke*	Bancha Twig Tea (Kukicha)
Turnips in Miso Sauce	

1. Vegetable Barley (Hatomugi) Soup

1 cup wild barley (hatomugi)
1 onion
1/4 cabbage
Daikon greens
1/3 daikon
2 carrots
8 cups water
1 6″ strip kombu
1/2 tsp. sea salt

Wash and drain barley. Cut all vegetables in 1/4-inch dice. Cut the kombu in 1/2-inch pieces. Water-sauté onion, cabbage, daikon greens, daikon, and carrot. Add barley and mix. Add water and kombu. Bring to a boil and boil hard 1 minute, uncovered. Add salt. Lower the fire, cover, and simmer for 1 hour. Adjust the salt to taste and cook 5 minutes more before serving.

2. Brown Rice

Pot-cook rice as in Menu I.

3. Whole Lotus Root Nitsuke

1 lotus root
2 tsps. sesame oil
Tamari soy sauce

Wash, dry, and trim lotus root. Sauté in sesame oil. Turn the lotus root as you sauté about 2 to 3 minutes. Then add water to cover half the lotus root. Boil hard, uncovered for 1 minute. Cover and simmer until tender. When water is 1/2 inch down, add tamari to taste and cook until dry, turning often.

To serve, cut in 1/4-inch circles. This is attractive because the inside is light and the outside is dark. Lotus root is good for dissolving mucus in the body, especially in the lungs.

4. Turnips in Miso Sauce

3 turnips
1–2 Tbsps. miso
1/2 tsp. grated lemon rind

Cut, dry, and trim turnips. Cut turnips in thin crescents. Cut greens in lengths equal to crescents. Water-sauté greens first in 1/4 inch of boiling salted water, then add turnips. Cover and let steam until tender. Purée miso in a little cooking water. Add grated lemon rind. When the turnips are tender and cooked dry, add the miso-lemon sauce. Toss together in a covered pot. Cook together 2 minutes without boiling.

5. Chinese Greens with Garlic

1 bunch Chinese greens
3 cloves garlic
Sea salt
Tamari soy sauce

Wash, dry, and cut the greens in 1-inch lengths. Mince the garlic and water-sauté. Add the greens. Mix together and lightly salt the greens. Let steam until tender. Sprinkle lightly with tamari to taste and mix.

6. Takuan or Other Pickle

See the Special Foods section.

7. Bancha Twig Tea (Kukicha)

> "Even the severed branch grows again, and the sunken moon returns; wise men who ponder this are not troubled in adversity."
>
> —Bhartrhari
> *Springs of Wisdom*

MENU XII

Miso Soup with Burdock and Leek	Kale with Tempeh
Bulgur Pilaf	Cabbage Pickle
Carrots à la Deer's Feet	Takuan or Other Pickle
(Shikagiri)	Bancha Twig Tea (Kukicha)

1. Miso Soup with Burdock and Leek

2 6″ strips wakame
1 medium burdock root
1 leek
2 Tbsps. miso or to taste

Soak, squeeze, and cut wakame into 1-inch pieces. Set aside. Wash burdock by brushing lightly with a natural-bristle brush, being careful not to rub off the skin. Trim any bad parts off the leek. Then slice the white end of the leek in half lengthwise and pull apart. Carefully wash the inside of the leek in cold running water, making sure to wash out any sand inside the leaves. If there are roots on the leek, wash them carefully, holding them upside down under the water and scrubbing them as if you were scrubbing your hair.

Mince the leek roots. Shave the burdock in thin 3/4-inch long pencil-like shavings. Slice the leek in 1/4-inch widths. Water-sauté the burdock 2 to 3 minutes until the strong smell becomes mild. Add minced leek roots. Then add the wakame and wakame soaking water, being careful to leave the last sandy tablespoon in the bowl. Bring to a boil, lower the fire, and simmer until the burdock is almost tender. Add the leek. When the leek becomes bright green and tender, add miso to taste. Refer to Menu I for details.

2. Bulgur Pilaf

2 cups bulgur
2 onions
1 Tbsp. sesame oil
Tamari soy sauce
3 cups water
1/4 cup roasted sunflower seeds

Cut the onions in 1/2-inch dice and sauté in sesame oil. Add tamari to make a slightly rich taste. Add bulgur and continue to sauté for several minutes until bulgur and onions become well mixed. Then add water, bring to a boil, lower flame, and simmer, tightly covered, for 1/2 hour. When done, mix lightly from bottom to top, and mix in the sunflower seeds. Arrange attractively in a ceramic bowl.

3. Carrots à la Deer's Feet (Shikagiri)

3 carrots
2 parsnip roots
1 pinch sea salt
1 Tbsp. kuzu
1/4 cup cold water
Tamari soy sauce
1 Tbsp. roasted sesame seeds

Cut carrots and parsnips in wedges with one side 1 inch long. Bring 1/2 inch of water to a boil, add salt and water-sauté parsnips until their smell becomes mild. Add carrot, and sauté quickly. Then cover and steam until tender, about 10 minutes.

Meanwhile, dilute kuzu in 1/4 cup of cold water. Add tamari to make a light tan color. Pour this mixture over the vegetables. Using a high fire, stir constantly until kuzu becomes thick and clear. Add a little water if necessary. To serve, garnish with roasted sesame seeds.

4. Kale with Tempeh

1 bunch kale
1 package tempeh
Tamari soy sauce

Wash kale well and pat dry. Cut in 1 1/2-inch lengths. Crumble tempeh in a bowl using a fork. Water-sauté tempeh first in 1/2 inch of boiling salted water. Steam 5 to

10 minutes. Add tamari to taste. Add kale. Mix lightly and steam until the stems are tender and the kale is still bright green.

5. Cabbage Pickle

1 head cabbage
3 cloves garlic
2 rounded Tbsps. sea salt

Cut the cabbage in quarters and remove the heart. Slice off the very bottom of the heart, as it is too fibrous. Cut hearts in half lengthwise and slice thin on the diagonal to make each slice the thickness of the leaves. Slice each quarter in half lengthwise, then cut in a fine julienne on the diagonal.

Crush each clove of garlic to release oil and facilitate peeling. Mince fine. Add garlic and salt to cabbage and mix well. Cabbage should become shiny with moisture. Taste should be a little too salty for eating, but salty enough for pickling. Add a little more salt if necessary.

Cover top of cabbage with a plate that will not touch the sides of the bowl as it is pressed down. Put weight on the plate using a heavy stone or a pot of water. Cover the bowl with a clean dish towel. Let stand a minimum of 1 hour. Overnight is better. The salt will draw water out of the cabbage, creating a pickling brine which will accumulate in the bottom of the bowl.

When the cabbage is ready to eat, take out your portion, squeezing it gently to leave the excess water in the bowl. If it tastes too salty, rinse and squeeze before serving. As you become proficient at pickling, the salt taste will become perfect.

6. Takuan or Other Pickle

See the Special Foods section.

7. Bancha Twig Tea (Kukicha)

> "Normal blood—pure and fresh blood—is the basal factor by which one's health is preserved and one's life is prolonged. And the digestive organs in which blood is produced are the root of life.
>
> "The villi in the digestive organs, especially in the intestinal mucous membrane, correspond exactly to the roots of a plant absorbing nutrients. And food is to the body what soil is to the plant. Therefore, it is necessary that we should try to improve or balance the quality and quantity of food in order to preserve our health and prolong our life."
>
> —Prof. Kikuo Chishima
> *Revolution of Biology and Medicine—Vol. 9*

MENU XIII

Miso Soup with Baby Daikon and Greens	Baked Turnips
Brown Rice	Savoy Cabbage and Turnip Greens
Black Beans with Garlic	Red Radishes
	Bancha Twig Tea (Kukicha)

1. Miso Soup with Baby Daikon and Greens

3–5 baby daikon roots
Daikon leaves
2 6″ strips wakame
Barley miso (mugi miso)

Cut the daikon in thin diagonal circles. Cut the leaves in 1-inch lengths. Soak and cut wakame. Then, using the soaking water for the soup stock, simmer wakame at least 15 minutes with the cover slightly ajar. Add the daikon leaves and boil hard, for 1 minute uncovered. Add the daikon and boil hard, for 1 minute, uncovered. Lower the fire. Replace the cover ajar and simmer until tender. Add miso to taste. Refer to Menu I for details.

2. Brown Rice

4 cups rice
5 cups water
2 pinches sea salt

Pressure-cook. Refer to Menu II for details.

3. Black Beans with Garlic

2 cups black beans
1 onion
3 cloves garlic
1 6″ strip of kombu
5 cups water
1/2 tsp. sea salt

Pick through, wash, and drain beans. Mince onion. Place knife blade over the clove of garlic and hit the blade with the heel of the other hand to crush the garlic. The skin easily comes off. Mince the garlic. Water-sauté the onion and garlic in the pressure pot. Add the beans, the kombu which has been cut in 1/2-inch pieces, and the water. Pressure-cook for 1 hour, or until the beans are tender. Add salt. Cook another 1/2 hour without pressure.

4. Baked Turnips

2 medium-size turnips
Sea salt

Wash, dry, and trim turnips, taking off the purple skin. Cut 1/2-inch circles from top to bottom. Arrange on an oiled stainless steel cookie sheet. Sprinkle lightly with salt. Add 1/4 inch of water. Cover with a second stainless steel cookie sheet. Bake at 450°F. for 20 to 25 minutes, or until tender. Serve 1 to 2 pieces per person. This is excellent for midafternoon snack for yang people.

5. Savoy Cabbage and Turnip Greens

1/2 Savoy cabbage
Turnip greens
Red radish greens (optional)

1 package tempeh
Tamari soy sauce

Cut the cabbage in 1-inch squares. Cut the greens in 1/2-inch pieces. Crumble tempeh and steam in 1/2 inch of boiling salted water. Add cabbage and steam 3 minutes. Add the hard greens and steam until partly tender, then the soft greens. Add tamari to taste and mix well.

6. Red Radishes

1 bunch red radishes

Wash and trim radishes. Boil 3 to 5 minutes in salted water. Rinse under cold water to stop cooking. Serve as is. This makes a great snack.

All radishes and turnips and their greens are suitable for dissolving excess animal protein and fat and for cleaning the body internally.

7. Bancha Twig Tea (Kukicha)

> Since Spring's energy is rising and nourishes the liver, smoking, which burns oxygen, counteracts rising energy and is injurious to the liver. In the case of liver cancer, smoking is dangerous.
>
> —Macrobiotic advice

MENU XIV

Clear Soup (Osumashi) with Tempeh	Arame with Onion and Carrot
Brown Rice with Wild Barley (Hatomugi)	Cabbage with Daikon and Scallion
Carrot-Burdock *Kinpira*	Takuan or Other Pickle
	Bancha Twig Tea (Kukicha)

1. Clear Soup (Osumashi) with Tempeh

1 6″ strip kombu
1 package tempeh
1–2 stalks broccoli
Sea salt
Tamari soy sauce

Wipe kombu clean with a damp cloth. Soak in water to soften, then cut into 1-inch squares. Fill the soup pot with water, add kombu, bring to a boil, and simmer 1/2 hour. (Soaking overnight or simmering 1 to 2 hours is better.)

Cut tempeh into 1/2-inch cubes. Cut broccoli into 1/2-inch wide strips lengthwise and 1/2-inch pieces widthwise to match tempeh. Cut broccoli flowers into 3/4-inch pieces.

Add tempeh to soup and cook 10 minutes. Add broccoli and cook with cover ajar until tender, but still bright green. Add salt to reach half the flavor. Then add tamari to fulfill the flavor, making it not too thin, but not too salty. This taste differs from individual to individual, from day to day, and season to season, according to one's condition. Tempeh is rich in B vitamins, as is tamari.

2. Brown Rice with Wild Barley (Hatomugi)

2 cups wild barley (hatomugi)
1 cup brown rice
4 1/2 cups water
1 pinch sea salt

Pot-cook as in Menu I.

3. Carrot-Burdock Kinpira

3 medium burdock roots
1 medium lotus root (optional)
1 large carrot
1 pinch sea salt
Tamari soy sauce

Wash the roots in cold water gently with a natural bristle brush. Dry with a towel and trim inedible parts, taking off as little as possible. Cut burdock, lotus root, and carrot into a fine julienne.

Bring 1/2 inch of water to a boil, add a pinch of salt, and sauté burdock until the strong smell evaporates. Add lotus root, if using, then carrot. Add water to 2/3 the volume of vegetables. Bring to a boil, boil hard 1 minute, uncovered. Lower the fire and simmer uncovered until the burdock is tender, about 20 minutes, and the water is down to 1/2 inch. Add tamari to taste and cook with cover ajar until dry.

4. Arame with Onion and Carrot

1 package arame
1 onion
1 carrot
1 pinch sea salt
Tamari soy sauce

Rinse arame. Carefully peel onion and carve off root and stalk ends, cutting off as little as possible. Trim carrot in the same way. Wash and dry the vegetables. Then cut them in a fine julienne to match arame. Squeeze arame and arrange on a cutting board. Cut in a 1 1/2-inch grid.

To 1/4 inch of boiling water add salt. Sauté onion until the strong smell evaporates. Then add arame and sauté several minutes until the smell is mild. Add carrots. Carrots are more yang and do not need to be sautéed so much.

Add arame soaking water, leaving the last sandy bit of water in the bowl. Water should reach the top of the vegetables. Add more if necessary. Bring to a boil, and boil hard 1 minute. Then lower flame and simmer, covered, about 30 minutes, or until water is down to 1/2 inch. Add tamari to make a mild, delicious taste, and cook uncovered until dry.

5. Cabbage with Daikon and Scallion

5 leaves cabbage
1/2 daikon
1 bunch scallions
1 bunch daikon leaves

Sea salt

Wash and dry all the vegetables. Scrub scallion roots in the water as if you were washing your hair. Cut the cabbage in 1-inch by 2-inch rectangles. Cut the daikon the same as the cabbage. Cut the scallions in 2-inch long diagonals to equal the length of daikon and cabbage. Mince the scallion roots and daikon leaves.

In 1/4 inch of boiling salted water, sauté the daikon, scallion roots, cabbage, and daikon leaves in that order. Sprinkle lightly with salt, cover, and steam several minutes until daikon is tender, but the cabbage is still bright green. Add scallions and steam 1 minute more.

6. Takuan or Other Pickle

See the Special Foods section.

7. Bancha Twig Tea (Kukicha)

> "Change doubt for faith, despair for hope, darkness for joy, sickness for radiant health, hate for forgiveness and loneliness for love."
>
> —CTL
>
> "Spirit governs mind, mind governs body, body harmonizes with nature, nature follows the Tao."
>
> —CTL
>
> "He who hath found peace with the body hath built a holy temple wherein may dwell forever the spirit of God."
>
> —*The Essene Gospel of Peace—Book Two*
> Edmond Bordeaux Szekely

MENU XV

Barley Bean Soup	Sesame Seeds
Rice Triangles (*Omusubi*)	Cauliflower Stems
Cauliflower in Miso Sauce	Collard Green Ohitashi
Carrots and Scallions with	Brown Rice Tea (Genmaicha)

1. Barley Bean Soup

1/2 cup barley
1/2 cup azuki beans
1 6″ strip kombu
3 cups water
1 onion
2 stalks celery
1 carrot
1/2 tsp. sea salt

Check barley and azuki beans for stones. Wash them in a bowl and drain in colander. Cut kombu into 1/2-inch pieces. Cook barley, beans, and kombu in 3 cups of water until the azuki beans are soft, about 2 hours. Meanwhile, cut the onion, celery, and carrot in 1/2-inch dice.

When the beans are soft, add vegetables and salt. Add enough water to make desired consistency for soup. Cook another 20 to 30 minutes.

2. Rice Triangles (Omusubi)

4 cups rice
5 cups water
2 pinches sea salt
Umeboshi plums
Unroasted nori

Pressure-cook rice as in Menu II. Rice should be cooked a little on the dry side to make omusubi. When the rice is cool, dip one hand into lightly salted cold water and rub hands together. Form rice into balls about 2 inches in diameter, pressing very firmly. Press thumb into the center of the ball and insert 1/2 umeboshi. Close the hole and press firmly again.

Form a triangle using the palm of the right hand and the opposing fingers to shape the two broad sides. Form the narrow side of the triangle with the index and third finger of the left hand on one side and the thumb on the other side, with the apex of the triangle formed at the angle between the thumb and index finger. Pressing firmly, turn the omusubi three times on one side, turn over and turn three times on the other side.

Form the corners sharply by pressing the index and third fingers of the left hand against the edge of the palm on the right hand. The resulting triangle should be approximately 3 inches on each side by 1 inch thick.

3. Cauliflower in Miso Sauce

1 head cauliflower
2 Tbsps. kuzu
1 cup water
1/4 cup miso
1 tsp. brown rice vinegar
1/2 cup minced parsley
1 pinch sea salt

Wash and dry cauliflower. Cut flowers off head and set stems aside. Boil the flowers in salted water several minutes until tender, and drain. Dilute kuzu in cold water, bring to a boil, and cook until thickened, stirring constantly with a wooden spoon.

In a separate bowl, dilute the miso with some of the cooked kuzu and pour it all back into the pot of kuzu. Cook together 2 to 3 minutes. Add vinegar and stir. Put the parsley in a strainer and steep it in boiling water for 3 minutes, or until the stems are tender. Drain well. Arrange cauliflower attractively in a serving dish and pour kuzu-miso sauce over it. Garnish with parsley.

4. Carrots and Scallions with Sesame Seeds

3 carrots
3 scallions
1 6″ strip kombu
Tamari soy sauce
1 1/2 Tbsps. roasted sesame seeds

Trim all the bad parts off the scallion. Wash and dry the scallions and carrots. Cut the carrots in deer's feet style, i.e., 1-inch wedges (shikagiri). Cut scallion in 1 1/2-inch lengths.

Cook the carrots in 1 inch of water on a bed of kombu until tender. Add scallion. Season lightly with tamari and cook together 1 minute more. Remove with a slotted spoon. Arrange in a serving bowl and garnish with sesame seeds.

5. Cauliflower Stems

Trim any excess fiber off the heart of the cauliflower. Cut the stems and the heart in 1/2-inch pieces. Cook this in the carrot, kombu, tamari broth leftover from recipe No. 4. Cook covered until dry. The kombu can be dried and used later.

6. Collard Green Ohitashi

1 bunch collard greens
1 pinch sea salt
Tamari soy sauce
1 Tbsp. roasted sesame seeds

Rinse the leaves in cold water and pat dry. Cook whole, uncovered, in boiling salted water several minutes until bright green and the stems are tender. Rinse in cold water and gently squeeze out excess water. Lay each stem alternately top to bottom. Press gently to form a roll and cut in 1 1/2-inch lengths. Sprinkle 1 or 2 drops of tamari on each portion. Garnish with sesame seeds. Serve one per person.

7. Brown Rice Tea (Genmaicha)

1/4 cup brown rice

Wash and roast rice until golden. Simmer 1/2 hour in a teapot of water.

> "A small-minded man weighs what can hinder him and fearful, dares not set to work. Difficulties cause the average man to leave off what he has begun. A truly great man does not slacken in carrying out what he has begun, although obstacles tower thousand-fold until he has succeeded."
>
> —Indian wisdom
> *Springs of Wisdom*

Spring—Breakfast Suggestions

I	1.	Miso Soup with Wakame, Tempeh, and Leeks
	2.	Soft Rice (Okayu) with Shaved Burdock
	3.	Gomashio with Kombu
	4.	Takuan Pickle
	5.	Grain Coffee (Yannoh)
II	1.	Miso Soup with Wakame, Parsley Roots, and Greens
	2.	Brown Rice with Hatomugi (Okayu)
	3.	Scallion Miso Condiment
	4.	Cabbage Pickle
	5.	Bancha Twig Tea (Kukicha)
III	1.	Brown Rice Okayu
	2.	Miso Condiment
	3.	Mugwort Mochi with Nori
	4.	Salt-pressed Pickle
	5.	Roasted Barley Tea (Mugicha)
IV	1.	Miso Soup with Wakame, Tofu, and Scallions
	2.	Oatmeal
	3.	Gomashio Condiment
	4.	Quick-boiled Mustard Greens
	5.	Bancha Twig Tea (Kukicha)
V	1.	Miso Soup with Wakame and Broccoli
	2.	Brown Rice Okayu with Bulgur
	3.	Umeboshi with Scallion Condiment
	4.	Quick-boiled Watercress
	5.	Roasted Barley Tea (Mugicha)

Spring—Lunch Suggestions

I	1.	Brown Rice with Condiment
	2.	Hijiki with Carrot and Baked Tofu
	3.	Tofu with Nori and Scallion
	4.	Chinese Mustard Greens
	5.	Pickle
II	1.	Brown Rice with Kasha Croquettes
	2.	Vegetable Stew
	3.	Roasted Nori
	4.	Kale with String Beans
	5.	Chinese Cabbage with Daikon Pickles
III	1.	Brown Rice with Roasted Barley
	2.	Celery Miso Condiment
	3.	Mixed Vegetable Nishime
	4.	Endive with Carrot and Tempeh
	5.	Pickle
IV	1.	Millet with Watercress
	2.	Steamed Kabocha
	3.	Kizami Kombu with Carrots
	4.	Broccoli with Sunflower Seeds
	5.	Pickle
V	1.	Brown Rice/Vegetable Sushi
	2.	Stuffed Turnips
	3.	Lotus Root
	4.	Chinese Greens with Garlic
	5.	Pickle

Summer Cooking

Summer is the ripening of the year in all its fullness. The rising potential energy of adolescent spring buds explodes in the bloom of realized maturity, blazoning their glory to the world. Not one strives, compares, desires. Each is complete in the very virtue of Being. Thus, summer is symbolized by the radiant energy of Fire.

At Summer Solstice, the sun is high and hot. Spring waters evaporate and the Earth becomes dry. The wild, fresh, and sour spring flavors ripen into a light and juicy sweetness, characterized by corn, sweet vegetables, and fruits. These are balanced by the strengthening bitterness of dark, leafy greens, such as lettuce, watercress, chicory, bok choy, dandelion-greens and roots. The bitter taste reflects the scorching quality of the sun. The complement of chlorophyll counteracts the heat, both inside and out.

The Heart and Small Intestine Meridians, as well as the Heart Governor (Pericardium) and Triple Warmer[1] Meridians, are activated by summer's heat. The small intestine, the "golden stove" of the body, the furnace of alchemical transmutation, transforms our food into blood. It is here that chlorophyll evolves into hemoglobin. The heart, the radiant sun of the body, circulates the red blood throughout the system and, with it, rays of warmth and love.

The cooking becomes still lighter than the cooking in spring. Less fire is needed, little to no oil, and less salt. Grains may be boiled or steamed and mixed with vegetables in colorful arrangements. Vegetables, too, can be quick-boiled or steamed. More vegetables may be taken in proportion to grains. Healthy people may eat small salads and fruits, such as apricots, berries, and watermelon.

Still it is necessary to maintain a balance between grains and vegetables, leaves and roots, liquids and minerals, raw and cooked foods. Otherwise, we lose our strong center, lose minerals, weaken the blood, and become tired. Then we have no resistance to withstand the cold winter.

In summer, three parts greens to one part roots is appropriate. Sea vegetables in salads provide minerals, which may be lost with excess liquids, fruits and acids. Though the salty taste is light and delicate, sea salt, tamari soy sauce, miso, and umeboshi are still useful.

In this way, summer cooking nourishes us and maintains our strength, while providing the refreshment we seek.

Note: Since the process of degeneration is generally yin, the menus for summer have been developed to strengthen the blood and immune system, the organs and body functions. Therefore, there is an inclusion of some yang element in each meal and a general absence of raw salads and fruits.

Since, within cancers, there are yin types and yang types, the menus herein may be adapted by adjusting the method and length of the cooking, as well as the flavor of salt. The use of garlic is for yang cancers only; please consult with your counselor.

---

1 Triple Warmer—the body temperature regulating system.

June

MENU XVI

Miso Soup with Broccoli Flowers	Cabbage with Scallions
Brown Rice with Pumpkin Seeds	Pickle: Cabbage, Red Radish, Watercress
Kabocha with Onions	Bancha Twig Tea (Kukicha)
Broccoli Stems with Carrots	

1. Miso Soup with Broccoli Flowers

2 6″ strips wakame
1 cup broccoli flowers
Barley miso (mugi miso)

Soak, squeeze, and cut wakame into 1/2-inch pieces. Use the wakame soaking water as a stock starter. Bring to a boil with added water to fill a pot, and simmer wakame at least 15 minutes. Meanwhile, cut broccoli flowers into 3/4-inch pieces. When stock is ready, add flowers and cook several minutes, until bright green and tender. The broccoli flowers should not lose their beautiful color, but the stems should be tender.

Dilute 1 to 2 tablespoons of miso in a portion of soup stock. Add slowly to the soup, enough to make a delicious taste. The amount of miso will vary according to season, weather, and the individual's condition.

2. Brown Rice with Pumpkin Seeds

3 cups brown rice
4 1/2 cups water
1 pinch sea salt
1/2 cup pumpkin seeds

Prepare and cook rice as in Menu I. While it is cooking, lightly roast the pumpkin seeds in a cast-iron skillet using a bamboo paddle or wooden spoon. When done, pour the seeds into a shallow dish and let cool. Mix gently into cooked rice, after allowing steam to escape from rice, or use as a garnish on top.

3. Kabocha with Onions

1 small or 1/2 large kabocha
1 onion
1 Tbsp. sesame oil
3 pinches sea salt

Wash kabocha with a vegetable brush and pat dry. Scrape off any bumps without taking off the skin. To remove stem, cut a circle around base of stem with heel of knife angling slightly inward. Using the butt of the handle, knock the loosened stem off. Slice pumpkin in half, scoop out and save the seeds. Trim off the navel at the bottom. Cut the kabocha into 1-inch-wide crescents from top to bottom. The 1 inch is measured at the equator. Slice the crescents into 3/4-inch pieces.

Cut the onion into 1/2-inch dice. To do this, carefully trim the top stem and the bottom core, taking off as little as possible. Peel the skin off carefully. With the core end up, slice the onion in half. Lay the cut side down with the core away from you.

Now cut lengthwise in 1/2-inch slices, up to, but not through, the core. Turn the onion sideways and cut through again in 1/2-inch slices, making a 1/2-inch dice. As you approach the core, hold both sides of the onion and continue cutting. Cut the core a little smaller. You will now have thin slices at the end. Turn these once more and cut into a dice.

Sauté onions in sesame oil until translucent and sweet. While sautéing, sprinkle with 1 pinch of salt. Add kabocha and continue to sauté until color deepens, 1 to 2 minutes. Add 1/2 inch of water and bring to a boil. Sprinkle lightly with salt, about 2 pinches. Then cover, lower fire, and simmer until tender, from 5 to 10 minutes. Yellow vegetables are high in vitamin A, which is oil soluble.

4. Broccoli Stems with Carrots

Broccoli stems left from soup flowers
1 carrot
1 pinch sea salt
Tamari soy sauce
1 Tbsp. roasted sesame seeds

Wash carrot with a natural-bristle brush, dry, and trim. Wash broccoli gently with hands. Do not use a brush on broccoli or any other leafy or delicate vegetable. Dry stems and trim off any hard, fibrous parts of the stalk.

Cut carrot and broccoli into 1/2-inch cubes. Bring 1/4 inch of water to a boil. Add a pinch of salt, and water-sauté broccoli stems until bright green. Add carrots, cover, and steam until tender, keeping bright color. Sprinkle lightly with tamari to taste. Mix and cook 1 minute more without cover. Allow steam to escape and garnish with roasted sesame seeds. Broccoli and carrot are high in vitamin A. Sesame seeds provide the oil for its absorption.

5. Cabbage with Scallions

1/2 green cabbage
1 bunch scallions
Sea salt

Wash, dry, and trim the cabbage. Trim the scallions before washing. Wash the roots well and mince fine. Wash and dry scallions. Cut out the heart of the cabbage. Slice the heart into thin diagonal strips and then in a 1/4-inch julienne. Slice cabbage into 1/4-inch julienne. Cut scallions in 2-inch lengths. Quick-boil cabbage with the scallion roots in lightly salted water until bright green and slightly tender. Add scallion and cook 1 minute more.

6. Pickle: Cabbage, Red Radish, Watercress

3 to 5 cabbage leaves
1 bunch red radishes
1/2 bunch watercress
1 tsp. sea salt

Cut cabbage leaves in 1-inch squares. Wash, dry, and trim red radishes and slice in thin circles from top to bottom. Cut watercress in 1-inch lengths. Mix with 1 heaping teaspoon salt. Mix well and taste. It should be too salty to eat, but salty enough for pickling.

Press in a large bowl, with a small plate with a weight on it, for a minimum of 3 hours. Overnight is better. When pickling, cover bowl with a clean, cotton cloth. Keep pickle in brine. Store in a jar in the refrigerator. Rinse each portion before serving if necessary.

7. Bancha Twig Tea (Kukicha)

> "Your first responsibility is to take care of your body and mind . . . . You must try to eat pure food and drink pure water . . . . The consecration of food governs what comes into the body. The consecration of activity governs what the individual does with the body and the mind, the muscles and the spirit."
>
> —Robert S. Mendelsohn, M. D.
> *Confessions of a Medical Heretic*

MENU XVII

Brown Rice Potage	Baby Daikon Pickle
Brown Rice with Arame	Takuan or Other Pickle
Chick-peas with Vegetables	Roasted Barley Tea (Mugicha)
Buckwheat Noodle Rolls (*Soba-maki*)	

1. Brown Rice Potage

1 cup brown rice
2 carrots
7 cups water
3 pinches sea salt
Watercress

Wash rice as in Menu I. Roast in a cast-iron skillet, stirring constantly with a bamboo paddle or wooden spoon until golden. Wash, dry, and trim carrots. Mince fine. Cook rice and carrots together in 7 cups of water in a regular pot. Bring to a boil and add 3 pinches of salt. Adjust salt to taste. Cover tightly and simmer quietly on a low fire for 1 hour. Mix gently before serving. Serve with watercress garnish.

2. Brown Rice with Arame

3 cups brown rice
4 1/2 cups water
1 pinch sea salt
1/4 package arame
Tamari soy sauce

Prepare and pot-cook rice as in Menu I. While rice is cooking, prepare arame. Rinse arame. Squeeze and cut arame in 1/2-inch pieces. Water-sauté it in 1/4 inch of water, until the strong smell evaporates. Add a little more water if necessary to continue sautéing. Add water to top of arame. Bring to a boil and boil hard for 1 minute before covering. Place cover ajar, lower flame, and simmer about 30 minutes. When water is down to 1/2 inch, add tamari lightly to taste, and cook uncovered until dry. When rice is done, mix arame lightly into rice without mashing it.

3. Chick-peas with Vegetables

2 cups chick-peas
1 6″ strip kombu
4 cups water
1 onion
1 carrot
Carrot tops
1/2 tsp. sea salt

Pick out stones and foreign debris from chick-peas. Soak overnight, or for at least 2 hours, before cooking. Wash thoroughly and drain in a colander. Wipe kombu clean with a damp cloth and cut kombu into 1/2-inch pieces. Peel onion. Wash, dry, and trim carrot and carrot tops, making sure to wash the sand out of the bottom of the carrot stalks. Cut onions and carrots into 1/4-inch dice. Mince carrot tops.

Pressure-cook chick-peas with kombu for 2 hours (1 hour if soaked). When tender, add onion and boil hard, uncovered, for 1 minute. Add carrot and carrot tops. Add salt. Mix into chick-peas, cover, and cook another 1/2 hour at low heat.

4. Buckwheat Noodle Rolls (Soba-maki)

1 package buckwheat noodles (soba)
Mustard greens
Nori
Tamari soy sauce

Cook noodles al dente. Drain and rinse in cold water in colander. Wash mustard greens in cold water, removing the roots. (Roots may be used later in a soup stock.) Quick-boil mustard greens in 1 inch of boiling water. Rinse in cold water to stop cooking and to keep bright green color. Gently squeeze out excess water and set aside.

Place unroasted nori on a bamboo sushi mat. Spread buckwheat noodles 1/4 inch high over the mat leaving 1 inch of the far side clear. Arrange 2 to 3 stems of mustard greens across buckwheat noodles on near side. Roll tightly and secure to nori on far side by dampening slightly if necessary. Trim ends.

Cut the noodle roll in half and each half in thirds. Make sure your knife is very sharp and clean, wiping it on a damp cloth between slices. Arrange cut side up on a platter. Sprinkle each portion with 2 drops of tamari.

5. Baby Daikon Pickle

1 bunch baby daikon with leaves
1 tsp. sea salt

Wash and dry the daikon and leaves. Slice daikon in thin diagonals. Cut leaves in 1/2-inch pieces. Add salt, and mix well. Press in a bowl, with a small plate and a weight, for 3 hours, or overnight. Rinse if necessary before serving.

6. Takuan or Other Pickle

See the Special Foods section.

7. Roasted Barley Tea (Mugicha)

"Macrobiotic medicine is a teaching of awareness of reality or the Order of the Universe through sickness."

"The highest dreams of man: happiness and health, freedom and peace, must have a firm foundation in biology, physiology and dialectics. Otherwise, they can never be fulfilled."

—George Ohsawa
Practical Guide to Far-Eastern Macrobiotic Medicine

MENU XVIII

Broccoli Noodle Soup
Brown Rice with Onion and Carrot
Azuki Kabocha
Broccoli Stems with Red Radishes
Carrot and Watercress Pickle
Takuan or Other Pickle
Bancha Twig Tea (Kukicha)

1. Broccoli Noodle Soup

1/2 package whole wheat noodles
1 6″ strip kombu
Sea salt
Tamari soy sauce
1 cup broccoli flowers

Cook noodles separately. Rinse and drain. Wipe kombu with a damp cloth, and cook whole at least 1/2 hour to make stock. (For stock, allow 1/2 to 1 cup water per person.)

Remove kombu, add salt and tamari to taste. Add broccoli flowers and cook until bright and tender. To serve, dip noodles in hot water and arrange in bowls. Pour soup over noodles.

2. Brown Rice with Onion and Carrot

3 cups brown rice
1 small onion
1 carrot
2 pinches sea salt
4 1/2 cups water

Clean rice. Mince onion and carrot. Add vegetables, salt, and water to rice and pot-cook all together. Follow instructions in Menu I.

3. Azuki Kabocha

1 cup azuki beans
1/4 kabocha
3″ strip kombu
3 cups water
1/4 tsp. sea salt

Clean azuki beans, removing any stones. Wash well and drain in a colander. Wash and dry kabocha and cut into 1/2-inch pieces. Cut kombu into 1/2-inch pieces after wiping with a damp cloth. Combine all ingredients with 2 cups of water in a pot or ceramic bean pot. You may use a ceramic bean pot on top of the stove if you use a metal flame tamer under it. In this case, warm the pot up slowly so it will not crack. Do not pressure-cook azuki beans as they are yang and the taste becomes bitter.

Bring the water to a boil and add 1/2 cup of cold water. This is called "shocking" the beans and facilitates cooking, making them become soft faster. Bring the water to a boil again and add 1/2 cup of cold water once more. Cover and cook 2 1/2 hours. Then add salt and cook 1/2 hour more.

4. Broccoli Stems with Red Radishes

2 broccoli stalks
1/2 bunch red radishes
1/2 tsp. sea salt

Wash, dry, and trim vegetables. Remove fibrous skin of lower stalk of broccoli. Cut broccoli in thin circles on a diagonal. Slice radishes top to bottom in thin circles. Quick-boil each separately in salted water until color is bright and broccoli stems are tender. Drain in a colander, mix together, and serve at room temperature.

5. Carrot and Watercress Pickle

1 carrot
Watercress equal to 1/3 of carrot
1/2 tsp. sea salt
1 Tbsp. lemon juice

Wash and dry vegetables. Trim carefully. Cut carrot into a fine julienne. Cut watercress to match length of carrot. Mix well with salt and lemon juice. Pickle with pressure for 1 hour minimum.

6. Takuan or Other Pickle

See the Special Foods section.

7. Bancha Twig Tea (Kukicha)

MENU XIX

Miso Soup with Broccoli and Carrot	Tempeh with Nori and Scallions
Brown Rice with Sesame Seeds	Daikon with Kombu Nitsuke
Carrot-Lotus Root-Burdock Nishime	Takuan or Other Pickle
	Roasted Barley Tea (Mugicha)

1. Miso Soup with Broccoli and Carrot

2 6″ strips wakame
2 quarts water
1 stalk broccoli
1 carrot
Barley miso (mugi miso)

Soak, squeeze, and cut wakame into 1/2-inch pieces. Then cook wakame in soaking water to make stock. Wash, dry, and trim broccoli and carrot. Cut broccoli in thin circles on a diagonal, continuing through the flowers. Cut carrot into flowers.

To cut flowers, select a carrot about 1 inch in diameter most of the way down. Cut the length into thirds, making it comfortable to hold in the hand. For a three-petalled flower, cut three equally spaced incisions along the length of the carrot, angled slightly inward. Turn the carrot over and repeat, removing long slender wedges. Now cut in 1/8-inch slices to create flowers. There are many variations of this form, and refinements are made according to your skill.

Add broccoli and carrot flowers to stock and simmer gently until tender. Add miso to taste as per Menu I.

2. Brown Rice with Sesame Seeds

3 cups brown rice
4 1/2 cups water
2 pinches sea salt
1/2 cup sesame seeds

Prepare and pot-cook rice as in Menu I. Meanwhile, wash sesame seeds in a fine-mesh strainer, patting the bottom of the strainer to remove excess water. Roast the sesame seeds in a cast-iron skillet, stirring evenly with a bamboo paddle or a wooden spoon until dry and a characteristic fragrance arises. To check if seeds are done, crush between thumb and fourth finger, then taste. The seeds should not taste raw or scorched. When the rice is done, mix the roasted seeds in. Do not mash the rice.

3. Carrot-Lotus Root-Burdock Nishime

3 burdock roots
1 carrot
1 lotus root
2 6″ strips kombu
Tamari soy sauce

Wash, dry, and trim burdock roots. Cut burdock and carrot in deer's feet-style, i.e., 1-inch wedges. Cut lotus root in quarters lengthwise, then in 1/4-inch triangles. Water-sauté in boiling salted water the burdock, lotus root, and carrot, in that order. Add water to 2/3 the level of the vegetables. Slip the kombu under the vegetables, place cover ajar, and cook until tender, about 20 minutes. When the water is down to 1/2 inch, add tamari lightly to taste and cook covered until dry, mixing the vegetables once or twice.

4. Tempeh with Nori and Scallions

1 package tempeh
2 6″ strips kombu
3 shiitake mushrooms
1″ water
Sea salt
Tamari soy sauce
1 sheet nori
3 stalks scallion

Cut tempeh into triangles 1 inch long. Wipe kombu with a damp cloth. Make stock with kombu and shiitake, and cook for 1/2 hour. Take out kombu and hang to dry. Add half salt and half tamari to stock to make a slightly strong flavor. Mince scallions.

Cook tempeh in broth for 15 to 20 minutes. Meanwhile, roast the nori and crumble into broth. Turn off fire and add scallions. Serve immediately. If you do not serve immediately, keep scallions in a side dish to use as a garnish later. Serve 2 to 3 pieces of tempeh per person.

5. Daikon with Kombu Nitsuke

1 small daikon
1 bunch daikon leaves
1/2 package shredded kombu (kizami kombu)
Tamari soy sauce

Wash and dry daikon and daikon leaves. Soak kombu. Cut daikon in a fine julienne. Mince daikon tops. Squeeze and cut kombu in lengths to match daikon. Water-sauté daikon in 1/4 inch of kombu soaking water. Add kombu and 1/2 of the kombu soaking water. Cook until tender and water is down to 1/2 inch. Add daikon leaves and tamari lightly to taste. Mix and cook until dry.

6. Takuan or Other Pickle

See the Special Foods section.

7. Roasted Barley Tea (Mugicha)

> "God said, 'See, I give you every seed-bearing plant that is upon all the earth, and every tree that has seed-bearing fruit; they shall be yours for food. And to all the animals on land, to all the birds of the sky, and to everything that creeps on earth, in which there is the breath of life, [I give] all the green plants for food.' And it was so."
>
> —*The Torah*
> *The Five Books of Moses*

MENU XX

Summer Garden Soup	Wakame-Cucumber Salad
Rice and Vegetable Croquettes	Takuan or Other Pickle
Chick-peas with Carrot Tops	Roasted Barley Tea (Mugicha)
Broccoli Stems with Atsuage	

1. Summer Garden Soup

1/2 cup dulse
3 shiitake mushrooms
1/2 cup daikon
1 carrot
1/2 cup broccoli flowers
Green beans—1 per serving

Lemon peel
Sea salt
Tamari soy sauce

Soak dulse. Wash gently while in water to remove sand. Let sand settle. Squeeze and cut dulse into 1-inch pieces. Soak shiitake until soft and cut in 1/4-inch julienne. Cut daikon in half lengthwise and in 2-inch lengths. Then cut into 2-inch-long rectangles. Cut carrot to match daikon. Cut broccoli flowers to 3/4-inch size.

Bring dulse soaking water, minus last sandy tablespoon, to a boil. Add water if necessary to make enough for soup, about 3 quarts. Cook dulse and shiitake about 15 minutes with cover ajar. Cut stem ends off string beans and quick-boil in stock for 1 to 2 minutes until bright green. Remove, rinse in cold water, and drain. Set aside.

To boiling stock add daikon and carrot. Cook several minutes until tender. Add broccoli flowers and cook until bright green and tender, about 2 to 3 minutes. Meanwhile, cut lemon peel in a very fine julienne. Season soup with half salt and half tamari to taste. To serve, garnish with 1 green bean and a pinch of lemon peel.

2. Rice and Vegetable Croquettes

1 cup brown rice
1 cup sweet brown rice
3 cups water
2 pinches sea salt
1 small onion
1 small carrot
2–3 scallions
sesame oil

Prepare and pot-cook rice (both types together) as in Menu I. Wash and dry vegetables. Peel onion carefully, taking off as little as possible. Mince vetetables, including scallion roots. Water-sauté in 1/4 inch of boiling salted water. Mix together with cooked rice and a pinch of salt. Dampen hands and form rice firmly into croquettes. Brush a cast-iron skillet with sesame oil and pan-bake, uncovered, on a medium fire. Do both sides until firm and golden.

3. Chick-peas with Carrot Tops

1 cup chick-peas
3 cups water
Carrot tops
1/4 tsp. sea salt
3″ strip kombu

Remove stones and any discolored peas from chick-peas. Wash, drain and pat-dry. Soak at least 2 hours, or overnight. Pressure-cook 1 1/2 hours with kombu. Wash the carrot tops well, removing sand inside the bottom of the stalks. Dry and mince. After the chick-peas are soft, add salt and carrot tops, and cook another 20 to 30 minutes.

4. Broccoli Stems with Atsuage

1 package atsuage (fried tofu)

Broccoli stems left from soup
1 tsp. sesame oil
Tamari soy sauce

Preboil the fried tofu to remove the oil. Drain and cool. Cut broccoli stems and tofu into 1/2-inch cubes. Sauté in sesame oil. Add 1/2-inch water, cover, and steam several minutes until tender and stems are still bright green. Season lightly with tamari and cook uncovered until dry.

5. Wakame-Cucumber Salad

2 6″ strips wakame
2 pickling cucumbers
Sea salt

Soak wakame 10 minutes, until tender. Squeeze and cut in 1-inch pieces. Wash, dry, and cut cucumbers in thin diagonal circles. Sprinkle the cucumbers lightly with salt. Press and pickle at least 30 minutes, or until water rises out of cucumbers. Remove cucumbers from brine and squeeze to remove excess liquid. Mix together with wakame.

6. Takuan or Other Pickle

See the Special Foods section.

7. Roasted Barley Tea (Mugicha)

"He who sows corn, grass and fruit, soweth the Law."

—*The Essene Gospel of Peace*—Book Two
Edmond Bordeaux Szekely

". . . and the cow and the bear shall feed; their young ones shall lie down together; and the lion shall eat straw like the ox . . . . They shall not hurt nor destroy in all my holy mountain; for the earth shall be full of the knowledge of the Lord, as the waters cover the sea."

—Isaiah 11: 7 and 9
Old Testament

July

MENU XXI

Soft Rice (*Okayu*) with Celery	Lentils with Nori and Cilantro
Brown Rice with Celery	Takuan or Other Pickle
Scallion Miso Condiment	Roasted Rice Tea (Genmaicha)
Carrot-Parsnip Nishime	

1. Soft Rice (Okayu) with Celery

1/2 cup brown rice

2 pinches sea salt
5 cups water
1 stalk celery
1 Tbsp. minced lemon rind
Tamari soy sauce

Prepare rice as in Menu I. Bring to a boil in a regular pot and cook 1 hour. Meanwhile, wash, dry, trim, and de-string celery. Mince and water-sauté celery in 1/4 inch of boiling water until bright green. Add minced lemon rind and cook together for 1/2 minute. Dot lightly with tamari. Serve 1/2 teaspoon as garnish on rice.

2. Brown Rice with Celery

3 cups brown rice
1 pinch sea salt
4 1/2 cups water
2 stalks celery

Prepare and pot-cook rice as in Menu I. Meanwhile, wash, dry, trim, and de-string the celery. Cut into 1/4-inch dice. Dip into boiling salted water 1/2 minute. Drain and cool. Mix gently with rice when done.

3. Scallion Miso Condiment

1 bunch scallions
Mugi miso, 1/4 amount of minced scallions
2 tsps. sesame oil

Mince scallions finely, including roots. Sauté in sesame oil. Add 1/4 inch of water. Cover and steam several minutes. Meanwhile, dilute miso in a little water to make a thick cream. Add miso to scallions, mix well, and cook together several minutes, stirring constantly until well married and consistency holds together.

Use 1/2 teaspoon per serving as a condiment on grain. This condiment is very good for cleansing the intestines, especially in the case of rheumatism, diverticulosis, parasites, and blood disease.

4. Carrot-Parsnip Nishime

Parsnip, equal amount as carrot
Carrot, equal amount as parsnip
2 tsps. sesame oil
1 pinch sea salt
1 Tbsp. roasted sesame seeds

Wash, dry, and trim vegetables. Cut roots on the diagonal 1/4 inch thick. Sauté parsnip in sesame oil. Then add carrot. Cover and steam in 1/4 inch of water for about 10 minutes or until tender. Sprinkle lightly with a pinch of salt. Mix lightly, cover and steam several minutes more. To serve, garnish with roasted sesame seeds.

5. Lentils with Nori and Cilantro

1 cup lentils
1 sheet nori

Several sprigs cilantro (or scallion)
1/4 tsp. sea salt
2 cups water

Remove stones and wash lentils. Drain off excess water. Cook together with crumbled nori for 40 minutes, or until tender. Add salt and cook 10 minutes more. Cut cilantro into 1/2-inch pieces. Mix in before serving.

6. Takuan or Other Pickle

See the Special Foods section.

7. Roasted Rice Tea (Genmaicha)

Wash and drain one handful (1/4 cup) brown rice. Roast until golden in a cast-iron skillet, stirring constantly with a wooden spoon. Bring a teapot of water to boil, add rice, and simmer for 1/2 hour.

"Lo! We have shown him the Way, whether he be grateful or disbelieving."
—Qur'an, LXXVI: 3

MENU XXII

Miso Soup with Dulse
Bulgur
Lentils with Carrot and Daikon
Burdock with Umeboshi
Boiled Salad
Salad Dressing
Bancha Twig Tea (Kukicha)

1. Miso Soup with Dulse

1/2 cup dulse
1 leek
Barley miso (mugi miso)

Soak dulse and gently rub off sand in soaking water. Allow sand to settle. Squeeze and cut dulse into 1/2-inch pieces. Simmer in soaking water, minus last sandy tablespoon, at least 15 minutes. Cut leek in half lengthwise. Wash well under running water, separating leaves to remove sand. Cut into 1/2-inch pieces. Add to soup and cook about 5 minutes. Add miso as per Menu I.

2. Bulgur

3 cups bulgur
4 1/2 cups water
2 pinches sea salt

Roast bulgur in a dry skillet. Add water and salt. Bring to a boil with cover ajar. Cover tightly, lower fire, and cook 40 minutes, until all water is absorbed. Mix lightly from bottom to top and cover with a clean cloth to allow steam to escape.

3. Lentils with Carrot and Daikon

2 cups lentils
1 carrot
3″ piece of daikon
3 1/2 cups water
1/2 tsp. sea salt

Cut carrot into eighths lengthwise and then into thin triangles. Cut daikon to match carrot. Water-sauté daikon, then carrot in 1/4 inch of boiling salted water. Add de-stoned, washed lentils, and water. Bring to boil, lower fire, and simmer 30 minutes. Add salt and cook another 10 minutes.

4. Burdock with Umeboshi

4 burdock roots
2 tsps. sesame oil
3 umeboshi, pits removed

Wash burdock gently with vegetable brush, being careful not to remove skin. Dry and cut into 1 1/4-inch lengths, then into thin rectangles lengthwise. Sauté burdock in sesame oil until strong, earthy smell evaporates. Add water to 2/3 the level of the burdock. Bring to a boil, lower the fire, and simmer until tender, about 20 minutes.

Meanwhile, mash three umeboshi. Dilute slightly with some of the burdock cooking water. Add to burdock and cook together. When burdock is tender, remove cover, and cook until dry. Serve three to five pieces per person.

5. Boiled Salad

2 cups whole wheat macaroni
1 bunch broccoli
1 head cauliflower
1/2 green cabbage
3 carrots
1 bunch watercress

Boil macaroni until al dente consistency. Rinse in cold water and drain. Separate broccoli and cauliflower flowers, cutting into bite-sized pieces. Cut broccoli and cauliflower stems into 1/2-inch by 1/4-inch pieces. Cut cabbage into 1-inch squares. Cut carrot into thin half-moons. Cut watercress into 1 1/2-inch lengths.

Boil the vegetables separately in boiling salted water until brightly colored and tender. Rinse in cold water and drain. Toss together in a mixing bowl with the macaroni. Add dressing described in next recipe.

6. Salad Dressing

3 tsps. umeboshi juice
2 tsps. sesame oil
1 tsp. tamari soy sauce
Water

Whip the ingredients together with chopsticks, adding enough water to make a light texture and taste. You may adjust ingredients slightly to suit your taste. Mix gently into the salad and serve all together in an attractive bowl. Decorate imaginatively.

7. Bancha Twig Tea (Kukicha)

"He that killeth an ox is as if he slew a man."

—Isaiah 66: 3
Old Testament

"For I tell you truly, from one Mother proceeds all that lives upon the earth. Therefore, he who kills, kills his brother. And from him will the Earthly Mother turn away, and will pluck from him her quickening breasts. And he will be shunned by her angels, and Satan will have his dwelling in his body."

—*The Essene Gospel of Peace*—Book One
Edmond Bordeaux Szekely

MENU XXIII

Soft Rice (*Okayu*) with Shiitake	Romaine Lettuce with Garlic
Brown Rice with Rye	Takuan or Other Pickle
Lentils with Burdock	Roasted Rice Tea (Genmaicha)
Cabbage with Turnip and Carrot	

1. Soft Rice (Okayu) with Shiitake

1/2 cup rice
5 cups water
3 shiitake mushrooms
1 bunch carrot tops
3 pinches sea salt

'lean and pot-cook rice as per Menu I, using 5 cups water. Soak, squeeze, and nince shiitake. Thoroughly wash, dry, and mince carrot tops. Add these to the rice ıfter it comes to a boil, together with salt. Lower fire and simmer, covered tightly, 'or 1 hour.

?. Brown Rice with Rye

2 2/3 cups rice
1/3 cup rye
1 1/2 pinches sea salt
4 1/2 cups water

'ot-cook as per Menu I.

ȝ. Lentils with Burdock

2 cups lentils
2 burdock roots
1 onion
1/2 bunch carrot tops
3 1/2 cups water
1/2 tsp. sea salt

/ash and dry vegetables. Carefully peel onion. Cut onion and burdock in 1/4-inch ice. Mince carrot tops. Water-sauté onion until translucent and sweet. Add burdock and sauté until its strong smell evaporates. Add lentils and water. Bring water to a boil. Lower the fire and simmer about 30 minutes. Add salt and carrot tops. Cook 10 minutes more.

4. Cabbage with Turnip and Carrot

4 leaves cabbage
1 turnip
1 carrot
Sea salt
Tamari soy sauce

Cut the cabbage into 1-inch squares. Cut the turnip and carrot into 1/2-inch cubes. Water-sauté turnip, cabbage, and carrot, in that order, in 1/4 inch of boiling salted water. Add a little more water, if necessary, and steam until tender.

Sprinkle lightly with salt while cooking. When tender, season lightly with tamari and cook until dry.

5. Romaine Lettuce with Garlic

1 bunch romaine lettuce
3 cloves garlic
Tamari soy sauce
1 to 2 Tbsps. sesame seeds

To wash romaine lettuce, thinly slice off the bottom core. Trim any remaining bad parts. Cut romaine lettuce in half lengthwise just through the heart and pull the leaves apart. Wash well under cold running water, separating the leaves to wash out the sand. Drain well and pat dry. Cut romaine lettuce in quarters lengthwise and in 1-inch strips widthwise. Slice the heart as thinly as the leaves. Crush garlic. Remove the skin and mince. Water-sauté the garlic in 1/4 inch of boiling salted water. Add romaine lettuce and sauté until bright green, about 2 minutes. Season lightly with tamari to taste and garnish with roasted sesame seeds.

6. Takuan or Other Pickle

See the Special Foods section.

7. Roasted Rice Tea (Genmaicha)

> "The Holy Land is within where we build our Holy Temple."
>
> —*The Essene Gospel of Peace*—Book Two
> Edmond Bordeaux Szekely

MENU XXIV

Black Bean Soup	Carrot-Burdock Kinpira
Brown Rice with Black Sesame Seeds	Broccoli with Nori and Ginger
	Swiss Chard Ohitashi
Wakame with Onions	Bancha Twig Tea (Kukicha)

1. Black Bean Soup

3/4 cup black beans
1/2 cup barley
1 onion
3 cloves garlic
2 stalks celery
1 carrot
1 6″ strip kombu
8 cups water
3/4–1 tsp. sea salt

Pick stones out of beans and barley. Wash well and drain. Wash and dry vegetables. Cut all the vegetables in 1/4-inch dice. Crush and mince the garlic. Water-sauté vegetables in the order given in the ingredients list. Add washed and drained barley and black beans. Cut kombu into 1/2-inch pieces and add. Bring to boil in 8 cups of water. Simmer 1 hour. When beans are tender, add salt to taste. Cook another 30 minutes. Adjust salt to taste.

2. Brown Rice with Black Sesame Seeds

3 cups brown rice
4 1/2 cups water
2 pinches sea salt
1/4 cup black sesame seeds

Pot-cook rice as per Menu I. Wash sesame seeds and roast in a dry skillet. When the rice is done, turn gently from bottom to top, lightly mixing in sesame seeds.

3. Wakame with Onions

1/2 package wakame
2 onions
Sea salt
Tamari soy sauce

Soak wakame until tender. Meanwhile, cut onions in thin crescents, making sure each slice includes a portion of the core. Squeeze and cut wakame into 1-inch pieces. Water-sauté onions in 1/4-inch of boiling water. Add wakame and wakame soaking water. Bring to a boil, lower fire, and simmer about 15 minutes. Add tamari to taste and cook until dry.

4. Carrot-Burdock Kinpira

1 large carrot
Burdock, 3 times the amount of carrot
1 Tbsp. sesame oil
Tamari soy sauce

Wash and dry carrot and burdock. Cut in a very fine julienne. Sauté burdock in sesame oil until the strong, earthy odor evaporates. Add carrot and sauté 1 to 2 minutes. Add water almost to cover burdock. Bring to a boil. Boil hard 1/2 minute without the cover. Lower the fire, cover, and cook until tender, about 20 minutes. When the water is down to 1/2 inch, add tamari to taste, and cook until dry.

5. Broccoli with Nori and Ginger

1 bunch broccoli
2″ piece of ginger
5 sheets nori
Sea salt
Tamari soy sauce

Wash broccoli well and pat dry. Remove any hard fibrous parts. Slice in half lengthwise. Cut flowers off leaving a 1/4-inch stem. Cut stalk on a thin diagonal. Peel ginger and mince finely. Water-sauté the broccoli flowers in 1/4 inch of boiling salted water. After the flowers have become bright green, add the stems. Break the nori into small pieces and add to the broccoli. Cover and steam several minutes, until the stalk is tender. Be careful to maintain the bright green color. Add ginger and tamari to taste. Cook together 1 minute, uncovered.

6. Swiss Chard Ohitashi

1 or more Swiss chard stems
Tamari soy sauce

Wash chard well and pat dry. Quick-boil whole in boiling salted water until bright green. Rinse in cool water, gently squeeze out excess water. Cut into 1-inch pieces and season lightly with tamari.

7. Bancha Twig Tea (Kukicha)

Note: Sometimes, in the middle of summer, there are a few cold, wet days. This menu is appropriate for such a time. Also, the upward-moving energy of the ginger and broccoli counteracts and balances the concentrating energy of the carrot and burdock.

> "For ten generations from Adam to Noah, no flesh of any creature was permitted to be eaten."
>
> —Rabbi Joseph Rosenfeld
> *Tree of Life*

> "From the day that the Holy Temple was destroyed it would have been right to have imposed on ourselves the law prohibiting the eating of flesh."
>
> —Rabbi Yishmael
> *Talmud*—Tracte Babba Bathra 608
> *Tree of Life*

MENU XXV

Cornmeal Lentil Soup	Wedged Cabbage
Brown Rice with Parsley	Red Radish Pickle
Cornmeal Mold with Tofu	Roasted Barley Tea (Mugicha)
Mixed Vegetable Nishime	

1. Cornmeal Lentil Soup

1/2 cup cornmeal

1/4 cup lentils
1 6″ strip kombu
1 stalk celery
1 small carrot
1/2 tsp. sea salt

Clean kombu with fingers to remove sand. Soak until soft and cut in 1/4-inch dice. Remove any stones from lentils. Wash and drain. Lightly roast cornmeal in a dry skillet until the harsh smell evaporates, about 1 to 2 minutes. Slowly add kombu soaking water, stirring constantly. Add lentils and kombu. Add water, bring to a boil, and simmer about 30 minutes. Add vegetables and salt. Simmer another 30 minutes. Adjust salt to taste. Amount of water is determined by consistency of soup desired.

2. Brown Rice with Parsley

3 cups brown rice
4 1/2 cups water
1 pinch sea salt
Parsley

Prepare and pot-cook rice as in Menu I. Wash, dry, and mince parsley. Mix into cooked rice while rice is still hot.

3. Cornmeal Mold with Tofu

1 cup cornmeal
1 12-oz. tub tofu
1 carrot
Carrot tops
2 cups water
1/2 tsp. sea salt

Wash, dry, and mince carrot and carrot tops separately. Mash tofu. Lightly roast cornmeal in dry pot until the harsh smell disappears, about 1 to 2 minutes. Slowly add water, stirring constantly. Add salt and carrot. Cover and cook on a small fire for 30 minutes, using a flame tamer. Add tofu and minced carrot tops. Cover and cook 10 minutes more. Pour into a mold and let set. To serve, cut into 2-inch squares.

4. Mixed Vegetable Nishime

1/3 daikon
2 stalks celery
1 large carrot
1/4 head romaine lettuce
1 pinch sea salt
Tamari soy sauce

Wash and dry vegetables, trimming where necessary. Cut daikon in half lengthwise and then in 1 1/2-inch diagonal half-moons. Cut celery and carrot to match. Cut romaine lettuce in 1/2-inch widths. Quick-boil in 1 inch of boiling salted water until color is bright and vegetables are still crispy. Season lightly with tamari.

5. Wedged Cabbage

1/2 green cabbage
1–2 pinches sea salt
1 tsp.–1 Tbsp. brown rice vinegar
1 tsp.–1 Tbsp. roasted sesame seeds

Cut cabbage into 1-inch wedges. Steam, sprinkling lightly with salt, until color is bright and leaves are at desired tenderness. Dot lightly with rice vinegar. To serve, garnish with roasted sesame seeds.

6. Red Radish Pickle

1 bunch red radishes
Radish leaves
1 tsp. sea salt

Separate leaves from radishes. Wash leaves several times in a bowl of water to remove sand. Wash radishes lightly with a vegetable brush. Trim radishes and leaves. Cut radishes in thin circles from top to bottom. Cut leaves in half. Mix with salt, and press in a bowl with a small plate and a weight for 1/2 to 1 hour. Longer is better. To serve, squeeze brine out of radishes and taste the pickle. If it is too salty, rinse in cold water and squeeze. Serve 1 tablespoon per person.

7. Roasted Barley Tea (Mugicha)

> "The Torah, realising that it would take many generations of special training before man's soul would become completely refined, permitted the eating of flesh after Noah but with many reservations and restrictions. . . . 'For blood is the soul.' Life, thought, character, behavior, are all contained in the chemicals comprised in the blood. The less of the animal blood in man, the purer his soul becomes, the nearer he gets to the Divine being. When the Israelites were near the Mishcon, the Sanctuary, the eating of flesh was forbidden to them (Orlah 2, Misnah 17). It is true, therefore, that the eating of flesh is looked upon as a lust and Jewish law aims to restrict and arrest that diet."
>
> —Rabbi Joseph Rosenfeld
> *Tree of Life*

August

MENU XXVI

Nori Soup with Black Radish
Rice Triangles (Omusubi)
Azuki-Udon Mold
Acorn Squash with Sunflower Seeds
Mustard Greens Ohitashi
Takuan or Other Pickle
Roasted Barley Tea (Mugicha)

1. Nori Soup with Black Radish

3 black radishes
6 cups water
6 sheets crumbled nori

1/2 bunch watercress
Sea salt
Tamari soy sauce

Wash, dry, and trim radishes. Cut in julienne style. Water-sauté in 1/4 inch of boiling salted water about 2 minutes. Add 6 cups water. Bring to a boil and boil hard for 1 minute uncovered. Add 6 sheets of crumbled nori. Lower fire and simmer about 20 minutes. Cut watercress into 1 1/2-inch lengths. Add an equal amount of salt and tamari to complete the taste of the soup. Makes a light, delicate flavor. Add watercress and serve.

2. Rice Triangles (Omusubi)

3 cups brown rice
3 1/2 cups water
1 tsp. sea salt
Umeboshi
1/2 cup roasted sesame seeds
1 bunch minced parsley
Nori

Pressure-cook rice as in Menu II. Always cook the rice a little dryer for omusubi or other style of rice balls. When the rice is done, gently turn it from bottom to top. Turn out into a tray and let cool.

To form omusubi see recipe No. 2 Rice Triangles, in Menu XLVII. Once the omusubi are formed, dip the top corners of half of them into roasted sesame seeds, and the top corners of the other half into the minced parsley. Arrange attractively on a platter.

3. Azuki-Udon Mold

3 cups azuki beans
2 packages whole wheat udon
1 6″ strip kombu
6 cups water
1 tsp. sea salt
1 bunch minced scallions
Nori

Break the kombu into small pieces. Pot-cook the azuki beans and kombu for 2 1/2 hours. When the beans are tender, add salt and cook for another 1/2 hour. Meanwhile, boil udon until tender, rinse in cold water, and drain. When beans are done, mix thoroughly with the udon and spread out in a 2- to 3-inch-deep baking tray, or any kind of molding tray. Let cool. Cut into 2 1/2-inch squares and serve garnished with minced scallions.

4. Acorn Squash with Sunflower Seeds

1 acorn squash
Sea salt
1/2 cup roasted sunflower seeds

Wash and dry acorn squash. Cut in half. Scoop out and save seeds. Cut into crescents of equal thickness, generally following the meridian lines. Arrange on a damp steaming towel in a steamer. Sprinkle lightly with salt, and steam until tender, about 20 minutes. Serve garnished with roasted sunflower seeds.

5. Mustard Greens Ohitashi

1 bunch mustard greens
Sea salt
Tamari soy sauce

Wash mustard greens well, removing the root which is too tough to eat. Save the roots for soup stock.

Quick-boil in boiling salted water until bright green and the stems are tender. Rinse in cool water. Gently squeeze out excess water. Cut into 1 1/4-inch lengths. Sprinkle lightly with tamari.

6. Takuan or Other Pickle

See the Special Foods section.

7. Roasted Barley Tea (Mugicha)

> "And the flesh of slain beasts in his body will become his own tomb. For I tell you truly, he who kills, kills himself, and whoso eats the flesh of slain beasts, eats of the body of death. For in his blood every drop of their blood turns to poison; in his breath their breath to stink; in his flesh their flesh to boils; in his bones their bones to chalk; in his bowels their bowels to decay; in his eyes their eyes to scales; in his ears their ears to waxy issue. And their death will become his death."
>
> —*The Essene Gospel of Peace*—Book One
> Edmond Bordeaux Szekely

MENU XXVII

Clear Soup (Osumashi) with Tofu and Watercress	Umeboshi Juice Dressing
Norimaki	Kombu Condiment (*Shoyu*-Kombu)
Whole Wheat Noodle Salad	Takuan or Other Pickle
	Roasted Barley Tea (Mugicha)

1. Clear Soup (Osumashi) with Tofu and Watercress

1 8″ strip kombu
3 shiitake mushrooms
1 carrot
1 tub tofu
Sea salt
Tamari soy sauce
Watercress

Cook kombu and whole shiitake mushrooms at least 1 hour to make soup stock. Amount of stock is determined by number of servings. Allow 1 cup per person.

Cut carrots into flowers. Cut tofu into flowers using a small cookie cutter or Japanese flower mold. Quick-boil carrot flowers in soup stock. Drain and set aside.

Boil tofu flowers until they float. Drain and set aside. Season the stock, half with salt and half with tamari, to make a delicious taste, not too weak, not too strong. Arrange one tofu flower, two carrot flowers and one sprig of watercress in each soup bowl. Pour hot soup over and serve.

2. Norimaki

3 cups rice
4 1/4 cups water
Sea salt
1 cucumber
1 carrot
1 bunch romaine lettuce
3 umeboshi, pits removed
Nori

Pot-cook rice with a pinch of salt as per Menu I. Wash and dry vegetables. Cut 1 inch off the stem end of the cucumber and rub it against the cucumber, holding the cucumber upside down. Dip the cut end in salt and rub against the cucumber to extract the white, bitter liquid. Rinse this off. Cut cucumber in 1/4-inch-wide strips lengthwise. Sprinkle with salt in a bowl, and press with a plate or weight to pickle at least 30 minutes. When done, rinse if too salty.

Cut the carrots also in 1/4-inch-wide strips lengthwise. Water-sauté in 1/4 inch of boiling salted water. Cover and steam until tender, several minutes. Quick-boil the romaine leaves for 1/2 minute and rinse in cold water to stop the cooking and to maintain their bright color. Mash umeboshi into paste, adding a little water to make creamy.

Press rice firmly onto a sheet of nori to 1/4-inch thickness, leaving 1 inch on long side clear. Lightly spread umeboshi paste on one long side of the rice closest to you. Place two strips of carrot, one cucumber pickle, and one leaf of romaine lettuce, rolled lengthwise, on top of the umeboshi paste. Roll rice tightly over the vegetables, with the nori forming the foundation. Press the vegetables firmly into the rice while rolling, keeping the norimaki even. Secure by pressing into the plain nori on the other end. Moisten lightly with water to secure nori, if necessary. Let sit for several minutes before cutting.

With a clean sharp knife, first trim the ends. Then cut the norimaki in half, and cut each half in thirds or fourths depending on the size desired. Wipe the knife clean on a damp cloth between each cut. The norimaki should be clean with no rice stuck to the outside. It should be firm so it does not fall apart. It should be dry and not mushy. It should be beautiful and tasty.

3. Whole Wheat Noodle Salad

1 package whole wheat spaghetti
2–3 stalks broccoli
1 cauliflower
1/2 bunch kale
2 carrots
4 leaves cabbage
1 cucumber
3 stalks celery

Cook the spaghetti until tender. Rinse in cold water and drain. Separate the flowers from the stems of the broccoli and cauliflower, leaving a 1/4-inch stem on each flower. Cut the broccoli and cauliflower stems on thin diagonals. If the stalks are too thick, cut them in half lengthwise first. Cut the kale into 1 1/4-inch lengths. Cut the carrots in half lengthwise and then in thin diagonals 1 1/4 inches long. Cut the cabbage into 1-inch squares. Cut the cucumbers in half lengthwise, then in thin diagonals to match the carrots. De-string the celery and cut in thin diagonals to match the carrots. All the vegetables should be cut approximately the same length.

Salt-press the cucumbers. Quick-boil the vegetables until bright and tender. Boil them from yang to yin so as not to cook the yang vegetable in the yin liquid. Rinse in cold water and drain. This vegetable-boiling water is good to use for soup stock. Mix all together.

4. Umeboshi Juice Dressing

5 umeboshi, pits removed
2 cups water

Boil umeboshi in 2 cups of water down to 1 cup. Mash umeboshi into the water. Pour over and mix into salad. Serve in a glass bowl. Store any left-over dressing in a jar in the refrigerator for later use.

5. Kombu Condiment (Shoyu-Kombu)

1 10″ strip kombu
1/2 cup tamari soy sauce
1/2 cup water

Brush kombu with fingers to remove any sand. Cut with scissors into 1/2-inch squares. Soak in a glass or enamel bowl in 1/2 cup tamari diluted with 1/2 cup water for at least 1 hour, or overnight. Then in an enamel saucepan, bring to a boil, lower fire, and simmer slowly until dry.

Spread kombu separately on a plate and allow it to dry thoroughly. Store in a glass jar, crock, or a ceramic-covered dish. Do not wash out the tamari remaining in the saucepan. Dilute it with cold water and use it for soup stock or flavoring when cooking vegetables.

Serve one or two pieces of shoyu-kombu per meal. This preparation is especially useful for cleaning the blood and strengthening the blood vessels.

6. Takuan or Other Pickle

See the Special Foods section.

7. Roasted Barley Tea (Mugicha)

> "... Daniel purposed in his heart that he would not defile himself with the portion of the king's meat, nor with the wine which he drank.... 'Prove thy servants, I beseech thee, ten days; and let them give us pulse to eat, and water to drink. Then let our countenances be looked upon before thee....' God gave them knowledge and skill in all learning and wisdom; and Daniel had understanding in all visions and dreams."
>
> —*The Book of Daniel* (1: 8–17)
> *Old Testament*

MENU XXVIII

Miso Soup with Celery Root	Broccoli and Cauliflower Flowers
Brown Rice	Tofu Dressing
Cornmeal Mold with Scallions	Broccoli and Cauliflower Stems
Country-style Daikon (Furofuki Daikon)	Bancha Twig Tea (Kukicha)

1. Miso Soup with Celery Root

3 6″ strips wakame
Celery
Celery root
Barley miso (mugi miso)

In a 1 1/2-quart soup pot, break wakame into water in small pieces. You can do this if wakame is not sandy. Bring to boil and simmer at least 15 minutes. Peel the celery root. De-string the celery. Slice both in thin diagonals. Add celery root and boil hard uncovered for 1 minute. Add celery, cover, and cook until tender. Add miso to taste as per Menu I.

2. Brown Rice

3 cups brown rice
4 1/2 cups water
1 pinch sea salt

Pot-cook as per Menu I.

3. Cornmeal Mold with Scallions

2 cups cornmeal
1/2 bunch scallions
1 onion
1 carrot
4 cups water
1/2 tsp. sea salt

Wash, dry, and trim vegetables. Cut onions and carrots into 1/8-inch dice. Mince scallions, including roots. In 1/4 inch of boiling salted water, sauté onions, then carrots. Add cornmeal and sauté 1 minute or until the harsh smell evaporates. Add water slowly while stirring and bring to a boil. Add salt. Cover and cook 40 minutes on low fire. When done, add scallions, mix well and pour into mold. Let the mixture become firm at room temperature or in a refrigerator. To serve, cut into 2-inch squares.

4. Country-style Daikon (Furofuki Daikon)

1 whole daikon
2 6″ strips kombu
3 shiitake mushrooms
Sea salt
Tamari soy sauce

Watercress

Wash, dry, and trim daikon and cut into 1-inch thick circles. Place two 6-inch strips of cleaned kombu on the bottom of a shallow pot. Cover with 1 inch of water. Add shiitake, bring to a boil, and simmer for at least 1/2 hour. Add salt to half the taste and tamari to complete the taste to make a strong broth.

Distribute daikon evenly in pot. Cover and cook until tender and translucent, turning daikon once. Check tenderness with chopstick. When done, add watercress cut into 2-inch sprigs. Serve one piece of daikon per person with watercress and a tablespoon of broth.

5. Broccoli and Cauliflower Flowers

I head cauliflower
1 bunch broccoli

Cut off flowers of both vegetables leaving 1/4-inch stems. Quick-boil separately in boiling salted water until bright and tender. Rinse in cold water and drain. Mix with Tofu Dressing.

Tofu Dressing

1 tub tofu
Sea salt
Brown rice vinegar

Quick-boil tofu. Drain well and mash in a suribachi. Add salt and brown rice vinegar gradually to taste. Keep the color light. Mix gently with vegetable flowers described above.

6. Broccoli and Cauliflower Stems

Broccoli stems
Cauliflower stems
1 tsp. kuzu
1/2 cup cold water
1 Tbsp. tamari soy sauce
2 Tbsps. sesame seeds

Cut stems into 1/2-inch cubes. Water-sauté in 1/4 inch of boiling salted water. Cover and steam until tender. Dilute kuzu in 1/4 cup of cold water. Add 1/4 cup of cold water and 1 tablespoon tamari. Add to vegetable stems and cook until translucent and slightly thickened, stirring constantly. Pour into serving bowl and garnish with roasted sesame seeds.

7. Bancha Twig Tea (Kukicha)

"Oh, the Ancient Truth!
Ages upon ages past it was found,
And it bound together a Noble Brotherhood.
The Ancient Truth!
Hold fast to it!"

—Goethe

MENU XXIX

Cabbage Soup with Dulse
Brown Rice with Millet
Rutabaga with Carrot
Hijiki with Sesame Seeds
Chinese Cabbage with Wheat Gluten (*Seitan*)
Gomashio with Wakame
Roasted Barley Tea (Mugicha)

1. Cabbage Soup with Dulse

3–5 cabbage leaves
1/2 cup dulse
1 leek
Sea salt
Tamari soy sauce

Soak dulse in water to cover until tender. Wash it in the soaking water to remove any sand. Squeeze and cut into 1/2-inch pieces. Pour soaking water into soup pot leaving last sandy tablespoon in bottom of bowl. Simmer soup for 15 minutes.

Meanwhile, trim and wash leeks, scrubbing roots as you would your hair under running water. Dry and cut into 1/2-inch pieces. Slice the heart of the cabbage in half and pull the leaves apart. Spreading the leaves, wash under water to clean out all the hidden sand. Cut cabbage leaves into 1/2-inch squares.

Add leeks and cabbage to soup and simmer several minutes until bright green and tender. Add salt and tamari to taste.

2. Brown Rice with Millet

1 cup brown rice
1 cup millet
1 pinch sea salt
3 cups water

Pot-cook as per Menu I.

3. Rutabaga with Carrot

1 rutabaga
1 carrot
Carrot tops
1 pinch sea salt

Wash, dry, and trim vegetables, peeling purple off top of rutabaga. Cut into 1/2-inch by 1/4-inch cubes. Water-sauté rutabaga in boiling salted water. Add carrot, cover, and steam until tender. Mince carrot tops and add. Sprinkle vegetables lightly with salt and cook until dry.

4. Hijiki with Sesame Seeds

1 package hijiki
Tamari soy sauce

Soak hijiki in water to cover about 10 minutes, or until tender. Gently wash the hijiki in the soaking water. Squeeze and cut it into 1 1/2-inch pieces. Water-sauté in

1/4-inch soaking water until the strong smell dissipates. Add remainder of soaking water minus the last remaining sandy tablespoon. Bring to a boil, cover, and simmer until tender, 30 to 40 minutes. When water is down to 1/2 inch, add tamari to taste and cook uncovered until dry, stirring once or twice.

5. Chinese Cabbage with Wheat Gluten (Seitan)

1/2 Chinese cabbage
1 strip kombu
4 cloves garlic
3 shiitake mushrooms
Sea salt
Tamari soy sauce
2 cups wheat gluten flour
5 scallions

Clean kombu with fingers or damp cloth to remove sand. Crush garlic and peel skin. Cook kombu, shiitake, and garlic in enough water to make stock, about 3 quarts. Add salt and tamari to taste.

Meanwhile, mix gluten flour with a pinch of salt. Add cold water a little at a time, until all the flour is absorbed and a spongy dough is created. Form gluten into 1-inch balls and simmer in stock for 30 to 40 minutes.

Cut cabbage into 1-inch strips widthwise. Mince scallions. Cook cabbage separately in 1 ladleful of stock. Sprinkle lightly with salt to reduce cabbage. Add cooked gluten balls and minced scallions. Mix together and serve three balls per person.

6. Gomashio with Wakame

14 Tbsps. sesame seeds
2 6″ strips wakame
1 scant Tbsp. sea salt

Wash and drain sesame seeds in a fine mesh strainer. Roast wakame in a cast-iron skillet on a small flame until brittle. Grind in a suribachi. Roast salt in skillet, stirring constantly with a bamboo paddle or wooden spoon. Grind together with wakame in suribachi. Roast sesame seeds until done, and grind while warm with salt and wakame.

Note: For more complete instructions on making gomashio, see "Condiments" in the Special Foods section.

7. Roasted Barley Tea (Mugicha)

> "What we have done will not be lost to all eternity. Everything ripens at its time and becomes fruit at its hour."
>
> —Divyavadana
> *Springs of Indian Wisdom*

MENU XXX

Soft Brown Rice and Barley (Okayu) with Umeboshi
Brown Rice with Millet and Carrot
Vegetable Nishime with Brussels Sprouts
Carrot Top Miso
Cauliflower-Carrot Pickle
Takuan or Other Pickle
Bancha Twig Tea (Kukicha)

1. Soft Brown Rice and Barley (Okayu) with Umeboshi

1/2 cup brown rice
1/2 cup barley
2 umeboshi
6 cups water

Clean rice as per Menu I. Pot-cook with umeboshi instead of salt for 2 hours. Garnish with 1/2 teaspoon carrot top miso (see recipe No. 4, below). Remove umeboshi pits before serving.

2. Brown Rice with Millet and Carrot

2 1/2 cups brown rice
1/2 cup millet
1 large carrot
4 1/2 cups water
1 pinch sea salt

Wash, dry, and mince carrot. Prepare rice and millet as in Menu I. Pot-cook all together. Mix well before serving.

3. Vegetable Nishime with Brussels Sprouts

1 onion
1 carrot
5 Brussels sprouts
Wheat gluten (*kofu*)
Sea salt
Tamari soy sauce
2 tsps.–1 Tbsp. kuzu
1/4 cup cold water

Wash, dry, and trim vegetables. Peel onion removing as little as possible. Cut onion from core to top in 1/2-inch crescents. Cut carrots into 1-inch wedges. Tear gluten in 1-inch irregular chunks to equal the size of the carrots.

Sauté the onions in 1/4-inch of boiling salted water. Add the Brussels sprouts. When their color becomes bright green, add the carrots and gluten. Add water to about halfway up. Cover and cook until the Brussels sprouts and onions are tender. Dilute kuzu in 1/4 cup of cold water. Stir in tamari to make a coffee color. Add to vegetable mixture and cook, stirring constantly, on a high fire until kuzu is thickened and translucent.

4. Carrot Top Miso

1 bunch carrot tops
Barley miso (mugi miso)

Remove any bad parts from the carrot tops. Wash well and pat dry. Mince. Water-sauté in 1/4 inch of boiling water for 1 minute. Cover and steam several minutes until the stems are tender.

Miso should equal 1/4 the volume of carrot tops. Dilute it in a little cold water. Add to the carrot tops, mixing well, and cook together about 5 minutes, stirring two to three times. Be careful not to burn it. Serve 1/2 teaspoon per serving on okayu or any grain.

5. Cauliflower-Carrot Pickle

1 cauliflower
1 large or 2 medium carrots
1 onion
1″ piece of ginger
Tamari soy sauce

Wash, dry, and trim vegetables. Cut cauliflower into small flowers. Set stems aside for other cooking. Cut carrots into quarters lengthwise and then into 2-inch strips. Blanch the vegetables in boiling salted water for 1 minute. Remove the vegetables with a slotted spoon. Carefully peel and mince the onion. Peel and mince the ginger. Put all the vegetables into a gallon jug. Pour the blanching water over them. Add enough tamari to make a strong taste. The tamari should equal about 1/4 the amount of water. The pickles can be kept in this brine, refrigerated, for up to 1 month.

6. Takuan or Other Pickle

See the Special Foods section.

7. Bancha Twig Tea (Kukicha)

"Where true principles lack, the results are imperfect."
—Henry Madathanas

Summer—Breakfast Suggestions

I.	1.	Mild Miso Soup with Wakame, Red Radishes, and Their Leaves
	2.	Brown Rice Okayu with Barley
	3.	Nori Condiment with Grated Lemon Peel
II	1.	Clear Soup with Nori, Broccoli, and Cauliflower Flowers
	2.	Cornmeal Potage
	3.	Roasted Pumpkin Seeds
III	1.	Brown Rice Noodles in Broth
	2.	Corn on the Cob
	3.	Roasted Nori
IV	1.	Mild Miso Soup with Wakame and Yellow Crook-neck Squash
	2.	Brown Rice Okayu with Corn Kernels and Watercress
	3.	Quick-boiled Dandelion Greens
V	1.	Millet Potage
	2.	Miso Condiment with Minced Lemon Peel
	3.	Chinese Cabbage Nori Rolls

Summer—Lunch Suggestions

I	1.	Brown Rice with Roasted Pumpkin Seeds
	2.	Pita Bread with Mashed Kabocha and Nori
	3.	Broccoli with Carrots
	4.	Quick-boiled Watercress
	5.	Roasted Barley Tea
II	1.	Brown Rice with Arame
	2.	Buckwheat Noodle Rolls with Mustard Greens (Soba Maki)
	3.	Cabbage with Scallions
	4.	Pickle
	5.	Bancha Twig Tea
III	1.	Brown Rice/Vegetable Croquettes
	2.	Tempeh with Nori and Scallions
	3.	Wakame Cucumber Salad
	4.	Pickle
	5.	Bancha Twig Tea
IV	1.	Bulgur Pilaf
	2.	Burdock with Umeboshi
	3.	Cabbage with Turnips and Carrots
	4.	Pickle
	5.	Roasted Barley Tea
V	1.	Cornmeal Mold with Tofu
	2.	Boiled Salad
	3.	Roasted Nori
	4.	Pickle
	5.	Roasted Corn Tea

Autumn Cooking

Indian Summer is the turning point from summer to fall. The cool nights temper the warmth of the days, gathering inward the radiant force. This gathering influence has a firming effect, creating squashes and pumpkins, onions and millet. These reflect the roundness of Earth and nourish the stomach, pancreas, and spleen, as well as the confidence and will. Thus, Indian Summer is symbolized by the gathering energy of Earth.

The Autumn Equinox brings time for the harvest. Full of sun, and condensed by cool nights, the flavors are full-bodied and sweet, rich-tasting and warm, turning the fresh sweetness of summer to the sweet starch of fall, as in parsnips and carrots, rice, beans, and chestnuts.

Gradually, the chlorophyll evaporates and minerals consolidate, transforming the once-green landscape to yellows, oranges, reds, and bronzes. The lush growth dries and withers as the cool days and crisp nights concentrate the life-force of the plants. The energy gathers from the roots, stems and leaves, from the soil and the sky, from the Heavens and the Earth, and crystallizes their essence in each tiny seed. These return to the Earth to await their rebirth, skillfully recycling all the forces at work.

By Autumn the gathering is complete and the energy, compressed by the cold, seeps deep in the Earth, as the downward thrust becomes dominant. Fruits become harder, such as apples and Bosc pears, leaves contract like daikon and kale, roots grow longer and stronger with minerals. Thus, autumn is symbolized by the consolidating energy of Metal.

As the weather cools, more fire is needed. Light oil-sautéing on cooler days, water-sautéing on warmer days, more boiling and less steaming is appropriate. Boiled cauliflower, cabbage, and strong-leaved greens replace summer salads. Sweet rice mochi, seitan (wheat gluten), and beans build strength for the cold. Dried fruits, nuts, and seeds are suitable snacks for the healthy.

The tastes are more concentrated, poignant, and spicy. Sourness is needed to curb spicy excess, such as sauerkraut or ume, *yuzu* or lemon.

In these ways, Indian Summer and Autumn cooking thicken the blood in preparation for the cold winter.

September

MENU XXXI

Pumpkin Soup	Romaine Lettuce with Sunflower Seeds
Brown Rice with Rye	Takuan or Other Pickle
Black Bean Stew	Bancha Twig Tea (Kukicha)
Dried Daikon with Atsuage	

1. Pumpkin Soup

1 kabocha or butternut squash
1 onion
Sea salt
Watercress

Wash and dry kabocha. Trim off stem and all bumps. Carefully peel onion, taking off only as little as necessary. Wash and dry. Cut onion into 1/4-inch dice. Cut pumpkin into 1-inch pieces. Save seeds. Water-sauté onion in boiling salted water until sweet. Add kabocha and sauté until color deepens, 1 to 2 minutes. Add enough water for soup, and cook until tender, 15 to 20 minutes.

Purée mixture in a Foley food mill. Hand-puréeing is preferred over electric blending. Return soup to pot, season with salt to taste, and cook 5 minutes more. To serve, garnish with watercress.

2. Brown Rice with Rye

2 1/2 cups brown rice
1/2 cup rye
1 pinch sea salt
4 1/2 cups water

Prepare rice and pot-cook as per Menu I.

3. Black Bean Stew

1 cup black beans
1 small onion
1 small stalk celery
1 small carrot
1 3″ strip kombu
3 cups water
1/4 tsp. sea salt

Peel onion. Wash, dry, and trim vegetables. De-string celery. Pick stones out of beans, wash, and drain in a colander. Cut vegetables into 1/2-inch dice. Wipe sand off kombu and cut into 1/2-inch squares.

Quickly sauté onion in 1/4 inch of boiling water. Add celery, carrot, beans, water, and kombu. Pressure-cook for 1 hour. When beans are tender, add salt. Adjust to taste and cook another 30 minutes.

4. Dried Daikon with Atsuage

1 package dried daikon (kiriboshi daikon)
1 package atsuage (fried tofu)
1 onion
Tamari soy sauce

Soak dried daikon in water to cover 10 minutes, or until soft. Boil fried tofu whole to remove oil, about 2 minutes. Drain. Carefully peel onion, wash, and dry. Cut into thin crescents, catching a piece of core in each slice. Squeeze daikon and cut in 1 1/2-inch pieces. Cut tofu in half lengthwise and in thin slices widthwise.

Water-sauté onion in 1/4 inch of boiling salted water until the smell is mild. Add tofu and sauté about 2 minutes, or until it becomes more firm. Add daikon and daikon soaking water. Bring to a boil, cover, and simmer 15 minutes. Add tamari to taste. Mix gently and cook, uncovered, until dry.

5. Romaine Lettuce with Sunflower Seeds

1 head romaine lettuce
1 bunch carrot tops
Sea salt
Tamari soy sauce
1/4 cup roasted sunflower seeds

Trim the bottom off the heart of the romaine lettuce. Cut the heart in half and pull the leaves apart. Wash well under cold running water and drain. Wash carrot tops well, removing sand from bottom of stalks. Dry and mince. Cut romaine lettuce into quarters and then into 1-inch slices widthwise, cutting through the heart more thinly.

Water-sauté carrot tops in 1/4 inch of boiling salted water. Add romaine lettuce, sprinkle lightly with salt, and steam 1 minute, until bright green. Season lightly with tamari. Garnish with sunflower seeds.

6. Takuan or Other Pickle

See the Special Foods section.

7. Bancha Twig Tea (Kukicha)

> "Those who rebel against the basic rules of the Universe sever their own roots and ruin their true selves. Yin and Yang, the two principles in nature, and the four seasons are the beginning and the end of everything, and they are also the cause of life and death. Those who disobey the laws of the Universe will give rise to calamities and visitations, while those who follow the laws of the Universe remain free from dangerous illness, for they are the ones who have obtained Tao, the Right Way."
>
> —*The Yellow Emperor's Classic of Internal Medicine*
> —Ilza Veith

MENU XXXII

Miso Soup with Parsley Roots	Arame with Onion
Lentil Rice	Cucumber Pickle
Gomashio with Kombu	Bancha Twig Tea (Kukicha)
Stuffed Daikon	

1. Miso Soup with Parsley Roots

1 6″ strip wakame
3 parsley roots with greens
1 Tbsp. barley miso (mugi miso)
Water

Soak, squeeze, and cut wakame into 1/2-inch pieces. Wash, dry, and trim roots and leaves of parsley. Separate leaves. Cut roots on a thin diagonal and cook until tender. Cut greens into 1/2-inch pieces and cook in soup until tender and bright green. Add miso by straining directly into soup or diluting in soup broth on the side. Adjust miso to taste.

2. Lentil Rice

2 1/2 cups brown rice
1/2 cup lentils
2 pinches sea salt
4 1/2 cups water

Prepare rice and beans and pressure-cook as per Menu II.

3. Gomashio with Kombu

15 Tbsps. sesame seeds
1 6″ strip kombu
1 scant Tbsp. sea salt

Wash sesame seeds in a fine-mesh strainer. Drain and pat dry. Wipe kombu clean and roast in a cast-iron skillet until brittle. Grind into powder in a suribachi. Roast salt in a skillet, stirring constantly with a bamboo paddle or wooden spoon. Grind in suribachi with kombu. Roast sesame seeds until dry and done. Grind in suribachi while warm.

Note: For more detailed instructions see "Condiments" in the Special Foods section.

4. Stuffed Daikon

1/2 daikon
2 6″ strips kombu
Sea salt
Tamari soy sauce
1 small onion
1 small carrot

1 tub tofu
3 scallions

Line bottom of a shallow pot with kombu. Add 1-inch of water and cook 30 minutes. Add salt and tamari to make slightly strong broth.

Wash and dry vegetables. Carefully peel onion, removing only as little as possible. Cut daikon into 1-inch circles. Scoop out center with spoon, leaving the bottom intact. Set aside. Set tofu in a colander to drain. Mince onion, carrot, and scallions. Put tofu in a bowl and mash. Add minced vegetables and 1/2 teaspoon salt.

Fill daikon with tofu mixture and arrange in broth. Place a wooden lid or a small plate inside the pot on top of the vegetables. Cook 20 minutes, or until daikon is tender.

5. Arame with Onion

1 package arame
1 onion
Tamari soy sauce

Rinse arame. Carefully peel onion, taking off as little as possible. Cut onion into thin crescents, catching a piece of core in each slice. Squeeze and cut arame into 1 1/2-inch lengths.

Water-sauté onion in 1/4 inch of boiling water until sweet. Add arame and sauté until the strong smell evaporates. Add water to cover. Bring to boil, cover, and simmer 20 to 30 minutes. When water is down to 1/2 inch, add tamari to taste and cook uncovered until dry.

Note: It is recommended to rinse arame instead of soaking.

6. Cucumber Pickle

Cucumbers
Sea salt

The best cucumbers, as far as taste and nutrition are concerned, are the Japanese cucumbers. If they are not available, use pickling cucumbers. American cucumbers are useful only if organic.

Cut 1 inch off the dark green stem end, dip in salt and, holding the cucumber upside down, rub the cut ends together to extract the bitter white foam. Throw the end away and rinse the cucumber.

Place the cucumber between two chopsticks. Slice thin circles down to the chopsticks making four slices. Cut all the way through on the fifth slice. Continue in this fashion until all the cucumber is cut. Place all the cucumber in a bowl and sprinkle with enough salt to pickle, approximately 1/2 teaspoon of salt per cup of sliced cucumber. Press with a small plate and a weight for about 1 hour. When the cucumbers are soft, gently squeeze each one between your palms, twisting slightly to open them into fans. Serve one or two per person.

7. Bancha Twig Tea (Kukicha)

"Alas! It is a foolish world that indulges itself in the acquisition of fame and wealth and regards life so lightly."

—Chang Chung-ching
Shang Han Lun
The Great Classic of Chinese Medicine

MENU XXXIII

Clear Soup (Osumashi) with Spiral Noodles
Brown Rice Mold
Hijiki with Tempeh
Egyptian Lentils
Chinese Cabbage with Chinese Pickled Turnip
Cucumber Rice Bran Pickle (*Nukazuke*)
Bancha Twig Tea (Kukicha)

1. Clear Soup (Osumashi) with Spiral Noodles

1 8″ strip kombu
5 shiitake mushrooms
1 cup whole wheat spiral noodles
1/3 daikon
Snow peas, 2 per person
Sea salt
Tamari soy sauce

Make stock with kombu and shiitake, simmering 1/2 to 1 hour. Cook and drain noodles separately. Wash, dry, and trim daikon and snow peas, removing strings from peas. Cut daikon into 1/8-inch julienne. Quick-boil snow peas separately, 1 or 2 minutes.

Remove kombu and shiitake from stock and dry for further use. Add salt and tamari, half and half, to make a good flavor. Cook daikon in stock several minutes, until tender. Arrange several noodles in a bowl. Pour soup, arrange daikon on top, and garnish with snow peas.

2. Brown Rice Mold

3 cups brown rice
4 1/2 cups water
1 pinch sea salt
1 onion
Shiitake from soup
1 carrot
1/2 bunch watercress
Umeboshi juice

Prepare and pot-cook rice as per Menu I. Wash and dry vegetables. Cut onion, shiitake, carrots, and watercress in 1/4-inch dice. Quick-boil the onion and carrot and drain well. Mix with cooked rice. Flavor lightly with umeboshi juice. (For umeboshi juice see recipe No. 4 in Menu XXVII.) Press firmly into a 2-inch-deep tray to mold. Cut in 2-inch by 3-inch rectangles to serve.

3. Hijiki with Tempeh

1 package hijiki
1 package tempeh
Tamari soy sauce

Soak hijiki in water to cover, about 10 minutes, or until soft. Squeeze and cut into 1/2-inch pieces. Crumble tempeh with a fork in a bowl. Sauté hijiki in 1/4-inch hijiki soaking water, until the strong smell evaporates. Add rest of soaking water minus the last sandy tablespoon. Bring to a boil, cover, and simmer about 20 minutes. Add tempeh. Mix and simmer together another 15 minutes, until water is down to 1/2 inch. Add tamari to taste, and cook uncovered until dry.

4. Egyptian Lentils

1 cup lentils
1 small onion
2 cups water
1/4 tsp. sea salt
1/2 sheet nori

Remove stones, wash, and drain lentils. Peel onion carefully, removing as little as possible. Cut in 1/4-inch dice. Water-sauté onion in 1/4 inch of boiling salted water. Add lentils and 2 cups of water. Bring to a boil, lower fire, cover tightly, and simmer 30 minutes or until tender. Add salt and nori, breaking it into small pieces. Cook 15 minutes more.

5. Chinese Cabbage with Chinese Pickled Turnip

1/4 Chinese cabbage
1 package Chinese pickled turnip
1 pinch sea salt

Wash, dry, and cut cabbage in 1/2-inch pieces widthwise. Steam in 1/2 inch of boiling salted water. Sprinkle with a pinch of salt to reduce cabbage. Add several pieces of pickled turnip, either whole or cut, enough to make a delicious, tantalizing flavor. Cook together several minutes more.

6. Cucumber Rice Bran Pickle (Nukazuke)

Pickling cucumbers (about 20), washed and dried
5 lbs. rice bran (nuka)
3 cups water
1 1/2 cups sea salt

Toast the nuka in a cast-iron skillet over low heat, stirring constantly with a wooden spoon for about 10 minutes, or until fragrant. Cool. Boil water, add salt and let dissolve several minutes. Cool. Add salted water to nuka to form a thick paste. Wash and dry cucumbers. Press them into the nuka, covering them completely. Cover with a wooden lid or clean cloth and keep in a cool place. The cucumbers may be eaten after 1 day. Add a little salt every time fresh cucumbers are added. Stir this mixture every day by hand to keep from spoiling.

7. Bancha Twig Tea (Kukicha)

"This is a changing world. You will disappear some day, this earth will disappear, this galaxy will disappear, this visible universe will change. But movement itself, change, is endless, constant and immortal. The law of change is Justice. . . . and you are the king [or queen] of this Universe. You changed yourself, within Infinity, into [human form.] You are a manifestation of Infinity. By your daily eating and drinking you are changing yourself. . . . Eating is the transmutation of life from nature, from Infinity. . . . You can change everything into [yourself], into your thinking and activity."

—Michio Kushi
The Spiral of Life

MENU XXXIV

Cornmeal Soup
Brown Rice with Black Sesame Seeds
Carrots with Tempeh
Savoy Cabbage with Nori and Ginger
Miso Condiment
Pumpkin *Kanten*
Bancha Twig Tea (Kukicha)

1. Cornmeal Soup

1 cup cornmeal
1 onion
7 cups water
1 1/2 tsp. sea salt
3 scallions

Carefully peel onion, taking off as little as necessary. Cut in 1/4-inch dice and water-sauté until mild. Add cornmeal and continue sautéing 1 minute more. Add water slowly, stirring constantly until smooth. Bring to a boil, stirring several times to prevent lumping on the bottom of pot. Add salt. Lower fire, cover, and simmer for 40 minutes. Garnish with minced scallions.

2. Brown Rice with Black Sesame Seeds

3 cups brown rice
2 pinches sea salt
3 3/4 cups water
1/4 cup black sesame seeds

Prepare rice and pressure-cook as in Menu II. Wash sesame seeds in a fine-mesh strainer and pat dry. Roast in a cast-iron skillet, stirring constantly with a bamboo paddle or wooden spoon until the seeds are dry and beginning to pop. Lower fire and stir faster. Check seeds by crumbling between the fourth finger and thumb. When they crumble easily, taste them. There is a fine line between not yet done and scorched. Be careful not to scorch the seeds. When done, pour into a wooden or porcelain bowl immediately. Mix together with cooked rice.

3. Carrots with Tempeh

3 carrots
1/2 package tempeh
Sea salt

Wash and dry carrots. Cut into 1/4-inch cubes. Using a fork, crumble tempeh in a bowl. Quickly water-sauté carrots in 1/4 inch of boiling salted water. Add tempeh, cover, and steam 10 minutes. Sprinkle lightly with salt. Mix and steam 5 minutes more.

4. Savoy Cabbage with Nori and Ginger

1 small cabbage
1″ piece fresh ginger
Sea salt
1 sheet nori
Tamari soy sauce

Wash and dry cabbage. Trim away any bad spots. Cut into quarters and remove heart. Slice heart on diagonal in fine julienne. Cut cabbage leaves in julienne on a diagonal.

Peel and mince ginger. Water-sauté cabbage in 1/4 inch of boiling water. Sprinkle lightly with a pinch of salt to reduce cabbage. Cover and steam 3 minutes. Add ginger and nori broken into little pieces. Add tamari lightly to taste. Mix well, and steam 2 minutes more uncovered.

5. Miso Condiment

1 bunch carrot tops
1″ piece fresh ginger
1 Tbsp. sesame oil
3 Tbsps. shaved kombu (*oboro* kombu)
Hatcho miso, 1/4 the amount of carrot tops

Wash, dry, and mince carrot tops. Peel and mince ginger. Oil-sauté carrot tops several minutes. Add 1/2 inch of water and bring to boil. Lower fire and add kombu. Cover and cook several minutes, or until carrot stems are tender. Put miso in a bowl, then pour cooking liquid into miso and dilute. Pour back into pot and add ginger. Mix well and cook several minutes more until well married.

6. Pumpkin Kanten

Kabocha or any winter squash (butternut, buttercup)
3 cups water
1/2 tsp. sea salt
5 Tbsps. agar-agar flakes or 2 1/2 bars
Roasted sesame seeds or crushed, roasted peanuts

Wash, dry, and trim pumpkin. Cut into 1-inch squares or crescents and steam until tender. Purée in a Foley food mill. Bring water to a boil, add salt and agar-agar. As soon as the agar-agar dissolves, add puréed pumpkin. Cook together several minutes. Pour into any tray or mold and chill in a cool place or in the refrigerator. To serve, cut into 2-inch squares. Garnish with roasted sesame seeds or crushed, roasted peanuts.

7. Bancha Twig Tea (Kukicha)

> "Cooking therefore is a vital skill—for men as well as women. . . . Macrobiotic cookery provides an opportunity for self-realization, and for a growing understanding of, and ability to use, the laws of nature.
>
> Cooking challenges our judgment as we blend colors, flavors, shapes, textures and fragrances of various foods into an integrated, harmonious whole. If music and painting are fine arts, the art of cooking stands at the pinnacle as the source of all human achievement. Life comes from food. . . . From the macrobiotic perspective, cooking is the supreme art, and its devoted practitioners deserve the highest respect and gratitude."
>
> —Lima Ohsawa
> *Macrobiotic Cuisine*

MENU XXXV

Lentil Soup	Gomashio
Millet Stew	Cabbage-Daikon-Carrot Pickle
Tempeh with Burdock	Bancha Twig Tea (Kukicha)
Hijiki with Onion and Carrot	

1. Lentil Soup

1 cup lentils
1 small leek
1 onion
3 cloves garlic
1/2 bunch collard green stems
1 carrot
5–6 cups water
1/2 tsp. sea salt

Cut the leek in half lengthwise and wash the sand from the inside of the leaves. Wash and dry all the vegetables. When peeling the onion, take off as little as possible. Crush the garlic to release the oil and remove the skin easily. Mince the garlic. Cut all the other vegetables in 1/4-inch dice. Remove the stones from the lentils. Wash and drain in a colander.

In 1/4 inch of boiling salted water, sauté the onion, garlic, collard green stems, leek, and carrot. Add lentils and water enough for soup according to desired consistency. Cook together until lentils are tender, about 30 to 40 minutes. Add salt and adjust to taste. Cook 5 minutes more.

2. Millet Stew

3 cups millet
1 onion
1 carrot
1/4 butternut squash

Collard greens
3 pinches sea salt
5 1/2 cups water

Wash and dry vegetables. Cut onions in 1/2-inch dice. Cut carrots into 1-inch wedges, deer's-feet style. Cut the butternut squash into 1-inch cubes. Check millet for tiny black stones. Wash and pat dry in a strainer.

In a large pot, water-sauté onion and millet. Add squash, carrot, salt and water. Bring to a boil, cover tightly, and simmer for 40 minutes. Meanwhile, quick-boil collard greens in salted water. Rinse in cold water and squeeze gently. Cut into 1 1/2-inch lengths and serve as garnish on each bowl of Millet Stew.

3. Tempeh with Burdock

1 package tempeh
1 medium or 2 small burdock roots
3 scallions
2 tsps. sesame oil
1 Tbsp. kuzu
1/4 cup cold water
Tamari soy sauce

Trim, wash, and dry the burdock and scallions. Shave the burdock like 1-inch long pencil shavings. When shaving burdock, always start at the thick end. Catch a portion of skin in each sliver, as well as a tip of core, so that each piece will be balanced between yin and yang. Cut the tempeh into 1/2-inch cubes. Cut the scallion into 1-inch lengths.

Sauté the burdock in the sesame oil until the strong, earthy smell evaporates. Add the tempeh and enough water to cover the burdock. Cook together until the burdock is tender. Dilute the kuzu in 1/4 cup cold water. Add enough tamari to make the color tan. Add kuzu to the burdock/tempeh mixture. Boil and stir until thickened and translucent. Adjust tamari to taste. Add scallions and cook 1 minute more. If there are scallion roots, they may be minced and used in the Millet Stew.

4. Hijiki with Onion and Carrot

1 package hijiki
1 onion
1 carrot
Tamari soy sauce

Soak hijiki in enough water to cover. Peel onion, taking off as little as necessary. Wash and dry onion and carrot. Cut both in a fine julienne. When hijiki is soft, squeeze and cut into 1 1/2-inch lengths.

Water-sauté onion until mild. Add hijiki and sauté until the strong ocean smell evaporates. Add carrot and sauté quickly. Add hijiki soaking water, minus the last sandy tablespoon. Cook, covered, about 30 minutes, or until hijiki is tender and water level is down to 1/2 inch. Add tamari lightly to taste, and cook, uncovered, until dry.

5. Gomashio

See the Special Foods section.

6. Cabbage-Daikon-Carrot Pickle

1/2 cabbage
1/3 daikon
1 carrot
Carrot tops
Sea salt

Wash, dry, and trim all the vegetables. Cut them in julienne style. Mince the carrot tops. Mix with enough salt to pickle, about 2 rounded tablespoons. Mix well. Cover with a small plate, leaving a 1-inch space between the plate and the sides of the bowl.

Place a weight on the plate and cover with a clean, cotton cloth. Pickle from 3 hours to 3 days.

7. Bancha Twig Tea (Kukicha)

"Macrobiosis (Longevity)"—a definition.

—*Biblical and Talmudic Medicine*
Julius Preuss

October

MENU XXXVI

Miso Soup with Broccoli and Scallions	Kale Ohitashi
Brown Rice with Millet	Gomashio
Mixed Vegetable Nitsuke with Daikon	Takuan Pickle or Other Pickle
	Bancha Twig Tea (Kukicha)

1. Miso Soup with Broccoli and Scallions

1 6″ strip wakame
1 1/2 quarts water
1 stalk broccoli
1–2 Tbsps. barley miso (mugi miso)
2 scallions

Soak wakame 5 minutes, or until soft. Squeeze out water and cut into 1/2-inch pieces. Add soaking water to soup pot, leaving the last tablespoon of sandy water at the bottom of the bowl. Add extra water if necessary. Bring to a boil. Add wakame. Lower the fire and simmer at least 15 minutes.

Wash, dry, and trim broccoli and slice in half lengthwise. Cut in thin diagonals including leaves and flowers. Add flowers and leaves to soup. Simmer 1 minute. Add stems. Simmer uncovered until just tender, not losing the bright green color. Add miso as per Menu I. Garnish with minced scallions before serving.

2. Brown Rice with Millet

2 cups brown rice
1 cup millet

4 cups water
1 pinch sea salt

Pressure-cook as per Menu II.

3. Mixed Vegetable Nitsuke with Daikon

1 onion
1/4 daikon
3 scallions
Tamari soy sauce

Peel onion, removing as little as necessary. Cut the onion into thin crescents. Cut daikon in julienne style to equal volume of onion. Cut scallions into 1-inch lengths, julienne style, on the diagonal. Water-sauté onion until translucent and the strong odor changes to sweet. Add daikon and sauté 2 minutes. Add 1 inch of water, cover, and cook until tender, about 10 minutes. Add scallions. Season to taste lightly with tamari.

4. Kale Ohitashi

Kale
Tamari soy sauce

Wash and dry kale. Trim off any bad parts. Quick-boil in 2 inches of boiling salted water. Cook until bright green and stems are tender. Remove from pot immediately. Rinse in colander under cold running water. Gently squeeze out excess water. Cut into 1 1/2-inch lengths. Season lightly with tamari and toss.

5. Gomashio

14 Tbsps. sesame seeds
1 Tbsp. sea salt

Wash and drain sesame seeds. Lay strainer of seeds on a sponge or towel to drain. Meanwhile, in a heavy cast-iron skillet, roast salt until crystalline. Pour salt into a suribachi and grind into powder. Salt is a Metal and will hold the heat.

Roast sesame seeds, stirring constantly with a bamboo paddle in a cross-grid fashion, holding the paddle firmly so as not to spill the seeds. Roast the seeds until they are dry. Continue roasting until they taste done.

There is a fine line between raw seeds and scorched seeds. When seeds are popping, lower the flame and stir faster. This is the time to test the seeds. Crush the seeds between the thumb and fourth finger. If they crush easily, taste the seeds. While tasting, gently blow air over the seed inside the closed mouth, so the air passes over the seeds and out the nose. The aroma gives a delicate and accurate indication of the degree of doneness of the seeds. As soon as the seeds are done, pour them into the suribachi.

Grind the seeds and salt together with a wooden pestle (*surikogi*). Use gentle pressure. If you are right-handed, hold the top of the pestle with the left hand, keeping it in a stable position. Hold the bottom of the pestle with the right hand, grinding the sesame salt in a counterclockwise direction; i.e., toward the body. If you are left-handed, grind in a clockwise direction. In either case, the purpose is to blend the ingredients together, thus using your own concentrating energy, moving inward toward the body. (To disperse ingredients, use an outward direction from the body.)

Continue grinding the seeds until they are 80 percent ground. Cool and store in an airtight crock. If necessary, the gomashio may be freshened by quickly reheating and regrinding. Perfectly-prepared gomashio can stay fresh up to 1 month.

6. Takuan or Other Pickle

See the Special Foods section.

7. Bancha Twig Tea (Kukicha)

> "For thousands of years grains have been man's fundamental food, the food which has distinguished him from the ape."
>
> —Herman Aihara
> *Learning from Salmon*

MENU XXXVII

Miso Soup with Turnip and Scallions	Lotus Root
Brown Rice	Turnip Greens Ohitashi
Mixed Vegetable Nitsuke with Cabbage	Takuan Pickle
	Bancha Twig Tea (Kukicha)

1. Miso Soup with Turnip and Scallions

1 6″ strip wakame
1 1/2 quarts water
1 turnip
2 scallions
1–2 Tbsps. barley miso (mugi miso)

Soak, squeeze, and cut wakame into 1/2-inch pieces. Pour soaking water into a 1 1/2-quart pot leaving 1 tablespoon of water in the bottom of the bowl, if sandy. Add water if necessary. Add wakame. Bring water to a boil and simmer 15 minutes with the cover slightly ajar.

Wash and trim turnip, trimming off the purple skin which holds excess potassium. Cut the turnip into thin crescents. Add to the soup and cook until tender. Cut the scallions into 1-inch lengths on a diagonal. When the turnip is tender, dilute miso in the soup broth in a separate bowl, and return to the soup. Adjust for taste, neither too weak nor too strong. (This changes from day to day, season to season, according to your condition.) Add scallions to the soup, simmering without boiling for 2 to 3 minutes to marry the soup.

2. Brown Rice

4 cups rice
5 cups water

2 pinches sea salt

Prepare and pressure-cook rice as in Menu II.

3. Mixed Vegetable Nitsuke with Cabbage

Onion
Cabbage
Carrot
Tofu
Sea salt

Trim the core and top of the onion as carefully as possible, carving off as little as necessary so as not to spoil the polar balance. Peel skin carefully. You may have to remove the first layer of flesh if it is bruised or withered. Carefully carve off any remaining skin on the onion. Cut the onion into thin crescents, catching a piece of core in each slice.

Cut the cabbage in 1-inch squares. Cut the carrot in thin diagonals. Mash the tofu. Bring 1/4 inch of water to a boil and add a pinch of salt. Add onion and sauté until it is translucent and sweet. Add cabbage and sauté until it is bright green. Add tofu and mix in. Add carrot. Do not mix. Cover and steam on medium fire until carrot is tender. Sprinkle lightly with salt. Mix lightly, and steam another 2 minutes.

4. Lotus Root

Fresh lotus root
1 pinch sea salt
Tamari soy sauce

When buying lotus root, make sure the root is brown and firm, and the skin and hairs are dark, not bleached. Wash the lotus root well, trimming the hairs. Cut into thin ovals on a slight diagonal. Bring 1/2 inch of water to a boil and add a pinch of sea salt. Add lotus root. Sauté about 2 minutes. Add water almost to 2/3 the volume of lotus root. Cover and cook on a medium-high fire until almost tender. Add tamari to taste. Mix well and cook until dry, mixing periodically. In some cases, sesame oil may be used for sautéing instead of water.

5. Turnip Greens Ohitashi

Turnip greens
Tamari soy sauce

Wash, dry, and trim turnip greens. Cook 2 minutes in boiling salted water until bright green and stems are tender. Rinse under cool water in a colander to stop the cooking. Gently squeeze out excess water and cut into 1 1/2-inch lengths. Sprinkle lightly with tamari and toss.

6. Takuan Pickle

See Special Foods section.

7. Bancha Twig Tea (Kukicha)

"By adhering to the Tao of the past, you will master the existence of the present."
—*Tao Te Ching*
Lao Tzu

MENU XXXVIII

Miso Soup with Daikon
Brown Rice and Sweet Brown Rice
Black Beans
Mixed Vegetable Nitsuke with Carrots
Mixed Greens Ohitashi
Scallion Miso Condiment (Negi Miso)
Bancha Twig Tea (Kukicha)

1. Miso Soup with Daikon

3″ piece daikon
1 6″ strip wakame
1 1/2 quarts water
1–2 Tbsps. barley miso (mugi miso)
2 scallions

Cut daikon in half lengthwise and then into thin diagonal slices. Continue preparation as in Menu II.

2. Brown Rice and Sweet Brown Rice

Prepare and pressure-cook the brown rice as in Menu II, substituting 50 percent sweet brown rice for regular brown rice.

3. Black Beans

1 cup black beans
3 cups water
1 6″ strip kombu
1/4–1/2 tsp. sea salt

Pick through beans to discard any stones, foreign matter, or damaged beans. Wash gently in cold water several times until the water runs clear. Pat dry in the colander. Add water and kombu. Cut kombu into 1/2-inch pieces. Combine beans, kombu, and water, and pressure-cook for 1 hour. Open lid after pressure has come down and add salt. Mix gently with a wooden spoon. Cover lightly and cook another 20 minutes. Black beans strengthen the reproductive organs, especially in women.

4. Mixed Vegetable Nitsuke with Carrots

1 onion
1 carrot
3″ piece daikon
Tamari soy sauce

Cut onion into 1/2-inch wide crescents. Cut carrot into 1/8-inch thick diagonals. Cut daikon in half lengthwise and into 1/8-inch thick diagonals. Water-sauté onion until translucent and sweet, the daikon until partly translucent, then the carrot. Add 1/2 inch of water. Cover and simmer until tender, about 10 minutes. Season lightly with tamari to taste. This is good for cleaning and strengthening the lower body.

5. Mixed Greens Ohitashi

1/4 head green cabbage
1–2 stalks celery
Carrot tops
Sea salt

Trim off any bad or fibrous parts of the cabbage. Wash and dry the cabbage. Remove the heart. Slice heart in half lengthwise and in thin diagonal strips. Cut the wedge of cabbage in half lengthwise and into 1/4-inch diagonal strips. Wash and dry the celery. Trim the bottom edge. Scrape down the top 2 inches and peel off the strings. Then slice into 1/4-inch diagonal slices. Wash carrot tops thoroughly and dry. Trim off any bad parts. Mince finely.

Bring to boil 1/4 inch of water. Add a pinch of salt. Add celery. As soon as celery turns bright green, add the cabbage. As soon as the cabbage turns bright green, add the carrot tops. Sprinkle lightly with salt. Mix well. Sauté on a high fire, stirring quickly, for 3 to 4 minutes, until carrot top stems are tender. This dish is good for cleaning and strengthening the upper body. It is also useful to help discharge excess water from the body.

6. Scallion Miso Condiment (Negi Miso)

1 bunch scallions
1 Tbsp. sesame oil
Barley miso (mugi miso)
1–2 Tbsps. water

Trim off bad parts of the scallions. Wash scallions well. Wash roots with your fingertips under running water as if you were washing your hair. Pat dry. Separate roots, whites, and greens. Mince each. Quickly sauté scallion greens in sesame oil. When they become bright green, add the whites. After 1/2 minute, add the roots. Cover and steam on medium fire for several minutes until tender. Add slightly diluted miso to equal 1/4 the volume of scallions. Mix well with scallions. Cover and simmer together several minutes. Let cool. Store in an air-tight crock. When cool, refrigerate. Use as condiment on grain. Serve 1/2 teaspoon for adults; 1/4 teaspoon for children aged seven to twelve. This is good for cleaning and strengthening the blood and intestines.

7. Bancha Twig Tea (Kukicha)

> "In ancient times those people who understood Tao [the way of self-cultivation] patterned themselves upon the yin and the yang [the two principles in nature]. . . .
>
> "There was temperance in eating and drinking. Their hours of rising and retiring were regular and not disorderly and wild. By these means the ancients kept their bodies united with their souls, so as to fulfill their allotted span completely, measuring unto a hundred years before they passed away.
>
> "Nowadays people are not like this; they use wine as beverage and they adopt recklessness as usual behavior. . . . Their cravings dissipate their true (essence); they

do not know how to find contentment within themselves; they are not skilled in the control of their spirits. . . . For these reasons they reach only one half of the hundred years and then they degenerate."

—*The Yellow Emperor's Classic of Internal Medicine*
—Ilza Veith

MENU XXXIX

Clear Soup (Osumashi) with Daikon	Arame
Brown Rice	Broccoli with Tempeh
Millet Stew	Red Radish Pickle
	Bancha Twig Tea (Kukicha)

1. Clear Soup (Osumashi) with Daikon

1 5″×3″ strip kombu
2 shiitake mushrooms
2 quarts water (2/3 cup water per serving)
1/3 daikon
1/2 bunch watercress
Sea salt
Tamari soy sauce

Soak kombu and shiitake overnight in a soup pot, or bring water to a boil and simmer 1 to 2 hours. Meanwhile, cut the daikon into 1 1/2-inch lengths. Slice each piece into 1/8-inch slices lengthwise. Then sliver each slice lengthwise up to 1/4 inch from the end to resemble pine needles. Cut the watercress into 2-inch lengths.

Add the daikon to the soup stock and cook until tender. When tender, remove the kombu and shiitake. Season with half sea salt and half tamari, adjusting to taste. Add watercress and serve, or garnish each bowl separately with watercress.

2. Brown Rice

Pressure-cook the rice as in Menu II.

3. Millet Stew

2 1/2 cups millet
1 onion
1/2 Hokkaido pumpkin (kabocha)
1 medium carrot
6 cups water
1/2 tsp. sea salt
Watercress

Wash and dry vegetables. Cut the onion in a 1/2-inch dice. Cut the kabocha into 1-inch cubes. Do not remove the skin. Cut the carrot in julienne style. Then set the vegetables aside. Pick through the millet to remove any stones. Wash thoroughly the same as for rice, using a fine strainer for rinsing. Pat the bottom of the strainer dry until all excess water is removed from the grain. Roast millet in a dry cast-iron skillet until golden brown. Put in a cooking pot and add 6 cups of water. Slowly bring to a boil. As the millet is coming to a boil, water-sauté the vegetables in the above order. Set aside.

When the millet comes to a boil, add 1/2 teaspoon salt. Simmer the millet on a low fire for 20 minutes. Add the vegetables to the millet and continue cooking another 20 minutes, until a stew- or porridge-like consistency is obtained. Garnish with a sprig of watercress.

4. Arame

1 package arame
Tamari soy sauce
3 Tbsps. sesame seeds

Rinse arame. Cut into 1 1/2-inch lengths. Water-sauté in 1/4 inch of water until the ocean smell is gone.

Add water up to the top of the arame. Bring to a boil with the cover slightly ajar. Then lower fire and cook on medium flame until the water level is down to 1 inch. Season lightly with tamari to taste and cook until dry.

While the arame is cooking, wash and roast the sesame seeds. When arame is done, mix in the seeds and serve.

5. Broccoli with Tempeh

1 bunch broccoli
1 block tempeh
Tamari soy sauce

Trim and wash broccoli. If the stalk is thick, you may need to trim the bottom two inches of fibrous skin. Cut the stalk in quarters lengthwise and slice into 1/2-inch pieces on the diagonal all the way up through the flowers. Separate the stalk from the leaves and flowers. Steam the stalks until half done.

Meanwhile, crumble the tempeh and add it to the broccoli stems. Cook several minutes. Then add the leaves and flowers. Season lightly with tamari and steam 2 to 3 minutes more. The vegetables should be tender, but still bright green.

6. Red Radish Pickle

1 bunch red radishes with leaves
2 tsps. sea salt

Separate radishes and leaves. Wash thoroughly. Drain and pat dry. Cut radishes in thin circles from top to bottom. Cut the leaves into 1/2-inch lengths on a slight diagonal. Mix together in a bowl and sprinkle liberally with salt.

Press with a plate and stone or in a pickle press. Leave overnight, or at least for 2 to 3 hours. To serve, rinse off excess salt and squeeze gently. Serve about 1 teaspoon per person.

7. Bancha Twig Tea (Kukicha)

"When the primitive ways of life are completely lost, as pertains to nutrition, the complete failure to maintain immunity to disease, associated with a very short life span, is seen."

—Arnold De Vries
Primitive Man and His Food

MENU XL

Okayu with Tekka Miso
Brown Rice with Kasha
Kabocha Crescents
Root Stew with *Konnyaku*
Chinese Cabbage with Umeboshi
Kale Ohitashi
Bancha Twig Tea (Kukicha)

1. Okayu with Tekka Miso

1 cup brown rice
5 cups water
1/4 tsp. sea salt
Tekka miso

Pick out stones from rice. Wash, drain, and pat dry in a strainer. Add water and salt. Bring to a boil with cover ajar. Then lower fire, cover, and cook 1 to 2 hours. Stir before serving. Garnish with a scant half-teaspoon of tekka miso. Tekka miso may be bought in a macrobiotic health food store. For homemade tekka miso, see the Special Foods section.

2. Brown Rice with Kasha

2 1/2 cups brown rice
1/2 cup kasha
3 3/4 cups water
2 pinches sea salt

Prepare and wash rice. Do not wash kasha. Pressure-cook as in Menu II. Mix lightly before serving.

3. Kabocha Crescents

1 small kabocha
Sea salt

Wash and dry kabocha. Remove stem and scrape off any bumps from skin. Cut in half from stem to root. Scoop out seeds and set aside. Cut crescents 1 inch thick at the equator. Line a steaming pot with a cotton steaming towel which has been wrung out in cold water. Arrange the crescents spirally in the pot. Sprinkle lightly with salt. Cover and steam until the kabocha skin is tender, about 20 minutes. The skin is nutritious and should be eaten together with the rest of the kabocha.

4. Root Stew with Konnyaku

1 onion
1 medium burdock root
1 carrot

6 small or 3 large Brussels sprouts
Wheat gluten (Kofu)
1 8″×4″ strip kombu
Konnyaku
Albi (*satoimo* or taro potato)
1 Tbsp. sesame oil
Sea salt
Tamari soy sauce

Wash, dry, and trim all the vegetables. Cut the onion into 1/2-inch crescents. Cut the burdock in half lengthwise and then into 1-inch straight pieces. Cut the carrot into 1/4-inch thick by 1-inch long diagonals. If the Brussels sprouts are large, cut in half lengthwise. Pull the wheat gluten into irregular 1-inch chunks. (The wheat gluten should already have been cooked in kombu-tamari broth with garlic and ginger. For wheat gluten, see the Special Foods section.) Soak the kombu until soft, about 15 minutes. Cut into 1/2-inch strips lengthwise. Tie each strip into a knot. Cut the konnyaku into 1-inch triangles. (Konnyaku is a special yam preparation.) Peel the albi and cut into 1-inch irregular chunks.

In sesame oil, sauté the onion, burdock, konnyaku and albi. Add the kombu soaking water. Then push the kombu knots to the bottom of the pot. Add water, if necessary, to reach the top of the albi. Bring water to a boil. Cook until burdock is almost tender. Then add the Brussels sprouts, carrots and gluten. Push the gluten into the stew. Cook until the carrots and Brussels sprouts are tender, about 5 to 10 minutes. Season with salt and tamari to taste, and cook 5 minutes more. Serve a variety of vegetables in each portion.

5. Chinese Cabbage with Umeboshi

1/2 small Chinese cabbage
2 umeboshi, pits removed

Wash and dry cabbage. Cut into 1-inch squares. Mash the umeboshi. Save the pits for sucking on, tea, or medicine. Bring 1/4 inch of water to a boil. Add the umeboshi and the cabbage. Cover and cook until tender, about 3 minutes. Toss the umeboshi and cabbage together. Transfer to a serving dish as soon as the cabbage is done.

Note: Sucking on the umeboshi pit is helpful in the case of sore throat, mouth sores, or acid indigestion.

6. Kale Ohitashi

Kale
Tamari soy sauce
Roasted sesame seeds

Wash, dry, and trim kale. Cook whole in boiling salted water until bright green and the stems are tender. Rinse in cold water and squeeze out excess water. Cut into 1/2-inch dice. Season lightly with tamari and garnish with sesame seeds.

7. Bancha Twig Tea (Kukicha)

"Five things alone are necessary to the sustenance and

comfort of the Indians among the children of the earth.
The sun, who is the Father of all,
The earth, who is the Mother of men,
The water, who is the Grandfather,
The fire, who is the Grandmother,
Our brothers and sisters the Corn and Seeds of growing things."

—Zuni belief

November

MENU XLI

Miso Soup with Leek	Tempeh
Rice Salad	Romaine Lettuce Ohitashi
Butternut Squash	Bancha Twig Tea (Kukicha)
Cabbage Rolls	

1. Miso Soup with Leek

3 6″ strips wakame
3 quarts water
1 12-oz. tub tofu
1 leek
Barley miso (mugi miso)

Soak wakame until tender. Squeeze and cut into 1/2-inch pieces. Pour soaking water into a 2-quart soup pot, withholding the last tablespoon of sandy water. Add more water if necessary. Add wakame, bring to a boil, cover, and simmer 15 minutes.

Meanwhile, cut the tofu into 1/2-inch cubes and set aside. Cut the leek in half lengthwise and wash well, opening the leaves to remove all soil. Cut the leek into 1/2-inch pieces on a slight diagonal. Add the leek to the soup. When it becomes bright green, add the tofu. When the tofu floats, add miso to make a delicate taste. (To check the quantity of miso, see Menu I.) Leek is good for releasing menses.

2. Rice Salad

4 cups brown rice
1 onion
2 stalks celery
1 carrot
3 pinches sea salt
2–4 Tbsps. umeboshi vinegar (umezu)
Nori

Pressure-cook the rice in 5 cups water with 2 pinches salt as per Menu II. When done, mix lightly and empty into a large bowl to cool. Meanwhile, dice onion, celery and carrot into 1/4-inch pieces. Water-sauté in that order in 1/4 inch of boiling salted water, then cover and steam until tender. Season with a pinch of salt while cooking. When done, mix lightly with rice, adding umezu to taste. Mix well and garnish with crushed, roasted nori.

3. Butternut Squash

1 medium butternut squash
Sea salt
1/2 bunch watercress

Wash and dry the squash, scraping off any hard parts on the skin. To remove stem, press down all around the stem with the heel of the knife. Then, with the butt of the handle, knock the stem off cleanly. Cut the squash in half lengthwise. Scoop out the seeds and reserve to wash and roast later. Cut each half in fourths and then into 1/2-inch triangles. Steam in 1 to 2 inches of salted water. Sprinkle lightly with salt while cooking. When tender, add watercress cut into 1/2 inch lengths. Steam 1 minute until bright green.

4. Cabbage Rolls

1 cabbage
1 onion
3″ piece daikon
1 carrot
1 bunch scallions
Tamari soy sauce
2 6″ strips kombu

Cut all the vegetables, except the cabbage, in thin julienne style. Cut out the cabbage heart and slice it in julienne style. Parboil the cabbage whole for 5 minutes, until the leaves are tender but still bright green. Rinse in cold water and drain well.

Water-sauté onion, daikon, cabbage heart, carrot and scallion, adding tamari to taste. Peel one leaf at a time from the cabbage. Shave the thick bottom vein to make the leaf more flexible for rolling. Fill with 1 to 2 tablespoons of cooked vegetables placed at bottom center of leaf. Fold over bottom and sides and roll tightly. Secure with a toothpick.

Place kombu in a shallow pot with 1/2 inch of water. Bring to boil. Add tamari to make a slightly strong broth. Place one layer of cabbage rolls over the kombu. The broth should come 3/4 of the way up the cabbage rolls. Cover and cook for 10 to 15 minutes. Remove with a slotted spoon and serve one per person.

5. Tempeh

1 block tempeh
Sesame oil
Tamari soy sauce

Cut tempeh in quarters. Cut each quarter in half on the diagonal to form triangles. Brush a skillet with sesame oil. Pan-bake tempeh on each side until golden. Add 1/4 inch of water, cover, and steam 10 minutes. Season lightly with tamari and cook uncovered until dry. Serve two triangles per person. Garnish with any green. Tempeh is high in B vitamins, including B_{12} and B_{17}.

6. Romaine Lettuce Ohitashi

Romaine lettuce

Tamari soy sauce
Roasted sesame seeds

Trim romaine lettuce and cut in half lengthwise to wash well. Drain and pat dry. Cut into quarters. Quick-boil until bright green. Rinse in cold water. Gently squeeze out excess water. Cut thinly through the heart. Cut leaves on a diagonal into 1-inch pieces. Sprinkle lightly with tamari. Garnish with roasted sesame seeds and toss gently.

7. Bancha Twig Tea (Kukicha)

"[You] must eat food to nourish the body so that [you] may hear and receive and explain the teaching, but [you] should not eat for mere enjoyment."

—Buddha

MENU XLII

Miso Soup with Burdock and Scallions	Carrot-Burdock Kinpira
Brown Rice with Watercress	Kiriboshi Daikon
Kombu Condiment (Shio-Kombu)	Turnips and Cabbage
	Bancha Twig Tea (Kukicha)

1. Miso Soup with Burdock and Scallions

2 6″ strips wakame
2 quarts water
1 whole baby burdock root or 1/2 mature burdock root
2 Tbsps. barley miso (mugi miso)
3 scallions

Soak, squeeze and cut wakame into 1/2-inch pieces. Cook in soaking water at least 15 minutes. Wash burdock gently with a natural-bristle brush just to remove dirt and not the skin. Dry burdock and trim the ends, cutting the top part off on the line where the root and stem meet. Hold burdock in the left hand allowing it to extend along the forearm. With your index finger under the end of the burdock, supporting it, shave the burdock as you would shave a pencil, making sure to get a piece of skin and a piece of core in each shaving. Each piece should be paper thin, about 1 inch long.

After the wakame has cooked, add the burdock. Boil hard, uncovered, 3 to 4 minutes, until the strong, earthy smell has evaporated. Then cover and simmer gently 15 to 20 minutes, until the burdock is tender. Lower the fire to stop the simmering. In a separate bowl, dilute the miso in soup broth and add it to the soup. Mix well and taste. Add more miso, if necessary, being sure to use a clean spoon. Cook the miso gently into the broth for 2 to 3 minutes. Do not boil. Garnish each serving with minced scallion.

2. Brown Rice with Watercress

4 cups brown rice
5 cups water
2 pinches sea salt
Minced watercress

See Menu II for pressure-cooked rice. After rice is done, turn out into a large bowl and mix in minced watercress. This dish is good for anemia.

3. Kombu Condiment (Shio-Kombu)

1 10″×4″ strip kombu
1/2 cup water
1/2 cup tamari soy sauce

Hold the kombu over the sink and brush it with your fingers, or wipe with a damp cloth, to remove any sand.

Cut the kombu into 1/2-inch squares. Combine water and tamari. Mix together with the kombu in an enamel saucepan and soak 1 to 2 hours. Then bring mixture to a boil and simmer gently, partially covered, until dry.

Spread the kombu out one by one on a plate to dry. This may take 1 to 2 days. Store in a crock or airtight container. Do not store in plastic. Serve one or two pieces per meal, 2 to 3 times a week. This is a condiment to be eaten with rice or other grain. Prepared in this way, kombu strengthens the blood vessels.

4. Carrot-Burdock Kinpira

Carrot
Burdock root
1 pinch sea salt
Tamari soy sauce

Proportions:

A) 2/3 burdock: 1/3 carrot—for more yin people
B) 1/2 burdock: 1/2 carrot—for more warmth

Cut the carrot and burdock in a very fine julienne style. Bring 1/4 inch of water to a boil. Add a pinch of sea salt. Sauté the burdock very well until the strong earthy odor evaporates. Add carrot and sauté 1/2 minute. Add water to 3/4 the level of the vegetables. Place the cover slightly ajar. Bring to a boil, then simmer until the burdock is tender and only an inch of water remains. Add tamari to taste. Cook until dry.

Kinpira is suitable for strengthening all lower organs, especially the intestines. For lung trouble, which often accompanies trouble in the large intestines, add lotus root to equal the amount of carrot. This dish is more tasty when sautéed in 1 tablespoon of sesame oil, and is especially good for yin people.

5. Kiriboshi Daikon

1 package dried daikon (kiriboshi daikon)
Minced scallion roots left from miso soup
Tamari soy sauce

Soak the dried daikon in water to cover until tender. Squeeze out the water and cut daikon into 1 1/2-inch lengths. Water-sauté in 1/4-inch soaking water 1 to 2 minutes. Add minced scallion roots left from the miso soup. Add soaking water and cook until tender, about 1/2 hour. Add tamari lightly to taste. Mix well and cook until dry. This dish is suitable for dissolving excess animal protein and animal fat. For this purpose, dried daikon is more suitable for yin people than fresh daikon.

6. Turnips and Cabbage

1 large or 2 small turnips
3–4 cabbage leaves
1 onion
Sea salt

Cut the onion and cabbage in 1/2-inch dice. Peel the purple skin off the turnip and cut into 1/2-inch cubes. Water-sauté the onion, turnip, and cabbage in that order. Lightly salt and steam until tender. This is good for cleaning the lower body, especially the kidneys, ovaries, and prostate.

7. Bancha Twig Tea (Kukicha)

> "From the corn we gather the pollen. The pollen that is like gold, reminds us of the color of anointment of the ancient ones. Grinding the corn it reminds us of heaven and it reminds us of earth. It reminds us that Father Sky and Mother Earth will unite forever.
>
> "From the corn we learn to live, we learn the life that is ours, by grinding the corn we learn the footsteps of life. We go through a purification, until we are like dust. The corn came from the dust, from Mother Earth, and it gives life, like from Father Sky.
>
> "We are like the kernel that comes from the corn. With it we bring life, like the seed of the corn. Corn is the fruit of the gods, it was brought to us by the creator, that we may remember him. Our lives, we must remember that they are holy. The corn is sacred. We are sacred. We hold the seeds of the gods to the future."
>
> —Taos Pueblo corn grinding song
> *Pueblo and Navajo Cookery*
> Marcia Keegan

MENU XLIII

Clear Soup (Osumashi) with Turnips and Cabbage	
Brown Rice with Carrot	Butternut Squash
Wakame Powder	Mustard Greens Ohitashi
Wheat Gluten (Kofu) with Onion	Bancha Twig Tea (Kukicha)

1. Clear Soup (Osumashi) with Turnips

1 6″×3″ strip kombu
2 quarts water
1 turnip
Turnip greens
1 carrot
Sea salt
Tamari soy sauce

Brush kombu with your fingers to remove sand and simmer in a 2-quart soup pot for at least 1 hour. Clean the turnip and trim off the purple skin. The purple part holds excess potassium. Slice in thin crescents 1/8 inch thick. Cut the turnip greens into 1 1/2-inch lengths on the diagonal. Cut the carrot into flowers and quick-boil in the kombu soup stock. Set aside. In the same stock, add the turnip and cook. Quick-boil the turnip greens and set aside.

Remove the kombu and hang somewhere to dry for later use, as in cooking beans. Season the soup stock, half with salt and half with tamari, to make a delicate taste. Arrange carrot flowers in the soup bowls, two flowers per person. Garnish with turnip greens. This soup is suitable for dissolving fat and mucous accumulations, and cysts and tumors in the ovaries and prostate.

2. Brown Rice with Carrot

4 cups brown rice
5 cups water
2 pinches sea salt
1 medium carrot

Shave the carrot into the brown rice before cooking, the same as shaving burdock in Menu XLII. Pressure-cook the rice as in Menu II. When done, turn rice bottom to top with a wet bamboo paddle, and cover with a bamboo mat or clean cloth to let the steam evaporate.

3. Wakame Powder

10″ strip wakame

Break the wakame into small pieces and dry-roast in a cast-iron skillet on a medium-low fire until easily crumbled, about 15 minutes. Grind into powder in a suribachi. Store in a covered ceramic dish or crock. Serve 1/4 to 1/2 teaspoon on grain or sprinkle into vegetables while cooking.

4. Wheat Gluten (Kofu) with Onion and Cabbage

1/2 cup wheat gluten flour
1 onion
3 leaves cabbage
1 4″×2″ strip kombu
4 scallions
Sea salt
Tamari soy sauce

Cook kombu in a 1 1/2-quart saucepan for 1/2 hour. Cut the onion in 1/4-inch julienne and the cabbage into 1-inch squares. Cut the scallion into 1-inch lengths on the diagonal. Remove the kombu and hang somewhere to dry for future use. Season the broth with half salt and half tamari to make a slightly strong taste.

Mix a pinch of salt into the flour and slowly add enough water to make dough. Form 1-inch-diameter dumplings from the gluten dough and cook in the broth until they float. Take out and set aside. Water-sauté the onion, cabbage, and scallion. Add the dumplings. Season lightly with tamari to taste. This dish promotes the building of strength in the body. It especially helps to strengthen muscle tissue.

5. Butternut Squash

1 butternut squash
1 onion
1 Tbsp. sesame oil
Sea salt
1–2 Tbsps. roasted sesame seeds

Cut the squash into 1/2-inch cubes and the onion into 1/2-inch dice. Sauté the onion in the sesame oil until it becomes translucent and sweet. Sprinkle 1 pinch of salt over the onions while sautéing. Add the squash and sauté until the color changes. Add about 1 inch of water. Sprinkle 1 more pinch of salt over the squash. Cover tightly and steam until tender. Remove the cover and boil hard until dry. Garnish with roasted sesame seeds. This dish is suitable for enhancing functions of the stomach, pancreas, and spleen.

6. Mustard Greens Ohitashi

1 bunch mustard greens
Nori
Tamari soy sauce

Wash the mustard greens well, separating the stems to clean out the sand. Pat dry. Cook 1 to 2 minutes in boiling water until bright green and the stems are tender. Remove quickly, put in colander, and rinse in cold, pure water. Gently squeeze out the excess water. Lay the greens out on the cutting board and cut into 1/2-inch pieces on the diagonal.

Roast one or two sheets of nori over a medium flame and break into small pieces over the mustard greens. Mix together with chopsticks. Dot lightly with tamari and mix again. This is suitable for dissolving fat and mucous accumulations in the lungs.

7. Bancha Twig Tea (Kukicha)

> "The seed of God is in us . . . . Pear seeds grow into pear trees, hazel seeds into hazel trees, and God seeds into God."
>
> —Meister Eckhart

MENU XLIV—Thanksgiving

Millet Potage	Chinese Cabbage Nori Rolls
Holiday Rice (*Chirashi Gohan*)	Nori Kanten
Stuffed Kabocha	Bancha Twig Tea (Kukicha)
Lotus Root with Sesame Seeds	

1. Millet Potage

1 1/2 cups millet
2 onions
2 parsnip roots
2 carrots
2 leeks
8 cups water
1/2 tsp. sea salt

Cut onions in 1/2-inch dice. Cut parsnip roots and carrots in uneven chunks (rangiri style). Cut leeks into 1-inch lengths on the diagonal. In a 5-quart soup pot, water-sauté the onion, parsnip root, and carrot in 1/4 inch of boiling salted water. Add the millet and enough water for soup, about 8 cups. Bring to a boil. Add salt and simmer covered for 40 minutes. When done, taste and add salt if necessary. Add the leeks.

Boil hard for 2 to 3 minutes without the cover, until the leeks are bright green and tender. Serve one or two pieces of each vegetable per portion.

2. Holiday Rice (Chirashi Gohan)

4 cups rice
5 cups water
2 pinches sea salt
3 onions
2 burdock roots
1 small daikon
1 large carrot
1/4 lb. string beans
Sea salt
Tamari soy sauce

Pressure-cook the rice as in Menu II. Cut all the vegetables julienne style. Water-sauté onions, burdock, daikon, and carrot in that order. Add 1 inch water. Cover and cook until tender, seasoning with half salt and half tamari to taste. Uncover and cook until dry. Quick-boil the string beans in salted boiling water until bright green and tender. Drain and set aside. When all the vegetables are done, mix in the string beans and arrange evenly on a platter to cool.

When the rice is done, use a bamboo paddle to turn from bottom to top. Leave rice uncovered so the steam can escape. Rinse the baking tray in cold water. Arrange the vegetables evenly on the bottom. Press the rice firmly into the tray on top of the vegetables. Let set until cool. Carefully invert onto a large platter or board. Cut into 2-inch squares and serve.

3. Stuffed Kabocha

1 kabocha (or winter squash)
Sesame oil
Sea salt
2 onions
1 carrot
1 bunch of scallions
1 tub tofu

Wash and dry the kabocha. Carefully scrape any hard bumps off the skin. Remove the stem as described in Menu XLI. Cut in half, top to bottom (yin to yang). Pare off the core on the bottom of the kabocha. Scrape out seeds and set aside for other use. Brush the whole kabocha lightly with sesame oil and lightly salt the inside.

Pan-bake at 375°F. in a covered baking dish for 20 to 25 minutes. Bake the kabocha face down until tender.

Mince all vegetables and mash tofu. Water-sauté onion, tofu, carrot, and scallion. Salt lightly, cover, and steam until the carrot is tender. When the kabocha is done, remove from oven and stuff with prepared vegetables. Replace in the oven and bake another 20 minutes until done. To serve, slice into 1-inch crescents.

4. Lotus Root with Sesame Seeds

2 fresh lotus roots
2 tsps. sesame oil

Tamari soy sauce
2 Tbsps. roasted sesame seeds

Wash lotus root with a natural-bristle brush and trim any black hairs around the neck. Cut the lotus root into 1/4-inch circles. Sauté in sesame oil. Add water almost to the top of the lotus root. Place cover slightly ajar and cook until the water level is down to 1/2 inch. Add tamari to taste and cook until dry. Garnish with roasted sesame seeds.

5. Chinese Cabbage Nori Rolls

Chinese cabbage
Nori
Tamari soy sauce

Quick-boil Chinese cabbage leaves in salted water. Spread out in a colander to drain and cool. Cut nori sheets in half lengthwise. Lay the nori on top of a cabbage leaf on a board. Roll tightly from the stem to the top of the leaf, turning the edges of the leaf in as you go. Slice the roll in thirds widthwise. Arrange spiral side up on a platter and dot lightly with tamari.

6. Nori Kanten

2 bars kanten (agar-agar)
2 quarts water
1 package nori
1 Tbsp. tamari soy sauce
1/4–1/2 cup roasted sesame seeds

In water, break up and dissolve kanten. Bring to a boil and simmer until completely melted. Break nori into small pieces and cook with the kanten. Add tamari to taste. Pour into molding tray and chill in the refrigerator. When partially set, sprinkle the top with roasted sesame seeds. Continue chilling until completely set.

7. Bancha Twig Tea (Kukicha)

> "Elijah once said to Rabbi Nathan: eat a third and drink a third and leave a third empty . . ."
> "The Talmud states: Chew well with your teeth and you will find it in your steps, and the drawing out of a meal prolongs a man's life."
>
> "People can exist without pepper, but not without salt. However, it must be used in the proper proportions."
>
> "Two men entered a shop. One ate coarse bread and vegetables while the other ate fine bread and fat meat and drank old wine. The one who ate fine food suffered harm, while the one who had coarse food escaped harm. Observe how simply animals live and how healthy they are as a result."
>
> —*Biblical and Talmudic Medicine*
> Julius Preuss
>
> "The well-resolved mind is single and one-pointed."
>
> —Bhagavad-Gita, II: 41

MENU XLV

Miso Soup with Tofu	(Seitan)
Brown Rice with Burdock	Chinese Cabbage Ohitashi with Nori
Stuffed Acorn Squash	Takuan or Other Pickle
Lentils with Wheat Gluten	Bancha Twig Tea (Kukicha)

1. Miso Soup with Tofu

2 6″ strips wakame
2 quarts water
1 tub tofu
1/2 bunch scallions
Barley miso (mugi miso)

Soak, squeeze, and cut wakame into 1-inch pieces. Cook in soaking water for 15 minutes. Cut tofu into 1-inch by 1/4-inch squares. Cut scallions into 1-inch lengths. Cook tofu 5 minutes, or until it floats. Add miso as in Menu I. Add scallion and cook together uncovered 2 to 3 minutes on a low fire.

2. Brown Rice with Burdock

3 cups brown rice
3 3/4 cups water
1 pinch sea salt
1 large or 2 small burdock roots
Tamari soy sauce

Prepare and pressure-cook rice as in Menu II. Wash burdock gently with a natural-bristle brush, being careful not to remove the skin. Shave burdock as if making 1-inch-long, thin pencil-shavings. Sauté in 1/2 inch of boiling salted water until the harsh smell evaporates. Cover and steam until tender. Add tamari lightly to taste and cook several more minutes until dry. Mix into cooked rice.

3. Stuffed Acorn Squash

1 acorn squash
1 carrot
Parsley
1 tub tofu
Sea salt
Sesame oil

Wash and dry vegetables. Drain and mash tofu. Mince the carrot and parsley, and mix them into the tofu with 1/2 teaspoon salt. Set aside. Cut out stem of squash and trim off bottom core. Cut the squash in half and remove the seeds. (These may be prepared as a snack later. See the Special Foods section.) Rub sesame oil around top edge of squash, then sprinkle the inside and edge of squash lightly with salt. Fill with tofu mixture and mound attractively. Bake in a pyrex baking dish with 1/2 inch of water, covered, at 400°F. for 30 to 45 minutes.

4. Lentils with Wheat Gluten (Seitan)

1 cup lentils
1/2 cup wheat gluten
1 small onion
1 carrot
1 ear corn
2 1/2 cups water
1/4 tsp. sea salt

Wash and dry vegetables. Peel onion, taking off as little as possible. Cut onion and carrot in 1/4-inch dice. Remove corn from cob with fingers. Cut seitan in 1/4-inch dice. Water-sauté onion until half-translucent. Add vegetables, seitan, lentils, and water. Bring to a boil, cover, and simmer 1 hour. Add salt and cook 15 minutes more.

5. Chinese Cabbage Ohitashi with Nori

1/4 Chinese cabbage
1/4 tsp. sea salt
1 sheet roasted nori

Wash and dry cabbage. Cut into long 1/4-inch-wide diagonal strips. Steam in 1/2 inch of boiling salted water. Sprinkle lightly with salt to reduce cabbage. Garnish with thin strips of roasted nori.

6. Takuan or Other Pickle

See the Special Foods section.

7. Bancha Twig Tea (Kukicha)

"These things are good in little measure and evil in large: yeast, salt and hesitation."
—*The Talmud*

Autumn—Breakfast Suggestions

I	1. Miso Soup with Wakame and Dandelion Leaves 2. Millet Potage with Kabocha 3. Gomashio with Nori 4. Quick-boiled Red Radishes with Leaves 5. Roasted Millet Tea
II	1. Miso Soup with Kabocha and Watercress 2. Brown Rice with Whole Wheat Okayu 3. Gomashio with Wakame 4. Roasted Nori 5. Roasted Wheat Tea
III	1. Pumpkin Potage 2. Pressure-cooked Brown Rice 3. Gomashio with Crushed Roasted Pumpkin Seeds 4. Roasted Nori 5. Bancha Twig Tea
IV	1. Clear Soup with Tofu, Carrot Flowers, and Watercress 2. Cream of Wheat 3. Nori Condiment with Sesame Seeds 4. Quick-boiled Kale 5. Grain Coffee
V	1. Buckwheat Noodles (Soba) in Broth 2. Mugwort Mochi with Nori 3. Grated Daikon with Tamari 4. Sauerkraut 5. Bancha Twig Tea

Autumn—Lunch Suggestions

I	1.	Brown Rice with Rye
	2.	Dried Daikon with Fried Tofu
	3.	Kabocha
	4.	Romaine Lettuce with Roasted Sunflower Seeds
	5.	Bancha Twig Tea
II	1.	Brown Rice Salad
	2.	Hijiki with Tempeh
	3.	Carrots with Black Sesame Seeds
	4.	Chinese Cabbage with Pickled Turnips
	5.	Bancha Twig Tea
III	1.	Brown Rice with Black Sesame Seeds
	2.	Miso Condiment
	3.	Carrots with Tempeh and Scallions
	4.	Savoy Cabbage with Nori and Ginger
	5.	Bancha Twig Tea
IV	1.	Brown Rice with Millet
	2.	Lotus Root
	3.	Baked Kabocha
	4.	Turnips with Greens Nishime
	5.	Roasted Brown Rice Tea
V	1.	Brown Rice with Sweet Brown Rice
	2.	Miso Condiment
	3.	Butternut Squash with Sesame Sauce
	4.	Quick-boiled Kale
	5.	Bancha Twig Tea

Winter Cooking

Winter is the time to withdraw, deep into the hidden recesses of Earth and self. The foliage falls and the Earth appears barren. It is the time to store energy and strengthen reserves. The long dark nights condense moisture from the air. Water gathers, dissolving minerals from dead plants on the way, and concentrates them as it freezes in the cold. In time, it fills the great ocean, the amniotic fluid of Mother Earth's womb. Water, the origin of life, gathering, floating, waiting to give birth. Thus, the floating energy of Water symbolizes winter.

The concentration of minerals creates salts, the essential taste in winter cooking. The kidneys control the mineral/salt-water balance in the body. The minerals not excreted are concentrated in the blood. This mineralized blood is condensed into bone marrow, which serves as a reservoir when more blood is needed. Thus, the kidneys nourish the bones. Courage and endurance ensue.

Buckwheat and beans, especially azuki, and sea salt, miso, and tamari soy sauce, nourish the kidneys and strengthen the blood. Miso soup with sea vegetables reiterates the ocean and starts each day with the origin of our birth.

More fire is needed in winter cooking. Stronger oil-sautéing, deep-frying, baking, pressure-cooking, and longer cooking are effective in maintaining strength and bodily warmth. Foods that store well, such as grains, beans, and roots predominate. Bread, seitan, and stews, and sweet brown rice mochi give added warmth to the body in winter. Three parts of roots to one part of greens is appropriate for winter, as nature's landscape reveals.

As more oil is used, more salt is essential. It strengthens the blood and enhances the flavors. To counteract excess saltiness, use the sweet taste of whole rice, azuki, black soybeans, and vegetables, cooked well to bring out their character.

The sea salt transmutes into iron, strengthening hemoglobin which, combining with oxygen, radiates with light. Thus, in the long darkness of winter, the sun is internalized and our spirit is bright. Accordingly, Winter Solstice celebrations permeate the land.

In this way, winter cooking helps us adapt to the cold.

Note: In cases of cancer and other yin illness, less oil is recommended, depending on the condition. Everyone's salt balance is slightly different, so adjust the salt measurements to your taste and need.

December

MENU XLVI

Wild Barley (Hatomugi) Soup	Strike Burdock
Brown Rice with Whole Wheat Berries	Wakame with Onions
	Boiled Salad
Azuki Kabocha	Roasted Rice Tea (Genmaicha)

1. Wild Barley (Hatomugi) Soup

2 cups wild barley (hatomugi)
1 6″ strip kombu
4 shiitake mushrooms
2 onions
2 stalks celery
1 medium carrot
8–10 cups water
1/2 tsp. sea salt

Wash and drain barley and set aside. Soak shiitake until tender. Cut the onions, celery, carrot, and shiitake in 1/4-inch dice. Water-sauté the onions, shiitake, celery, and carrot. Add the shiitake soaking water, discarding the bottom teaspoon, if sandy. Add barley. Add 8 to 10 cups water depending on desired thickness. Bring to boil, add salt and kombu, and simmer 1 hour. Taste, and add more salt if necessary, cooking another 5 minutes. This soup is good for reducing tumors.

2. Brown Rice with Whole Wheat Berries

3 1/2 cups brown rice
1/2 cup whole wheat berries
5 cups water
2 pinches sea salt

Pressure-cook as in Menu II. This rice enhances the vitamin B supply in the body.

3. Azuki Kabocha

3 cups azuki beans
1 small kabocha
1 6″ strip kombu
6 cups water
1/2 tsp. sea salt

Pick clean and wash azuki beans. Cut the kabocha into 1/2-inch cubes. Cut the kombu into 1/2-inch pieces. Mix all together in 6 cups water. Bring to a boil with the cover ajar. Lower the fire. Cover tightly and simmer 2 1/2 hours. When beans are tender, add salt, mix in, and cook another 1/2 hour. This dish is good for strengthening kidney functions and facilitating discharge of body toxins.

4. Strike Burdock

1 bunch medium-sized burdock roots

3 umeboshi, pits removed
1 Tbsp. sesame oil

Wash, dry, and trim the burdock. Cut in 1 1/4-inch lengths. Place the blade of the knife flat on 2/3 the length of the burdock. Strike the blade with your fist in order to crush that part of burdock. Mash umeboshi and set aside. Sauté burdock in the sesame oil. Add water almost to the top of the burdock. Cover, bring to a boil, and simmer until tender. Mix mashed umeboshi into the remaining water and cook until dry. This dish is good for neutralizing poisons and strengthening the intestines.

5. Wakame with Onions

2 oz. wakame
2 onions
Enough water to cover wakame
Tamari soy sauce

Soak wakame until tender. Squeeze out water and cut into 1-inch pieces. Cut the onions in thin julienne style. Water-sauté onions until translucent and sweet. Add the wakame and wakame soaking water. Cook together until the wakame is tender, 10 to 15 minutes. Add tamari to taste. Cook until most of the water is gone.

6. Boiled Salad

2 stalks celery
1 carrot
1/2 bunch watercress
Umeboshi juice (umezu)

Wash, dry, and trim vegetables. De-string celery. Cut the celery and carrots in julienne style. Cut the watercress into 1/2-inch lengths. All vegetables should be the same length. Quick-boil each separately until the color is bright and the texture is almost tender. Rinse to cool and drain well. Toss together with umeboshi juice to taste.

7. Roasted Rice Tea (Genmaicha)

1/4 cup brown rice

Wash and roast rice until golden. Cook in a teapot of water for 1/2 hour. Stir before serving. This is a very soothing tea, and is nourishing for babies, elderly people, and people with weak digestion.

> "Biologically speaking, we are children of the Vegetal Mother, and spring from the vegetal. Without vegetable life, no animal on the earth would survive. We depend upon vegetal products. Our hemoglobin is derived from chlorophyll. All vegetal foods are virgin materials for the purpose of maintaining or constructing our body. Neither meat nor animal products are pure virgin material for us. We must eat vegetables and their direct products. This is the biological principle and fundamental law: vegetables are the superior food."
>
> —George Ohsawa
> *The Philosophy of Oriental Medicine*

MENU XLVII

Lentil Vegetable Soup
Rice Triangles (Omusubi)
Hijiki with Onion and Carrot
Japanese Turnips (*Kabu*) in Miso Sauce
Carrots with Leeks
Pickle: Chinese Cabbage with Turnip Greens
Bancha Twig Tea (Kukicha)

1. Lentil Vegetable Soup

2 cups lentils
2 onions
2 stalks celery
2 carrots
Leek roots
1 6″×4″ strip kombu
3–3 1/2 quarts water
Sea salt

Cut the kombu into 1/2-inch pieces. Cut the onion in 1/4-inch dice. Cut celery in fourths lengthwise and in 1/4-inch dice on the diagonal. Cut the carrot in eighths lengthwise and then in 1/8-inch-diagonal triangles.

Mince leek roots left from recipe No. 5. Pick clean, and wash lentils. Water-sauté onions, leek roots, celery, carrots, and lentils in a 5-quart soup pot. Add kombu and enough water for soup. Bring to a boil and simmer 40 minutes. Add salt to taste, about 1 flat teaspoon. Then cook another 15 to 20 minutes.

2. Rice Triangles (Omusubi)

3 cups brown rice
3 3/4 cups water
1 pinch sea salt
Umeboshi
Nori

Prepare and pressure-cook the rice as in Menu II. To form the triangles, follow the instructions in Menu XV.

3. Hijiki with Onion and Carrot

1 package hijiki
1 onion
1 carrot
Tamari soy sauce

Soak the hijiki in water to cover for 15 minutes or until soft. Cut both onion and carrot in thin julienne style, making sure the carrot is equal in length to the onion. Squeeze excess water from hijiki and cut into the same lengths as the onion. Water-sauté the onion, hijiki, and carrot using 1/4-inch hijiki soaking water. Sauté the hijiki well until the strong odor changes to mild.

Add soaking water to the top of the vegetables, discarding the last tablespoon of water. Add more water to the cooking pot, if necessary. Cover and cook until tender.

When the water level is down to 1/2 inch, remove the cover. Add tamari to taste and, with the cover ajar, cook until dry.

4. Japanese Turnips (Kabu) in Miso Sauce

1 bunch turnips
1 Tbsp. sesame oil
Barley miso (mugi miso)

Wash and trim the turnips. Japanese turnips are small, round, pure white globes and are milder than the purple-topped American turnips. Cut the turnips into 1/4-inch crescents. Cut the greens into 1/2-inch diagonals. Oil-sauté in sesame oil. Add 1 inch of water. Cover and steam until tender. Season lightly with barley miso, diluting it in the remaining water.

5. Carrots with Leeks

3 carrots
1 leek
Sea salt
Roasted sesame seeds

Cut the carrots into 1/4-inch-thick diagonals. Cut the leeks into 1-inch lengths. Water-sauté leeks quickly, first the greens, then the whites. Add carrots, cover, and steam until tender. Sprinkle lightly with salt. Mix and steam 2 minutes more uncovered. Sprinkle with roasted sesame seeds.

6. Pickle: Chinese Cabbage with Turnip Greens

1 bunch turnip greens
1/2 Chinese cabbage
2 tsps. sea salt

Wash the vegetables well and dry. Slice julienne style on the diagonal. Put in a bowl and sprinkle with approximately 2 teaspoons salt. Mix well and taste. The taste should be slightly too salty to eat, but salty enough to pickle. Press with a small plate, leaving 1/2-inch space between the plate and the bowl. Place a heavy weight on the plate. A heavy rock used just for pickling is best. Leave for at least 3 hours. Overnight is better. Three days is excellent. After 3 days, put the whole contents in a glass jar or crock and refrigerate. To serve, squeeze out the portion needed and taste. If too salty, rinse in cold, pure water and squeeze again. Arrange lightly on a plate. With experience you will learn to make perfectly salted pickles that do not taste salty.

7. Bancha Twig Tea (Kukicha)

> "For the power of God's angels enters into you with the living food which the Lord gives you from his royal table. And when you eat, have above you the angel of air, and below you the angel of water. Breathe long and deeply at all your meals, that the angel of air may bless your repasts. And chew well your food with your teeth, that it become water, and that the angel of water turn it into blood in your body.

And eat slowly, as it were a prayer you make to the Lord. For I tell you truly, the power of God enters into you, if you eat after this manner at his table."

—*The Essene Gospel of Peace*—Book One
Edmond Bordeaux Szekely

MENU XLVIII

Butternut Squash Soup	Romaine Lettuce and Watercress Salad
Kasha	Takuan Pickle
Azuki-Udon Casserole	Bancha Twig Tea (Kukicha)
Daikon with Pickled Turnip	

1. Butternut Squash Soup

2 onions
1 butternut squash
1 bunch watercress
3 quarts water
Sea salt

Cut the onion in a fine dice. Cut the butternut squash into 1/2-inch pieces, reserving the seeds for further processing. Break watercress into 2-inch sprigs and set aside.

Bring 1/4 inch of water to boil and add a pinch of salt. Sauté onions until translucent and sweet. Add squash and sauté until the color becomes bright. Add enough water for soup in a 4-quart pot. Cover and simmer until tender. Purée onions and squash in a Foley food mill. Return to pot. Season with 1/2 teaspoon salt or to taste. Cook another 5 minutes. To serve, garnish with watercress.

2. Kasha

2 onions
1 bunch scallions
4 cups kasha
8 cups water
5 pinches sea salt

Cut onions in 1/2-inch dice. Cut scallions into 1/2-inch diagonals. Mince scallion roots. Water-sauté onions and scallion roots and half of the scallions. Add kasha and water.

Bring water to a boil. Add 1 pinch of salt per cup of kasha, plus 1 pinch for the pot. Cover and cook 20 minutes on a small fire. When done, add the other half of the scallions, mix well, and let steam in the hot kasha 2 to 3 minutes before serving.

3. Azuki-Udon Casserole

1 package Japanese unbleached udon or macrobiotic udon
2 cups azuki
5 cups water
1/2 tsp. sea salt
Sesame oil
Scallions

Boil udon al dente. Drain and rinse in cool water. Cook azuki in 5 cups of water for 2 1/2 hours. Add salt and cook another 1/2 hour. In a large bowl, mix the udon and beans thoroughly. Place in an oiled baking dish and bake at 400°F. for 1/2 hour. To serve, cut into 2-inch squares. Garnish with minced, quick-boiled scallions, if desired.

4. Daikon with Pickled Turnip

1 round Chinese daikon or 1 long Japanese daikon
3 Chinese pickled turnips

Cut the daikon into thin 1/2-inch by 1-inch rectangles. Cut the turnip julienne style. Water-sauté the daikon. Add the turnip and steam together until the daikon is tender. No further seasoning is necessary. Homemade pickled turnips may also be used.

5. Romaine Lettuce and Watercress Salad

1 bunch romaine lettuce
1 bunch watercress
1 carrot
Umeboshi juice

Cut the romaine lettuce in half in order to wash the insides well. Dry all the vegetables after washing. Cut the romaine hearts in eighths. Cut all the romaine lettuce into 1-inch lengths on the diagonal. Cut the watercress in 1 ½-inch lengths. Cut the carrot julienne style to match watercress.

Quick-boil the carrot and set aside. Steam the romaine lettuce and watercress in 1/4 inch of boiling salted water until bright green. Rinse greens in cold water to stop cooking and to set the color. Gently squeeze out the excess water. Mix together with the carrots. Mix with umeboshi juice to taste, about 2 to 3 teaspoons.

6. Takuan Pickle

See the Special Foods section.

7. Bancha Twig Tea (Kukicha)

> "Gluttony, overdrinking, and overeating, especially the overeating of animal protein, animal fat, and white sugar, dilute digestive juices, then bring about the putrefaction of the intestinal contents, then lead to the acidosis of blood, and at last develop bacterial toxins in the intestines. And besides, gluttony, overeating, and overdrinking may be the cause of all sorts of chronic diseases including cancer. This will be well shown by the fact that the occurence rate and death rate of cancer both were extremely low at the time of a food shortage during the second World War, but with the favorable turn of the food situation in postwar times, various kinds of diseases have rapidly increased in number and, as a result, hospitals which were once almost empty in wartime are now filled with patients who are suffering from various kinds of diseases including cancer."
>
> —Prof. Kikuo Chishima
> *Revolution of Biology and Medicine*—Vol. 9

"When you relax your attention for a little, do not imagine that you will recover it wherever you wish."

—Epictetus

MENU XLIX

Rice Potage (Okayu) with Lotus Root
Baked Wild Barley (Hatomugi)-Rice Casserole
Arame with Lotus Root
Baked Daikon
Dandelion Ohitashi
Takuan Pickle
Bancha Twig Tea (Kukicha)

1. Rice Potage (Okayu) with Lotus Root

2 cups brown rice, washed
12 cups water
1 lotus root
1/2 tsp. sea salt
Watercress

Add water to rice and bring to a boil. Meanwhile, grate the lotus root. After the water boils, add the grated lotus root and boil hard for 3 minutes without the cover in order to evaporate the yin quality. Then add the salt. Lower the fire and cook 1 to 2 hours with the cover slightly ajar. To serve, garnish with watercress. This dish is good for respiratory problems.

2. Baked Wild Barley (Hatomugi)-Rice Casserole

2 cups wild barley (hatomugi)
3 cups brown rice
6 1/4 cups water
2 pinches sea salt
2 onions
2 carrots
1/3 package shredded kombu (kirikombu)
4 shiitake mushrooms
1 bunch scallions
2 pinches sea salt
Tamari soy sauce

Pick clean and wash the barley and rice. Pressure-cook in 6 1/4 cups water with 2 pinches of salt. Cut the onion and carrots julienne style. Soak kombu in water until tender. Squeeze out kombu and cut into 1-inch lengths. Soak the shiitake, squeeze, and cut julienne style. Cut the scallions into 1 1/2-inch lengths. Mince the roots. Water-sauté the onions, scallion roots, shiitake, kombu, and carrots in that order. Cover and steam until tender. Season lightly with tamari.

When the rice and vegetables are done, mix them together. Pat down firmly in an oiled baking dish. Bake at 400°F. for 20 minutes. To serve, cut into 2-inch squares.

3. Arame with Lotus Root

1 package arame
1 lotus root
Tamari soy sauce

Rinse the arame. Wash the lotus root and cut in thin half circles on the diagonal. Cut the arame into 1 1/2-inch lengths. Water-sauté the lotus root 2 to 3 minutes. Add the arame and sauté until the strong smell becomes mellow. Add water and cook covered approximately 40 minutes until water level is down to 1 inch. Add tamari to taste. Cook until dry.

Note: It is recommended to rinse arame instead of soaking.

4. Baked Daikon

Daikon
Hatcho miso
Sesame seeds

Wash and cut the daikon into 1-inch circles. Place on a cookie tray with 1-inch sides, in 1/2 inch of water. Dilute miso in a little water and spread thinly on top of daikon circles. Sprinkle with raw sesame seeds. Cover with stainless-steel cookie tray. Bake at 400°F. for 25 minutes.

5. Dandelion Ohitashi

1 bunch dandelion leaves
Tamari soy sauce
2 Tbsps. sesame seeds, dry-roasted

Cut dandelion hearts into quarters. Wash well and pat dry. Cut the length of the dandelions into thirds. Quick-boil in 1 inch of salted water until they are bright green and the stems are tender, about 2 to 3 minutes. Rinse in cold, pure water. Squeeze out excess water. Cut into 1 1/2-inch lengths. Dot lightly with tamari and sprinkle with sesame seeds which have been dry-roasted in a cast-iron skillet. Toss lightly.

6. Takuan Pickle

See the Special Foods section.

7. Bancha Twig Tea (Kukicha)

MENU L

Miso Soup with Turnips and Greens	Savoy Cabbage with Bulgur and Sunflower Seeds
Brown Rice with Barley	Watercress Ohitashi
Burdock and Carrot	Bancha Twig Tea (Kukicha)
Kiriboshi Daikon with Onion	

1. Miso Soup with Turnips and Greens

2 6″ strips wakame
3 quarts water
1 large turnip
Turnip greens
Barley miso (mugi miso)

Soak, squeeze, and cut wakame into 1/2-inch pieces. Simmer the wakame in the soaking water for a minimum of 15 minutes while preparing the vegetables. Wash and dry turnip greens. Trim turnip removing only the inedible portions from the top and the root. Carefully peel off only the purple portion of the skin. The purple part is holding excess potassium. The turnip itself has enough potassium in it for our needs. Cut the turnip from top to bottom into 1/2-inch slices. Cut these slices again from top to bottom into 1/2-inch strips. Cut the strips into 1/2-inch cubes widthwise. Cut the greens into 1/2-inch pieces.

Cook the turnips in the wakame stock until tender. Add the greens. As soon as they become bright green, add miso a little at a time to taste. For further details see Menu I. Cook together 2 to 3 minutes without boiling to marry the soup.

2. Brown Rice with Barley

1 1/2 cups brown rice
1 1/2 cups barley
3 3/4 cups water
1 pinch sea salt

Prepare and pressure-cook the two grains together as in Menu II.

3. Burdock and Carrot

4 burdock roots
2 carrots
Tamari soy sauce
1 Tbsp. roasted sesame seeds

Wash, dry, and trim roots. Slice burdock and carrot on a thin diagonal about 1 1/2 inches long. In a 1/4 inch of boiling salted water, sauté the burdock until the strong earthy smell evaporates. Add carrot and sauté lightly about 1 minute. Add water just to the top of the burdock. Bring to a boil, lower the fire and simmer, covered, until the burdock is tender and the water is down to 1/2 inch. Add tamari to taste, mix gently and cook, uncovered, until dry. Garnish with roasted sesame seeds.

4. Kiriboshi Daikon with Onion

1 package kiriboshi daikon (dried daikon)
1 onion
Tamari soy sauce

Soak, squeeze, and cut daikon into 1 1/2-inch pieces. Cut onion in fine julienne style. In 1/4 inch of boiling salted water sauté onion until mild. Add daikon and daikon soaking water. Bring to a boil with cover ajar. Tighten cover and lower fire, cooking about 20 to 30 minutes until daikon is tender. Add tamari lightly to taste and cook until dry.

5. Savoy Cabbage with Bulgur and Sunflower Seeds

1 Savoy cabbage
1/2 cup bulgur
1/2 cup roasted sunflower seeds
3/4 cup water
1/4 tsp. sea salt

Bring the water to a boil and add the salt and bulgur. Cover and cook on a low fire for 30 minutes. Wash the savoy cabbage very well, inspecting for aphids. Dry and cut into 1-inch squares. Steam the cabbage in 1 inch of boiling salted water until bright green and tender. Roast the sunflower seeds, stirring constantly until they are golden. When the bulgur is done, lightly toss together with the cabbage and roasted sunflower seeds.

6. Watercress Ohitashi

Watercress
Tamari soy sauce

Rinse the watercress well, picking off any yellow leaves. When the watercress greens turn yellow, they become toxic. Dip the watercress into boiling salted water until bright green, about 1/2 to 1 minute. Rinse in cold running water and gently squeeze out the excess water. Serve two to three stems whole, depending on size. Dot lightly with tamari.

7. Bancha Twig Tea (Kukicha)

> "For the sake of healthy life, everyone . . . must preserve his blood normally by taking natural food and by well-balanced mental life, because by these factors' influence the condition of blood changes remarkably.
>
> "By physical exercise, the lungs and heart increase their activity; accordingly, circulation of blood is promoted and the oxygen content and freshness of the blood increase. . . . Cancer cells develop under oxygen-deficient conditions, as has been pointed out by Warburg. As the river's water is purified by its flowing, blood also is refreshed by its active circulation.
>
> ". . . spraying of dangerous insecticides, pollution of air, water and soil by . . . chemical poisons and radio-isotopes from waste products of factories, foods polluted by artificial staining, . . . harmful chemicals, or irradiation treatments, . . . are absorbed into [the] blood through the digestive canal or other parts of [the] body and give dangerous effects to every [person] and even to fetal life."
>
> —Prof. Kikuo Chishima
> *Revolution of Biology and Medicine*—

> "There is a vast preponderance of those who wander downwards unliberated."
> —*The Tibetan Book of the Dead*

January

MENU LI

Miso Soup with Red Radish Leaves	Arame with Sesame Seeds
Brown Rice	Red Radishes
Root Vegetable Stew with *Jinenjo*	Takuan or Other Pickle
	Bancha Twig Tea (Kukicha)

1. Miso Soup with Red Radish Leaves

1 6″ strip wakame
Water
2 bunches red radish leaves
Barley miso (mugi miso)

Soak, squeeze, and cut wakame into 1/2-inch pieces. Pour soaking water into a 1 1/2-quart pot, leaving sandy residue in bottom of bowl. Add water if necessary. Add wakame and bring to boil. Simmer 15 minutes with the cover slightly ajar.

Meanwhile, wash radish leaves well and pat them dry. Separate leaves and add them, without cutting, to the soup. Cook for 2 or 3 minutes. Add miso by either straining it directly into the soup or by diluting it in soup broth in a separate bowl and pouring it back. Adjust to taste. If miso is too strong, add boiled water a little at a time.

2. Brown Rice

Pressure-cook rice as in Menu II.

3. Root Vegetable Stew with Jinenjo

2 6″ strips kombu
4″ piece of jinenjo
2 burdock roots
3 carrots
1 small daikon
Wheat gluten (optional)
1 butternut squash
Sea salt
Tamari soy sauce

Cut all vegetables into 3/4-inch pieces. Layer all ingredients in the order given. Add water to top of gluten. Cook on a high flame 7 to 10 minutes uncovered. Sprinkle lightly with salt. Cover and cook 7 to 10 minutes more. Add tamari to make a mild delicious taste and cook another 2 to 3 minutes. Turn off fire, remove cover and let stand a few minutes until steam escapes.

This method of cooking is called "layering." It makes a vegetable dish that is good for strengthening the whole body and is especially recommended for weak people. It is best in cold weather.

4. Arame with Sesame Seeds

1 package arame
Tamari soy sauce
1 1/2 Tbsps. brown sesame seeds

Rinse arame, arrange on cutting board, and cut into 1 1/2-inch lengths. Bring 1/4 inch of water to a boil and water-sauté arame until strong smell dissipates. Add water, bring to a boil, and boil hard 1 minute uncovered. Lower fire, cover, and simmer about 20 to 30 minutes or until water is down to 1/2 inch. Taste arame to check for tenderness. If still a little hard, cover and cook another few minutes until tender. Add tamari to make mild, delicious taste. Mix well and cook uncovered until dry. Meanwhile, wash and roast sesame seeds. Mix into arame when done.

Note: It is recommended to rinse arame instead of soaking.

5. Red Radishes

2 bunches red radishes
1 pinch sea salt

Wash radishes well under cold, running water with a natural-bristle brush. Trim top and bottom, cutting off tail but leaving a 1/4 inch of stem. Bring 2 inches of water to a boil, add salt and radishes. Cook radishes 2 to 3 minutes. Rinse in cold water, drain and serve as is. This is also good for a mid-afternoon snack.

6. Takuan or Other Pickle

See the Special Foods section.

7. Bancha Twig Tea (Kukicha)

MENU LII

Broccoli Nori Soup
Brown Rice with Wild Barley (Hatomugi)
Turnip Miso Stew
Kiriboshi Daikon with Kombu
Cabbage with Old Cabbage Pickle
Takuan or Other Pickle
Bancha Twig Tea (Kukicha)

1. Broccoli Nori Soup

Broccoli
3 quarts water
5 sheets nori
Sea salt
Tamari soy sauce

Wash and dry broccoli. Trim fibrous parts off the lower stalks and cut the stalk lengthwise in thin slices. Then cut into 1-inch lengths, including the leaves and flowe[rs.] Separate stalks from leaves and flowers.

Bring water to a boil in a 2-quart soup pot. Tear the nori into small pieces. Simmer for 5 minutes, add broccoli flowers and leaves. When the color turns bright green, add thinly sliced stems and simmer until tender, uncovered. Season half with salt, half with tamari, tasting to balance the flavor. The flavor should be delicate and delicious.

2. Brown Rice with Wild Barley (Hatomugi)

2 1/2 cups brown rice
1 1/2 cups wild barley
6 cups water
2 pinches sea salt

Wash and drain the grain. Roast in a dry skillet stirring constantly until golden. Put into a cooking pot with water and salt. Bring to a boil and simmer for 40 minutes. See Menu I for details.

3. Turnip Miso Stew

2 turnips
Turnip greens
1 onion
1 carrot
1 4″ square of kombu
1–2 Tbsps. Hatcho or mugi miso

Cut all vegetables in 1/2-inch dice. Water-sauté onion, turnips, and carrot. Add kombu and 1 to 2 inches of water. Cook until carrots are tender. Add turnip greens. Boil hard 1 minute without the cover. When the leaves are bright green, dilute miso in the stew broth in a separate bowl. Return to stew and cook gently for several minutes.

4. Kiriboshi Daikon with Kombu

1 package dried shredded daikon (kiriboshi daikon)
1/2 package dried shredded kombu
Tamari soy sauce

Soak daikon and kombu until tender in separate bowls. Squeeze out and cut into 1 1/2-inch pieces. Put all but the last teaspoon of kombu soaking water in the pot. Add kombu and bring to a boil. Add daikon and as much daikon soaking water as is necessary to bring water to top of daikon. Boil hard, uncovered, for 1 minute, lower fire, place cover slightly ajar, and simmer until vegetables are tender and water is down to 1 inch. Add tamari to taste, mix well, and simmer uncovered until dry.

5. Cabbage with Old Cabbage Pickle

1/4 head green cabbage
2 Tbsps. old cabbage pickle

Shred cabbage. Water-sauté in 1/4 inch of boiling salted water. Add the old cabbage pickle, mix together until cabbage is tender. No other seasoning is necessary.

6. Takuan or Other Pickle

See the Special Foods section.

7. Bancha Twig Tea (Kukicha)

> "The finest weapons can be the instruments of misfortune,
> and thus contrary to Natural Law.
> Those who possess the Tao turn away from them,
> Evolved leaders occupy and honor the left;
> Those who use weapons honor the right."
>
> —Lao Tzu
> —George Ohsawa
> *The Order of the Universe*

MENU LIII

Roasted Rice Soup with Nori	Kale with Pumpkin Seeds
Brown Rice with Barley	Takuan Pickle
Vegetable Miso Stew	Bancha Twig Tea (Kukicha)
Squash-Cabbage Nori Rolls	

1. Roasted Rice Soup with Nori

1 cup brown rice
4 quarts water
1 tsp. sea salt
Nori
Minced scallions

Wash and roast brown rice until golden. Bring to a boil in 4 quarts of water. After the water boils, add 1/2 teaspoon salt. Add 2 to 3 sheets of nori broken up into small pieces. Lower the fire, cover and cook 1 hour. After it is done, add salt to taste, about 1/2 teaspoon and cook another 15 minutes. Garnish with minced scallions.

2. Brown Rice with Barley

3 cups brown rice
1 cup barley
5 cups water
2 pinches sea salt

Pressure-cook as in Menu II.

3. Vegetable Miso Stew

1 onion
3 shiitake mushrooms
2 burdock roots
1 turnip

6 baby daikon
Turnip greens
1 Tbsp. sesame oil
Water
1 6″ strip kombu
1/2 tsp. minced ginger root
2 Tbsps. barley miso (mugi miso)

Wash, dry, and cut all vegetables in 1/2-inch dice. Oil-sauté onion, shiitake, burdock, turnip, daikon, and turnip greens in that order. Add water to cover. Push kombu into bottom of pot. Cover, bring to a boil, and simmer until tender. Add 1/2 teaspoon minced ginger and about 2 tablespoons diluted miso, or enough to make a delicious taste. Continue to cook without boiling for several minutes.

4. Squash-Cabbage Nori Rolls

1 butternut squash, washed
1 Chinese cabbage, washed
1 package nori
1/4 tsp. sea salt

Cut squash into 2-inch squares. Steam and purée. Add salt. Quick-boil Chinese cabbage leaves. Drape leaves over edge of a colander to drain and cool. Holding the knife horizontally, slice through the thick end of the stem to facilitate rolling. Spread out one leaf at a time on the cutting board. Place 1/2 sheet of nori over the leaf. Spread 1/4 inch of squash over the nori. Roll from stem to leaf, folding the sides in as you go. Using a sharp knife, slice in half on the diagonal.

5. Kale with Pumpkin Seeds

1 bunch kale
1 pinch sea salt
2 Tbsps. roasted pumpkin seeds
Tamari soy sauce

Clean and wash kale well. Shake off excess water and pat dry. Trim edges off the stems. Quick-boil whole leaves in boiling water with salt until bright green and the stems are tender. Remove quickly and rinse in cold water. Gently squeeze out excess water. Cut the stems in thin diagonal slices. Cut the leaves in 1/2-inch wide diagonals. Add roasted pumpkin seeds to garnish. Add a few drops of tamari and toss.

6. Takuan Pickle

See the Special Foods section.

7. Bancha Twig Tea (Kukicha)

> ". . . strait is the gate, and narrow is the way, which leadeth unto life, and few there be that find it."
>
> —St. Matthew, VII: 14

MENU LIV

Millet Stew	Broccoli Ohitashi
Brown Rice	Takuan or Other Pickle
Kinpira with Lotus Root	Bancha Twig Tea (Kukicha)
Chick-peas	

1. Millet Stew

1 cup millet
1 onion
1 carrot
1/2 acorn squash
5 cups water
1/2 tsp. sea salt
Watercress

Pick clean, wash, and roast millet. Cut onions into 1/4-inch crescents. Slice carrot 1/4 inch on slight diagonal. Cut squash into 1-inch cubes. Water-sauté onion, squash and carrots in this order. Add millet and water. Bring to a boil and add salt. Cover tightly, lower fire, and simmer 40 minutes to 1 hour. When done, adjust the flavor with salt. Do not use tamari soy sauce. Cook another 5 minutes. To serve, garnish with watercress.

2. Brown Rice

3 cups brown rice
3 3/4 cups water
1 pinch sea salt

Pressure-cook as per Menu II.

3. Kinpira with Lotus Root

3 medium burdock roots
1 lotus root
1 medium carrot
1 Tbsp. sesame oil
Water
Tamari soy sauce

Cut vegetables in a fine julienne style. In sesame oil, sauté burdock well, until strong, earthy aroma subsides. Add lotus root and sauté until aroma becomes mild, 2 to 3 minutes. Add carrot and sauté 1 minute. Add water up to 1/4 inch from the top of the vegetables. Boil hard, uncovered, for about 3 minutes. Then lower fire, cover, and cook 40 minutes. When the burdock is tender and water is down to 1 inch, add tamari to taste and cook until dry. It is imperative that the tamari cook into the roots. Serve 1 to 2 tablespoons per meal.

4. Chick-peas

3 cups chick-peas

7 cups water
1 4″ square kombu
Carrot tops
Sea salt

Pick through, wash, and drain chick-peas. Soak overnight or at least 2 to 3 hours before cooking. Bring to a boil and boil hard without the cover for about 3 minutes. Lower the fire, add kombu which has been cut into 1/2-inch squares, and pressure-cook for 1 1/2 hours. If you prefer, you can use fresh water, add the kombu and pressure-cook directly. While the beans are cooking, wash, dry, and mince the carrot tops. When the beans are tender, cool pot under running water. Open lid and add salt, 1/4 teaspoon per cup of beans. At the same time, add minced carrot tops. Mix well. Replace the cover without using pressure and cook another 1/2 hour.

5. Broccoli Ohitashi

1 small bunch broccoli
1–2 cloves garlic
1 pinch sea salt
Tamari soy sauce

Wash and dry broccoli. Cut the broccoli lengthwise in strips as thick as your little finger. Then cut into 2-inch lengths. Mince garlic and water-sauté in 1/4 inch of boiling salted water. Add broccoli and sauté until bright green. Sprinkle with salt. Cover and steam until stems are tender. Remove cover, sprinkle lightly with tamari, and cook until dry.

6. Takuan or Other Pickle

See the Special Foods section.

7. Bancha Twig Tea (Kukicha)

"Drs. Shleiden and Shwann proved that cells grow by budding. Dr. Haeckell proved that cells grow from a protoplasmic state of matter which does not have cell structure, i.e., monera. O.B. Lepeshinskaya proved that the cell is generated from living matter, not from another cell. Dr. Chishima proved [the differentiation of the non-nucleated red blood corpuscle into the nucleated body cell.]

"Recently, Professor Halpern, a member of the French Academy of Medicine, stunned the cancer researchers of the world by saying that cancer cells grow not by division but by fusion. His theory is close to ours. However, it will be more perfect if he will add the concept of transformation from [degenerated] blood cell to cancer cell.

"I have been claiming that orthodox medicine must be corrected by this 'spontaneous cell generation' theory. Our 'spontaneous cell generation' theory is not [a] widely accepted theory yet; however, nature itself reveals its validity."

—*The Hidden Truth of Cancer*
K. Morishita, M. D.
(Herman Aihara, Translator)

MENU LV

Clear Soup (Osumashi) with Cauliflower	Lotus Root with Arame
Brown Rice with Lotus Seeds	Kiriboshi Daikon with Koya-dofu
Carrot-Parsnip Nishime	Dandelion Leaves Ohitashi
	Bancha Twig Tea (Kukicha)

1. Clear Soup (Osumashi) with Cauliflower

1 6″ strip kombu
3 quarts water
1 cauliflower
Sea salt
Tamari soy sauce

Brush kombu with fingers to remove sand. Simmer in 3 quarts of water for 1/2 hour. Wash, dry, and trim cauliflower. Cut flowers into small flowerettes. Cut stems and heart into 1/2-inch cubes. Remove the kombu from the stock. Add salt and tamari to taste, each comprising half of the flavor. Cook the cauliflower in the stock until the stems are tender. This makes a simple but elegant soup.

2. Brown Rice with Lotus Seeds

3 cups brown rice
1/2 cup lotus seeds
4 1/2 cups water
1 pinch sea salt

Prepare rice and pressure-cook with lotus seeds as in Menu II.

3. Carrot-Parsnip Nishime

3 carrots
1 large parsnip
Carrot tops
Sea salt

Wash, dry, and trim vegetables. Cut carrots and parsnip into equal 1-inch irregular pieces. Mince carrot tops. Water-sauté parsnip in 1/4-inch of boiling salted water. Add carrot and 1/4 inch more water. Bring to a boil, cover, and steam until almost tender. Add carrot tops, sprinkle lightly with salt, shake pan to distribute evenly, cover and cook until dry.

4. Lotus Root with Arame

1 package dried lotus root
1 package arame
Tamari soy sauce

Soak lotus root for 2 hours. Rinse arame and cut into 1 1/2-inch lengths. Water-sauté arame in 1/4 inch of boiling water until strong odor evaporates. Add lotus root and sauté 1 to 2 minutes. Add water to cover vegetables and bring to a boil. Lower fire, cover and simmer about 40 minutes or until lotus root is tender and liquid is reduced. Add tamari lightly to taste and cook until dry.

Note: It is recommended to rinse arame instead of soaking.

5. Kiriboshi Daikon with Koya-dofu

1 package dried daikon (kiriboshi daikon)
3 thick or 6 thin dried tofu cakes (koya-dofu)
Tamari soy sauce

Dried daikon and dried tofu may be found in health food stores or Oriental food markets.

Soak tofu and daikon separately in water to cover until soft. Squeeze tofu and cut into strips 1/4 inch wide by 1 inch long. Squeeze daikon and cut into 1 1/2-inch lengths. Sauté tofu in 1/4 inch of boiling water. Add tamari lightly and mix until evenly absorbed. Add daikon and daikon soaking water. Bring to a boil, lower fire and cook with cover ajar about 30 minutes or until water is down to 1/2 inch. Adjust tamari to taste and cook uncovered until dry.

6. Dandelion Leaves Ohitashi

1 bunch dandelion leaves
Umeboshi juice
Roasted sesame seeds

Make sure to wash sand out of bottom of leaves. Dry and trim away bad parts. Cut dandelion into 2-inch lengths. Simmer in boiling water 3 to 5 minutes, covered. Do not lose bright green color. If you raise the lid to peek and replace it, especially more than once, the green color will become dark and muddy looking. Rinse in cold water. Drain and squeeze out excess water. Season with umeboshi juice to taste. Garnish with roasted sesame seeds. Toss lightly to mix evenly.

7. Bancha Twig Tea (Kukicha)

> "God wrote not the laws in the pages of books, but in your heart and in your spirit. They are in your breath, your blood, your bone; in your flesh, your bowels, your eyes, your ears, and in every little part of your body. They are present in the air, in the water, in the earth, in the plants, in the sunbeams, in the depths and in the heights. They all speak to you that you may understand the tongue and the will of the living God. But you shut your eyes that you may not see, and you shut your ears that you may not hear. I tell you truly, that the scripture is the work of man, but life and all its hosts are the work of our God."
>
> —*The Essene Gospel of Peace—Book One*
> Edmond Bordeaux Szekely

February

MENU LVI

Clear Soup (Osumashi) with Tofu and Scallions	Carrot-Daikon Greens Condiment
Brown Rice with Rye	Takuan or Other Pickle
Root Stew with Lotus Root	Vegetable Trimmings Tea
Dandelion with Tofu	

1. Clear Soup (Osumashi) with Tofu and Scallions

1 5″ strip kombu
3 shiitake mushrooms
2 quarts water
1/2 tub tofu
Sea salt
Tamari soy sauce
3 scallions

Brush any sand off kombu with fingers. Soak overnight, or simmer kombu and shiitake in water for at least 1 hour. Cut tofu into 1/2-inch cubes. Remove kombu and hang up to dry for use in bean cooking. Season stock with half salt, half tamari to taste. Add tofu. Cook several minutes or until it floats. Meanwhile, mince scallions, reserving the roots for the root stew. Serve three or five cubes of tofu per bowl, and garnish with scallions.

2. Brown Rice with Rye

2 1/2 cups brown rice
1/2 cup whole rye kernels
3 3/4–4 cups water
1 pinch sea salt

Pressure-cook in 3 3/4 to 4 cups water depending on consistency desired. The 4-cup measure includes a little extra water for the rye. Follow details in Menu II.

3. Root Stew with Lotus Root

1 8″ strip kombu
1 large burdock root
1 lotus root
1 small daikon
Scallion roots (optional)
1 small kabocha
2 carrots
Tamari soy sauce

Clean kombu and place in 2 inches of water in the bottom of stew pot. Bring to a boil, cover, lower the fire and simmer. Meanwhile, cut vegetables into 1/2-inch irregular pieces. Bring the water back to a boil, add burdock and boil hard 1 minute, uncovered. Add lotus root and boil hard 1 minute. Add daikon and boil hard 1 minute.

Add scallion roots. Add kabocha and boil hard 1/2 minute. Add carrots. Cover and cook at least 10 minutes or until burdock is tender. Add tamari to taste, and cook 2 to 3 minutes more.

4. Dandelion with Tofu

1/2 bunch cultivated dandelion leaves or 4–5 bunches wild dandelion leaves
1/2 tub tofu
2 pinches sea salt

Wash dandelion well and shake dry. Cut into 1/2-inch lengths. Mash the tofu. Water-sauté tofu in 1/4 inch of boiling salted water until firm, stirring constantly, breaking up with chopsticks to prevent sticking. Add 1 pinch salt while cooking. Add dandelion leaves, sprinkle with 1 pinch salt, and steam until bright green and tender. Mix well before serving.

5. Carrot-Daikon Greens Condiment

Carrot and daikon greens from the Root Stew
Tamari soy sauce
1 Tbsp. roasted sesame seeds

Wash, dry, and mince carrot and daikon greens from Root Stew. Water-sauté daikon greens in 1/4 inch of boiling salted water. Add carrot tops, cover, and steam until tender. Add tamari to taste, a little on the strong side. Cook until dry. Add roasted sesame seeds. Serve 1/2 teaspoon per person as a condiment on grain.

6. Takuan or Other Pickle

See section on Special Foods.

7. Vegetable Trimmings Tea

Vegetable trimmings from the Root Stew
2 umeboshi pits
3 cups water

Wash and drain the trimmings from the Root Stew vegetables. Add umeboshi pits and water. Bring to a boil and simmer for 1/2 hour. Strain before serving.

> "Therefore the first curing method for these diseases is to devise a countermove for the recovery of physiological function of [the] whole body, especially of [the] digestive canal.
>
> "But orthodox medical sciences overlook utterly this principle.
>
> "For the planning of recovery of digestive function, especially the villi-function of intestinal mucous membrane, we must devise dietary cure and improvement of living for promoting health.
>
> "For these diseases the application of radioactive isotopes and chemotherapy make the condition of the patient worse and no effect can be expected.
>
> "Even if temporarily improved, after all, it causes the vitality of the whole body to decrease."
>
> —Prof. Kikuo Chishima
> *Revolution of Biology and Medicine*—Vol. 9

MENU LVII

Barley and Black Soybean Soup
Sesame Seed Rice
Kabocha Crescents
Chinese Cabbage with Gluten (Kofu)
Romaine Lettuce with Garlic
Takuan or Other Pickle
Roasted Barley Tea (Mugicha)

1. Barley and Black Soybean Soup

1 cup barley
1/2 cup black soybeans
1 6″ strip kombu
1/3 daikon
1 carrot
8 cups water
1/2 tsp. sea salt
4 scallions

Pick clean, wash, and drain barley and beans. Cut kombu into 1/2-inch pieces. Cut daikon and carrot into 1/4-inch triangles the size of the beans. Put all together in the pressure cooker with water and salt. Pressure-cook 2 hours. Serve garnished with minced scallions.

2. Sesame Seed Rice

2 2/3 cups brown rice
1/3 cup raw sesame seeds
3 3/4 cups water
1 pinch sea salt

Pressure-cook. See instructions in Menu II.

3. Kabocha Crescents

1 kabocha
Sea salt
Roasted sesame seeds

Scrape any hard parts off the skin of the kabocha. Wash and dry, remove the stem, cut in half, remove the seeds, and set aside. Cut into 1-inch crescents. Bring water to a boil in a steaming pot. Wet and wring out a steaming towel and line the steamer with it. Arrange the kabocha crescents in a spiral in the pot, with the thin ends of each crescent under the adjoining piece. Sprinkle lightly with salt. Fold the sides of the towel over the squash. Cover and steam until tender, about 20 minutes. To serve, garnish with roasted sesame seeds.

4. Chinese Cabbage with Gluten (Kofu)

3 large or 5 small Chinese cabbage leaves
3 shiitake mushrooms
3″ daikon

1 carrot
1 cup wheat gluten (kofu), or you may substitute tempeh
1 Tbsp. sesame oil
1 pinch sea salt
Tamari soy sauce

Wash and dry vegetables. Soak the shiitake until tender. See section on Special Foods for making kofu. Cut the cabbage leaves into quarters. Cut the hearts out and slice thinly on diagonal. Cut the cabbage into 1-inch pieces. Cut the daikon in half lengthwise and in thin 1/8-inch half-moons on a slight diagonal. Cut the shiitake in 1/8-inch julienne, cut the carrot in 1/16-inch julienne. Cut the kofu or tempeh in 1-inch by 1/8-inch squares. Sauté shiitake, daikon, cabbage, carrot, and tempeh or kofu in sesame oil, in that order. Add 1 to 2 inches of water, bring to a boil, add salt, and simmer until tender. Add tamari to taste. You can leave this a little juicy.

5. Romaine Lettuce with Garlic

1 head romaine lettuce
3 cloves garlic
Tamari soy sauce

Cut the romaine lettuce in half, wash well, shake, and dry. Cut into quarters. Cut the hearts into thin diagonal slices. Cut romaine lettuce into 1-inch pieces. Crush and mince garlic. Water-sauté in 1/4 inch of boiling salted water. Add romaine lettuce and mix with garlic while sautéing. Cook until bright green. Add tamari lightly, mix, and cook 1 minute more. Garlic helps the blood to hold oxygen.

6. Takuan or Other Pickle

See the Special Foods section.

7. Roasted Barley Tea (Mugicha)

> "If we want to grasp what life is, we must pattern our search after life itself. The secret of life is Order. This is the backbone of Oriental philosophy. We must first master our own self, and then bring order to our home, peace to the nation, and harmony to the world. Thus, order should begin within us, and spread from us in ever-widening circles. All of our acts are evidence of our understanding of life; if we are chaotic, we are showing that we have made ourselves ignorant of life's purpose. Order begins in our blood cells and soon manifests itself in our daily life; once this has happened, we can find it in our human relationships, and finally, metaphysically, in world and cosmological order. But those who do not follow this pattern, who do not order their lives first, are not qualified to speak of peace in the world and spiritual happiness."
>
> —Michio Kushi
> *The Spiral of Life*

MENU LVIII

Miso Soup with Gluten Cake (*Shonai-bu*)
Brown Rice with Black Soybeans
Onion with Sesame Miso Sauce
Burdock with Scallions
Romaine Lettuce and Watercress with Tofu Sauce
Salt-pressed Pickle
Bancha Twig Tea (Kukicha)

1. Miso Soup with Gluten Cake (Shonai-bu)

2 6″ strips wakame
1 1/2–2 quarts water
1 sheet flat gluten cake (Shonai-bu)
6 stems watercress
1 Tbsp. barley miso (mugi miso)

Soak wakame until soft, squeeze and cut into 1/2-inch pieces. Use soaking water for soup stock, less the last teaspoon, if sandy. Add water, if necessary, for 2-quart soup pot. Add wakame, bring to a boil, simmer for at least 15 minutes. Meanwhile, soak gluten cake in water for 1 minute, wrap in clean cotton towel and leave until soft, 5 to 10 minutes. Then slice widthwise into 1/2-inch strips. Wash, dry, and cut watercress into 1 1/2-inch lengths. Add gluten cake to soup and cook several minutes. Add miso and adjust to taste. Cook into soup 2 to 3 minutes without boiling. Add watercress at the end.

2. Brown Rice with Black Soybeans

2 1/2 cups brown rice
1/2 cup black soybeans
1 small carrot
4 1/4–4 1/2 cups water
2 pinches sea salt

Pick through, wash, and drain rice and beans. Wash, dry, and cut the carrot as in making pencil shavings. Add water and salt. Pressure-cook. (See details in Menu II.)

3. Onion with Sesame Miso Sauce

2 onions
1–2 Tbsps. barley miso (mugi miso)
1–2 Tbsps. sesame seeds

Cut onions in half and cut each half in thirds from bottom to top. Boil in 1 inch of water until tender. Add miso diluted in cooking water. Add roasted sesame seeds. Mix together. Serve one or two pieces per person.

4. Burdock with Scallions

3 medium burdock roots
1 bunch scallions
1/2″ ginger root
1 Tbsp. kuzu

1/4 cup cold water
1 Tbsp. tamari soy sauce

Wash and dry burdock and scallions. If the burdock is thick, slice in half lengthwise. Cut into 1-inch lengths straight across. Cut scallions into 1-inch lengths straight across. Water-sauté burdock in 1/4 inch of boiling salted water until earthy smell evaporates. Add water to almost the top of the burdock. Cover and cook until tender. Mince ginger and add to burdock. Dilute kuzu in 1/4 cup cold water. Add tamari to kuzu, mix well, and add to burdock cooking water. Bring to boil and stir until thickened and translucent. Taste and add tamari if necessary. Add scallions and cook 1 minute more.

5. Romaine Lettuce and Watercress with Tofu Sauce

1 head romaine lettuce
1/2 bunch watercress
12 oz. tub tofu
3 umeboshi
Brown rice vinegar

Cut romaine lettuce in half. Trim, wash, and dry. Remove yellow leaves from watercress, as they become toxic. Wash and dry watercress. Cut romaine hearts in half and pull the leaves apart. Boil in 2 inches of boiling salted water until bright green and the hearts are tender. Rinse in cold water immediately. Dip watercress in boiling salted water until bright green. Rinse in cold water immediately.

Squeeze excess water from romaine lettuce and watercress. Cut romaine lettuce in 1-inch pieces and watercress into 1/2-inch pieces. Toss together. Cut tofu into 1-inch cubes. Cut umeboshi in half. Remove pits. Mince umeboshi. Boil tofu and umeboshi together in 1 cup water. Cook 15 minutes until tofu becomes fluffy. Remove tofu with a slotted spoon and put in a suribachi with umeboshi. Grind, adding a little cooking water to make creamy consistency. Add 2 to 3 drops brown rice vinegar to taste. Spoon over romaine lettuce and watercress and mix together.

6. Salt-pressed Pickle

1/4 green cabbage
3″ daikon
2–3 stalks celery
1/3 bunch watercress
1 carrot
1 Tbsp. sea salt

Cut all vegetables julienne style. Sprinkle with salt. Mix well and taste. This should be too salty to eat as is, but just salty enough to pickle vegetables. With the vegetables in a bowl, place a small plate directly on the vegetables and then a weight on the plate in order to press the pickle. Cover with a clean, white towel. Leave to pickle from 1 hour to 3 days. After 3 days, put the pickled vegetables with the brine in a jar in the refrigerator. To serve, remove portion and rinse if too salty.

7. Bancha Twig Tea (Kukicha)

"God casts no soul away, unless it cast itself away. Every soul is its own judgment."
—Boehme

MENU LIX

Buckwheat Cream Potage	with Fried Tofu (Atsuage)
Norimaki	Chinese Cabbage Nori Rolls
Daikon with Leek	Takuan or Other Pickle
Bok Choy Leaves and Carrot	Roasted Barley Tea (Mugicha)

1. Buckwheat Cream Potage

1 cup buckwheat flour
3 1/8 cups water
1/2 tsp. sea salt
1 onion
Carrot tops
1 tsp. sesame oil
Tamari soy sauce
1 Tbsp. roasted sesame seeds

Using a flame tamer under the pot, roast the buckwheat flour, stirring constantly until a nice aroma arises. Let the flour cool about 15 minutes, or set the bottom of the pot in cold water, stirring the flour to cool it quickly. Add 3 cups of cold water, a little at a time, stirring constantly to make a creamy consistency. Bring to a boil stirring constantly so as to prevent lumping. Add salt, stir, and lower fire. Cover tightly and simmer at least 30 minutes. If too thick, add boiling water slowly to achieve desired consistency.

Meanwhile, mince onion and carrot tops. Sauté in sesame oil. Add 1/8 cup of water, cover, and steam until tender. Add tamari to taste, a little bit on the strong side, and roasted sesame seeds. To serve, garnish buckwheat cream potage with 1/2 teaspoon of the vegetable condiment.

2. Norimaki

3 cups brown rice
A little less than 3 3/4 cups water
1 pinch sea salt
1 carrot
4 bok choy stems
Nori
Umeboshi paste or mashed umeboshi

Pressure-cook rice as in Menu II. When cooking rice for Norimaki, a little less water should be used to make it more dry. Measure carrot and bok choy stems against the length of the nori and cut to match. Cut the carrots lengthwise into eighths and the bok choy lengthwise into fourths. Cook each in 1/2 inch of water, just until tender and drain. Cool the cooked rice and spread out 1/4 inch thick on a sheet of nori, leaving 1 inch along the far side. Spread a thin line of umeboshi paste or mashed umeboshi along the near side of the rice. Place one piece of carrot and two pieces of bok choy along the line of the umeboshi.

Roll the Norimaki tightly and evenly from the near edge to the far side. Let set several minutes before cutting. With a clean, sharp knife, cut in half widthwise, wipe the knife, and cut into quarters. Wipe the knife again and cut into eighths. Arrange attractively on a platter, spiral side up. Serve five to seven pieces per person as a main dish.

3. Daikon with Leek

3″ daikon
1 leek
1 onion
1 6″ strip kombu
1 Tbsp. kuzu
1/4 cup water
1 Tbsp. tamari soy sauce

Cut the onion into 1/4-inch crescents. Cut the daikon into 1/4-inch half-moons. Cut the leek into 1 1/2-inch julienne-style diagonals. Water-sauté onion, daikon and leek in that order. Add 1/2 inch of water and place kombu underneath vegetables. Cover and cook several minutes until tender.

Meanwhile, dilute kuzu in 1/4 cup water and add tamari. Remove kombu and hang up to dry. Pour kuzu over vegetables, stirring constantly until thickened and translucent. Add a little boiling water if necessary. This dish should be light and succulent.

4. Bok Choy Leaves and Carrots with Atsuage

Bok choy leaves
1 carrot
Atsuage (fried tofu)
Tamari soy sauce

Pile bok choy leaves one on top of another, matching center vein. Cut in half down the center. Cut each half into 1-inch strips lengthwise. Gather all the strips together and cut across into 1-inch lengths. Cut carrot julienne style. Cut fried tofu into 1-inch squares. Water-sauté tofu in boiling water. Add bok choy leaves and carrot. Steam until leaves are bright green and carrot is tender. Season lightly with tamari.

5. Chinese Cabbage Nori Roll

Chinese cabbage
Nori
Tamari soy sauce

Quick-boil Chinese cabbage leaves, rinse under cold water, and drain. Gently squeeze out excess water. Shave thick part of stem to facilitate rolling. Lay half sheet of unroasted nori over Chinese cabbage. Roll tightly and fold in edges of leaves as you go. Cut in half. Dot each center with tamari. Arrange attractively to show spiral.

6. Takuan or Other Pickle

See the Special Foods section.

7. Roasted Barley Tea (Mugicha)

> "Heaven and earth do nothing, yet there is nothing which they do not accomplish."
> —Chuang-tse (Ch. XVIII)

MENU LX

Kasha Potage	Mushrooms
Brown Rice with Sunflower Seeds	Kohlrabi
Hijiki with Tempeh	Shoyu-Kombu Condiment
Carrots with Shiitake	Bancha Twig Tea (Kukicha)

1. Kasha Potage

1 cup kasha (buckwheat groats)
2 6″ strips wakame
1 onion
1 carrot
1/4 green cabbage
Carrot tops
6 cups water
1/2 tsp. sea salt

Wash, dry, and trim vegetables. Soak, squeeze, and cut wakame into 1/2-inch pieces. Cut the onion and carrot into 1/4-inch dice. Cut the cabbage in 1/4-inch julienne. Be sure to use the heart of the cabbage. Mince the carrot tops.

Water-sauté the onion, cabbage, carrot, and carrot tops. Add the kasha and mix together. Add the wakame soaking water and enough fresh water to total 6 cups. Add the wakame. Bring to a boil. Add salt, and cook with cover ajar on a medium-low fire, about 40 minutes.

2. Brown Rice with Sunflower Seeds

3 cups brown rice
3 3/4 cups water
1 pinch sea salt
1/2 cup roasted sunflower seeds

Prepare and pressure-cook rice as in Menu II. When done, lightly mix in sunflower seeds without mashing the rice.

3. Hijiki with Tempeh

1 package hijiki
1 package tempeh
Tamari soy sauce

Soak hijiki in water to cover. Wash it gently in the soaking water to remove any debris and let the water settle. When the hijiki is soft, squeeze and cut into 1/2-inch pieces. Crumble the tempeh in a bowl with a fork. Water-sauté the hijiki until the strong ocean odor evaporates. Add tempeh and sauté 1 minute more. Add the hijiki soaking water minus the last sandy tablespoon. Bring to a boil and boil hard, uncovered, 1 minute. Lower the fire, cover, and cook about 40 minutes, until the hijiki is soft and the water is down to 1/2 inch. Add tamari lightly to taste. Mix well and cook uncovered until dry.

4. Carrots with Shiitake Mushrooms

3 carrots
3 shiitake mushrooms
1 Tbsp. sesame oil
Sea salt

Soak shiitake to soften. Wash, dry, and trim carrots. Cut carrots on a 1/4-inch-thick diagonal, the same length as the shiitake. Squeeze shiitake and cut the same as the carrot. Sauté shiitake in sesame oil several minutes. Add carrots and continue to sauté 1 to 2 minutes. Add 1/4 inch of water, cover, and steam until tender. Sprinkle lightly with salt. Mix evenly. Cover and steam several minutes more. Sesame oil facilitates absorption of the vitamin A in the carrots.

5. Kohlrabi

1 or more kohlrabi, as needed
Sea salt
Tamari soy sauce
1–2 Tbsps. roasted sesame seeds

Wash, dry, and trim the kohlrabi. Separate the stems from the bulb. Remove any fibrous portions from the skin of the bulb. Slice from top to bottom in 1/4-inch circles. Cut these from top to bottom into 1/4-inch strips. Cut the stems into 1-inch lengths. Sauté in 1/4 inch of boiling salted water, first the stems, then the strips. Sprinkle lightly with salt, cover, and cook until tender, about 5 minutes. Add tamari to taste and cook until dry. Garnish with sesame seeds.

6. Shoyu-Kombu Condiment

1 4″×6″ strip kombu
1/2 cup water
1/2 cup tamari soy sauce

Brush kombu with fingers to remove sand. Soak until soft. Cut into 1/2-inch squares. Put kombu in a pot with 1/2 cup soaking water and 1/2 cup tamari. Cook with the cover ajar for about 1 hour. Then cook half-covered until dry. Spread each piece of kombu out on a plate or a tray and allow it to air dry. The residue of tamari in the cooking pot can be diluted and used in soup. Do not wash it away. Serve one or two pieces kombu with grain. Shoyu-kombu strengthens the blood and the blood vessels.

7. Bancha Twig Tea (Kukicha)

> "Change is unlimited. There is no such thing as good or bad. Man can change anything into himself. To attain this endless liberty, not the curing of sickness, is the final goal of macrobiotics. The purpose of macrobiotics is to become free to change all of this world into what we want—unhappiness to happiness, sickness to health, war to peace, misery to love. When you attain this real freedom, you really become the children of the Kingdom of Heaven."
>
> —Michio Kushi
> *The Spiral of Life*

Winter—Breakfast Suggestions

I	1.	Miso Soup with Wakame, Burdock, and Leeks
	2.	Brown Rice with Whole Wheat Berries
	3.	Gomashio with Kombu
	4.	Quick-boiled Watercress
	5.	Burdock Root Tea
II	1.	Miso Soup with Wakame, Sweet Rice Dumplings, and Scallions
	2.	Pressure-cooked Brown Rice
	3.	Shoyu-Kombu
	4.	Country-style Boiled Daikon (Furofuki Daikon)
	5.	Kombu Tea
III	1.	Miso Soup with Wakame, Carrots, and Kale
	2.	Kasha with Onions
	3.	Cabbage with Sauerkraut
	4.	Roasted Nori
	5.	Bancha Twig Tea
IV	1.	Miso Soup with Wakame, Mochi, and Scallions
	2.	Fried Brown Rice with Onions, Tempeh, and Scallions
	3.	Savoy Cabbage
	4.	Roasted Nori
	5.	Bancha Twig Tea
V	1.	Miso Soup with Kombu, Shiitake, and Daikon
	2.	Brown Rice Vegetable Stew (Ojiya)
	3.	Collard Green Nori Rolls
	4.	Pickle
	5.	Grain Coffee

Winter—Lunch Suggestions

I	1. Rice Triangles (Omusubi) 2. Hijiki with Sesame Seeds 3. Turnips in Miso Sauce 4. Carrots with Leeks 5. Pickle
II	1. Kasha 2. Gomashio 3. Vegetable Noodle Casserole 4. Romaine Lettuce and Watercress Salad 5. Pickled Turnips
III	1. Baked Barley Rice Casserole 2. Arame with Lotus Root 3. Baked Turnips 4. Broccoli 5. Pickle
IV	1. Brown Rice 2. Nori Condiment with Ginger 3. Root Stew with Jinenjo 4. Boiled Cabbage with Radish Leaves 5. Radish Pickle
V	1. Millet Stew 2. Kinpira with Lotus Root 3. Parsnips with Sesame Seeds 4. Kale with Tempeh 5. Pickle

Thoughts on Breakfast and Lunch

To maintain strong blood, good digestion, stamina, and endurance, it is advisable to drink miso soup at least once everyday. I prefer to have miso soup in the morning for breakfast. This way, the protein can be utilized by the body all day. Whether you have miso soup in the morning or evening is up to you. You can even alternate the soup between breakfast and dinner. It is less convenient to have soup for lunch if you have to carry it.

I have suggested hearty breakfasts for most seasons except summer. It is better to eat more lightly in the hot weather. For those people who generally eat a lighter breakfast, miso soup and grain cereal is enough. Some people may want to skip breakfast altogether, finding they have more energy as a result. This is an excellent practice if you thrive on it.

I generally recommend cooking two meals a day, breakfast and dinner. This way, lunch can be taken from the previous night's meal. This not only cuts time, but makes it easy to pack a lunch the night before for those who have to take it to work or school.

Arrange the food attractively, filling the container with one-half to two-thirds grain garnished with a condiment. Umeboshi is famous for keeping the grain fresh and tasty. Arrange several side dishes, in portions of one to two tablespoons each, in the remaining space. It is better not to pack beans, as they tend to spoil. Do not forget to tuck a pickle in the corner.

Children's rice can be decorated with their name, a flower, or a smiling face, using a variety of land and sea vegetables. Use your imagination. I call this "lunch box art.

Sometimes, the rice and vegetables can be stuffed into whole wheat pita bread and carried as a sandwich. They can be rolled in nori to make Norimaki Sushi. Or the rice can be firmly formed into rice balls or triangles, stuffed with vegetable surprises, and wrapped with nori. These types of lunches are easy to carry and there is no container to bring home.

Hot tea can be carried in a glass-lined thermos or tea bags of bancha or mugicha, or instant grain coffee, can be carried lightly and prepared with naturally boiled wate (not electric heated or microwaved).

This way, each lunch time is a treat.

Part 3

Special Foods

All life is ultimately dependent on the seed. If we eat predominantly only parts of the whole, in the form of fruits, leaves, grasses, barks, roots, polished grains, dairy or other parts of animals; or any extracted and concentrated foods, such as tofu, tempeh, wheat gluten, vitamins and minerals, sugar or other sweeteners; or if we eat these things second hand through eating animals which eat these foods first; then we ourselves are only partial in development. This is why we experience some kind of deficiency or hidden hunger. Hidden hunger gives rise to the further eating of other unbalanced foods, in an effort to complete us.

In truth, we have all we need to be complete already within us. Once we have established our independent wholeness (health), harmony, and happiness, then we can share it with others in abundant joy. Anything less than this leads to some kind of addictive eating and behavior.

Teachers can help us find the way, but the way is there for us to master and make our own. In truth, we are the Way; the Way is within us. To fully comprehend this, we must clear our channels of reception and perception, in order to achieve a state of direct experience, without having to think about it too much. Conceptualization often gets in the way and obscures our insight.

In order to help us to cleanse, strengthen, and balance our system, transitional foods and special foods and applications are useful. Various side dishes, as have been presented in the Menus, work in harmony, as extensions of grain, to balance the various parts of the body.

Together with side dishes, there are a variety of condiments, pickles, and preparations—such as wheat gluten, tofu, tempeh, natto, and mochi, among others, to supplement our daily food. (Since tofu, tempeh, natto, and mochi are readily available in macrobiotic and health food stores, their methods of preparation are not presented here.) A section on Light Desserts is included to satisfy occasional cravings for dessert, while not jeopardizing the healing process.

Sections on Teas, Internal Remedies, and External Remedies round out, though do not exhaust, the section on Special Foods.

Condiments

> A Chinese cookbook for self-development teaches:
> "Food, when seen as medicine for preserving life, has no deleterious side effects . . . . Therefore, if one falls sick, one should first examine one's diet, then choose well, chew carefully, and give thanks. In this way, the curative powers of nature, with which mankind is blessed, are given full rein to act, and nearly all diseases are conquered."
>
> Saei Yoneda
> —*Good Food from a Japanese Temple*

Condiments play unique and varied roles in macrobiotic cuisine. Their great variety add color, flavor, and zest to foods. They aid in the digestion of grains through their contribution of alkaline elements, which balance the inherent acidity of most grains. They add an important source of amino acids, in the form of seeds, nuts, beans, sea vegetables, miso, and tamari soy sauce, which, together with whole grains, make complete proteins. Umeboshi, the salt-pickled plum of innumerable virtues, has the ability to preserve the grain for several days, making it ideal for work, travel, or camping.

There are condiments for all kinds of physical and emotional conditions, as well as condiments appropriate for summer or winter, wet weather or dry, elders, children, thinkers or laborers.

Condiments have the unique ability to turn the energy of the grain toward a specific direction, to serve a specific purpose in the body. For instance, if we are feeling tired and low, a condiment such as Umeboshi with Scallions can revive our energy and enthusiasm. If we are feeling tense and agitated, a condiment such as Nori with Shiitake, seasoned lightly with tamari soy sauce, can relax us.

As our body becomes clean and balanced, condiments and pickles can begin to substitute for the variety of side dishes taken up to that point. They can supply the particular stimulation needed to adjust the balance of the body. However, it may take some time before this stage is achieved.

Some kind of condiment can be taken with the grains everyday. They can be used, one by one, in small amounts. It is best not to mix them all together or to use tamari soy sauce directly on grain, unless it is something like vegetable fried rice, in which case the oil and vegetables balance the tamari soy sauce. Use the condiments with sensitivity toward their effect on the body, as well as their appropriateness to the season. In this way, whole grains become an unending source of surprise and delight.

1. Gomashio

15 Tbsps. brown sesame seeds
1 Tbsp. sea salt

Gomashio has been used for centuries to aid the digestion of rice and other grains. Since grain generally tends to be acid, it needs to be cooked with, and complemented by, a small amount of salt. Sesame seeds together with whole grain make a complete protein.

The combining of sesame seeds with sea salt is based on the ancient wisdom of yin and yang, sesame seeds being yin and sea salt being yang. To arrive at the proper proportion between the two depends on an understanding of one's physical and mental condition. Generally speaking, children from the ages of 1 to 5 can take gomashio in a 20 to 1 ratio. Older people from the age of 60 or 65 can take the same proportion. If someone is too yang from a previously heavy meat or salt diet, this 20 to 1 proportion is also appropriate. Such a person should be careful not to take too much in quantity at one serving. A greater than 20: 1 proportion may be too weak and add too much oil to the diet.

Gomashio can be used on grains year round, changing the proportions to suit the season, weather, and our condition. Stronger gomashio is suitable for cold climate and weather, and for weak, yin adults. Milder gomashio is suitable for hot climate and weather, for children and elders, and for more yang adults.

In very cold climates or seasons, a proportion of between 8 and 12 to 1, according to the person's condition, is appropriate. In hot climates or seasons, 14 or 15 to 1 is appropriate, according to the person's condition. It is important to keep in mind the basic ratio of 7 parts potassium to 1 part sodium when making any modification to suit the particular circumstances at hand. Serving: ½ to 1 teaspoon on grain.

Method: After measuring out the seeds carefully, pick through them to remove any stones, twigs, or other foreign matter that does not belong. It is not easy to wash seeds in a bowl of water since they generally all float. It is much more effective to wash them in a fine-mesh strainer under cold, running water to allow any sand to wash out. The bottom of the strainer should be patted with a cloth or sponge repeatedly until the excess water is removed. Then the strainer should be set to one side, resting on a cloth or a sponge to allow any remaining moisture to drain calmly without being disturbed. During this time the salt can be measured and roasted. When measuring the salt, the spoon should be leveled without packing the salt down too firmly. The salt should be roasted first since it is a Metal and will hold the heat. Use a medium-high flame.

Roast the salt in a cast-iron skillet. The thick bottom prevents salt or seeds from scorching as easily as in a thin stainless steel pot or pan. A bamboo paddle should be held in the hand firmly, not loosely, so as to become a part of the hand itself. Move the salt back and forth in a grid-like pattern in order to insure even heating. The purpose of roasting the salt is to eliminate excess yin elements gathered from the air during storage, and to prepare the yang salt to combine with the yin elements of the sesame seeds. The salt should be roasted lightly until it is crystalline. The salt should not become yellow or brown. When the salt is done, put it into the suribachi and grind it into powder. There it can await reception of the seeds.

Now roast the seeds. Again hold the bamboo paddle firmly in the hand and move the seeds back and forth in a grid-like pattern to insure even roasting. In the beginning, while the seeds are wet, the fire can be moderately high. As the seeds begin to dry and the pan retains heat, the fire can be reduced to medium. As the seeds continue to roast and begin to pop, it is important to move the paddle faster and to lower the flame. At this point, a characteristic fragrance will begin to arise. This only indicates that the seeds are beginning to become done, but in fact are not yet done. However, it is important to pay close attention at this time as there is a fine line between raw and scorched seeds. The crucial test is in crushing the seeds between the fourth (weakest) finger and the thumb. If the seeds crush easily, they are done. Put the crushed seeds into the mouth, biting them with the front teeth. While exhaling through the nose, cause air to rise from the lungs into the mouth and over the seeds. In this way you can discern the subtle fragrance of the seeds and control the degree to which they are cooked. The color should remain golden.

When done, pour the seeds over the sea salt in the suribachi. The seeds must be ground while warm in order to facilitate the spread of oil over each grain of salt. This makes well-harmonized gomashio and prevents thirst. Whether you are right-handed or left-handed, grind in a direction toward the body so as to create fusion between the ingredients, i.e., you are channeling energy toward the inside. (When you wish to disperse ingredients, it is more effective to stir toward the outside.) Continue grinding until the seeds are 80 percent ground.

Make sure your shoulders are low and relaxed and your breathing is even and deep. The quality of energy channeled into the food affects the healing quality of the food as well as the taste.

Poorly made gomashio often looks too dark or too pasty, or tastes scorched or raw. Making gomashio well is an exercise in concentration, one-mindedness, centered breathing, relaxation, and harmony, both inwardly and outwardly.

Allow the gomashio to cool before storing. The best container for storage is a ceramic crock or ceramic cheese container with a tight-fitting lid. Well-made gomashio should last up to 1 month. If the taste changes before then, quickly roast the gomashio again and grind the remaining 20 percent of the seeds. The taste should become refreshed. Store in a cool place.

Sesame seeds have been used in the West since Babylonian times to promote sexual virility among men, beauty among women, strength among soldiers, and clarity of mind. These virtues have also been known and enjoyed for thousands of years in the East.

A) Gomashio with Kombu

14–15 Tbsps. brown sesame seeds
2 tsps.—1 Tbsp. sea salt
1 4″–6″ strip kombu

Wash seeds in a fine mesh strainer. Pat dry and drain. Wipe kombu clean and roast in a dry cast-iron skillet slowly, until it becomes brittle and easily crumbles. Be careful not to burn it. Grind into powder in a suribachi, enough to make 1 tablespoon. Roast salt in the skillet several minutes, stirring constantly with a bamboo paddle. Grind into a powder in the suribachi with the kombu. Roast the sesame seeds until dry and done. Grind while still warm together with salt and kombu in the suribachi. Follow detailed instructions in recipe for Gomashio. See also Menus VI and XXXII.

B) Gomashio with Wakame

14 Tbsps. brown sesame seeds
2 6″ strips wakame
1 scant Tbsp. sea salt

Follow instructions for Gomashio with Kombu. See Menus XXIX and XXXVI.

2. Nori Condiment (Nori Tsukudani)

1 package nori
Tamari soy sauce
2 cups water
1/2 tsp. ginger

If wild nori is used, wash it very well. Cut or break nori into small pieces. Cover with water and cook 30 to 60 minutes until pasty. Add tamari lightly to taste and cook several more minutes. Nori condiment is useful for dissolving animal fats in the body. You may add a little grated ginger for more yang conditions or for hard tumors. No ginger should be added for more yin conditions.

Nori condiment can be used on grain year round. The tamari flavor can be lighter in warm climate and weather, and stronger in cold climate and weather. Cool and store in a glass jar in the refrigerator. Serve 1/2 teaspoon per serving on grain.

3. Scallion Miso Condiment

1 bunch scallions
Mugi miso, 1/4 amount of minced scallions
2 tsps. sesame oil
Water

Mince scallions finely, including roots. Sauté in sesame oil on medium flame 1 to 2 minutes until bright green. Add 1/4 inch of water. Cover and steam several minutes. Meanwhile, dilute miso in a little water to make a thick cream. Add miso to scallions, mix well, and cook together several minutes, stirring constantly until well-married and consistency holds together. You may use onion instead of scallion.

Scallion Miso Condiment can be used on grain year round, using milder miso in warm climate and weather and stronger miso in cold climate and weather. While cleansing and strengthening the blood, this condiment tends to warm the body. This condiment is very good for cleansing the intestines, especially in the case of rheumatism, diverticulosis, parasites, and blood disease. See also Menu XXXVIII. Serving: 1/2 teaspoon.

4. Umeboshi Juice Dressing

5 umeboshi, pits removed
2 cups water

Boil umeboshi in 2 cups of water down to 1 cup. Mash umeboshi into the water. Pour over and mix into salad. Serve in a glass bowl. Store any left-over dressing in a jar in the refrigerator for later use.

Umeboshi Juice Dressing can be used on vegetables year round, though it is especially appropriate in spring and summer on boiled salads to cleanse the liver and refresh the body. Umeboshi in general is a very good anti-bacterial. It is useful in counteracting gastrointestinal acidity from poorly digested grains or beans, as well as problems resulting from the intake of excessive summer fruits or alcohol.

5. Carrot Top Miso

1 bunch carrot tops
Barley miso (mugi miso)

Remove any bad parts from the carrot tops. Wash well and pat dry. Mince. Water-sauté in 1/4 inch of boiling water for 1 minute. Cover and steam several minutes, until the stems are tender. Miso should equal 1/4 the volume of carrot tops. Dilute it in a little cold water. Add to the carrot tops, mixing well, and cook together about 5 minutes, stirring two to three times. Be careful not to burn it.

Carrot Top Miso can be used on grain year round, but is especially appropriate in the autumn and winter. Most people throw away carrot leaves. However, carrot is no more complete without its top than we are without our head. Carrot leaves are almost as high in nutritional value as carrot roots, especially in vitamins A and C. Serve 1/2 teaspoon per serving on Okayu (Soft Rice) or any grain.

6. Miso Condiment

Hatcho miso, 1/4 the amount of carrot tops
1 bunch carrot tops
1″ piece fresh ginger
1 Tbsp. sesame oil
3 Tbsps. shaved kombu (oboro kombu)

Wash, dry, and mince carrot tops. Mince ginger. Oil-sauté carrot tops several minutes. Add 1/2 inch of water and bring to a boil. Lower fire and add kombu.

Cover and cook several minutes or until carrot stems are tender. Put miso in a bowl, pour cooking liquid into miso, and dilute. Pour mixture back into pot and add ginger. Mix well and cook several minutes more until well-married. See also Menu XXXIV.

Miso Condiment can be used on grain year round, but is especially appropriate in the autumn and winter. Many different varieties of Miso Condiment can be prepared by varying the vegetable or vegetables used according to season. In spring and summer, barley miso can be substituted for Hatcho miso, and grated lemon or orange rind can be substituted for ginger. Serving: 1/2 teaspoon on grain.

7. Kombu Condiment (Shoyu-Kombu)

1 10″×4″ strip kombu
1/2 cup water
1/2 cup tamari soy sauce

Over the sink, brush the kombu with your fingers, or wipe with a damp cloth, to remove any sand. Soak and cut the kombu into 1/2-inch squares. Mix together 1/2 cup water and 1/2 cup tamari. Add to the kombu in an enamel saucepan and soak 1 to 2 hours. Then bring to a boil and simmer gently, partially covered, until dry. Spread the kombu out individually on a plate to dry. This may take 1 to 2 days. Store in a crock or air-tight container. Do not store in plastic. See also Menu LX.

Kombu Condiment can be used with grain year round. It can be prepared more strongly with tamari for winter or cold weather and for yin people, or more mildly for summer, warm weather and more yang people. It has the tendency to strengthen the heart and blood vessels, which are often weakened by summer indulgences in cold beverages, fruit juices, fruits, and ice cream. Serving: one to two pieces, two to three times per week.

8. Nekombu

Nekombu is the root or "stronghold" of the kombu frond. It is very yang and dense with minerals. Pressure-cook 1/2 to 1 package for 1 hour. Then prepare it in the same way as Shoyu-Kombu.

Nekombu can be used with grain primarily in the winter. It can also be included in root stews and bean stews, in which case it does not need to be cooked with tamari soy sauce first. As a condiment, serve one piece with grain.

9. Carrot and Daikon Greens Condiment

1 bunch daikon greens
1 bunch carrot greens
Tamari soy sauce
1 Tbsp. roasted sesame seeds

Wash, dry and mince carrot and daikon greens. Water-sauté daikon greens in 1/4 inch of boiling salted water until bright green. Add carrot tops, cover, and steam until tender. Add tamari to taste, a little on the strong side. Cook until dry. Add roasted sesame seeds.

Carrot and Daikon Greens Condiment can be used with grain year round. As the vegetables change with the season, other combinations can be used. Following the same method, for example, combinations can include carrot and carrot tops, daikon and daikon tops, parsnip and parsnip tops, burdock and scallions, onion and scallions, and dandelion root with its greens. Serving: 1/2 to 1 teaspoon on grain.

10. Wakame/Kombu Powder (A)

10″ strip wakame or kombu

Break the sea vegetable into small pieces and dry-roast in a cast-iron skillet on a medium-small fire until easily crumbled, about 15 minutes. Grind into powder in a suribachi. Store in a covered ceramic dish or crock. Serve 1/4 to 1/2 teaspoon on grain or sprinkle into vegetables while cooking. This condiment can be used as a mineral supplement.

11. Wakame/Kombu Powder (B)

Wash wakame or kombu to remove sand and excess salt. Hang on line until dry. Lay kombu or wakame flat on a stainless steel or enamel tray. It can be stacked up to 6 inches high. Bake in a 250°F. oven for 2 to 3 minutes. Turn off the fire and let sit. Repeat every hour until the sea vegetable is crispy and crumbly, about 2 to 3 hours. Or you can leave the oven on for 2 to 3 hours at the lowest setting. Watch that it does not burn.

The best traditional way of baking sea vegetables is in an unglazed ceramic pot. The cover is sealed with dough. Bake the whole pot in a fireplace, covering it with hot coals and ashes. The sea vegetable will carbonize.

In either case, grind the sea vegetable to powder in a suribachi. It can be used plain or ground with roasted sesame seeds. Instead of grinding into powder, the sea vegetable can be broken into small pieces and carried as a travel snack.

Wakame Powder and Kombu Powder can be used year round as a mineral supplement on grain, or added to vegetable dishes or soups. As a condiment, serve 1/4 to 1/2 teaspoon on grain.

12. Umeboshi with Scallion or Onion

Mash eight large umeboshi and mix with one raw, minced onion or one bunch raw, minced scallions. If the onion or scallion tastes is too harsh, put it into a cotton bag and squeeze it under cold, running water, then mix it with the mashed umeboshi.

Umeboshi with Scallion or Onion can be used on grain year round. While the taste of this combination may appear to be strong, it is actually quite delicious with brown rice. It serves to purify the blood and to center and focus the energy. This combination is also very effective in cleaning the intestines of harmful bacteria and parasites. Serving: 1/2 teaspoon on grain.

13. Grated Daikon

Grate 1 to 2 teaspoons of raw daikon and mound it attractively on the plate. Dot it lightly with tamari soy sauce. This is a good digestive aid for fried foods, seafood, mochi, or any heavy meal. The daikon should be placed next to the particular food it is complementing. If it is used as a general "digestif," it can be placed at the top of the plate to be eaten at the end of the meal. It is sometimes accompanied by an equal amount of raw, grated carrot. This adds a yang balance to the yin daikon.

Grated daikon can be used year round. This may not be necessary for people who are too thin, whose condition is yin, or whose bowels are loose. On the other hand, it is effective in dissolving excess animal protein and fat, and is helpful in achieving weight loss. In this case, serve 1 tablespoon, dotted lightly with tamari, at the end of the meal.

14. *Furikake*

Furikake comes from the general image of rain falling from the sky. As a condiment, it denotes the myriad variety of delightful and tasteful ingredients used to embellish grain. Combinations include: gomashio with kombu or wakame, nori, shiso leaves, shiso seeds, iriko (tiny dried sardines), sansho seeds (Japanese pepper seeds), red pepper, ao-nori (green river nori), and roasted crushed peanuts with nori. There are many other varieties. Each has its own specific taste as well as effect on the body.

Furikake can be used year round, selecting ingredients in harmony with the season. Serving: 1/2 to 1 teaspoon on grain.

Example 1: Shiso Leaves with Sesame Seeds
Use shiso leaves taken from pickled umeboshi. Dry and crush them in a suribachi. Use them in the same proportion as salt in making gomashio.

Example 2: Shiso Seeds with Ginger
Pickle shiso seeds with sea salt and a little minced ginger for 2 to 3 weeks. This can be sprinkled over rice, or used in making rice balls (Omusubi) or added to miso condiments. See directions for Salt-pressed Pickles in Pickle Section.

15. Onion Butter

Finely mince at least 6 onions. Sauté in 1/4 inch of boiling salted water or 1 tablespoon sesame oil. Add enough water to cover the vegetables and cook on a low fire for 2 to 3 hours. You may need to use a metal flame tamer. Cook until the onion becomes a sweet brown paste. Add 1/4 to 1/2 teaspoon sea salt. Stir and cook another 15 minutes. Be careful not to scorch the bottom. This condiment is good for strengthening the intestines and reproductive organs.

Onion Butter can be used mainly in the autumn and winter. Onion Butter may not be appropriate for young children or healthy teenagers as it may have aphrodisiac effects. Serving: 1/2 to 1 teaspoon on grain or bread.

16. Scallions

Wash, dry, and mince a bunch of scallions. Put into a cotton bag and squeeze under cold, running water to remove excess chlorophyll and modify the pungent taste. This can be sprinkled over grain, salad, soup, or even used as a spread on bread or crackers. It is very refreshing for summer. Scallions are antiseptic and help to kill parasites and harmful bacteria as well as to neutralize the toxins excreted by those parasites or bacteria.

Scallions can be used year round. They may be used raw as garnish for healthy or yang people, but should be slightly cooked for more yin people. Serving: 1 teaspoon

17. Natto

3 cups dried soybeans
10 cups water
6 1-pint Chinese white paper containers

Wash and soak soybeans overnight. Next day, drain soybeans and put into a deep pot. Add fresh water to cover beans by 1 1/2 inch. With cover ajar, bring to a boil, lower fire, and simmer 30 minutes. Skim off foam and loose skins, cover, and simmer another 4 to 5 hours, until beans are tender. Do not stir or the beans will break and stick to the bottom of the pot. Check tenderness by crushing one bean between the thumb and fourth finger.

Strain the beans, reserving the liquid for soup stock or other cooking. Place 1 cup of hot beans in each container, close the covers and stack them in a large double brown paper bag. Close the bag and secure it firmly with string. Place it in the oven, using only the heat of the pilot light. The heat should be maintained between 98° to 104°F. Leave the soybeans in the oven to ferment for 3 nights. After the second night, rotate the stacking order of the containers to insure even heating and fermentation.

After the third night, remove the containers and let the natto cool. If the oven or weather are too warm and the beans become too fermented, an ammonia smell may develop. In this case, spread the beans out and let dry in a cool place until the strong ammonia odor evaporates, leaving a pleasant smell.

Fermented soybeans have a dark rich color with a stringy texture holding the whole beans together. This is natto. To store, refrigerate 1 week or freeze several months. To serve, mash natto lightly in a suribachi, season with tamari soy sauce, and garnish with raw minced scallions or red or white radish leaves. Serve 1 teaspoon on rice. Natto, together with brown rice, provides complete protein and satisfies cravings for animal food and sometimes sugar.

Natto can be used year round, but is most appropriate in the spring. The short fermentation period and relative lack of salt is a yin preparation, compared with miso, whose fermentation period is from 1 to 3 years, with greater use of salt. The energy of natto is more upward, while the energy of miso is more downward.
Serving: 1 or 2 tablespoons on grain.

18. Soft Tekka Miso (Shigure Miso)

2 lbs. burdock roots
1 lb. carrots
4 oz. fresh ginger root
1 cup soybeans
1/2 lb. dried lotus root
2 cups sesame oil
2 lbs. Hatcho miso (or barley or rice miso)

Mince burdock, carrots, and unpeeled ginger very finely into powder. Set each one aside separately. Soak soybeans in boiling water to cover, about 1 hour. As beans soak up water, add hot water to keep them covered. Crush lotus root into powder in the suribachi.

In a cast-iron skillet or deep, heavy enamel pot, boil oil. Add soybeans and cook, stirring constantly, for 10 to 15 minutes on a medium-high flame. Cool one soybean to taste. It is done when crisp on the outside and soft on the inside. Add burdock. Stir and cook 10 minutes. Add carrot, cook, and stir continuously for 10 minutes. Add extra oil if necessary, up to 1/2 cup. Add lotus root powder. Cook and stir constantly for 10 minutes. Add ginger. Mix in and cook another 10 minutes. Now add miso and stop the fire. Mix in thoroughly. At this point you may put the whole mixture in the oven on the lowest setting. Be very careful not to overheat the miso. Stir every hour. Make a well in the center of the tekka to collect excess oil. Do not let it burn.

This tekka is sweet and rich. Together with rice or other grain, it provides complete protein.

Soft Tekka Miso can be used primarily in the winter or cold climate and by more yin people. It has the tendency to warm the body. It is not advisable for children, as it may be too yang for them. This delicious Tekka came down to me from Mr. Muramoto, author of *Healing Ourselves*. It should be stored in a glass container or ceramic crock. Serving: 1/2 teaspoon on grain.

19. Tekka Miso

6 burdock roots
lotus root equal to 2/3 of burdock
carrot equal to 1/2 of burdock
4 cups sesame oil
5 cups Hatcho miso
6 Tbsps. finely minced ginger

Wash and dry vegetables. Mince them finely into powder. In hot oil sauté burdock, lotus root, and carrot about 10 minutes each, adding one to the other. Add miso and mix in well. Then add ginger dispersing it evenly throughout the mixture. Continue sautéing and stirring constantly for 10 to 12 hours. Be very careful not to let the Tekka Miso burn.

Tekka Miso can be used primarily in the winter or cold climate. This preparation is a very yang medicine. It strengthens the blood and the body and is excellent for yin people. It is not advisable for healthy children, as it may be too yang for them. Serving: 1/4 teaspoon on grain.

20. Oil Miso (Abura Miso)

3 Tbsps. miso (Hatcho miso is best)
1 Tbsp. sesame oil

Sauté miso in oil gently until well mixed. This condiment may be used as is or may be embellished with any one of a variety of ingredients such as: minced scallion, red pepper, lemon rind, ginger, Japanese horseradish (wasabi) or American horseradish. In this case, sauté the vegetable several minutes before adding miso. In the case of lemon rind or ginger, add after miso and cook together several minutes.

Oil Miso can be used primarily in the winter or cold climate and by more yin people. It is not advisable for children, as it may be too yang for them. Serving: 1/4 to 1/2 teaspoon on grain.

Pickles 

Pickles represent one of the most ancient ways of preserving vegetables after the harvest, tiding people over the long winter months until fresh vegetables become available again in the spring. Almost every country has its special recipes for pickles, handed down generation after generation within a household, family, or community.

Pickling has long been a significant technique for adapting to environmental and seasonal changes. Grain- and vegetable-eating cultures have traditionally used salt-based pickles to counteract the acidity of grain. Meat-based cultures have applied sugar, wine, and vinegar to pickle, ferment and marinate animal and vegetable foods, both to preserve them as well as to break down the proteins and kill inherent toxins. The fermenting and marinating of animal proteins tends to vegetalize them, making them more suitable for human consumption.

In cold countries like Russia, Germany, and the Balkan and Slavic countries, sauerkraut is famous; in the United States, dill pickles and various relishes are popular accompaniments to meats; in Japan, takuan, salt, bran, and miso types of pickles have traditionally enhanced the rice; in Korea, kim chee continues to be a hot and spicy addition to meat and vegetable meals. Most meat-eaters also drink fermented beverages, such as wines and beers, which traditionally provided further digestive enzymes. This is no longer the case since the advent of pasteurization.

Among nomadic herders and dairy eaters, fermented milk products, such as buttermilk, kefir, yogurt, and various cheeses have been prepared, not only for preservation, but also to cultivate the growth of lactobacillus, used to promote digestive enzymes and bacteria. However, this type of milk-based food tends to be acidic and mucus-forming.

Among agriculturally stable grain- and vegetable-eaters, miso, soy sauce, natto, and tempeh were cultured in order to promote the growth of digestive enzymes and bacteria. This type of salted and fermented vegetable-based food tends to be alkaline and mucus dissolving.

All pickles are used to aid digestion. They all stimulate the flow of saliva, the first fermenting and digesting element. Some are effective in promoting the metabolism of animal proteins and fats. Some promote the assimilation of grains and beans. Others are used to stimulate strong peristaltic motion in the stomach and intestines, especially after their activity has been slowed down by excessive eating and drinking.

There must be hundreds of different kinds of pickles, as well as methods for their preparation. Some may take only a few minutes to prepare. Others may take days, weeks, months, or even years.

Pickling is accomplished macrobiotically through the use of salt, pressure, and time in varying proportions. Miso, soy sauce, grain vinegars, and grain brans are themselves used to pickle other foods.

Any vegetable may be pickled, as well as grains, beans, fruits, and nuts. The more yin vegetables are most appropriately prepared in more yang pickling mediums, such as salt or miso, while the more yang vegetables are most appropriately prepared in more yin pickling mediums, such as grain vinegar, and/or tamari soy sauce.

Pickling can be done year round. In the summer, the treasures of excess produce can be preserved for the more lean months of winter. Miso and bran pickling, which are slower and take a longer time, are best begun in autumn, after the first cold spell and before the Winter Solstice. After the Winter Solstice, the essence of the vegetables changes radically, the yin rising energy is exhausted and the downward yang energy is strongly concentrated. It is best to begin the pickling when the moon is waxing, before it reaches the peak of fullness.

It is essential to use the best ingredients and appropriate utensils for pickling. Balanced sea salt and pure deep-well or spring water are critical. All utensils, such as spoons, chopsticks, and covers should be of hardwood. The best containers are wooden tubs, kegs, or barrels that allow the free flow of air, moisture, and energy. Unglazed clay and earthenware crocks are also acceptable and are preferred over porcelain and glass containers. Plastic and metal containers and utensils are to be avoided.

Non-porous stones of various weights are useful for different kinds of pickles. Stones should be kept clean and cared for in the same way as other cooking utensils. Pots or gallon jugs of water can also be used as weights, adjusting the pressure on the pickles by changing the volume of water.

If weights are used, it is necessary to cover the pickles directly with a wooden lid that fits inside the crock or tub. The weights are then placed on this lid. Cover the whole thing with clean, unbleached muslin cloth to keep the dust out. Store the pickles in a cool, dry place. Do not store near fresh vegetables or near the cooking area or in any other area where airborn spores may be active, as they may alter the fermentation process.

The following are a small sampling of a variety of pickles to tempt your palate and enhance your meals. They are arranged in order of length of preparation time. The quicker pickles are appropriate for summer, warmer climates, and more yang physical conditions. The longer pickles are appropriate for winter, colder climates, and more yin physical conditions.

Serve pickles at the end of meals, in small quantities, from one to several pieces or from a teaspoon to a tablespoon. Enjoy.

1. Twenty-four Hour Pickles (Asa-zuke) (*2–24 hours*)

Cut turnip or daikon in thin half-moons or squares. Coarsely chop leaves. Salt-press the leaves first and squeeze out the excess liquid. Cut 1 carrot julienne style. Cut 1 teaspoon of lemon peel julienne style. Mix all together with enough salt for pickling, 1 to 2 teaspoons, depending on volume of vegetables. Taste to check the necessary amount of salt. Press 2 to 24 hours. See also Menus XVI, XVII, XXV, XXXII, XXXIX.

2. Salt-Pressed Pickles (Achara-zuke) (*1–3 days*)

This pressed salad may be varied with different combinations of vegetables. One example: minced onion, cabbage cut in 1-inch squares, romaine lettuce cut in 1/2-inch strips, thin cucumber circles, carrots cut in thin half-diagonals, watercress cut in 1/2-inch pieces. Mix with 1 to 2 teaspoons of sea salt. It should be a little too salty to the taste. Press 1 to 3 days. See also Menus XII, XXXV, XLVII, LVII.

3. Brine Pickles (*3 days*)

A variety of seasonal vegetables may be used. It is best to select vegetables whose flavors are harmonious with each other. You may use cauliflowerettes, minced onion, carrot sticks, turnip sticks, and garlic. Season with salt alone, or salt together with 2 tablespoons umeboshi juice. Place all the vegetables in a jar and pour salted boiling water over them. The salt water taste should be on the strong side. Or use 1 part water to 1/4 part tamari soy sauce. This pickle is ready in 3 days. See also Menus III, XXX.

4. Umeboshi Pickles (*3–5 days*)

Soak 8 umeboshi in 2 quarts of water in a 1-gallon jar for 3 hours, or until the water becomes pink. Add washed and dried vegetables: daikon, carrot, onion, cauliflower, cucumber, sliced ginger, or other appropriate vegetables. Cover with a cotton cloth and keep 3 to 5 days in a cool place.

5. Rice Bran Pickles (Nuka-zuke) (*2 days–1 week–1 month*)

This pickle is usually made in the spring and summer. You can use plain rice bran or seasoned rice bran (*nuka-no-moto*). Seasoned rice bran may include ground soybeans, powdered sea vegetable, sea salt, powdered mustard, and powdered or crushed red chili peppers. These seasonings act as a preservative. If plain rice bran is used, the mixture must be mixed daily. Toast 10 cups of rice bran in a cast-iron skillet over low heat, stirring constantly about 10 minutes or until fragrant. Put rice bran into a large bowl to cool. Meanwhile, boil 3 cups of water, add 1 1/2 cups of sea salt, and continue boiling until salt is dissolved, about 2 to 3 minutes. Let water cool. Mix the water and the rice bran gradually to form a paste which can be placed in a pickling crock.

Prepare a variety of vegetables by washing, drying, and sometimes cutting them into appropriate pieces. You may use whole pickling cucumbers, cabbage leaves, jicama sticks, carrot sticks, cauliflower flowerettes, daikon, onion, and seasonal vegetables. Push these vegetables down into the rice-bran mixture pressing the rice bran firmly down around them. Keep the vegetables well covered with bran. Be sure to mix daily if unseasoned bran is used. If liquid rises, either drain it out or absorb it with more roasted bran.

The cucumber pickles and other yin vegetables can be used in 1 day. Turnips and cabbage may be used after 2 days. Roots take longer, from 1 week to several months. When new vegetables are added, always add more salt. This mixture may be used continuously for years. The older it gets, the better it is. To serve, rinse the vegetables in cold water, drain them, and cut either thinly or in a variety of interesting shapes. Only one to three pieces of pickle are sufficient per meal. These pickles promote lactic acid bacteria, which is essential to the digestive process and promotes the assimilation of our food. There are two variations for making rice bran pickles:

A) 5 lbs. bran, 1 lb. salt, water, no pressure

B) 5 lbs. bran, 5 lbs. salt, no water, 5 lbs. pressure

See also Menu XXXIII.

6. Chinese Cabbage Pickles (Hakusai-zuke) (*10 days*)

Cut the cabbage in quarters. Wash and drain it in a cool dark place for 1 day. Salt the bottom of the crock. Sprinkle the bottom of the crock with lemon peel cut julienne style. Layer the cabbage tightly, alternating with salt and lemon peel. Place the second layer of cabbage in a direction opposite to the first layer, forming a grid pattern. Repeat this layering until all cabbage is used. Cover with a wooden lid directly on top of the cabbage and place a heavy stone 5 to 10 pounds in weight according to the amount of cabbage used. Pickle 10 days or more. To serve, rinse in cold water, squeeze, and cut in a coarse julienne style.

7. Dill Pickles (*2 weeks–1 month*)

Wash and dry or quickly blanch 1 dozen or more pickling cucumbers. Boil 1 quart of water with 1 tablespoon sea salt and cool. Add 3 sprigs of fresh dill and a package of pickling spices, or enough salt to make the water salty to the taste. Spices are optional. Pickle 2 weeks to 1 month before eating. Not advisable for yin people.

8. Miso Pickle (Miso-zuke) (*1 month*)

Use whole vegetables or roots, cut to fit the container. Carrot and burdock should be blanched in boiling water 30 seconds and cooled. They may be pickled in miso 10 days and then eaten. Daikon should be dried 1 day, cut to size and pickled in miso 1 month before eating. Cucumber and ginger root should be salt-pressed 1 day, then pickled in miso 1 month before eating. All the vegetables should be rinsed and cut before serving.

9. Sake-kasu Pickle (Kasu-zuke) (*1 month*)

Any vegetable may be used such as cucumber, turnip, daikon. Wash, dry, and cut the vegetables. Mix with 1/10 their weight of salt and press 24 hours, until the liquid comes up. Remove from the brine and layer in another crock with saké-kasu, the dregs left from making sake. Pickle 1 month. No weight is necessary. The same kasu may be used with new salt-pressed vegetables.

10. Sauerkraut (*7 days–6 months*)

Sauerkraut is one of the most important fermented foods used throughout the ages and around the world. It promotes digestive bacteria and the assimilation of essential nutrients. It can be made with or without salt, and can take from 7 days to 6 months to ferment.

A) Salted Sauerkraut: Wash and dry cabbage. Cut in julienne style. Add salt alone or together with whole or ground caraway seeds.

B) Saltless Sauerkraut: Wash, dry and cut cabbage. Add 2 tablespoons caraway seeds, 2 tablespoons dill seeds, and 2 tablespoons celery seeds for each cabbage. These spice seeds help produce lactic acid. You may also add 1 tablespoon each of kelp powder and garlic powder. Layer the cabbage, other vegetables, and seasonings alternately and firmly in an earthenware crock or large glass jar. Do not use any metal, as the salt or acid will corrode it and the metal will interact chemically with the food. Leave 3 to 4 inches of space between the top of the vegetables and the top of the container. Place the large, uncut cabbage leaves over the top of the vegetables to reduce oxidation during fermentation. Weigh the vegetables down with a clean plate and stone and cover the top of the container with a clean, white cotton cloth.

Store in a warm room between 70° and 80°F. If the room is too cool, wrap the jar in a blanket. You may need to place the jar or crock in an enamel tray to catch any overflow of fermenting juices. Remove any scum that may appear. When done, store sauerkraut in a cool place, keeping the vegetables submerged in the brine. Be sure to keep the plate, stone, and covering cloth clean. Sauerkraut can be served as is, or used as a seasoning in lightly cooked vegetables, especially fresh cabbage. Do not cook too long as this will kill the enzymes so essential to health.

11. Daikon Pickle (Takuan) (*3 months–5 years or more*)

This pickle is usually made in the fall. Use organic daikon with leaves. For 5 pounds of daikon, use 5 pounds of nuka (rice or wheat bran) or brown rice flour and 2 to 2 1/2 pounds of sea salt. Wash and dry daikon and leaves. Hang the daikon to dry in a cool, dark place where there is a light breeze or wind. The daikon should be strung with a heavy string or light rope tied around the center of each daikon one above the other as if forming a ladder.

Dry the daikon in this manner for about 2 weeks, or until it can be easily bent in a full circle. Cut the leaves off the daikon. Mix salt and rice bran and sprinkle a thin layer on the bottom of a clean, dry crock. Line up the daikon in the crock on top of this layer without letting them touch. Sprinkle bran on top of and in-between each daikon. Continue layering the daikon and bran in this manner, but as tightly as possible. Place the dry leaves on the top and cover them with bran. On top of this, place a wooden cover and a weight equal in pounds to the daikon—in this case 5 pounds. You may use a pickling rock.

After 2 to 4 weeks water rises; if too much water comes up, strain it and use for seasoning in vegetable cooking or making light pickles. Let the daikon pickle 1 year. If you use less salt, however, 1 part salt to 3 parts rice bran, you can start using the pickles in 3 weeks to 3 months. The more salt you use the longer the pickling. For example, use 3 cups of salt for 3 year pickles, 5 to 10 cups of salt for 3 to 5 year pickles.

To serve any of these pickles, rinse and drain. If the pickles are too salty, soak in pure cold water for 5 to 10 minutes. Cut them in 1/8-inch thin slices and serve one to two slices per person. Takuan is very strong and should not be eaten in quantity. It is used as a digestive aid, as a B-vitamin supplement, and to strengthen the digestive system.

This is only a small sampling of the infinite variety of pickles that may be made. Pickles should be used everyday. Not only to promote digestion and assimilation of our food, but also to add zest and variety to any meal. Pickles are a constant source of surprise and delight.

Wheat Gluten

In macrobiotic cuisine, which is based primarily on grain and vegetables, there are many varied sources of protein. Combinations such as whole grains and beans, whole grains and seeds, whole grains and sea vegetables, whole grains and vegetables (especially leafy greens), and whole grains and nuts, make complete proteins. Also, whole grains and bean products, such as miso, tamari soy sauce, tofu, tempeh, natto, and yuba (dried soymilk skin) make complete proteins.

By comparison, there are only a few sources of protein in a meat-based diet, mostly animal in origin. These are mainly beef, pork, lamb, goat, poultry, eggs, fish and dairy. This type of protein, with the exception of white-meat fish, is not only high in saturated fats, but is also very acidic and mucus-forming. Therefore, it tends to make the body congested and hard. Stagnation occurs and organ and nervous sytem functions are impeded. The life-force energy is blocked and sickness is produced. Hardness and inflexibility are signs of physiological death.

Vegetable-based proteins are relatively less acidic and mucus-forming than animal-based proteins. They are also lower in saturated fats and cholesterol. They tend to create a more alkaline condition in the body. Therefore, the body is able to remain more flexible. In the macrobiotic approach, protein takes a subordinate role to carbohydrate and starch, which never harden the body. All these factors facilitate the smooth functioning of the organs and nervous system and the life-force energy can flow more readily. Flexibility and adaptability are signs of an active life.

Wheat gluten is one kind of vegetable protein. It is made from whole wheat. The process involves washing away the starch and the bran until only the protein remains. Because of this, wheat gluten is no longer a whole food, but is useful as a supplemental food. Due to its glutenous quality, it has a strengthening effect on the body. Its innate elasticity gives elasticity to the tissues and tends to strengthen the muscles, thus helping the body to maintain its youthful vigor.

Wheat gluten can be prepared in a number of ways, several of which are presented here. It can then be added to vegetable dishes, soups, and noodle dishes, in the same way that fish, chicken, or other animal protein would be used. It is best cut or torn into small bite-size pieces. Since wheat gluten is not a whole food, but is concentrated protein, it is not used as a main dish. Its virtue is in complementing side dishes, contributing a unique and distinctive taste and texture.

It is advisable to use any vegetable protein in a 1 : 7 ratio with other vegetables. The addition of daikon, radish, cabbage, green leafy vegetables, and, for more yang people, a bit of grated ginger, will help in the digestion of vegetable protein.

Those people who suffer gluten intolerance or some allergic reaction to wheat can avoid wheat gluten temporarily until their condition clears up. They can enjoy it occasionally thereafter, with no ill effect.

Wheat gluten is usually considered to be a treat and can be used 1 to 2 times per week, especially in the winter and cold climate or by weak people. In the summer or hot climate, it can be enjoyed several times per month. Please chew it well.

Wheat gluten may be made in a variety of ways. The following is a description of the basic simple production of raw protein from wheat, as well as a simple procedure for its long-time preservation.

A) Basic Gluten (Kofu)

10 cups red hard winter wheat flour alone or with 2 cups pastry flour or 2 cups unbleached white flour or 2 cups gluten flour
2 tsps. sea salt
Water

Mix flours and salt. Add water a little at a time, enough to make firm dough, mixing constantly by hand. Knead dough 20 minutes or longer to create gluten. It is important to knead firmly with the heel of the hand, putting strong energy into the dough with the weight of your body. When the dough is formed and elastic and the surface is clean and shiny, let it sit for 40 minutes or longer. Cover with a clean white cotton cloth.

Place the dough in a large bowl and cover with plenty of good water. Now wash the dough by stretching and pulling, pushing and pulling to separate the starch from the protein. In the beginning, plenty of starch will come out and the water will become milky. Pour this water off into a large container. Add fresh water and continue washing out the starch from the protein. Pour all the milky water into the other container. Add fresh water and repeat the process until the water becomes light. Save only the thick starchy water.

The heavy, starchy water can later be poured into shallow trays and sun-dried until the water evaporates and the solid starch is left. This starch can be broken up and stored in glass jars for use as a thickener in cooking. Make sure it is thoroughly dry.

The lighter water can be saved for soup stock, vegetable cooking, or bread, if it can be used within 1 or 2 days. Or you can wash your face in it to make a smooth complexion. Otherwise, it can be discarded.

After all the starch has been washed out of the dough, what is left is vegetable protein. To make a smoother product, it is useful to wash the protein or gluten under cold running water, stretching it repeatedly to expose and wash out the bran.

This is kofu. It can be used in a variety of ways. Various cooked grains or seasonings can be added to the gluten before further preparation in order to add texture and flavor. Small pieces can be torn off, cooked in a seasoned stock, and served alone, with vegetable accompaniment, or together in vegetable stews. Or the gluten may be molded in a rectangular Pyrex dish and refrigerated several days until it becomes more compacted by dehydration. It can then be sliced into 1/2-inch slabs and prepared as cutlets.

Note: Generally speaking, fresh winter wheat has enough gluten to make other added flour unnecessary. However, if the crop is weak or the wheat is yin or too old, strong gluten will not form as easily, necessitating the use of additional flour.

B) Wheat Gluten Stock

1 10″ strip kombu
5 shiitake mushrooms
5 cloves garlic
1″ piece ginger
Sea salt
Tamari soy sauce

C) Preserved Gluten (Seitan)

Tear uncooked kofu into 1/2-to 1-inch pieces and cook in a strong broth seasoned with sea salt and tamari soy sauce from 1 to 3 hours, or until dry. This is seitan. In this way, wheat gluten can be easily stored in glass jars in the refrigerator. It is better to use jars with glass or plastic lids as salt corrodes the metal lids. Seitan can be used in vegetable cooking as a seasoning, cooking it into the vegetables long enough to evenly distribute the salt. In this way no other salt or tamari is needed for the dish.

Note: Another way to preserve gluten, especially for winter cooking, is to deep-fry it. Use sesame or corn oil for frying. Form the gluten into either hand-sized patties or mold it half-way up in an oiled bread-loaf pan. Remove and fry the whole loaf at one time. This fried gluten can be stored in the refrigerator for a month or more.

In preparation for cooking, just cut or slice the amount needed, in the appropriate size and shape for the planned dish. The possibilities are endless.

Light Desserts

The concept of dessert is connected to the idea of eating for entertainment, both sensory and emotional. When eating for entertainment is inharmonious with the life process, it falls into the category of hedonism, living for pleasure alone. The word "hedonism" comes from the Greek *hedys*, meaning "sweet," and *hedone*, meaning "pleasure."

The Romans brought the idea of eating for pleasure to the peak of practice in their Dionysian and Bacchanalian festivals. Dionysius and Bacchus were the Greek and Roman gods of wine, originally honored at the time of the harvest.

In ancient Greece, the Epicureans of Athens believed that mealtime was a time to nourish the spirit as well as the body. They believed that pleasure was best achieved by practicing self-restraint and controlling the indulgence in desires. They practiced moderation in all things and used the festivals to develop their great drama.

By contrast, though the Roman citizens lived primarily on wheat, barley, pine nuts, and fish, the emperors and wealthy aristocrats gorged themselves obscenely on enormous quantities of foods and wines at ostentatiously lavish banquets. These practices filtered down to the public and, at festival time, debasing the original intent, the whole populace joined together in gastronomically indulgent, wild, and sensuous orgies, which were prolonged by the practice of disgorgement. Such practices ultimately led to the biological degeneration of the Roman Empire.

The craving for sweets originates biologically from the ingestion of animal flesh. Animal protein and fats create thick blood and heat in the body, due to their yang qualities and the mucus and stagnation they create. This condition creates a biological attraction for its opposite: any food, drink, or other substance which disperses stagnation and cools the body. These carry the counteracting forces of yin energy.

With the increase in animal food consumption since the Industrial Revolution, and the relative decrease in the use of grains and vegetables, there has been a concurrent increase in the production and consumption of sweets and alcoholic beverages. Over the course of generations, as people became more affluent, the quantity of animal-quality protein has accumulated logarithmically in the human body, creating a greater biological demand for yin substances which counteract the increasing physiological and psychological tension created in the body by animal foods. This basic factor, together with the increase in daily stress and world tension, has caused the escalation in the search for, and indulgence in, yin "foods." This has led to the overwhelming increase in the use of sugar in all forms, including soft drinks, pastries, ice cream, and chocolates; alcohol, medications and, finally, drugs. It is not uncommon to find Westerners beginning the day with desserts, such as pastries and fruits, even soft drinks and alcohol.

The problem is further complicated by the degeneration of basic daily foods themselves, due to the agricultural application of chemicals and the commercial processing and refining of foodstuffs.

This brings us to the present crisis in human history. Between the extreme yang of char-broiled flesh, leading to violence, and the extreme yin of sugar, medications, and drugs, leading to suicide, we are experiencing human degeneration in epidemic proportions, and the subsequent decline of society and civilization as we know it.

> "In order, then, at this point in his Evolution, to advance any further, man must first fall; in order to know, he must lose. In order to realize what Health is, how splendid and glorious a possession, he must go through all the long negative experience of Disease; in order to know the perfect social life . . . he must learn the misery and suffering which come from mere individualism and greed; and in order to find his true [Hu] Manhood, to discover what a wonderful power it is, he must first lose it—he must become a prey and a slave to his own passions and desires. . . ."[1]

> "For the restoration of the central vigour when lost or degenerate, a diet consisting mainly of [vegetables] and grains is most adapted. Animal food often gives . . . a lot of nervous energy . . . of a spasmodic and feverish kind; the food has a tendency to inflame the subsidiary centres, and so to diminish the central control. Those who live mainly on animal food are specially liable to disease—and not only physically; for their minds also fall more easily a prey to desires and sorrows. In times therefore of grief or mental trouble of any kind, as well as in times of bodily sickness, immediate recourse should be had to the more elementary diet. The body under this diet endures work with less fatigue, is less susceptible to pain, and to cold; and heals its wounds with extraordinary celerity."[2]

It is always in times of great darkness, and in the depths of despair, that we seek for the true path back to Life. We look for what has worked before and listen to the words of the great teachers. Thus, decline is always followed by rebirth, and the Fall of Civilization will be followed by the Resurrection of Man.

In our search, we find that, among peoples whose sustenance depends more on grains and vegetables than on animal foods, there is simultaneously less dependence upon, or need for, sweets. Just the opposite is used: salt. The meal is concluded with a salt-pickled vegetable, which serves as an aid in the digestion of grain and insures strong digestive activity itself. By contrast, sugar has the tendency to slow down or even stop digestion, which leads to putrefaction and disease.

For the sake of those who have been accustomed to taking a sweet dessert at the end of the meal, and who may still be attached to, and craving, such sweet taste, I have included a section on Light Desserts. These are presented with due consideration for the healing process and should be taken only when really craving such sweetness. This is in keeping with the ancient Greek principle of "macrobiotics"—the art of longevity, "eating to support life and practice the way of God."

Generally speaking, it is best to satisfy such desires with sweet vegetables, such as cooked onions, carrots, parsnips, squashes, cabbage, and greens, or their broths. However, the following desserts are suggested to help you make the transition through withdrawal to a sugar-free, addiction-free, and disease-free, life.

Please prepare them with a touch of elegance.

---

1 Edward Carpenter, *Civilisation: Its Cause and Cure* (Los Angeles: Tao Books and Publication, Inc., 1971), p. 31.

2 Ibid. p. 46.

Summer

1. Watermelon Kanten

Bring 1 quart of water to a boil and slowly add 6 tablespoons of agar-agar flakes. Lower the fire and let simmer until completely dissolved. Add a pinch of sea salt. Meanwhile cut 1/4 of a watermelon into 1/4-inch cubes. Add to the agar-agar and cook 5 minutes. Pour into an enamel cooling tray with 2-inch sides. Put into the refrigerator to gel. Serve either in 2-inch squares, or shave three to five thin layers with a round tablespoon and pile them in a serving dish one on top of another in the shape of a flower. Garnish with two or three leaves of watercress.

2. Stewed Fruit

Organic fresh or dried fruit can be cut and cooked in about 1-inch water for 1/2 hour. Add a pinch of sea salt while cooking. Sea salt neutralizes the acidity of fruit and makes the fruit sweeter. Among fruits, you can use apples, apricots, strawberries, and cherries. Just cook one at a time.

3. Rice Syrup Kanten (Ame Kanten)

Bring 1 quart of water to a boil. Add 4 tablespoons of agar-agar flakes and cook several minutes until dissolved. Then add 1/2 cup of brown rice syrup, sold as *Yinnie Syrup*. Add 1 pinch of sea salt and cook until the syrup is completely dissolved. Pour into a tray or individual serving molds and refrigerate to gel. To unmold gel, place each mold in a pan of hot water for 1 minute. Loosen the edges with a knife and invert quickly onto a dessert dish. Garnish with roasted sesame seeds.

4. Summer Vegetable Kanten Delight (Vegetable Mitsumame)

Bring 1 quart of water to a boil, add a pinch of sea salt and 6 tablespoons of agar-agar flakes. Dissolve thoroughly. Pour into a molding tray up to 1/2 inch high and gel in the refrigerator. When firm, cut into 1/2-inch cubes.

Meanwhile, wash, dry, and cut daikon, cauliflower, and string beans into 1/2-inch cubes. Slice red radishes thinly from top to bottom. Cut the kernels off one ear of corn and cut watercress into 1/2-inch pieces. Quick-boil each of them separately from 1/2 minute to several minutes, depending on the vegetable, until tender but still bright color. Drain well. Arrange 1 tablespoon of each ingredient attractively in individual serving dishes.

Mitsumame is traditionally made with fruits and red beans, but for sickness, Vegetable Mitsumame is better. You may vary your choice of vegetables using not more than five kinds. Make sure to use a variety of colors.

5. Apricot Kanten Parfait

Soak dried apricots until soft. Grind into paste in the suribachi. Bring 1 quart of water to a boil and add 5 tablespoons agar-agar flakes. Simmer until completely dissolved. Add the apricot purée and cook together 2 or 3 minutes with a pinch of sea salt. Pour into a molding tray and put it in the refrigerator. When firm, break it up into a mixing bowl and whip with a whisk. Spoon into parfait glasses and garnish with three thin slices of fresh apricots.

Winter

1. Applesauce

Wash, dry, and cut several apples into small pieces. Cook in 1/2 to 1 inch of water together with the seeds and a pinch of sea salt for 1/2 to 1 hour. Mash through a strainer or colander. Do not add cinnamon. Serve warm.

2. Kabocha with Applesauce Surprise

Wash, dry and cut kabocha into 2-inch squares. Cook in a steamer with a steaming towel. First wring out the towel in pure cold water and line the steamer with it. Arrange the kabocha on it. Sprinkle the kabocha lightly with sea salt, cover the kabocha with the rest of the towel and place the lid on the steamer. Cook until tender about 15 to 20 minutes. Prepare applesauce as in No. 1. Serve one square of kabocha with 2 tablespoons of applesauce spooned over the center. Garnish with roasted sesame seeds.

3. Kabocha Kanten

Of all the winter squashes, the Japanese kabocha is by far the most delicious. Ironically, it originated in Boston and was transported to Japan where it found a home in Hokkaido, where the flavor improved.

Bring 1 quart of water to a boil and add 6 tablespoons of agar-agar flakes. Simmer until completely dissolved. Meanwhile, steam the kabocha as in No. 2. Purée the kabocha and add to the agar-agar water. Mix thoroughly and pour into a cooling :ray. Gel in the refrigerator until firm. To serve, cut into diamond shapes 3 inches ong. Serve two per person. Garnish with several roasted pumpkin seeds arranged ıttractively.

4. Azuki Kabocha Kanten

Pick clean, wash, and drain 1/2 cup of azuki beans. Bring to a boil in 2 cups of water. Add 1/2 cup of cold water, and bring to a boil. Add a second 1/2 cup of cold water, bring to a boil again, lower fire, and simmer for 2 1/2 hours. Add a pinch of ea salt and cook for another 1/2 hour. Add 4 tablespoons of agar-agar flakes and : cups water and cook all together until agar-agar is dissolved. Meanwhile, make :abocha kanten as in No. 3. When the kanten is firm, layer the azuki beans firmly on op of the kanten in an equal thickness. Continue gelling in the refrigerator. When irm, place tray in 2 inches hot water in the sink for 1 or 2 minutes. Separate the dges with a knife. Then invert quickly on a serving platter. To serve, cut into 2-inch quares. To garnish, dot the center with a few azuki beans.

5. Cabbage and Apple Casserole

Vash, dry, and cut 1 small cabbage julienne style. Wash, dry, and thinly slice two to hree apples into crescents, removing the seeds. On a lightly oiled baking tray, layer abbage, apple, and cabbage. Lightly sprinkle with sea salt and top with raw sunower seeds. Cover with a stainless steel cookie sheet or use a Pyrex casserole dish. ake at 375°F. for 30 to 40 minutes.

Meanwhile dilute 1/4 cup of kuzu in 1/2 cup of water. Add 1 1/2 cups of water, bring to a boil, add a pinch of sea salt, lower the fire and simmer, stirring constantly with a wooden spoon until thick and translucent. Spoon kuzu sauce over the casserole and serve.

Note: Kanten is made from agar-agar, which is a gelatinous sea vegetable used for aspic-type preparations. Since it is rich in yang minerals, it balances the yin elements, such as vitamins, glucose, and fructose, in the grain syrup and fruits.

Snacks

Snacking has become an international pastime. Multi-billion-dollar industries have been built up around the "snack." The desire for snacking comes primarily from eating unbalanced and partial foods. The subsequent lack of complete nutriment leads to hidden hunger. The result is the constant desire to eat. Unfortunately, most commercially prepared snacks are also comprised of unbalanced and partial foods. Thus, the cycle continues. This pattern is totally unconducive to health and longevity.

The way out of this conundrum is to eat carefully selected and prepared meals using whole foods, such as whole grains and vegetables, and to chew them well. Grains and vegetables provide the body with a steady supply of energy distributed evenly over a long period of time. It is easy to be satisfied on three, two, or even one meal a day. The truth is, the less we burden our body with digestion, the more energy we have for other activities. This is especially important in the process of healing. It is as important for the digestive organs to rest periodically as it is for us to rest every night. More illness is created by overeating than by undereating. And overeating never leads to long life.

When we establish a consistent rhythm of eating, working, and sleeping, in attunement with the day and night, and the sun and moon, then all our physical and mental processes will function harmoniously. As a result, we experience smooth energy, endurance, calm mind, and mental clarity, all through the days of our lives.

There will be occasions when snacks are appropriate, to satisfy normal (as opposed to hidden) hunger between meals, to share with friends, or to make up for missed meals when traveling or working. However, it is generally not advisable to make a habit of substituting snacks for meals.

The following are a small example of various types of snacks that we can enjoy. They are divided into four categories: Cooked Snacks, consisting of mini-meals, which can be eaten in or packed for travel; Succulent Snacks, appropriate for warmer weather, due to their cooling effect on the body; Dry Snacks, which can be eaten any time, any place, and are appropriate for more yin people; and Sweet Snacks, which can help to balance a temporarily over-yang condition.

For the purposes of healing, I have suggested mainly whole grains, vegetables, and seeds and have omitted baked flour products. Still, the possibilities of creativity are limited only by your imagination. Be inventive.

Generally speaking, it is better, and more orderly, to eat well-balanced meals at regular intervals. The nervous system and entire body functions in a more harmonious way when meals, eliminations, activity, and rest, fall into a rhythmic pattern. There are times, however, when small snacks may be necessary or desired. The best between-meal snacks can be taken from balanced portions leftover from the previous meals. Even a small bowl of rice or noodles, with or without a little vegetable, will suffice. If you are not at home, this mini-meal can be easily taken with you in a small stainless steel or ceramic container with a plastic lid, like a Japanese "o-bento."

Cooked Snacks

1. Norimaki Sushi

Brown rice sushi is a very convenient mini-meal or snack to carry. It is a complete meal in itself. Place nori on top of a sushi mat. Spread cooked brown rice to 1/4-inch thickness onto a sheet of unroasted nori, leaving 1 inch of the far side clear. Spread a little umeboshi plum or paste along the long edge nearest you. Arrange cooked vegetables or pickled cucumber sticks on top of the line of umeboshi. Roll the nori firmly as in forming a jelly roll, keeping the vegetables tightly within the first roll. Usually sushi is sliced in 1/2-inch to 1-inch widths, but it is sometimes fun to leave it whole. After all, sushi is the Oriental sandwich.

2. Rice Balls (Omusubi)

Omusubi means "knot" or "connection" and is traditionally formed in the shape of a triangle. It is formed by the two hands of yin and yang, or heaven and earth, and the triangles representing the symbols for yin and yang.

The American version of rice balls is a result of a lack of skill in forming these triangles. Nevertheless, rice balls, when properly made, are just as nutritious and delightful to eat. Please follow instructions for making rice balls or Omusubi in Menu XV.

As a treat, you may insert a variety of vegetables or beans as surprises, instead of umeboshi, in the center of the rice ball. However, if you plan to travel with this food, umeboshi is more effective as a preservative. Also, umeboshi rice balls that are formed with a strong power by the hand, give a special energy to the body, and make the digestive system strong.

3. Mochi

If you want something hardy and chewy, mochi is very satisfying.

Mochi is sweet pounded rice cake. Use either plain brown rice or green mugwort mochi. Mugwort is an herb high in iron and is useful to strengthen the blood in the case of anemia as well as to discharge worms and parasites from the body.

Place mochi in a dry cast-iron skillet on a small fire. Cover and pan-bake on top of the stove until it becomes soft and puffs up a little. Turn it over once and continue baking until the other side is soft. It is not necessary to leave it until it explodes.

Dot mochi lightly with tamari soy sauce and wrap in half sheet of roasted nori. Mochi warms the body and is more appropriate for colder weather. A tablespoon of raw grated daikon helps to digest mochi.

4. Noodles

Use whole wheat, brown rice, or buckwheat noodles. Boil in a large pot in enough water to allow the noodles to move actively. Cook, uncovered, 10 to 15 minutes until done. The noodles should be tender, but firm enough to not fall apart and become mushy. The Italians call the right texture "al dente," which is chewy. Rinse the noodles in pure cold water and drain to remove the excess starch which causes them to stick together. The noodles may be served in a variety of ways:

A) Soup Broth

Cook a 6-inch piece of kombu and 2 shiitake mushrooms together for 20 minutes. Remove kombu and hang to dry. Season broth with half sea salt and half tamari soy sauce, tasting to check the flavor.

Dip noodles in a separate pot of boiling water to warm up. Arrange in individual serving bowls. Add soup broth, garnish with minced scallions, and serve.

B) Vegetable Kuzu Sauce

Slice any vegetable you like, such as onion, daikon, cabbage, carrot, and scallions. You may add fresh or fried tofu. Sauté the vegetables in sesame oil or water in the order given. Add water almost to top of vegetables, cover and cook until tender, keeping bright color.

Dilute 1 tablespoon kuzu in 1/4 cup of water. Add 1/2 to 1 cup more water and 2 to 3 tablespoons of tamari soy sauce, to make light brown color. Add this to the vegetables. Bring to a boil on a high fire and stir until thickened and translucent. Dip noodles in boiling water to warm up, and arrange in individual serving bowls. Ladle Vegetable Kuzu Sauce over noodles.

C) Vegetable Fried Noodles

Cut and sauté vegetables as for Vegetable Kuzu Sauce. Add the cooked noodles and fry together. Season lightly with tamari soy sauce. Arrange in individual serving bowls. Garnish with minced scallions.

Succulent Snacks

5. Vegetables and Pickles

If you prefer something juicier, you may choose among a variety of boiled vegetables. Red radishes, daikon, turnips, broccoli, cauliflower, cabbage, watercress, or squash make succulent refreshments. They may be boiled for 1 to several minutes in lightly salted water until tender. Squash may be boiled or steamed, and eaten as is or spread onto rice cakes. This may be topped with roasted sesame or pumpkin seeds for an elegant hors d'oeuvre. In the summer, lightly pickled cucumbers are more cooling and refreshing than watermelon. See Pickle Section for instructions.

6. Deluxe Party Platter

Wash, dry, and cut into various and interesting bite-sized shapes, a variety of vegetables such as broccoli, cauliflower, daikon, winter squash, cabbage, parsnip root, carrot, lotus root, rutabaga, bok choy stems, and rolled green leaves such as Chinese cabbage, collard greens, bok choy leaves, mustard and turnip greens. Secure with toothpick.

Cook each one in a broth of kombu, sea salt, and tamari soy sauce until tender and bright in color. Arrange attractively on a serving platter. Or quick-boil in salted, boiling water. Dress with umeboshi juice, lemon juice and tamari, brown rice vinegar with sesame oil and tamari, or mashed tofu flavored with any of the above dressings. Mix together in a separate bowl before arranging on the platter. Surround the vegetables with quick-boiled watercress, the stems of which have been tied in a knot. The whole platter can be garnished with minced parsley and/or roasted sesame seeds. Enjoy the party!

Dry Snacks

If you are desiring only something small to nibble on, you can choose from several dry snacks such as rice cakes, roasted grains, roasted seeds, popcorn, or sea vegetables. The following is a small variety of suggested snacks:

7. Rice Cakes

Among all of the health food and macrobiotic crackers and chips available, I feel rice cakes are the most balanced. They are not deep-fried and have no oil. You can choose between salted and unsalted varieties. They can be eaten plain or as open-faced sandwiches spread with rice and gomashio, beans, cooked vegetables, pumpkin, or squash. See section on Succulent Snacks.

8. Roasted Brown Rice

Clean and wash rice as per Menu I. Soak in 5 percent salt water for several hours or overnight. Drain well. Let the strainer sit on a sponge or a cloth for 1 hour without disturbing to complete draining. Dry-roast in a cast-iron skillet using a bamboo paddle to evenly heat the rice. Continue roasting until the rice becomes golden brown. Some of the rice may even pop open like popcorn. At this point it is done. Do not allow the rice to become dark brown. Cool and store in a glass jar or ceramic crock.

9. Pumpkin and Squash Seeds

When preparing Hokkaido pumpkin, called kabocha, or any other winter squash, uch as butternut, acorn, turban, or buttercup, carefully remove the seeds, wash hem, and spread them out to dry. You may dry them in the sun or in the oven by he heat of the pilot light. If you spread them in a wide-mesh strainer, they will dry aster and will not tend to mold. After they are dried, soak them overnight in a 5 perent salt solution, using unrefined sea salt of good quality. Drain them well and roast hem in a dry cast-iron skillet, moving them evenly and continuously with a bamboo addle. When the shells puff up and begin to pop open, they are done. If the seeds egin to jump out of the skillet, simply lower the fire and stir faster. The more tender hells can be easily chewed and eaten. The tougher shells can be discarded while the eeds are enjoyed.

0. Shelled Seeds

umpkin or sunflower seeds bought in the store should be obtained in the raw state nd roasted at home. In this way, you can control the quality of salt if it is used, or ou may make unsalted, roasted seeds. It is not necessary to roast seeds in oil and is preferable not to do so. If your condition is more yin, you may take some sunflower seeds as well as pumpkin seeds. If your condition is more yang it is better to avoid sunflower seeds.

Simply roast the seeds carefully in a cast-iron skillet, moving them evenly and continuously with a bamboo paddle or a wooden spoon. In this way, the seeds will become evenly roasted until they are a beautiful golden color. If the seeds are roasted unevenly, some will be raw while some will be scorched, and they will cause disharmony inside of you.

It is better to eat the seeds a little at a time, not taking more than a small handful at one sitting. Eating them one by one will help you to chew well while marveling at their complexity. All pumpkin and squash seeds are useful as a vermifuge, to get rid of intestinal parasites.

11. Sesame Seeds

When buying sesame seeds, choose the brown or black variety. White sesame seeds have been de-hulled and are equivalent to white rice. When choosing black seeds, make sure their color is mottled and not jet black, which indicates dyeing. Sesame seeds need to be washed before roasting. Run cold water over them in a fine-mesh strainer while sifting through them with your fingers to allow any sand to wash out. Pat the strainer dry with a sponge, squeezing often to remove excess water. Let the strainer rest on a sponge for 1/2 hour without disturbing to remove any remaining water. Roast the seeds in a dry cast-iron skillet until they become dry and start to jump. At this point, lower the fire and stir faster. Crush the seeds between the fourth finger and thumb and, if they crush easily, taste them. They should taste just right, neither raw nor scorched. The seeds should be a beautiful golden color. Be careful not to overroast them.

When used as a snack, sesame seeds can be mixed with other food. Do not use more than 1 or 2 teaspoons straight. Sesame seeds are high in lecithin, which is an emulsifier and helps break down accumulated fats in the body.

12. Popcorn

Organic popcorn is best. If the popcorn is old and dry and does not pop well, store it in a glass jar in the refrigerator with a few drops of water sprinkled in it. Let it stay several days so it can absorb moisture. It is the expanding moisture in the corn that causes it to pop.

Spread the corn one layer thick in a dry cast-iron skillet. I like to use a round splatter-control screen to cover the pot so I can watch the corn popping. It is light weight so it allows the moisture to evaporate, which makes the popcorn crispy. It is not necessary to use oil to pop corn. As soon as the corn is popped, put it in a brown paper bag with a sprinkle of sea salt. It is better to use sea salt which has been roasted and powdered in a suribachi. Shake vigorously and enjoy. Be careful, if you eat the whole bag at once, your bowels may become loose from so much fiber. One or two handfuls at a time should suffice.

13. Sea Vegetable

Nori, wakame, or kombu may be roasted and eaten as snack as is. The wakame or kombu should be wiped well to remove excess salt before roasting.

Put wakame or kombu in a dry cast-iron skillet and let bake until dry and brittle, either on top of the stove or in the oven. This snack is very good as a mineral supplement. It also discharges radiation and heavy metals and builds up the blood.

In the case of nori, wave the purple sheet over an open fire, quickly and carefully until it becomes green. Do not let it catch fire. One-half to one sheet of nori per day is very useful in dissolving animal fats.

14. Popcorn Snack Deluxe

Mix popcorn with lightly roasted pumpkin, squash, or sunflower seeds, sesame seeds, crushed roasted nori, and sea salt. Share with friends.

Sweet Snacks

15. Fruits and Vegetables

Dried or cooked fruit such as apples, cherries, and strawberries, or sweet vegetables such as parsnip root with carrot, onion, squash, either cut or puréed into a spread, often satisfy a taste for sweets.

They can be used alone or on rice cakes. Although vegetables can be eaten together with noodles or grains, fruit should not be mixed regularly with grains or beans.

If you are not really hungry and want something warm to soothe your stomach and help you relax, settle down to a cup of hot tea.

Teas

Teas have been brewed throughout the ages from almost anything that could be boiled or steeped. The origin of their use dates back to the Stone Age, some 25,000 to 35,000 years ago. Even at that time, various herbs were found to have special effects on the body.

The Chinese began to cultivate specific tea plants around 2700 B.C., using them to flavor the water essentially boiled for purification. The cultivation and use of tea was brought from China to Japan around A.D. 800, where it ultimately developed into an art form, the Japanese imbuing it with highly stylized, formal, and ceremonial aspects, culminating in the Tea Ceremony. Gradually, the knowledge, cultivation, and use of tea spread throughout Asia.

It was not until the early 1700s that tea, as it is commonly known in the West, was first served in Holland and England, and not much later transported to the English colonies in America. It was an English duchess who created the custom of afternoon tea around 1840.

Over the centuries, tea has played important parts in history, war, economics, philosophy, culture, and medicine throughout the world. There has been almost no aspect of life that tea has not entered or influenced. Yet, as ancient and worldly as it may be, it never ceases to be interesting or effective.

Almost every traditional people has developed a pharmacopoeia of teas to be used for healing. Volumes have been written on the properties, methods of preparation, and effects on the body of probably thousands of ingredients used in these decoctions. Yet, very little is known about them in the Western world, beyond what comes in bags and boxes from the supermarket or tea shop.

The greatest development of medicinal teas has taken place in the agricultural societies of India, Tibet, China, Japan, and Korea. In countries where grains and vegetables form the primary basis of nutrition, it has been conducive to use teas coming from similar sources to make the necessary adjustments in the body. The teas are decocted from all forms of animal, mineral, and vegetable elements.

After food, tea is considered to be the second level of medicine. Massage, acupressure, acupuncture and moxabustion are considered to be the third level of medicine. The use of drugs and chemicals as medicine is relegated to the fourth level. And surgery is considered to be the last resort, to be avoided whenever possible.

The practice of self-reflection, meditation, and visualization, on the part of both patient and healer, is essential at every stage of treatment and is a significant part of the healing process itself.

In the *Shang Han Lun*, the most highly revered medical classic in China, written over 1,800 years ago (in the third century A.D.), the author, Chang Chung-ching, exclaims, "I don't quite understand why scholars today do not pay more attention to these formulas and techniques when treating their elders, healing the poor, and maintaining their own health. They do little but vie for fame and power and delight themselves with improving their physical appearance while neglecting their spiritual development."[3]

The macrobiotic approach to healing has always incorporated the use of various teas, along with dietary adjustments, to correct imbalances in the body and mind. The teas are made from a variety of ingredients, each with its own effect upon the body. Some are more yin, relaxing the body; some more yang, strengthening the body. Some have very powerful cleansing properties and can dissolve and discharge heavy accumulations of excess proteins and fats from the body. Some discharge heavy metals and radiation. Some eliminate parasites. Some strengthen the blood. There are even teas which enhance clarity of thinking, as well as teas which insure good sleep. The teas listed below are those most commonly used in daily life as simple beverages or for specific healing purposes.

To find the most appropriate and harmonious way to accomplish any task is the heart of Zen. To practice that way is to bring the performance of that task to the level of art. There is even a way to boil water.

All water used for cooking, especially in preparing medicinal teas, should be pure deep-well or spring water. Considering the quality of most water in the world today, it may be necessary to purify the water through a solid carbon-block water purifying system. The best teapots for boiling water or brewing tea are made of unglazed ceramic, glazed ceramic, enamel, or glass. It is not suitable to prepare teas in metal pots. Aluminum is to be avoided altogether.

The best fire for all cooking is wood fire. The next best, and most versatile for our purposes, is gas. Electric "fire" is disorienting to the blood stream and interferes with the healing process, and is best not utilized. Microwave cooking should be avoided altogether.

---

3 *Shang Han Lun*, Chang Chung-chin. Translated by Hong-yen Hsu (Los Angeles: Oriental Healing Arts Institute, 1981), p. 2.

Daily Teas

1. Bancha Stem or Twig Tea (Kukicha)

This tea is rich in minerals and it is used after mealtime to strengthen the whole body. It is also good for calming the nervous system and creating a state of relaxation.

The tea should be roasted before using. You can roast a whole package in a dry cast-iron skillet lightly until a nice fragrance arises. Cool the tea and store it in a glass or ceramic container. Bring 1 quart of water to a boil, add 1 tablespoon of tea and simmer at least 5 minutes. This makes a bracing brew. For more yin people, simmering for 15 to 30 minutes makes a more mellow brew.

2. Roasted Barley Tea (Mugicha)

Roasted barley tea is made from whole barley which still has the husk on it. It comes already roasted and is sold in Oriental food stores as well as macrobiotic markets. This tea may also be made at home from pearl barley. Just roast it in a dry cast-iron skillet, stirring constantly until golden brown and fragrant. This tea is good for yang people and also as a daily drink in summer. It also aids in melting animal fat from the body and reducing fever.

To 1 quart of boiling water, add 1 to 2 tablespoons of roasted barley. The strength may be varied according to desire, ranging in taste from a light tea to a rich quasi-coffee. Simmer 10 to 20 minutes according to strength desired.

3. Rice Tea (Genmaicha)

Clean and wash 1/4 cup of raw, brown rice. Add to 1 quart cold water. Bring to a boil, adding a tiny pinch of sea salt. Lower fire and simmer 30 to 40 minutes. Stir before serving. You may strain the tea if you like, but it is not necessary. This tea is good for pregnant women and nursing mothers as well as their babies, although anyone can enjoy this delicious tea. It is also very soothing to upset stomachs.

4. Roasted Rice Tea (Yaki Genmaicha)

Clean and wash brown rice, drain well, and roast in a dry cast-iron skillet, stirring constantly until golden, not brown. Cook the same as rice tea. Roasted rice tea is more yang than rice tea and is more suitable for yin people.

5. Rice Milk (Omoyu)

Omoyu is the heavy rice milk that accumulates on the top of Okayu. See Menu VI for Okayu. In this case, make Okayu with 7 parts of water instead of 5. This rice milk is very good for sick people who have no appetite.

6. Wheat Tea (O-Mugicha)

Wheat tea is a cooling summer tea and can be used as a relaxing drink for yang people and children. It can be made raw or roasted in the same way as rice tea.

7. Grain Coffee (Yannoh)

Yannoh is a type of coffee made from roasted grains, beans, and roots. It has been used traditionally throughout the Orient and was popular in Europe as an ersatz-coffee during the war. It can be prepared in a variety of ways, using different grains, beans, and roots in varying proportions. The general proportions are: 1 part grain, 2/3 part beans, 1/6 part roots. For more yin people, the proportion of roots can be increased to one-third. The grain portion can be made from brown rice, winter wheat, or millet, or a combination of grains, with rice predominating.

The bean portion can be made from azuki, black beans, chick-peas or a combination of beans. The root portion can be made from burdock, carrot, dandelion, or chicory, or a combination of roots. The most common combination has been 3 parts brown rice, 5 parts winter wheat, 4 parts chick-peas, 3 parts azuki beans, and 2 parts chicory.

Clean and wash all ingredients separately. Mince the roots. Roast each ingredient separately in a dry cast-iron skillet, stirring constantly until they reach a rich brown color. Mix all the ingredients together and grind into powder in a grain mill.

To prepare, dissolve 1 tablespoon of Yannoh into a cup of cold water. Bring to a boil and immediately lower the flame. Gently simmer for 5 to 10 minutes according to desired strength.

8. Yannoh with Kuzu

Kuzu is a root starch used primarily for strengthening the lower organs. It helps in the case of yin colds and diarrhea. This is a yang drink, good for warming the body on a cold, raw day.

Dilute 1 teaspoon of kuzu in 1/4 cup of cold water. Add 1 tablespoon of Yannoh and 3/4 cup of cold water. Bring to a boil, lower flame immediately, and simmer gently 5 to 6 minutes, stirring constantly until the kuzu is smoothly thickened. More or less kuzu can be added according to the thickness desired.

9. Dandelion Root Tea (Tampopo-Cha)

Dandelion root tea can be either bought or made at home. There are two kinds: raw for a more yang condition, or roasted for a more yin condition. It is used to strengthen the heart, intestines, and reproductive organs.

To prepare the root at home, wash, dry, and cut several dandelion roots into tiny pieces. Spread out on a bamboo mat to dry in the sun. In this state it is considered raw. If roasted root is desired, sun-dry and roast it in a cast-iron skillet until it is dark brown, stirring constantly with a wooden spoon. Cool completely before storing.

To make tea, bring 1 tablespoon of dandelion root to boil in 1 quart of water, reduce flame, and cook 10 minutes or to desired strength.

10. Burdock Tea (Gobo-Cha)

Burdock tea can be either bought or made at home. To make at home, wash and dry the burdock roots. Either shave or mince them and spread them out to dry.

To prepare tea, add 1 to 2 tablespoons of burdock to 1 quart of cold water, bring to a boil, lower fire, and simmer 10 to 20 minutes. You may add more tea for a stronger taste as desired. Burdock tea is also used for strengthening the body.

11. Azuki Bean Tea (Azuki-Cha)

Azuki bean tea can be made from raw or roasted beans. The raw tea is useful to adjust kidney imbalance and to release excess water from the body. Use raw beans for a yang kidney condition. The roasted tea is useful to strengthen yin kidneys. Do not roast beans too much as azuki beans are already yang. Add 2 tablespoons of beans to 1 quart cold water and simmer down to one pint, cooking for 2 to 3 hours. You may add a pinch of sea salt if necessary.

12. Kombu Tea (Kombu-Cha)

Kombu tea is used for cleaning and strengthening the blood. You may use either dried kombu or baked-powdered kombu, which is useful as an instant tea for traveling. For instant tea, add I cup of hot water to 1 teaspoon kombu powder; otherwise, bring 3 inches of kombu to a boil in 1 quart of water, reduce fire, and simmer 10 minutes. The same kombu can be used for tea two or three times. It is better to dry used kombu than to refrigerate it for further use.

13. Corn Silk Tea

Corn silk tea may be either bought or made at home. To make at home, simply collect the silk from summer corn and spread it out to dry. It can be stored indefinitely in a glass jar. To prepare tea, add 1/4 cup of corn silk to 1 1/2 cups of water and cook down to 1 cup. Corn silk tea, if made more strongly, can be used as a mild diuretic. Made less strongly, it is a refreshing summer drink.

14. Umeboshi Plum Tea (Ume-Cha)

Umeboshi plum is really made from Japanese or American apricot. You may make this tea either from whole umeboshi or from the pits left over from other preparations. Use either 3 whole umeboshi or 5 to 6 pits in 1 quart of water. Bring to a boil, lower fire, and simmer 1/2 hour. Refrigerate in a quart jar or covered pitcher. This tea can be taken at room temperature for a refreshing summer drink.

15. Vegetable Tea

Vegetable tea can be made from a variety of unsalted vegetable cooking broths. Do not use strong-tasting broths, especially with high potassic taste, made from Swiss chard or mustard greens. You may use the broths from watercress, broccoli, corn, carrots, and sometimes daikon and red radishes, if your condition is too tight. In this way nothing is wasted.

Medicinal Teas

16. Salt Bancha

Salt bancha can be taken as a tea to counteract fatigue. It can also be used to wash out the inner cavities of the eyes, nose, throat, and vagina, and can be used occasionally as an enema. It helps loosen stagnation and discharge mucus.

As a body cleanser, warm up bancha tea and add enough sea salt to make it a little less salty than sea water. Make sure it is completely diluted before using.

17. Tamari (Shoyu) Bancha

Put 1/2 to 1 teaspoon of tamari soy sauce in a 4-ounce teacup. Add hot bancha tea over this. This tea neutralizes blood acidity, improves circulation, counteracts fatigue, and promotes good sleep. It is good as a 3 o'clock pick-me-up.

18. *Ume-Sho-Bancha*

Mash 1/2 umeboshi in the bottom of a teacup. Add 1/2 to 1 teaspoon of tamari soy sauce. Add 1 cup of hot bancha tea and stir. This tea regulates digestion, strengthens the blood, and improves circulation. It is also useful to calm indigestion.

19. *Ume-Sho-Kuzu*

Mash 1/2 to 1 umeboshi in the bottom of a teacup. Dilute 1 to 2 teaspoons kuzu in 1/4 cup of cold water. Add 1 cup of cold water and 1 teaspoon tamari soy sauce. Bring to a boil, lower fire, and simmer, stirring constantly, until kuzu is thickened and translucent. Pour over umeboshi and stir before drinking.

20. Ume-Sho-Bancha with Kuzu/Tamari/Ginger

Mash 1/2 umeboshi on the bottom of the teacup. Dilute 1 to 2 teaspoons kuzu in1/4 cup of room-temperature bancha tea. Add 1 cup bancha tea and 1/2 to 1 teaspoon of tamari soy sauce. Bring to a boil, stirring constantly until kuzu becomes thickened and translucent. Put 1/4 teaspoon grated ginger juice into teacup. Pour hot Kuzu-Sho-Bancha over this. Stir and drink. This tea increases blood circulation and helps make the body feel warm.

21. Mu Tea

Mu Tea comes in two varieties, sixteen-herb and nine-herb. Sixteen-herb is the original formula. Mu Tea comes prepackaged in the health food stores. It is not used as an after-dinner tea, but as a medicinal tea to yangize and energize a weak condition. It should only be used occasionally, when necessary. For instance, if you are suffering menstrual cramps from yin cause and are swollen and bloated, Mu Tea helps to counteract this condition. It can also be used double-strength as a diuretic. Yang and red-faced people should not take Mu Tea.

22. Mugwort Tea (Yomogi-Cha)

Mugwort is a green, leafy herbal plant which grows wild in many places, north or south. It has a characteristic bitter taste, although it is a yin plant. The leaves are collected and dried at home, or they can be bought in a health food store. Mugwort is high in iron and is useful for strengthening the blood, especially in the case of anemia, in which case it is taken as food.

In the form of tea, it is useful for dispelling parasites and in treating yang conditions such as jaundice. Excessive use may cause yin constipation. To prepare, boil 1 tablespoon of tea in 1 quart of water and simmer for 5 to 10 minutes.

23. Shiitake Mushroom Tea

Shiitake Mushroom Tea cools the body and helps to reduce excessive energy. It is especially useful for hyperactive children, violent or hysterical people. Shiitake tea can be used to counteract internal stress and tension. It is also useful in helping to dissolve excess animal fat.

Cook 1 or 2 shiitake mushrooms in 2 cups of water, down to 1 cup for 30 to 35 minutes. Add 1 scallion cut in 1-inch pieces, and cook 1 minute more. Add a drop of tamari soy sauce. The shiitake and scallion may be eaten after the tea has been drunk.

24. Daikon Tea No. 1

Originally, daikon had more potent healing properties. It used to be hard and with a strong, pungent taste. Today's daikon is more highly cultivated making it watery and weak with a mild taste.

If you have good strong organic daikon, grate 2 tablespoons. Add 1 1/2 pints of hot water and 1 to 2 tablespoons of tamari soy sauce with 1/2 to 1 teaspoon of grated ginger.

If you have only commercial daikon, grate 1/2 cup, add 1 tablespoon of tamari soy sauce and 1/4 to 1/2 teaspoon grated ginger. Pour 1 cup of hot bancha tea over this mixture. Stir and drink while hot.

In either case, this drink is useful for promoting perspiration and urination to break the fever of a cold.

25. Daikon Tea No. 2

Grate fresh daikon and squeeze out 1/4 to 1/2 cup of juice, depending on the strength of the daikon. You may use cheesecloth to squeeze out the juice. To this add two to three times the amount of water, again depending upon the strength of the daikon. Bring to a boil, adding a pinch of sea salt. Cook 1 or 2 minutes more.

Drink one time per day for no more than 3 days. Never take without boiling. This is useful to release tight kidneys and reduce swollen legs.

26. Daikon Tea No. 3

Put 1 tablespoon grated daikon in a teacup. Add 2 or 3 drops of tamari soy sauce. Add hot bancha tea and drink. This tea helps dissolve fat and mucus, and is most effective when taken at bedtime. Do not use more than 1 week without macrobiotic guidance.

27. Daikon Carrot Tea

Grate 1 tablespoon each of raw daikon and raw carrot. Bring to a boil in 1 cup of water and simmer with a pinch of sea salt or 1/2 teaspoon of tamari soy sauce. This drink helps discharge excessive fats and dissolves hardened accumulations in the intestines.

28. Lotus Root Tea (Kohren)

Lotus root tea can be made from either fresh lotus root, grated and squeezed, or dried and/or powdered lotus root. When using fresh lotus root juice, mix with half as much water. Bring to a boil, add a pinch of sea salt, lower fire, and simmer about 5 to 10 minutes. Drink hot. This can dissolve protein congestion in the kidneys.

When using dried lotus root, cook in 1 cup of water about 15 to 20 minutes. Add a pinch of salt or 1/2 teaspoon of tamari soy sauce and drink hot.

When using dried powdered lotus root, add 1 teaspoon to 1 cup of water. Bring to a boil and simmer several minutes. Drink hot.

In either case, take three times per day eliminating all other liquids. Lotus Root Tea helps to dissolve mucus in the lungs and relieve coughing. Lotus Root Tea with Kuzu is effective for deep bronchial congestion. Add 1 tablespoon kuzu to Lotus Root Tea and cook until thick and translucent.

29. Black Bean Tea (Kuro-Mame-Cha)

Black Bean Tea is used for throat problems such as hoarseness and laryngitis. It is also used to regulate irregular menstruation and to strengthen women's reproductive organs.

In the latter case, it should be taken for a period of 2 to 3 months. To 1 quart of cold water, add 2 tablespoons of black beans. Bring to a boil, lower the fire, and simmer about 2 hours, reducing the liquid down to 1 pint. Drink 1/2 cup warm tea 1/2 hour before meals.

30. Baked Ume Tea (Yaki-Ume-Cha)

Use either whole umeboshi or pits left over from other preparations using umeboshi. Bake them in a 350°F. oven until charred. Crush the carbonized umeboshi and/or pits into powder. Add 1 tablespoon to 1 cup of hot water and drink. This tea is very effective in neutralizing acidity and relieving intestinal problems including those caused by parasites.

31. Carbonized Hair Tea

Many things in nature may seem strange but are nevertheless effective. One of these is carbonized hair tea. This tea is very effective in controlling hemorrhaging. A woman should take the hair from the back of a man's head. A man should take the hair from the back of a woman's head.

Bake 1 tablespoon of hair in a small cast-iron skillet in the oven until completely carbonized. Crush into powder. Mix with 1 cup warm water that has been boiled and drink.

32. Bamboo Leaf Tea

Use dried bamboo leaves from the top of the trees, or buy dried bamboo leaves from the local Chinatown. For 1 1/2-quart teapot, add about 20 leaves to cold water. Bring to a boil and simmer 3 to 5 minutes. Drink 1/2 cup warm tea 1/2 hour before meals. This tea is effective in controlling hemorrhaging.

33. Ranshio

This is not a tea, but is an effective drink for strengthening the heart and promoting heartbeat and blood circulation. This is especially useful for yin heart attack accompanied by fibrillation. It should not be used in the case of constriction of the heart.

Ranshio (A)

For yin or weak heart, mix one whole egg with 1 tablespoon tamari soy sauce, using 2 to 3 chopsticks or a small wooden spoon. Drink slowly teaspoon by teaspoon. You should soon feel stronger. Take once a day for no more than 3 days.

Ranshio (B)

This preparation is stronger than Ranshio (A) and is used in the emergency of a yin heart attack.

Break an egg carefully in half. Pass the yolk back and forth between the two half shells, letting the egg whites fall between them into a bowl. Discard the egg whites. Place the yolk in a cup, fill the smaller half of the shell with tamari soy sauce and add this to the egg yolk. Mix together with chopsticks and drink slowly. Do not take more than once a day for 3 days.

34. Green Drink

Many women suffer bladder infection either periodically or consistently over a long period of time. The main cause of this is not only poor hygiene, but also stagnation of the blood in the bladder. This is caused by heavy, salty, oily foods such as meat or cheese, together with sweet, pasty foods such as pastries. Green Drink has been beneficial in alleviating bladder infection, whether acute or chronic.

First, it is necessary to follow the standard macrobiotic diet with no animal food. Then, take Green Drink for 3 days. Blend raw romaine lettuce, cucumber, celery, watercress, and parsley with a little water. Drink one glass two or three times a day. Make fresh each time. Do not take more than 3 days.

For a stronger remedy using less liquid, take Daikon Tea No. 3.

Other Internal Remedies

For every condition there is a remedy. However, no two conditions are identical, considering the differences in individual sex, age, constitution, condition, background, and present circumstances, including geography, climate, weather, social relationships, emotions, and mentality. Therefore, no two remedies can be identical. The astute healer will vary the ingredients, proportions, methods of preparation, and times of ingestion to harmonize and balance each condition, changing the recommendations as the condition and circumstances change. This is why patent formulas are not suitable for everyone, even if two people have the same symptoms.

In the macrobiotic approach to health, the specific naming of various diseases is not so important. Rather, to understand the nature and cause of the problem is essential. Therefore, all problems are differentiated into two categories, yin or yang. Many problems are dominated by an imbalance of either yin or yang energy, while some problems involve disharmony in both the yin and yang energies in the body. By harmonizing these energies, the body's natural self-healing mechanism is facilitated. In this way, we are working with the universal order of creation and no dangerous side-effects are produced.

The following Internal Remedies are suggested as an adjunct to the previous section on Teas. They will be found to be helpful in more exceptional circumstances.

For a more comprehensive coverage of Macrobiotic remedies, see *Macrobiotic Home Remedies* by Michio Kushi and Marc Van Cauwenberghe, M.D.

1. Umeboshi

Umeboshi, next to miso, is one of the most ingenious creations of mankind. It is the Oriental equivalent to the Western aspirin, yet is infinitely more useful and effective.

Technically, umeboshi is in the apricot family, but has been mistranslated as "plum." It has the fuzzy skin of an apricot, not the shiny, smooth skin of plum. It is picked green, while it is still sour, then dried and pickled with sea salt and beefsteak leaves (shiso), which give it its color. It develops a strong salty, sour taste, which is the key to its healing power.

Among its many virtues, umeboshi counteracts infection, kills bacteria, and neutralizes acidity. It can soothe a sore throat, reduce inflamed tonsils, ease indigestion, and dispel gas. It can counteract a cold, dismiss a headache, prevent air or sea sickness, and purify bacterially polluted water.

For a common cold, use umeboshi in tea, such as Ume-Sho-Bancha or Ume-Sho-Bancha with Kuzu and Ginger, as described in the section under Medicinal Teas.

For acid stomach, indigestion, gas and discomfort after overeating, simply eat a whole umeboshi by itself. Umeboshi also kills harmful intestinal bacteria and microorganisms. For sore throat and swollen glands, suck on an umeboshi and its pit for as long as possible.

To alleviate thirst and help diminish water in the body, suck on an umeboshi pit for an hour or more and swallow your saliva. This also comforts the stomach.

Carry umeboshi in your backpack or car when hiking or traveling. If you cannot boil your water, soak several umeboshi in a quart of water to purify it before drinking. In this way, it has saved many people's lives.

2. Sesame Oil

Sesame oil is the most yang, stable, nutritious, and delicious of all oils. It is used for beautification and medication as much as it is for food.

For yang constipation, mix 1 to 2 tablespoons of raw sesame oil with 1/4 teaspoon ginger and 1/2 teaspoon or so of tamari soy sauce and eat this on an empty stomach. This will help to discharge hard, stagnated bowels. For external uses, see section on External Applications.

3. Vermifuges (Parasite Cleansers)

A. Common Parasites

This preparation is very effective in eliminating pin worms and round worms and other parasites and microorganisms. Do not eat or drink anything for breakfast. Instead, eat the following mixture: 1 handful of raw brown rice, 1/2 handful of raw pumpkin seeds, 1/2 handful of raw minced onion, scallions and garlic mixed together. Mix all the ingredients together. Eat this for breakfast, chewing well. Eat this when you are very, very hungry. You may eat your regular meal after 2 P.M. Repeat this procedure for 3 days. If you are thirsty, take Three Taste Tea or Corsican Seaweed Tea, available at macrobiotic markets.

B. Tapeworm

Tapeworm is probably the most difficult parasite to eliminate. There are very strong medicines for this, but in taking them, one runs the risk of destroying essential digestive bacteria. Jesus had a much more interesting and gentle method of attacking this problem.

Fast, taking nothing but hot water for 3 days. On the morning of the fourth day, boil whole milk and with a towel draped over your head to catch the vapors, deeply breathe in the sweet steam. The famished tapeworm will rise to the occasion, attracted by the sweet rich aroma and will make its exit through your mouth. It is best for the worm to come out head first, in this way, so it will not regenerate itself.

4. Carp Soup (Koi-Koku)

Koi-Koku is used when necessary to strengthen people who have lost vitality. It helps new mothers regain strength more quickly after childbirth and stimulates the flow of rich, thick milk. It is also sometimes used for weak people who have lost energy through illness.

1 lb. carp, whole
3 lbs. burdock root
2 Tbsps. sesame oil
1 cup used bancha tea twigs (kukicha)
1/2 cup miso
1 tsp. fresh ginger juice

The carp should be purchased live. Ask the fish seller to remove only the green gallbladder, as it is bitter, leaving the rest of the fish intact—scales, fins, head, and tail included. At home, wash the fish well. Cut it into bite-size pieces and set aside.

Wash, dry, and cut burdock in julienne style. Sauté in sesame oil, using the pressure-cooker pot until the strong earthy aroma evaporates. Add water to cover and bring to a boil. Add carp and bancha tea twigs, which have been tied in a cheesecloth bag. Cover, bring to pressure, lower fire, and simmer for 2 hours. Cool pot to lower pressure. Remove lid and check to see if the bones and scales have become soft. If not, cook longer. If they are soft, remove bag of tea. Then add enough water to reach 2 inches above the ingredients and boil into soup.

In a separate bowl, dilute miso in 1/2 cup of soup broth. Add to soup without boiling and simmer gently for 15 to 20 minutes. Add juice of freshly grated ginger, stir into soup and turn off fire. Let sit several minutes before serving.

Koi-koku will keep 1 week in the refrigerator.

5. Special Rice Cream

Clean, wash, and drain 1 cup of organic short grain brown rice. Add 20 cups of water. Bring to a boil, add 1/2 teaspoon sea salt. Lower fire and simmer 2 hours. When done, cool slightly and pass through a cotton muslin bag, turned with the seams toward the outside. A triangular bag is easiest to use with a wide mouth and a long stem. After all of the rice cream has passed through the bag, squeeze the remaining dregs until all the starch is drawn out. The dregs left over in the bag may be used in soup or other grain cooking. Stir the rice cream several times until even and smooth.

This special rice cream is highly nourishing and readily absorbed. It is very good for babies and sick people who cannot hold any other food. It helps vitalize a weakened condition.

Special Rice Cream is also very helpful in assuring smooth transition when one is ready to pass over into the next life. It creates a feeling of deep calm and peaceful mind.

External Applications

The realm of External Applications is endless. Their use dates back to the animals in the dawn of Man. Man was the great observer. He saw and he imitated. What he saw was this: When animals roll in the grass, they are massaging their own backs; when they rub themselves against trees, they are stimulating certain meridians; when they lie on the earth, the earth is absorbing toxins from their digestive organs; when they wade and soak in the mud or water, they are cleansing themselves of excesses discharging through the skin; when they stand with one leg up, they are stimulating certain points; when they prepare nests of leaves, they are preparing, not only sleeping places, but simple poultices to cool the body after a heavy meal. They saw mothers lick, stroke, and hold their babies when they were frightened or hurt, or just to share affection. In this way, Man learned from the animals and from nature. Those who learned well became medicine men, medicine women, shamans, hilots, curanderos—healers.

We all have the ability to heal. We have only to take responsibility and learn how to heal ourselves. In the macrobiotic way of life, remedies are made out of ingredients commonly found in nature and in the kitchen. They are easy to make and easy to use. Do not let initial unfamiliarity breed procrastination. Doing something takes a shorter time than thinking about it. Benjamin Franklin said, "Well done is better than well said." Good efforts bear good fruits.

1. Hot Towel Body Rub

Every morning and evening, rub your whole body with a towel wrung out in hot water. This helps dissolve accumulated fat under the skin. It opens the pores and stimulates circulation, so that excess toxins in the body can be discharged through the skin.

2. Salt Bath

Fill the tub with hot water waist high. While the water is running, add 2 big handfuls of coarse salt. Do not use your good cooking salt. Soak in this salt bath for 5 minutes before bedtime. It helps loosen stagnation and stimulate circulation in the lower body.

3. Daikon Leaf Bath (Hiba Bath)

If you cannot find daikon leaves, ask the produce man to save the leaves cut from the daikon in the market and give them to you. String the bunches up separately to dry in the shade until they become brown and brittle. If you cannot find daikon leaves, you can substitute turnip leaves.

Boil 5 bunches of leaves in a gallon of water about 1 hour until the water becomes brown. Add 1 handful of coarse salt. (For instance, kosher salt.)

Fill the tub to waist height and add the daikon leaf water without the leaves. Soak in this at least 10 minutes before bed, covering the upper body with a towel. As circulation is stimulated in the lower body, the body will grow warm and begin to sweat. This is very good for healing the sexual and reproductive organs. It is also useful for skin problems and for drawing out odors and excessive oils from the body. If the bath makes you weak, you may use the water as a compress in the same way as a Ginger Compress.

4. Salt Bancha Lemon Douche

To 1 quart of warm bancha tea, add enough sea salt to make slightly salty taste. Add the juice of 1 lemon and use as a douche following the Daikon Leaf Bath. This douche is effective in cleaning mucous accumulation in the vagina.

Without the lemon juice, Salt Bancha can also be used to cleanse the nasal cavity and the eyes, as well as making a good gargle for sore throats.

5. Salt Pack

Use coarse salt rather than good sea salt. Roast 2 to 3 cups in a dry cast-iron skillet until very hot. Wrap it in a doubled old bath towel or in a bag fashioned from a doubled bath towel secured with Velcro. Fold the Velcro over when putting hot salt in the bag so as not to melt it.

Salt pack is very soothing to any painful part, such as earache, menstrual or muscle cramps, and is helpful in the case of diarrhea or other intestinal upset or gas. Do not use in the case of appendicitis. It can also be used for yin kidney pain, but not yang kidney pain. The salt stays hot for about 1/2 hour and helps promote good sleep.

6. Ginger Compress

Ginger Compress promotes the discharge of toxins from the nucleus of the blood cell, as well as stimulates the circulation of the blood and other body fluids. The action of the intense heat and the penetrating quality of ginger helps loosen and dissolve hardened, stagnated accumulations, cysts, and tumors. It can be used on any part of the body below the head, except in the case of appendicitis.

In a large, wide, enamel pot, boil 2 gallons of water. Meanwhile, grate 2 large fistfuls of fresh ginger root and tie it in a cotton bag such as a 5-pound muslin flour sack. After the water has boiled, lower the fire and put in the sack. Cover and let steep 10 minutes. Never boil ginger or it will lose its healing power. After 10 minutes, press the ginger sack with a wooden spoon to release the yellow liquid into the water.

Use an old, white, 100 percent cotton terry cloth bath towel cut in half. Grasp the two diagonal corners and twist the towel. Dip it into the hot water until it is thoroughly soaked and continue to twist the towel to discharge excess water. Open and fold in half or into a square and apply to the painful part. Cover with another towel and a blanket to keep in the heat. Never use plastic or nylon. Also, you may need to keep the pot on a low flame to maintain the heat, especially if you are applying the compress for 15 to 20 minutes.

While the first towel is on the body, prepare the second towel. Do not allow the first towel to cool before applying the second towel. Keep the temperature on the body even. Continue applying the hot Ginger Compress until the skin becomes red. In the case of cancer, apply only 3 to 5 minutes in preparation for Albi (Taro) or Potato Plaster.

7. Ginger Towel Body Rub

Make Ginger Water as in No. 6 and use for Hot Towel Body Rub No. 1. This is especially useful for spinal problems such as scoliosis.

8. Ginger Foot/Hand Soak

Prepare Ginger Water as in Ginger Compress No. 6 and soak the hands and feet in it for 10 to 20 minutes before bed to stimulate circulation, counteract coldness in the hands and feet, and to alleviate pain in the feet and legs.

9. Tofu Plaster

You can use commercial tofu for external application. Drain the tofu and mash it. Add a little white flour to bind it. Spread 1/2 inch thick on a thin cotton cloth, the thickness of a man's handkerchief, or use fine cheesecloth. Spread it about 1/2 inch larger than the area to be covered. Apply to the painful part following Ginger Compress. This cold plaster picks up the toxins dislodged from the tissues by Ginger Compress.

If Tofu Plaster does not follow Ginger Compress add 5 percent grated ginger. This is effective for drawing out fever in the forehead, in a local inflammation, or in a bruise.

Tofu Plaster is also effective in preventing blood clot in the case of a bodily injury or blow to the head. It is much more effective than an ice pack. Change the Tofu Plaster every 1 to 3 hours or when it becomes hot.

10. Albi Plaster (Taro Potato)

The best potato to use is called *sato-imo* in Japanese. Albi is sato-imo. It is shaped like a small, dark brown hairy egg, round on one end, pointed on the other. If you cannot find this type of potato, you may use taro, but make sure it is a small rather than large variety. Peel and grate the potato. If it does not sting the fingers strongly, add 5 percent grated ginger. Spread to 1/2-inch thickness on fine cheesecloth a little larger than the area to be covered. If the skin is very sensitive, lay the plaster on the skin with one layer of cloth between the skin and the plaster. If it is still uncomfortable, apply sesame oil to the skin first. You may wrap the plaster with a cotton towel to prevent bedding from becoming wet. Change the plaster every 4 hours. In some cases you can sleep with it.

Albi Plaster is stronger than Tofu Plaster. As it draws toxins and poisons out of the body, it may change color from light yellow to dark brown. As the condition improves, the color becomes lighter. It is usually applied following Ginger Compress. If the body becomes too cold, place a hot salt pack on top of the Albi Plaster.

11. Potato and Greens Plaster

If there is no albi, you may substitute white potato. It is not as strong as albi but is still useful. In order to make it stronger, mix 50 percent grated green leafy vegetables with 50 percent grated potato and 5 percent grated ginger. Add enough white flour to bind it. Apply in the same way as Albi Plaster.

12. Brown Rice Plaster

Brown Rice Plaster can be used on local inflammations such as boils or infections where the skin is not broken. It is useful in reducing fever around the affected area.

Grind together in the suribachi 70 percent cooked brown rice, 20 percent minced raw green leafy vegetables and 10 percent raw nori torn in small pieces. Add a little water, if necessary, to make smooth paste. Apply this plaster directly to the skin. After it absorbs heat from the inflammation and becomes hot, remove it with warm water.

13. Buckwheat Plaster

The virtue of Buckwheat Plaster lies in its ability to draw out retained excess fluid rom swollen areas of the body.

Mix buckwheat flour with just enough hot water to form a hard, stiff dough. Apply o the swollen area in a 1/2-inch-thick layer and cover with clean white cotton cloth, ither wrapped around the body or tied in place. Leave for 4 hours. To be effective, Buckwheat Plaster must be used repeatedly from several times up to 3 days. Vater will begin to drain out of the skin.

In the case of cancer, such as abdominal swelling, swelling of the neck, arm, or ymph nodes associated with breast or other organ removal, apply a 5-minute Ginger ompress to the swollen area. Then apply Buckwheat Plaster renewing it every hours.

This is a much safer procedure to reduce water retention than mechanical raining in the hospital, which suddenly depletes essential body energy and can leave e patient in a precarious and critical condition.

4. Lotus Root Plaster

otus Root Plaster has proved very effective for dissolving accumulations of mucus in chronic cases of asthma, allergy, sinus trouble, bronchitis, and congestions of e nose and throat which impair breathing.

Grate enough fresh lotus root to cover the affected area. Add 10 to 15 percent hite flour or just enough to bind it, and 5 percent fresh grated ginger. Spread this ixture onto a clean white cloth to 1/2-inch thickness and apply directly to the skin. eep on for several hours or overnight. This may be used repeatedly for several days ing a new plaster each time.

To enhance the effectiveness of Lotus Root Plaster, first apply a 5-minute Ginger mpress to stimulate circulation and loosen stagnated mucus.

. Carp Plaster

nce carp has a special quality of coldness, it has the ability to draw fever out of body. It is especially useful for pneumonia and bronchitis, even advanced cases.

With prayerful apologies, crush and mash a whole live carp and mix in enough ole wheat flour to bind it. Spread this mixture onto oiled paper such as wax paper, or the special paper used for cooking found in Spanish markets. You may even try fish- or meat-wrapping paper. Place the plaster paper-side down onto the chest and leave for 1 to 3 hours. The body will begin to cool. As the temperature falls, check it every half hour and remove the plaster immediately at 97°F.

In the case of pneumonia, drinking 1 to 2 teaspoons of blood from the freshly killed carp is also effective in reducing the fever.

If no carp is available, you can substitute Tofu, Chlorophyll or Potato Plaster. Even an ice pack or fatty hamburger-meat plaster can be helpful to reduce fever. Do not eat the meat.

16. Cabbage Plaster

Cabbage or any dark green leafy vegetable can be used to reduce fever or heat in the body. Cabbage is convenient because a leaf can easily sit like a cap on the head. However, any dark green leaf will do, even from nearby trees.

17. Mustard Plaster

Mustard Plaster is very penetrating because of its pungency in a similar way to ginger. It creates heat in the body and is used to increase blood circulation and loosen various forms of stagnation. You can obtain dried mustard powder in a supermarket; a two-ounce can should suffice. Mix it with enough hot water to make a thin paste. Spread this onto a paper towel and cover it with another paper towel. Then slip this between the two halves of a folded white cotton bath towel. Apply this to the congested area and leave until the skin becomes red and warm. Do not allow the skin to burn. When removing Mustard Plaster, wipe off any juice that may have seeped through to the skin.

18. Miso Plaster

Miso has a high level of active bacteria and is therefore effective in controlling more yin bacteria. You can apply it directly to fungus, such as athlete's foot or other bacterial infections. Cover lightly with a clean white cloth or sock. Renew everyday until the skin is healed.

19. Dentie

Dentie is a black powder made from carbonized eggplant and sea salt. It acts as disinfectant, suture, and bandage in one. It is useful to heal wounds and eliminate fungal and bacterial infections, as well as to get rid of lice and scabies. It is also used on a daily basis as a dentifrice, strengthening the gums and counteracting pyorrhea.

20. Sesame Oil

Dark sesame oil is more effective than the overrefined light sesame oil popularly available. Sesame oil is high in lecithin which, as an emulsifier, not only helps to melt fats, but also helps to dissolve scars. Massage sesame oil into scars caused by surgery or wounds on a daily basis until they disappear. It may take up to 1 year.

During natural childbirth, purified sesame oil can be used to lubricate, massage, and ease the stretching of the perineum by a skillful and sensitive helpmate. It can also eradicate abdominal stretch marks with massage after childbirth. Sesame oil is ideal for lubricating nursing nipples and protecting the baby's body from diaper rash. It may also be useful as an internal as well as external lubricant during sexual intercourse.

Apply sesame oil to burned skin, after the heat has been drawn out by green leaves. It can also be used to ease the discomfort of tight skin after a sunburn has cooled down, and to soften dry skin.

Use sesame oil to reinsert external hemorrhoids and to heal cracked skin anywhere on the body.

To eliminate water retention in the eyes, put 1 or 2 drops of purified dark sesame oil in the eyes at bedtime. Continue every night for about a week until the eyes improve.

To purify sesame oil, bring it to a gentle boil without burning it. Pass it through a pre-boiled, dry, multi-layered cheesecloth, repeating up to five times. It can be stored in a small, brown glass jar. Use at room temperature.

A subtle touch of sesame oil on the eyelashes will make the lashes look longer and darker and is safer to use than mascara. For use on the scalp for baldness, psoriasis, earaches and scoliosis, see Ginger Sesame Oil.

21. Ginger Sesame Oil

This combination stimulates the activity of the capillaries and nervous system as well as general circulation. It also relieves aches and pains caused by bruises or tightness of the muscles or tissues.

Grate fresh ginger root and squeeze out the juice. Add an equal amount of sesame oil. Whip together with three chopsticks. With the fingertips, massage this into the scalp to heal the skin of dandruff and psoriasis. The dissolving and penetrating action also stimulates the growth of new hair in the case of baldness caused by hardened animal fats.

For scoliosis, dip cotton into the Ginger Sesame Oil, and massage the spine and both sides of the spine vigorously until the skin becomes red. Do this nightly for the first 2 weeks and 3 times a week for 3 to 6 months.

For earache, gently warm the oil before mixing with the ginger juice. Put several drops in the painful ear and plug the ear with absorbent cotton saturated in the Ginger Oil. If the ear is very painful, make a salt pack and lay the ear on it as a pillow.

22. Dark Leafy Greens/Sesame Oil

For any kind of burn, cool the skin immediately with some dark green leafy vegetable. After the heat is reduced, apply sesame oil, which is high in vitamin E, to heal the damaged skin.

23. Umeboshi

Umeboshi has been discussed in Other Internal Remedies. It has a variety of other uses. For headache, cut an umeboshi in half, put the pit in your mouth and plaster the two halves of the umeboshi on the temples. Lie down and relax. Breathe deeply, and channel the pain right out of the doorways of your temples.

To prevent air- or seasickness, paste an open umeboshi on your navel. You can cover it with gauze. It will dry and stay there. Strange as it may seem, it works.

Carry umeboshi in your backpack or car when hiking or traveling. If you cannot boil your water, soak several umeboshi in a quart of water for at least 1 hour to purify it before drinking. In this way, it has saved many people's lives.

24. Daikon Slices

For yang constrictive heart pain, apply several pieces of 1/4-inch thick sliced daikon on and around the heart area. It should be room temperature rather than cold from the refrigerator. Lie down and relax with this application until the pain disappears. Drink 1 cup of hot bancha tea.

25. Green Clay

Dried powdered green clay, such as that made by Cattier, can be mixed with enough water to make paste. Apply this to boils or pimples to draw out the pus and dry up the skin. Make just a little bit at a time.

26. Daikon, Onion, Scallion Juice

Grate or slice any of these vegetables and squeeze out the juice. This is good for insect bites and bee stings.

27. Mud

When the above vegetables are not available, mud is effective for insect bites and bee stings. Dig down in the earth a little to get clean, moist mud.

28. Vinegar

To prevent mosquito bites in the evening, rub your exposed skin with vinegar. Healthy macrobiotic people are never attacked by mosquitoes.

29. Pine Needles Decoction

This is effective for poison oak and poison ivy. Use long pine needles that grow 3 to a cluster. Collect about 1 quart of them and boil in 2 gallons of water down to 1 gallon. The water should become brown. Paint the affected skin with this decoction.

30. Cold Salt Water

Cold salt water is useful in contracting burned skin. Soak the burned part in cold salt water until all irritation disappears. Then seal the wound from air with Sesame Oil. This will prevent blistering.

31. Warm Salt Water

Use warm salt water as an enema or douche to relieve retained bowel or fat accumulations in the colon, and to cleanse the vagina of mucus. It is also effective as a gargle for sore throat.

32. Nuka Face Wash

Nuka is rice polishings and has been traditionally used to cleanse the skin, to lighten dark spots and leave the skin feeling soft. You can use rice polishings or oatmeal for this purpose. Put 1/4 to 1/2 cupful in a small cotton bag. Soak this in water for 1/2 minute, squeeze the starch to the surface of the bag and wash the face with it. It can be used on the whole body.

33. Cucumber Juice

Grate fresh cucumber and squeeze out the juice. Apply this to the face with the fingertips after washing the face with nuka. Cucumber juice is a mild astringent and leaves the skin feeling fresh and soft without drying.

Basic Nutrient Charts

The information in the following charts was derived from various sources, including *Composition and Facts About Foods* by Ford Heritage, *Standard Tables of Food Composition* compiled by The Japan Dietetic Association Corp. and the unpublished oral teachings of my teachers of philosophy and Oriental Medicine, both in America and in Japan.

Vitamins	Food Sources	Use in Body
A (Oil Soluble)	Leafy greens, esp., dandelion, collard, mustard, Swiss chard, watercress, lettuce (Boston/Bibb/Butter), New Zealand spinach, parsley, chicory, endive, turnip; green vegetables, esp., broccoli, peas, scallion, chives, celery; yellow vegetables, esp., corn, pumpkin, carrot, squash; yellow fruits, esp., dried apricots; tofu, egg yolk	Promotes growth and reproduction, good for eyes esp., night vision; good for skin, lungs, gallbladder, kidney, blood pressure; is stored in liver; body tissue reparation and maintenance (resists infection), good for hair, teeth, and bones. Abscisic acid, a vitamin A analog, seems to control the proliferation of cancer cells. It is found in all root vegetables, mature green leafy vegetables, onions, lima beans, sweet potatoes, yams, seeds, nuts, apples, pears and strawberries.
B COMPLEX (Water Soluble)	Whole grains, miso, tamari, natto, tempeh	Promotes energy, metabolism (carbohydrate, fat, protein), muscle tone maintenance (gastrointestinal tract); good for eyes, hair, liver, mouth, skin, nerves.
B_1 Thiamine (Water Soluble)	Whole grains, esp., barley, wheat, millet, rye, brown rice, corn; seeds, esp., sunflower, whole sesame, pumpkin and squash; beans, esp., lentils, pinto, white, red, lima, soy, mung; nuts, esp., Brazil, peanuts; dried peas; bamboo shoots, leafy greens, esp., collard, dandelion, kale; all sea vegetables, esp., dulse, kelp; miso, wheat germ	Builds energy and appetite, aids digestion (hydrochloric acid production), carbohydrate metabolism, aids muscle tone maintenance (heart, intestine, stomach), aids proper function of heart, liver, circulation; promotes growth, learning capacity, is good for brain, ears, eyes, hair, nervous system.
B_2, G Riboflavin (Water Soluble)	Whole grains, esp., millet, rye; leafy greens, esp., turnip, collard, dandelion, parsley, kale, mustard, watercress; broccoli; seeds, esp., sesame, sunflower, pumpkin, squash; beans, esp., white, lentils, soy, red, lima, mung, pinto; dried peas, rice polish, wheat germ, mushrooms, wheat bran, nuts, esp., chestnuts; sea vegetables, esp., kelp, dulse	Antibody and red blood cell formation; cell respiration; metabolism (carbohydrate, fat, protein); delays degeneration; improves skin and eyes, liver, kidneys, heart.

Deficiency	Herbs	Destroyed by:
Slow growth, poor bone and tooth development; night blindness, reduced ability to resist infection; keratosis (clogged hair follicles on arms, legs, buttocks); skin lesions from excess sun; warts, xerophthalmia (damaged cornea), allergies, appetite loss, fatigue, itching and burning eyes; rough, dry skin, sinus trouble	Alfalfa, dandelion root, paprika, parsley, watercress, yellow dock, sorrel	Fertilizer (nitrogen), nitrogen dioxide (air pollution), alcohol, coffee, cortisone, excessive iron, mineral oil, vitamin D deficiency
Acne, anemia, constipation, cholesterol (high), digestive disturbances, fatigue; dull dry falling hair, insomnia, rough, dry skin		Alcohol, birth control pills, coffee, infections, sleeping pills, stress, sugar, sulfa drugs
Lack of appetite; fatigue, constipation, beriberi, nervous instability, depression, polyneuritis, cardiac failure, edema, irritability, numbness of hands and feet, pain and noise sensitivity, pain around heart, shortness of breath	Bladder wrack, dulse, fenugreek, kelp, wheat germ	Sugar, antibiotics, unhappiness, stress, alcohol, coffee, surgery, fever, pregnancy, lactation, tobacco, raw clams
Sores and cracks at lip corners, inflammation of lips and tongue; burning, itching eyes; photophobia; blurred vision; cataracts, poor digestion, retarded growth	Bladder wrack, dulse, fenugreek, kelp, saffron	Sugar, antibiotics, alcohol, tobacco, coffee, contraceptives

Vitamins	Food Sources	Use in Body
B_3 Niacin (Water Soluble)	Whole grains, esp., wheat, millet, brown rice, barley, sorghum, rye; leafy greens, esp., kale, collard, parsley, watercress; beans, esp., soy, mung, white, red, lima; seeds, esp., sesame, squash, sunflower, pumpkin; corn, taro, mushroom, dried peas; chick-peas, rice polish, wheat bran, kelp, chestnut	Builds mental health, aids nervous system, helps maintain appetite; good for adrenal glands, pancreas, circulation, cholesterol level reduction, growth, hydrochloric acid production, metabolism (protein, fat, carbohydrate), sex hormone production, good for skin, liver, tongue, soft tissue.
B_5 Pantothenic Acid (Water Soluble)	Whole grains, beans, esp., soy; rice polish, wheat germ, cooked mushrooms, raw elderberries	Promotes healthy skin, hair, liver; promotes energy, vitamin utilization, growth of adrenal hormones, production of antibiotics; stimulates nervous system, growth, good for digestive tract.
B_6 Pyridoxine Hydrochloride (Water Soluble)	Whole grains, rice polish, wheat germ, corn oil, peas, cooked prunes, green leafy vegetables, esp., cabbage	Good for muscles, skin, fat and protein utilization (weight control), appetite, teeth, gums, blood vessels, red blood cells, liver, antibody formation, digestion (hydrochloric acid production), nervous system (maintains sodium/potassium balance). For iron deficiency take B_6 together with iron.
B_{12} Cobalamin (Water Soluble)	B-complex foods, miso, kelp, dulse, tempeh, buckwheat	Prevents nerve cell degeneration; aids metabolism of carbohydrates, fats, and protein; promotes appetite, blood cell formation and longevity, healthy nervous system.
B_{15} Pangamic Acid (Water Soluble)	Whole grains; sunflower, sesame and pumpkin seeds	Cell oxidation and respiration: metabolism (protein, fat, sugar); glandular and nervous system stimulation; good for heart, kidneys.

Deficiency	Herb	Destroyed by:
Indigestion, gastrointestinal, skin and neurologic change; appetite loss, canker sores, depression, halitosis, headaches, pellagra, insomnia, muscular weakness, nausea, nervous disorders, skin eruptions	Alfalfa, parsley, blueberry leaves, burdock seeds, fenugreek, watercress	Sugar, refined starches, antibiotics, alcohol, coffee, corn, sickness (Intestinal absorption is decreased during sickness.)
Loss of appetite; indigestion, nausea, abdominal pain, moodiness, depression, restlessness, nerve problems, fainting sensations, rapid pulse, pain in arms and legs, repeated infections, respiratory infections, lowered blood pressure, loss of hair, muscle cramp, premature aging, kidney trouble, duodenal ulcers, eczema, hypoglycemia, disturbed electrolyte and water balance, diarrhea		Alcohol, coffee; insecticides, fumigation (even in health food warehouses. In China and Viet Nam all produce is farm fresh, no stocking. Market from 5 A.M. to noon.)
Depression, sleepiness, loss of appetite, nausea, vomiting, convulsions, esp., in babies, hair loss, dizziness, sore lips and tongue, acne, irritability, pain in arms and legs, hypochromic anemia, weakness, arthritis, conjunctivitis, learning disabilities, seborrheic dermatitis		Cortisone, codeine, coffee, alcohol, sugar, tobacco, radiation, birth control pills, estrogen, aging (After 50, B_6 assimilation becomes difficult.); food processing and high protein diet, which create anemia and aging.
General weakness, nervousness, pernicious and macrocytic anemia, dermatoses, neurititis, walking and speaking difficulties	Alfalfa, bladder wrack, dulse, kelp	Alcohol, coffee, laxatives, tobacco, oral contraceptives, stress, eating only vegetables and fruits, iron deficiency
Heart disease, nervous and glandular disorders		Alcohol, coffee

Vitamins	Food Sources	Use in Body
B_c, M Folic Acid (Water Soluble)	Whole grains; green leaves, mushroom, wheat germ, soybeans, dried dates	Helps build strong blood, aids intestinal tract, digestion, body growth and reproduction, protein metabolism, red blood cell formation, glands, liver.
B_x, Paba Para-Aminobenzoic Acid (Water Soluble)	B-complex foods, wheat germ, rice polish and rice bran	Helps maintain natural hair color, aids blood cell formation, intestinal bacteria activity, protein metabolism, good for glands, skin.
C Ascorbic Acid (Water Soluble)	Peas, leek, garlic, onion, turnip, daikon, pumpkin, scallion, horseradish, leafy greens, esp., parsley, watercress, kale, collards, turnip greens, broccoli, Swiss chard, lettuce, dandelion greens, mustard greens, Brussels sprouts, cabbage and Chinese cabbage	Forms and maintains intercellular substance, aids bones, teeth and gums, collagen production, digestion, iodine conservation, healing burns and wounds, red blood cell formation (hemorrhaging prevention), shock and infection resistance (colds), vitamin protection (oxidation), good for adrenal glands, heart, connective tissue (skin, ligaments, bones).
D (Oil Soluble)	Sunlight, watercress, egg yolks, wheat germ	Promotes normal bone and tooth development, regulates absorption and fixation of calcium and phosphorus, aids normal blood clotting, skin respiration, nervous system maintenance, heart action, good for thyroid gland.
E Tocopherol (Oil Soluble)	Whole grains, esp., barley, brown rice, buckwheat, rye; dark green vegetables, leafy greens, esp., dandelion greens, watercress; sesame seeds, nuts, beans, vegetable oil, wheat germ, kelp, dulse, eggs	Prevents liberation of hemoglobin from red blood cells, aids heart, reproduction, utilization of fatty acids, aging retardation, anticlotting factor, blood cholesterol reduction, blood flow to heart, capillary wall strengthening, fertility, male potency, lung protection (antipollution), muscle and nerve maintenance, good for skin, pituitary gland, blood vessels.

Deficiency	Herbs	Destroyed by:
Sprue (malabsorption of nutrients), megaloblastic anemia (inability of DNA to divide due to lack of B_{12} and folic acid together), indigestion, graying hair, growth problems		Alcohol, coffee, stress, tobacco, unhappiness, worry, oral contraceptives, vitamin C deficiency (cannot produce B_c without C)
Loss of hair, failure of growth, reproductive failure, constipation, depression, digestive disorders, fatigue, headache, irritability, gray hair		Alcohol, coffee, sulfa drugs
Cutaneous hemorrhage, poor bone development, weakened cartilages, muscle degeneration, anemia, stunted growth, susceptibility to infection, bleeding gums, scurvy, bruise easily, nose bleeds, poor digestion, capillary wall ruptures, dental cavities	Burdock seeds, capsicum, marigold flowers, oregano, paprika, parsley, rose hips, watercress, elderberries	Excess water, aspirin, cortisone, fatigue, stress, smoking, coffee, alcohol, antibiotics, high fever, breathing smoke and air pollution
Rickets (bowed legs, enlarged joints), tetanic convulsions, osteomalacia	Watercress	Lack of sunlight, mineral oil
Dry, dull or falling hair, sterility, enlarged prostate gland, gastrointestinal disease, heart disease, impotency, miscarriage, muscular degeneration	Alfalfa, bladder wrack, dandelion leaves	Oral contraceptives, food processing, too much fat, rancid fat and oil, chlorine, mineral oil

Vitamins	Food Sources	Use in Body
F Unsaturated Fatty Acids (Oil Soluble)	Vegetable oil, wheat germ, sunflower seeds	Promotes artery hardening prevention, blood coagulation; blood pressure normalizer, cholesterol destroyer, aids glandular activity, growth, vital organ respiration, good for mucous membranes, nerves, skin, adrenal and thyroid glands, cells, hair.
K Menadione (Oil Soluble)	Leafy greens, safflower oil, oatmeal	Aids blood coagulation, good for liver.
P Bioflavanoids (Water Soluble)	Fruits (skins and pulp), esp., apricots, cherries, grapes, citrus, plums, prunes, black currants; parsley, walnut	Aids blood vessel wall maintenance, bruising minimization, cold and flu prevention, strong capillary maintenance; combats disease of joints, diabetes, tuberculosis, good for connective tissue (skin, gums, ligaments, bones), teeth.
Rutin	Buckwheat	Blood coagulation.
U	Cabbage, celery, raw greens	Helps combat ulcers.
Hormones	Sea vegetables	

Minerals	Food Sources	Use in Body
Calcium Ca	Seeds, esp., sesame, sunflower; leafy greens, esp., watercress, dandelion; sea vegetables, dandelion root, beans, almonds	Bone and tooth formation, blood clotting, aids heart rhythm, nerve tranquilization, nerve transmission, muscle growth and contraction; activates some enzymes, aids blood coagulation, normalizes metabolism, good for skin, soft tissue. (It is the most abundant mineral in the body.)
Carbon C	Nuts, olives, roasted seeds, and sea vegetables	Good for teeth, connective tissue, skin, hair, nails.
Chlorine	Celery, kelp, carrot, dock, parsnip, turnip, leafy greens, esp., kale, lettuce, watercress, dandelion, cabbage; cucumber	Good for digestion and elimination, normalizes osmotic pressure in blood and tissues, sustains normal heart activity, aids acid/alkaline balance, good for blood, epithelium, nerves.
Chromium	Whole grain cereals, corn oil	Maintains blood sugar level, glucose metabolism (energy), good for circulatory system.

Deficiency	Herbs	Destroyed by:
Acne, allergies, dry skin, dry brittle hair, diarrhea, gallstones, nail problems, eczema, underweight, varicose veins		Radiation, x-rays
Diarrhea, increased tendency to hemorrhage, miscarriages, nosebleeds, hemorrhagic disease in infants	Alfalfa, chestnut leaves	Antibiotics, diarrhea, colitis, radiation (from x-ray, TV, microwave oven), aspirin, mineral oil, rancid fats
Anemia, bleeding gums, capillary fragility and permeability, easy bruising, dental cavities, low infection resistance (colds), nosebleeds, poor digestion	Paprika	Antibiotics, aspirin, cortisone, high fever, stress, tobacco
Capillary fragility	Paprika	
	Aletris root, alfalfa, clover, false unicorn root, garlic, ginseng, tropical yam root	

Deficiency	Herbs	Destroyed by:
Heart palpitations, insomnia, muscle cramps, nervousness, arm and leg numbness, tooth decay, retarded bone and tooth development, fragile bones, stunted growth, rickets, osteomalacia, osteoporosis	Arrowroot, plantain, chamomille, dandelion root, flaxseed, horsetail grass, nettle	Excessive liquid and juices, lack of exercise, stress
		Excessive liquid and juices
		Excessive liquid and juices, alcohol, sugar
Atherosclerosis, glucose intolerance in diabetes and hypoglycemia		Excessive liquid and juices

Minerals	Food Sources	Use in Body
Copper Cu	Nuts, esp., Brazil; legumes, esp., soybeans; whole grains, raisins	Good for liver, gallbladder, blood, lungs, heart, absorption and metabolism of iron, oxidation of fatty acids and of tyrosine to melanin pigments, aids metabolism of ascorbic acid, good for hair, skin color, healing process of body, hemoglobin and red blood cell formation, circulatory system.
Fluorine F	Almond, carrot, leafy greens, esp., beet greens, turnip greens, dandelion	Good for bones, teeth, blood, skin, nails, hair.
Hydrogen* H	Carrot, celery, spinach, cabbage	Good for blood, all cells.
Iodine I	Leafy greens, esp., Swiss chard, turnip greens, kale, mustard greens; kelp, dulse, agar, summer squash, cucumber, watermelon, blueberries, sea salt	Constituent of thyroxine which regulates rate of energy exchange, aids oxidation of fats, proteins; stimulates circulation, aids physical and mental development, good for hair, nails, skin, teeth, thyroid gland.
Iron Fe	Leafy greens, esp., parsley, watercress, shiso greens; sea vegetables, esp., nori, wakame, dulse, hijiki, river nori, kelp; beans, seeds, esp., sunflower, squash, sesame; eggs, wheat germ, whole grains, sun-dried sliced daikon, dried red pepper	Aids hemoglobin and myoglobin production, stress and disease resistance, good for oxidative enzymes, bones, brain, muscles, nails, skin, teeth.
Magnesium Mg	Leafy greens, esp., parsley, kale, mint, watercress, cabbage, carrot tops, spinach; whole grains, beans, whole sesame seeds, nuts, esp., almond; sea vegetable, bran	Strengthens nerves and muscles, conditions liver and glands, stimulates elimination, activates enzymes in carbohydrate metabolism, aids acid/alkaline balance, blood sugar metabolism (energy), calcium and vitamin C metabolism; good for arteries, bones, heart, teeth and blood albumin.

* Particular gases are listed due to their essential function in the body.

Deficiency	Herbs	Destroyed by:
Retarded hemoglobin production, defective respiration, general debility, limited growth, skin sores		Excessive liquid and juices
Tooth decay, spinal curvature, weakened eyesight	Garlic, watercress	Excessive liquid and juices
		Disturbed by intense heat, such as fever, fire and radiation, and intense cold.
Cold hands and feet, dry hair, irritability, nervous disturbances, obesity, goiter (enlarged thyroid), cretinism (subnormal basic metabolism), sensitivity to infections, general weakness, low body and mental activity	Bladder wrack; dulse, kelp and other sea vegetables	Excessive liquid and juices
Anemia, breathing difficulties, brittle nails, chlorosis, constipation, paleness, limited growth, inferior vitality	Watercress, yellow dock, burdock root, meadowsweet, parsley, strawberry leaves	Excessive liquid and juices; coffee, excessive phosphorus and zinc, tea
Confusion, disorientation, easily aroused anger, nervousness, rapid pulse, tremors, soft bones, digestive disorders, exhaustion, poor complexion, convulsions	Carrot leaves, dulse, dandelion leaves and root tea, flaxseed (as tea or in food), kelp, bladder wrack, meadowsweet, parsley, peppermint, walnut leaves	Excessive liquid and juices

Minerals	Food Sources	Use in Body
Manganese Mn	Leafy greens, esp., parsley; carrot, celery, beet, cucumber, chive, legumes, bran, whole grains, egg yolk	Aids thyroxine formation, urea formation, lipotropic activity of choline, utilization of thiamine, metabolism of carbohydrates, strengthens tissues and bones, aids sex hormone production, reproduction and growth, vitamin E utilization, enzyme activation; good for brain, mammary glands, liver, kidneys, pancreas, spleen, heart, lymph, muscles, nerves.
Nitrogen* N	Leafy greens, alfalfa	Good for muscles, cartilage, tissue, ligaments, tendons, lean flesh.
Oxygen* O	Fresh air	Good for bones, teeth, skin, red blood cells, circulation, optimism.
Phosphorus P	Leafy greens, seeds, esp., pumpkin, squash, sesame, sunflower, safflower; nuts, beans, whole grains, sea vegetables, dried fruit, eggs	Aids bone and tooth formation, cell growth and repair, energy production, heart muscle contraction, kidney function, calcium and sugar metabolism, nerve and muscle activity, vitamin utilization; activates some enzymes, promotes fat and carbohydrate metabolism, transportation of fatty acids; good for brain, nervous tissue, hair.
Potassium K	Beans, nuts, rice bran, sunflower and sesame seeds, wheat bran, dates, figs, peaches, banana, all vegetables, esp., leafy greens, carrot, beet, radish; sea vegetable, dried fruit	Promotes intercellular fluid balance, regulates heart rhythm, nervous and muscular irritability, aids elimination, aids formation of glycogen from glucose, fats from glycogen, proteins from peptones and proteoses, good for rapid growth, nerve tranquility, blood, kidneys, skin.
Silicon Si	Leafy greens, esp., lettuce, dandelion, savoy cabbage; onion, leek, parsnip, pumpkin, cucumber, strawberry, sunflower seed, rice bran	Good for blood, muscles, skin, nerves, nails, hair, connective tissue, pancreas, tooth enamel, antiseptic action.

* Particular gases are listed due to their essential function in the body.

Deficiency	Herbs	Destroyed by:
Ataxia (muscle coordination failure), dizziness, ear noises, loss of hearing, weak tissue respiration, restricted growth, defective reproductive functions, glandular disorders, general weakness, skin sores		Excessive liquid and juices, excessive calcium/phosphorus
Improper growth		Disturbed by intense heat, such as fever, fire and radiation, and intense cold
Asphyxiation and death		Disturbed by intense heat, such as fever, fire and radiation, and intense cold
Poor mineralization of bones, appetite loss, irregular breathing, poor growth, rickets, fatigue, nervous disorders, decreased as well as overweight, general weakness	Caraway seeds, garlic, chickweed, licorice root, marigold flowers, meadow-sweet, sesame seeds, watercress, sorrel	Excessive liquid, juices, iron, aluminum, magnesium; white sugar
Disturbed growth and elimination, weak muscular control, incomplete digestion, constipation, acne, continuous thirst, dry skin, slow irregular heartbeat, insomnia, nervousness, weak reflexes, general weakness	Carrot leaves, German camomile flowers, comfrey leaves, dandelion leaves, eyebright, watercress (best raw), fennel, parsley, oak bark, nettle leaves	Excessive liquid, juices and salt; stress, sugar, alcohol, coffee, laxatives, diuretics, cortisone
Reduced resistance to infectious diseases	Horsetail grass	Excessive liquid and juices

Minerals	Food Sources	Use in Body
Sodium Na	Kelp, celery, carrot, salt, radish, sesame seed, watercress, kale, beet greens, dandelion greens	Aids formation of digestive juices, aids elimination of carbon dioxide, regulates osmotic pressure, maintains water balance, promotes nerve irritability, normal cellular fluid level, proper muscle contraction, good for blood, lymph system.
Sulfur S	Kelp, turnip, leek, radish, celery, Brussels sprouts, watercress, lettuce, cabbage, raspberry, bran, eggs, nuts, wheat germ, kale	Promotes body tissue formation, collagen synthesis, aids digestion and elimination, oxidizing agent in hemoglobin, good for hair, nails, nerves and skin.
Zinc Zn	Whole grains, pumpkin and sunflower seeds, mushroom, kelp	Effects transfer of carbon dioxide from tissues to lungs, is constituent of digestive enzyme for hydrolysis of protein, aids healing of wounds and burns, aids carbohydrate digestion, prostate gland function, reproductive organ growth and development, sex organ growth and maturity, vitamin B_1 and phosphorus metabolism, good for blood, heart, brain, thyroid, liver, kidneys.

Trace Elements and Minerals				
Aluminum	Bromine	Lead	Neon	Silver
Argon	Cerium	Lithium	Nickel	Strontium
Arsenic	Cobalt	Mercury	Rubidium	Tin
Beryllium	Helium	Molybdenum	Scandium	Titanium
Boron	Lanthanum	Neodymium	Selenium	Vanadium

Deficiency	Herbs	Destroyed by:
Nausea, vomiting, diarrhea, muscular cramps, digestive disorder, general debility, decreased weight, appetite loss, intestinal gas	Fennel seed, watercress, meadowsweet	Excessive liquid and juices, lack of chlorine and potassium
Restricted growth, eczema, dermatitis, poor nail and hair growth	Calamus, eyebright, fennel seed, garlic, meadowsweet, watercress	Excessive liquid and juices
Restrictive and retarded growth, loss of taste, poor appetite, prolonged wound healing, sterility, defective intestinal absorption, delayed sexual maturity, fatigue		Excessive liquid and juices; alcohol, high intake of calcium, lack of phosphorus

Amino Acids	Food Sources	Use in Body
Alanine	Alfalfa, carrot, celery, dandelion, lettuce, cucumber, turnip, watercress, apple, apricot, grapes, olive, orange*, strawberry, almonds	Good for skin and adrenal glands.
Arginine (essential)	Alfalfa, green vegetables, esp., celery, lettuce, leek; carrot, beets, radish, parsnip, potato*	Aids muscle contractions, controls body cell degeneration, good for reproductive organs, is cartilage constituent.
Aspartic	Carrot, celery, cucumber, parsley, radish, turnip greens, watercress, lemon, apple, apricot, watermelon, almonds	Retards bone and tooth destruction, aids lung and respiratory functions, good for heart and blood vessels.
Cystine	Alfalfa, carrot, beet, cabbage, cauliflower, onion, garlic, kale, horseradish, Brussels sprouts, apple, currants, raspberry, Brazil nut, hazelnut, filbert	Good for hair, red blood corpuscles, mammary glands, aids tissue resistance to infection.
Glutamic	String beans, Brussels sprouts, carrot, cabbage, celery, beet greens, dandelion greens, parsley, lettuce, spinach, papaya*	Promotes digestive juice secretion, glycogen formation and its change to energy sugar, aids production of insulin, prevents anemia, has disinfectant properties.
Glycine	Carrot, dandelion, turnip, celery, parsley, spinach, alfalfa, garlic, raspberry, watermelon, potato*, orange*	Good for cartilage, muscle fiber; controls sex hormone.
Histidine (essential)	Horseradish, radish, beet, carrot, celery, dandelion greens, turnip greens, cucumber, endive, alfalfa, leek, garlic, onion, apple, sorrel	Aids liver formation of glycogen, controls mucus, semen and hemoglobin component.
Hydroxyglutamic	Carrot, celery, parsley, lettuce, spinach, grapes, raspberry, plum, tomato*	Controls generation of gastric juice; is similar to glutamic acid.
Hydroxyproline	Carrot, beet, lettuce, dandelion greens, turnip greens, cucumber, olive, almond, Brazil nut, apricot, cherry, orange*, raisin, grapes	Good for liver and gallbladder, aids fat emulsifying and formation of hematin and globulin in red blood corpuscles.
Iodogorgoic	Carrot, celery, lettuce, spinach, sea lettuce, kelp, dulse, tomato*	Good for all glands (thyroid, pituitary, lymph, adrenals, etc.).
Isoleucine (essential)	Nuts, *except* peanut, cashew, chestnut; olive, avocado*, papaya*	Regulates thymus, spleen, pituitary and metabolism, good for hemoglobin.

* These foods should be used with discretion.

Amino Acids	Food Sources	Use in Body
Leucine	Same as Isoleucine	Counterbalances Isoleucine.
Lysine (essential)	Carrot, beet, cucumber, celery, parsley, spinach, dandelion greens, turnip greens, alfalfa sprouts, soybean, apple, apricot, pear, grapes, papaya*	Good for liver, gallbladder and fat metabolism; aids regulation of pineal and mammary glands, corpus luteum, oophoron and ovaries; prevents cell degeneration.
Methionine	Brussels sprouts, cabbage, cauliflower, dock, kale, horseradish, chive, garlic, watercress, apple, Brazil nut	Aids function of spleen, pancreas and lymph; is constituent of hemoglobin, tissues and serum.
Norleucine		Helps to balance Leucine functions.
Phenylalanine (essential)	Carrot, beet, spinach, parsley, apple, tomato*	Aids elimination of waste, good for kidney and bladder functions.
Proline	Carrot, beet, lettuce, dandelion greens, cucumber, turnip, olive, almond, Brazil nut, raisin, grapes, cherry, orange*	Good for white corpuscles, regulates emulsifying of fats.
Serine	Horseradish, radish, leek, garlic, onion, carrot, cucumber, beet, celery, parsley, spinach, cabbage, alfalfa, apple	Promotes tissue cleansing of mucous membrane; good for lungs and bronchials.
Threonine (essential)	Carrot, alfalfa, green leafy vegetables, papaya*	Aids exchange of amino acids to establish balance.
Thyroxine	Carrot, celery, lettuce, spinach, turnip, kelp, sea lettuce, tomato*	Aids activity of thyroid, pituitary, adrenals and orchitic glands; regulates metabolism and speed of reactions.
Tryptophane (essential)	Carrot, beet, turnip, endive, celery, dandelion greens, fennel, snap beans, Brussels sprouts, chives, spinach, alfalfa	Aids generation of cells and tissues, gastric and pancreatic juices; good for optic system.
Tyrosine	Carrot, cucumber, lettuce, beet, alfalfa, dandelion greens, parsnip, leek, parsley, watercress, spinach, green pepper*, almond, strawberry, apricot, watermelon, cherry, apple	Aids generation of red and white blood corpuscles, promotes development of cells and tissues; is active in adrenals, pituitary, thyroid; good for hair.
Valine (essential)	Carrot, turnip, lettuce, dandelion greens, parsnip, parsley, squash, celery, beet, almond, apple, tomato*	Aids function of corpus luteum, mammary glands and ovaries.

* These foods should be used with discretion.

Vegetable Sources of Protein

(Grams per 100 grams edible serving.*)

GRAINS and CEREALS

28.5 Wheat gluten, dried (fu)
27.9 Wheat germ
13.9 Buckwheat
13.5 Oatmeal
13.2 Rice bran (nuka)
13.0 Whole oats
12.7 Proso millet (kibi)
12.7 Rye
12.0 Hard wheat
10.8 Buckwheat noodles (soba, dried)
10.4 Soft wheat
10.3 Sorghum
10.0 Barley
9.9 Foxtail millet
9.9 Popcorn
9.6 Wheat gluten, wet
9.5 Millet
8.2 Corn, whole dried
7.6 Glutenous brown rice
7.4 Brown rice
6.9 Half brown rice (hakumai)
6.2 White rice
6.0 Koji (*Aspergillus oryzae*, fermenting enzyme)

BEANS and BEAN PRODUCTS

34.3 Soy bean, dried
24.7 Broad bean
24.7 Lentil
23.0 Mung bean
22.9 Pinto bean
22.8 Cow pea
22.5 Red bean
22.3 White bean
21.7 Peas
21.5 Azuki bean
20.5 Chick-pea (garbanzo)
20.4 Lima bean
20.2 Kidney bean
10.9 Soy bean, fresh
8.4 Lima bean, fresh
6.5 Green pea, fresh
52.3 Soy milk skin (yuba)
38.4 Soy flour, roasted (kinako)
19.5 Fermented soybean cake (tempeh)
18.6 Soybean curd, fried (aburage)
16.5 Fermented Soybean Condiment (natto)
6.0 Soybean curd (tofu)
3.6 Soy milk
3.5 Soybean solids (okara)

MISO

32.2 Dehydrated
23.6 Powdered
21.0 Hatcho
19.4 Soybean
17.6 Low salt
16.1 Peanut
13.5 Red
13–11 Mellow red, yellow, white
12.8 Barley
12.7 Sweet red
11.1 Sweet white
20.0 Tamari soy sauce

VEGETABLES

6.5 Peas, fresh
6.2 Garlic
5.2 Daikon greens
5.2 Mugwort
5.0 Kale
4.9 Brussels sprouts
4.8 Lily root
4.5 Collards
4.5 Shepherd's purse
4.1 Burdock
3.8 Corn, fresh
3.6 Broccoli
3.6 Parsley
3.1 Pumpkin
3.1 Horseradish
3.0 Bean sprouts
3.0 Spinach
2.9 Salsify
2.7 Dandelion greens
2.7 Cauliflower
2.7 Mushroom
2.7 Turnip greens
2.6 Mustard greens
2.5 Bamboo shoots
2.5 Shallot
2.4 Lotus root
2.4 Savoy cabbage
2.4 Watercress
2.4 Swiss chard
2.3 Autumn squash
2.2 Beet greens
2.2 Leek
2.1 New Zealand spinach
2.1 Potato
2.1 Yam
2.1 Dock (sorrel)
2.0 Kohlrabi

* All measurements are approximate, varying with geographical location, climate, season and crop.

1.9 Taro
1.9 Scallion
1.9 String bean
1.8 Celeriac
1.8 Chicory
1.8 Chives
1.7 Escarole
1.7 Parsnip
1.6 Cabbage
1.5 Turnip
1.4 Chinese mustard greens
1.4 Chinese cabbage
1.4 Sweet red pepper
1.4 Olive
1.4 Water chestnut
1.3 Carrot
1.2 Onion
1.1 Rutabaga
1.1 Daikon
1.1 Radish
1.1 Summer squash
0.9 Celery
0.9 Cucumber

SEA VEGETABLES
35.8 River nori
35.6 Purple nori, superior
34.2 Purple nori, ordinary
29.0 Purple nori, inferior
20.7 Green nori
12.7 Wakame
7.5 Arame
7.3 Kombu
5.6 Hijiki
2.3 Agar-agar

SEEDS
29.7 Pumpkin, squash
24.0 Sunflower
19.7 Sesame
18.9 Watermelon
8.1 Lotus
5.3 Ginkgo

NUTS
31.1 Pignolia
26.0 Peanut
23.1 Walnut
21.0 Almond
19.6 Cashew
19.3 Pistachio
17.4 Brazil
13.2 Hickory
13.0 Pinon
12.7 Hazelnut (filbert)
11.0 Pecan
7.8 Macadamia
6.7 Chestnut

Note: Beans, nuts and seeds, miso, tamari soy sauce, and tofu protein counts are generally equivalent to, or higher than, all animal protein, including beef, lamb, goat, turkey, duck, chicken, eggs and fish. They are lower in fat and ecologically more economical.

Part 4

AIDS, Candida, and the Common Cold

All life is nothing but an aggregation of that which has come before it. Just as our personality is a composite of all our experiences and dreams, past, present, and future, so our body is a composite of all the stages of evolution, from primitive microorganisms to human form. We carry the manifestations of these stages within us, beginning with the ocean, from which all life evolved.

Every human being passes through the approximately three billion years of biological evolution on earth in the nine months of gestation. As embryos, we grow from microorganisms through the Piscean to the mammalian stages of life in the ocean, swimming within the amniotic mini-ocean of our mother's womb. As we develop, we begin to carry the ocean within us, as salty blood, saliva, tears, and digestive bacteria.

Bacteria and viruses are primitive life forms occurring naturally in nature. The more primitive a life form, the more ubiquitous is its adaptability, that is, the more capable it is to live anywhere, under any conditions. Primitive algae also has this capability. Different strains of bacteria and virus are produced by different environments.

The main function of these primitive organisms is photosynthesis and digestion. They flourish on elemental forms of protein and carbohydrate, water and often, though not always, sunlight. They carry on this digestive process in the ocean and on the land, as well as in our digestive organs. They develop into various forms, according to the quality of the environment and the variety of food that surrounds them.

In nature, as they eat, they grow and evolve. As they develop, their food changes accordingly. The more complex in development a species becomes, and the more differentiated its life systems, the more selective it is of the type of environment it depends upon for support. Thus, primitive forms evolve into more complex structures, from one-celled to many-celled, immobile to mobile, invertebrate to vertebrate, sea animals to air and land animals, four-footed to two-footed and two-winged, to two-footed and two-armed, and from a horizontal nervous system and posture to a vertical nervous system and posture, as in man.

The blueprint of the structure of ocean and land creatures and systems is imprinted in our genes, such as: intestines that undulate as snakes, ears and cochlea reminiscent of snails, villi absorbing nutrients like sea anemone, ovaries with seeds like fruit-bearing trees, lungs which act as respirators, like the leaves of the plant kingdom, and so on. In this fashion, all the various forms of creation grow and develop, cumulatively, out of the great undifferentiated ocean, into the unification of Man as a species, the ultimate form.

At birth, the baby is land-born and eventually crawls on all fours like an animal. It gradually pulls itself up and walks slightly bent, holding on until it grows stronger and can stand on its own. Thus, Man evolves in the spiral of humanization.

At each stage of evolution, each life form has its particular food. It consumes what is less evolved than it, and is, in turn, consumed by what is higher than it. Life evolves from lower to more complex forms through digestion and transmutation, the two primary functions of all creatures. These are the mechanisms through which life is manifest and the universe pulses from potential to matter to potential again.

The process of evolution is increasingly complex. Each species evolves out of, and is, therefore, dependent upon, the phase of evolution that precedes it for its sustenance.

It can be said, then, that the main mechanism of evolution is based on digestion and transmutation. In the ocean, where life begins, the primitive digestive system is external: the ocean itself is swarming with digestive bacteria and enzymes. As life develops, and the digestive system grows more complex, it becomes internalized in subsequently higher life forms. As life evolves from ocean to land, the ocean is carried forward, internally, to continue its function of digestion, as various fluids in the body and digestive organs.

Among the myriad and innumerable types of digestive bacteria and enzymes, some thrive in a more yin environment, some in a more yang environment; some thrive in a sweet, saccharine environment, some in a salty, saline environment; some in an acid environment, some in an alkaline environment; some in warm or hot temperatures; some in cool or cold temperatures; some in dark, some in light; some in oxygen, some in nitrogen; some in fermented, spoiled and decayed matter, some in strong and vital systems. In other words, all bacteria, viruses, enzymes, molds, yeasts, fungi, and so on are the offspring of the environment which produced them, just as we are the offspring of our mother and father, and the Earth is the offspring of the heavenly forces of yin and yang.

Therefore, the environment that we create in ourselves produces and supports the life forms that thrive there. We create our internal environment through all the food and other substances that we eat, drink, smoke, inhale, or otherwise ingest. We even absorb chemicals, smoke, pollutants, and various vibrations through the skin, just as we absorb vitamin D from the sun. These all gather and accumulate to form our internal quality. This is reflected in our internal and external condition: how we feel, how we look, how we think, and how we behave.

The right food creates strong and healthy organisms. Inappropriate, incomplete or degenerate forms of food weaken the whole system, beginning with the blood. In a degenerated state, our blood devolves to a lower form of organism. In this state, it easily becomes food for other organisms and we become hosts to harmful bacteria, viruses, and parasites. They do not only come from outside, however. We also create them internally through the devolution of our blood. Then, like all primitive organisms, they reproduce rapidly and prolifically. For example, the AIDS virus reproduces 1,000 times faster than any known gene.[1]

Many "destructive" bacteria and viruses are nothing more than degenerate forms of our own hemoglobin doing their job of cleaning up and digesting pathological, spoiled, and decayed tissue, just as insects perform in nature.

If our lifestyle includes the ingestion of extreme yin substances, such as chemically produced and adulterated foods and drinks; high-sugar foods and beverages, such as tropical fruits and fruit juices; milk and milk products; pastries, ice cream, soft drinks, candy, and gum; or such foods containing other types of sugar or sugar-substitutes, such as honey, molasses, date sugar, corn, raisin, or maple syrup, fructose, sucrose and lactose, especially in extracted and concentrated forms, or saccharine and other similar artificial substances, our blood quality will deteriorate. Simple sugars are primary food for primitive life forms, such as bacteria, viruses, molds, fungi, and yeasts. They are not appropriate food for human beings and destroy the red blood cell. As long as we continue to eat them, along with other degenerate forms of "food," we will support the growth of these destructive microorganisms within us, and our blood will degenerate into similar primitive forms of life.

[1] Dr. Mahler, Chief, World Health Organization.

If we also ingest acid food and drinks, such as alcohol, vinegar, sodas and citric acid beverages, as well as excessive animal or vegetable protein, our blood quality will become acidic and we will lose the minerals which bind the cell structure together. If, together with this, we ingest or absorb medications, such as vaccinations and antibiotics, drugs of any kind, excessive creams, lotions, perfumes, and other cosmetics, as well as yin bodily secretions such as sperm, then our blood, tissue, and cell quality will begin to deteriorate. We will, for all practical purposes, regress the quality of our blood and tissues to a lower, more yin, stage of evolution. Instead of creating a life-supporting ocean-like internal environment, we create a swamp-like environment in which life systems break down, decay, and disintegrate. At this point, various fusions may take place, creating mutations in cell structure, as in cancer.

In other words, if we work all day in an artificial environment, such as an hermetically sealed, air-conditioned, fluorescently lighted, electric appliance- and possibly radiation-charged, positive-ion-rich environment (from computer screens, microwaves, televisions, etc.); eat artificially produced and adulterated foods; smoke or breathe smoke; snack on acids and sweets, such as coffee with milk and/or sugar, soft drinks, pastry, ice cream, and candy; enjoy an alcoholic "Happy Hour" after work; go out with friends at night, which means absorbing more moon energy than sun energy; gather in dark, crowded, smoke-filled rooms where the oxygen is depleted and carbon dioxide is increased together with smoke exhalation; take drugs; expose ourselves to strong vibrations, such as motorcycles and other vibrating machines, which act as a centrifuge to the body cells; or to loud and discordant sounds which traumatically disturb our sensitive life-force field; or, in some other way, lower our resistance, then we have created the appropriate environment in which lower, more yin, forms of bacteria and virus can thrive on disintegrating matter. We have not created an appropriate life-support environment for human beings and the weakened sodium- and mineral-poor immune system can no longer protect us. It is at this point, as in the case of AIDS, that the HTLV-III virus destroys the white blood cells.

In this way, we set the stage and become the food for lower forms of life. These primitive life forms are produced within the environment we provide for them. They arrive by personal invitation. They do not enter as a hostile invading army. They come to fulfill their natural function. To greet them as an enemy and blame them for our deterioration is a mistake. It is egocentric and dualistic. We are responsible for our condition. No one created it but ourselves. Even if we "catch" a "contagious" virus from someone else, it is because we have already provided the internal environment in which that prolific primitive organism can thrive. We create the deficiencies within us by taking incomplete and unsuitable foods and substances. AIDS itself is an auto-immune deficiency disease. If our systems are strong and alkaline, we never "catch" such viruses. We do not invite parasites to devour us, even long after we die. They are not attracted to us. This is how survivors walked through the Black Plague unscathed.

"Whenever blood or blood corpuscles change into a pathological state, numerous bacilli always arise spontaneously in the blood by putrefaction, even when no bacillus intrudes into the blood from the outside.

"Most of the diseases which are called 'epidemic' do not occur due mainly to the infection of bacteria or viruses, but, as a matter of fact, due to ill health, irregular habits, unseasonable weather, and other bad circumstances including 'milieu.'"[2]

This is possibly the origin, mechanism, function, and cause of a plethora of yeast, bacterial, and viral "infections," such as candida, AIDS, influenza, and the common cold.

The use of antibiotics to kill these "invading hordes of enemies" is also against life and further deteriorates our body, killing necessary and useful bacteria and enzymes within us.

It behooves us to cooperate with, support, and harmonize ourselves with nature instead of going against the natural forces which created us.

"Therefore, it is necessary that in order to promote our health and enjoy longevity, we should try to take an adequate quantity and quality of diet to improve the useful symbiotic bacteria in the intestine, or the intestinal symbiotic bacterial flora, rather than be afraid of bacteria."[3]

As human beings, we have a certain degree of free will. We have a choice to make at every moment of our lives. That choice either promotes life, peace, health, harmony, prosperity, and happiness, or death, war, sickness and disease, conflict, poverty, and misery. Every thought, image, expectation, desire, dream, and goal that we create in our silent fantasies; every word, phrase, and quality of expression that we use to project those fantasies into the world; and every action and type of behavior, seen or unseen, that we perform, manifest as our personal reality and create the world we live in.

In this way, out of the illusive fabric of life itself, we create either positive experiences or negative experiences; we either enrich and develop ourselves and others as human beings, or we degenerate ourselves and others into a lower world of subhuman beings; we either live in an inner world of revelation and compassion or in an inner world of nightmares and hallucinations; we either grow toward the angelic and godly or toward the monstrous and demonic. In other words, thought by thought, word by word, action by action, and step by step, we create, for and by ourselves, Paradise or Hell. The choice is up to us.

---

[2] Kikuo Chishima, *Revolution of Biology and Medicine* (Japan: Neo-Haematological Society Press, 1972), p. 277.

[3] Ibid.

Part 5

Self-Transformation

Stand Guard at the Gateways to Heaven

There is an ancient saying in Japan: *Shin do fuji no gensoku.* This is the principle of no difference between mind, heart, and earth. It means: The environment and I are one. We are so intimately connected with our environment that there is virtually no dividing line. The environment nourishes us as we nourish the environment.

There are many different levels of food, both visible and invisible, tangible and intangible. We are constantly being influenced by, and absorbing, infinite vibrations, cosmic rays, emanations of stars and planets, sun and moon. We are affected by climate and season, geographical conditions, mountains and valleys, deserts and oceans, water and wind, heat and cold. We are influenced by the various formations of air, water, and earth. We are affected by the red blood and flesh of animals, and by the chlorophyll and substance of vegetables, by fire and ice, cooking and freezing, yin foods and yang foods.

We are equally conditioned by what we think, feel, see, hear, say, and do. What we think, feel, see, hear, say, and do at the time we are eating is impressed on the newly formed cells and becomes what we are.

We become that which we absorb or allow to enter into us, whether tangible or intangible, visible or invisible. As we absorb, so we emit. As the food we absorb becomes us, so we become food to everything within and around us. The quality of what we eat and channel determines the quality of what we emanate. We are catalyzers of the universe.

Our mind, our senses, our emotions, our mouth, our actions, are all gateways to Heaven or Hell.

> Jesus said, "Hear and understand: Not that which goeth into the mouth defileth a man; but that which cometh out of the mouth, this defileth a man. . . .
>
> ". . . those things which proceed out of the mouth come forth from the heart; and they defile the man.
>
> "For out of the heart proceed evil thoughts, murders, adulteries, fornications, thefts, false witness, blasphemies:
>
> "These are the things which defile a man. . . ."

Macrobiotically, we say, that which goes into the mouth and that which comes out of the mouth reflect each other and are inextricably connected. They are a continuous flow and transmutation of the same energy.

We live within, and are one with, the great ocean of infinite energy, in a constant flux of transmuting itself from one state to another. We are part of this great flux and, as human beings, may be the only creatures capable of channeling and directing that energy at will.

God gave us all we need. It is up to us whether we direct that energy to create Heaven, or we direct it to create Hell. Therefore, let us take a conscious stand to guard the gateways to Heaven.

On Letting Go and Being

Everyone has some kind of unhappy memory, some difficulty he or she has lived through in the past. Most people carry those bad memories with them, even to the end of their lives, continuing to be stuck in, and living in, the past.

We carry memories of frightening events, real or imagined, that happened either to ourselves or to someone else. We carry the feelings themselves of fear or rejection, even though the circumstances no longer exist in which they were born. We carry every imaginable description of negativity within us, from the slightest projection of our own mind to traumatic experiences of catastrophic proportions.

The very process of reliving and maintaining these memories as fixed entities creates physiological tension and stress of immeasureable extent in our body. We often speak of torn, broken, or scarred hearts. There is probably more truth in this than one suspects.

And so we live in our silent world, accumulating more and more scars to nourish our despondency. And we ask: What is there to live for?

People have dealt with this problem in many ways: through overeating, drugs, alcohol, sugar, sex, or work addiction; through suicide, through armoring and through neglect. Or they have tried psychotherapy of various styles.

In working through unresolved residual emotional conflicts, it is not necessary to bathe ourselves in their intensified energy. This only leads to more physiological imbalance, harming the energy and the organs.

Life is ephemeral. We live in a sea of dreams, which are the fantasies and projections of our mind. It is the mind that interprets a situation as stressful and that reacts in a stressful way. Thus, it is the mind that creates stress, not the situation. Therefore, it is the mind that can let it all go, seeing it all as ephemeral illusion. It is the mind that can release the negative energy and transform it into a positive, creative, dynamic force.

One way to achieve this is through forgiveness. Forgiveness is a very powerful tool for self-healing. Forgiveness means that we are not judging and negating the entire person or particular circumstance because of specific shortcomings. Forgiveness means that we accept and embrace that person or circumstance in its entirety, no matter what. The bigger the misdeed, the bigger the forgiveness. Then, within that realm of consciousness, in whatever ways are appropriate, we can help them, guide them, inspire them, or encourage them to overcome those shortcomings or misdeeds, or try to find a way to change the circumstances. This may take transcendent patience and insight, as well as time. The benefit to us is that as our compassion grows, so do we.

We must also achieve forgiveness within ourselves. Until then, negative emotions will linger: resentment, bitterness, hatred, anger, depression. Whatever form they may take, they are self-poisoning. The object of our negativity does not necessarily feel what we are harboring secretly in our heart. Who feels that? We do. Who is poisoned by that? We are. When we feel negative emotions rising within us, we can seize the opportunity for self-purification. We can forgive that person or circumstance for all the harm he or it has done us, intentionally or unintentionally, and forgive ourself for our negative reaction to that person or situation. Once we have done that, the way is cleared and the energy can flow freely to be used in a creative, positive way.

It was with this mind that Jesus cried from the cross, "Forgive them, for they know not what they do."

No energy is ever lost in the universe. All energy is in a constant state of flux and transmutation. It is not sufficient to just ignore, deny, or dismiss negative energy. It must be changed according to our higher guidance. The creative way to handle negative emotions is to transform them into positive energy. The act of forgiveness clears the way for this to take place. The result is a feeling of emotional and physical clarity and vitality. The accumulation of this positive energy paves the way for rejuvenation and happiness.

We are all made of the same life-force. We are all made from the same infinite, universal, creative energy. We are all crystallizations of one Spirit. What we have done through improper eating, improper thinking, and improper action is to have buried, blocked, obstructed, and deviated that energy so that our understanding, interpretation, and expression are also inaccurate.

The most direct way to approach this problem on the causal level is, macrobiotically, to discharge the excess that causes blockage and deviation of energy; to strip away the plaque: the excess meat, fat, dairy, and sugar. As we discharge old body cells, the memories imprinted on them are also discharged. Then, we replace those old, tainted cells with new, fresh cells, carrying the imprint of purified, positive, and loving thoughts. In this way, we rebalance the system, clarifying the body in preparation for perceiving and expressing the pure energy again in an accurate way. Fasting and illumination have always gone hand in hand.

The reason everyone loves babies is because their energy is pure: it is not distorted yet. Since a baby's energy is flowing freely, without obstruction, we feel whole and joyful when holding it. We laugh when the baby laughs because this laughter is the bubbling spring of God's pure energy, which is love. Jesus taught, "Behold, the Kingdom of God is within you." (St. Luke 17: 21). Where is the Kingdom of Heaven that we enter? It is inside. Our body is nothing but pure crystallization of spiritual energy, and our mind is nothing but pure undifferentiated spiritual energy, which we channel into thought and action. There are not two separate entities, two separate worlds. There is only one universe in different states, different densities of materialization or spiritualization.

Once we clearly see our oneness with all Life, the act of forgiveness becomes easy, natural. There is a very effective, formal ceremony, that we can use to seal this state of awareness. It is a Forgiveness Ceremony.

Choose a suitable place for the ceremony. It should be a place to which you are attuned inwardly. It could be your bedroom, a special corner of your living room, a place where you keep special or sacred books, or an altar which you have prepared. It could be a garden or a meadow, under a special tree, at the ocean, or in the mountains. It could be right where you are, sitting quietly, alone.

Purification is more easily achieved through fasting. It is best to fast for three days, drinking only bancha tea. If this is difficult, you may make a partial fast, eating at your regular mealtimes, only whole grains in small servings, and chewing well.

During this period, it is necessary to physically clean any space or objects connected to the person or situation involved. The cleaning must be thorough, inside and outside, underneath and behind; in effect, cleaning all the corners of your mind, especially what is hidden. Make everything clean and in order. As we clean, we can feel in our consciousness that we are cleaning away the veil of illusions from our eyes and can now see the true realities of life. Our kinship with all that there is, is experienced and understood with new depth.

After the area is cleaned, purify it with incense or sagebrush. Light the end, wave the fire out, and leave it smoking. Walk around the ceremonial area, waving the smoking incense to purify any negative influence that might be lingering, both in the atmosphere and in your own mind.

Place the smoking incense securely in a focal point and light two candles, one on either side. Sit comfortably facing this with your back straight. Then visualize all the people, situations, and circumstances, one at a time, that have triggered negative reactions in you and say, silently or outloud, whichever is more effective, "I forgive you. I forgive myself for harboring ill-will toward you. I love you and pray for your happiness. May God bless you." Feel your unhappiness dissolve. Repeat the same thing for each person and each circumstance toward which you have carried ill feelings. Go back in your life as far as possible. Cleanse yourself as deeply as you can. For each one, say, "I forgive you for all the harm you have done to me. I forgive myself for the harm I have done to you, in action or in silence. I love you and pray for your happiness, all the rest of your life, in this life and in the next life, now and forever." And let it go. You may elaborate in whatever way feels the most deeply satisfying.

Repeat the whole process until you feel empty, peaceful, and clear. Then, sit very quietly, breathing deeply, and experience the long-awaited peacefulness within. In this way, you begin to nourish yourself.

The inner healing has begun.

Testimonials

Testimonial of Allen Goldstein

In November 1982 I discovered a small cyst on the right rib cage and had it lanced. The area swelled and I became concerned. I had it partially cut out and it was found to be malignant. I was given a 50 percent chance of living. Radiation was recommended, but I was not guaranteed a cure.

I found out about macrobiotics through Dr. Sattilaro's book *Recalled by Life*. I was inspired to start macrobiotics and saw Michio Kushi in Denver, Colorado, in February 1983. Michio said, "Don't worry. No problem." He said I was pre-cancerous in other areas, too, such as the prostate. He explained that the primary cause was animal fat, chicken, sweets, and dairy. He recommended lighter cooking, more variety of vegetables, boiled salads, pressed salads, and raw salads once or twice a week.

This way of cooking and eating helped me to feel more relaxed. I had always been very tense. I lead a high-tension life and began not to internalize it as much as I had before. My internal condition was becoming less sticky and hard, due to the change in food. As a result, it was easier for me to let go of psychological tension.

Under the guidance of Cecile Levin, I followed the diet very carefully over the next two years, including the use of specific external applications. In those two years, I lost 30 pounds. My body became very clean and the tumor grew, collecting the body's poisons in one place. Finally it opened and began to discharge to the outside. At this point, I had two choices: either allow the tumor to continue draining until it was completely discharged, which would take some time and attention, or, since the body had become completely clean and the tumor had become externalized and encapsulated, I could just have it cut off. I understood that if the tumor were removed surgically before the body was clean, the cancer would reappear elsewhere. If the tumor was left on and the diet was broadened too much, the poisons being discharged could become reabsorbed into the blood and cause trouble, such as metastasis.

I decided to save time and have the tumor removed surgically. For some reason, all the lymph nodes in and under the right armpit were also removed. This was unnecessary, since they were non-malignant. The surgery was followed by fifty sessions of low-grade radiation one minute daily for three months. All the hair on the right rib cage was permanently burned off by the radiation. I was careful to eat very well macrobiotically during my recovery. I would never have gone ahead with the surgery if I had not been sure my body was totally clean beforehand. The surgery simply removed what my body had already started to discharge, thanks to Macrobiotics.

Testimonial of Carl Melikian

During a physical examination I was informed of a tumor on my prostate. A biopsy was taken and the pathologist's report was positive. The following week (November 1981, at age 58) surgery was performed removing my prostate. After surgery I experienced radiation treatment for a two-month period. Shortly after the radiation treatment a bone scan was taken indicating no abnormalities.

During another routine physical examination of February 1984, a lymph node lump was discovered in the lower portion of my neck. Surgery was performed removing the tumor. This was followed by another bone scan indicating cancer activity on my spine and in the rib cage. As a result of the above developments, it was recommended that my testicles be removed. This was done in March 1984. The prognosis did not look too good for me at this point.

A friend of the family mailed me a book written by Dr. Sattilaro, *Recalled by Life.* My health problems were similar to that of Dr. Sattilaro: similar operations, similar pains, similar complications. Along with the book was included a flyer on Macrobiotics from the W.L.A. East West Center describing the educational activities of Cecile Levin.

Prior to my introduction to Macrobiotics, my diet was a typical American diet: meat, heavy on dairy products, fruits, vegetables. At this point, my energy was somewhat at a low point. I did have pains in the back and also required naps in the afternoon on a daily basis.

I met with Cecile in February 1985 and received instruction in macrobiotic cooking, as well as personal guidance. As a result, my style of preparing and eating foods has changed and my diet now consists primarily of whole grains, vegetables, beans, and sea vegetables. Approximately a year after being introduced to Macrobiotics, I noticed an improvement in my energy level and I no longer required afternoon naps. Furthermore, there have been no more pains in my back.

Another bone scan was taken in December 1985. There was no change from the previous test. A subsequent scan in May 1986 showed no evidence of metastatic disease. A last bone scan in May 1987 showed no evidence of metastatic disease. I am in complete remission. My health and energy level are good and the blood pressure is normal.

Testimonial of Mel Edel

I thought I was on a good diet, but I was mistaken. I took lots of red meat, steak almost every night, salads with oil and vinegar, frozen vegetables, butter, and lots of cheese. I was a great eater of cheese, in which I overindulged. I also took quite a bit of alcohol—whisky, double vodka and tonics, and beer daily. Then I switched to wine, thinking it was less harmful. I was under a lot of stress due to my wife's brain tumor surgery and heart problems. I was also taking care of my sister after her husband died.

I was suffering intermittent back pain and fatigue. A full physical examination had revealed a healthy condition, but I was not feeling well. A subsequent blood test revealed prostate cancer, fourth stage advanced. It was too late for surgery or chemotherapy. A top doctor recommended estrogen to counteract the high testosterone and to slow down the growth of cancer in the prostate. This was in September 1985.

Then I found the book *Recalled by Life* by Dr. Anthony Sattilaro. The next day I went cold turkey on vegetables and grains and cut out all red meat and dairy. After finding out about Cecile Levin in October, my way of eating was adjusted more accurately.

In December 1985, I had my quarterly examination. The prostate had lost its hardness and become softer. By March, the alkaline phosphatase had reduced by one-half. By June, it had reduced more and I experienced a great general improvement. By December I reached full remission.

The March 1987 test showed my cholesterol level was down to 118 from the previous 200 to 250 level. The prostate was totally soft and normal. The doctor said that if he had not known that I had had cancer, he would never have guessed it. My social life has increased with very happy results.

Testimonial of Kenneth Minton

When I was 25 years old, working for Shell Oil Company, I was in the habit of eating just about anything and everything. I was overweight at 155 pounds and had a chronic sinus infection. An irregular mole appeared on my back and started to spread in a clover-leaf pattern. During a routine medical check-up, the mole was biopsied and confirmed as Clark's level 1 melanoma. The doctor said it was nothing to worry about and removed it by surgery.

Two months later, I found a lump in my right armpit. It was diagnosed as an infection and antibiotics were prescribed. They were useless. I had the lump biopsied and it was found to be a malignant melanoma. Several lymph nodes were found to be involved. I had already found more lumps after the initial surgery.

I was frightened by the prospect of having cancer and, on the same day, made appointments for interviews at the John Wayne Clinic at UCLA and with Cecile Levin at the East West Center for Macrobiotic Studies. Cecile explained the macrobiotic way of life and dietary practice to me. Everything she told me made sense and I felt more at ease. She told me my body could heal itself if I gave it a chance.

At UCLA, only surgery was recommended. I was told no other way existed. When I told them I wanted to try macrobiotics first, the doctors became infuriated. One doctor told me my chances for survival were one in a million. I was warned that no diet could help and was given two years to live. Further tests revealed I had Clark's level 2 melanoma. Later, when I requested my records, I found half of them had been lost.

I started the macrobiotic diet. Within five weeks I lost 25 pounds of fat and felt pretty good. Within three to four months, I felt more stamina and found the tumor shrinking. When the original surgeon discovered that I had refused further surgery, he offered to examine me free of charge. After six months of macrobiotics, he found no more tumor. He did not want to know how I had achieved this. He did not want to know anything about the diet. Nevertheless, I returned to him for another examination after one year. Nothing was found.

I was so excited about the diet and the way I felt. My hair grew thicker, my nails grew stronger, and, more importantly, my long-standing chronic sinus infection disappeared. After the first month all constipation was alleviated. I found that exercise helped a lot during the process of discharging. Now, five years later, I work out and exercise daily, weigh 145 pounds, and the sinus trouble has never returned. I have been gratefully enjoying the macrobiotic way of eating with my family, who have also benefitted, for these five years, and am glad to be alive.

Testimonial of Elaine Gyorke

In 1976 I was seeking a cure for a number of ailments which were being medically treated, but were not being cured. I was 26 years old, had severe acne, was overweight, very fatigued, and was suffering from leg muscle spasms, which my father also suffered as a result of multiple sclerosis. I had been suffering with this problem for nine years and feared that I, too, might be developing multiple sclerosis. The doctor told me there was no way he could treat me, but that if my eyes began to fail, this would be a sure sign of multiple sclerosis and then he would have something to treat. Later on I experienced an expansion and separation of bone, both in my knees and in the breast plate. Again, there was no treatment for this. The doctor did prescribe drugs for the acne, but they had little or no effect, so I began to experiment with vitamin therapy. I continued with my usual way of eating, which consisted of meat, potatoes, dairy products, eggs, baked goods, some vegetables, desserts, ice cream, and some wine. I took very little grain. I did eliminate red meat within the year, but I saw little change in my condition.

Fortunately, I was introduced to Cecile Levin and began studying macrobiotic cooking. Within ten days of eating grains and vegetables my skin cleared up. I made whole grains my primary food and included vegetables, beans, sea vegetables, and fermented products, such as pickles, miso, and tamari soy sauce. My weight dropped and the muscle spasms ceased for the first time in nine years. Later, my bones began to contract and feel solid again.

Within a few months I experienced increased energy, clarity of thought, and creative inspiration. With the physical illness and blockages removed, I now desired to achieve a calm, psychologically sound, state of mind on a continuing daily basis. I feel that the removal of animal foods and fats, refined and processed foods, chemicals and medications, as well as caffeine and spices, relieved my body of the toxins, acids, and sugars which had contributed to my weak condition. By eating whole grains and organic foods, I became relaxed and began to feel unified. Stressful situations no longer stimulated tension, anxiety, and fears in me.

For many years I had been pursuing a stressful career in film production. Then my career desires shifted, enabling me to have a more personal means of expression with a feminine emphasis. I returned to school, entered a design program and have since been employed as a designer of clothing and interior spaces. This field has provided me with personal rewards which eluded me in the film industry and which I would not have been able to accomplish in my previous condition.

Today, twelve years since meeting Cecile, I am eternally grateful for her teachings, insight, wisdom, and support, which have enabled me to develop a strong core from which I have cultivated physical and psychological health, vitality, creative talent, a calm and peaceful state, and never-ending gratitude.

Testimonial of Mary Cordaro

During most of my life, I never felt well. Even as a child, I felt tired and lifeless. After several years of alternating with bouts of chain smoking and bingeing on food, I only became more fatigued and depressed. I eventually relied on Western medicine for relief. By the time I was 27, I was taking antibiotics for bladder infections about every two months. Two years later, I contracted severe allergies, periodic asthma, dizziness, and nausea. I finally found a "wholistic" doctor who diagnosed me as having candida and started me on an elaborate diet with vitamin therapy, in addition to daily testing and allergy shots. This approach got me on my feet again, but it was only temporary.

Two years before I met Cecile, my father died of liver and kidney cancer. While researching healing methods for him, I stumbled upon Macrobiotics. I was not able to use it for him, but I began to experiment with it, continuing to fall into patterns of self-abuse. I ate a typical vegetarian diet, free of most dairy, but loaded with sugar and caffeine.

At 32, I was desperate for help. I had just returned from a lengthy series of business trips, completely exhausted. One day during the last trip, I had a shock. I was freshening up my lipstick outdoors after lunch and, as I looked in the mirror in the full daylight, I could not believe how I looked. I realized that I was aging rapidly and looked like a dying person. I checked with my husband for confirmation and he also saw the rapid aging. I became very frightened. This was the turning point for me.

I decided to see Cecile for guidance in Macrobiotics. The first few weeks on my new diet were fine. Literally overnight, I gave up caffeine, sugar, flour products, oil, and all other unnecessary foods. I started to feel better, my energy increased, and my allergies disappeared. My life at home and at work began to run smoothly. Then, it happened. I became obsessed with becoming well.

Having read about the many miracle cures in macrobiotic books, I became tense from the worry that if I did not do everything perfectly, I would never become healthy. I had no idea at the time that the stress I was creating for myself was inhibiting my healing process. As a result, I unconsciously became overly yang from worry, lack of joy, and the consequent unconscious tendency to cook overly strong dishes. About three months into the diet, my body became so cold that during fairly mild weather I had to wear up to six layers of clothing just to keep from shivering. I became chronically constipated. Then my skin went wild. The slight case of beginning psoriasis that I started with became an all-over-body itch, as the psoriasis spread over my entire body from shoulders to feet. My legs became so inflamed and swollen that I could not bend them. I cried several times a day from the twenty-four hour agony of itching, scratching, bleeding, and oozing. I slept no more than an hour at a time. I became an emotional basket case, with the added worry that I would not be able to continue working. My obsession with doing things right only increased, and I constantly berated myself for not improving. After all, people dying of cancer were becoming well faster than I was. I knew my kidneys were in deep trouble, but I was not dying! Every week, I had a telephone "check-up" with Cecile to discuss the changes and ways to slow down the discharge. As Cecile suggested, I started to cook with more water, included some fish occasionally, and cut out some of the more yang dishes. Whenever I cooked with too much salt, overate grains, or deviated in the least from the guidelines, I would suffer all over again with the itching, bleeding, and constipation. Although I continued to have interrupted sleep, I slowly started to regain my strength and could leave the house for short periods of time.

Then one day, about six months into the diet, things started to change. After spending a week in bed, and having made several changes in my diet with valuable coaching and support from Cecile, I started to feel a little better and was able to partially resume work. After a business meeting, I was alone in the office when I saw a box of wheat crackers. I was not hungry. I told myself that if I even touched those crackers, I would have to face weeks of incapacitating swelling, bleeding and increased itching. I knew that the crackers could constrict the kidneys, which would affect my skin. I watched myself in horror as I proceeded to eat most of the box of crackers, in the blinding way that I used to binge. When I finished the box, I panicked. What had I done! As I started to drive home, I made a decision. What if I bathed myself in self-love and completely erased the fear, the guilt, and the panic? That night I discovered the wisdom of macrobiotics with the incredible healing power of self-love. Because I allowed myself to truly relax, I did not become sick from the crackers. The energy was not cut off by tension and I realized how good it felt to love myself. I said affirmations about my health, my goodness, and my capacity for love.

After that night I decided to change my thinking. I went through a slow process of realization. Along with a healing diet there must exist the desire to live and to experience life. I became very easy on myself. I allowed myself to eat widely and to give in to my cravings for more yin foods, such as barley malt, fruit, oil, and tahini, which I had avoided in order to heal the psoriasis. Although I continued to cook and eat the basic diet, if I found myself eating handfuls of granola, or several rice cakes with tahini and apple butter, I began to recognize these needs as signals that I needed to love myself. I also made more effort to include more balanced, good-quality yin dishes in my meals. No matter what I did, I practiced unconditionally loving myself. My health continued to improve! My skin began to clear up, my body warmed up, and I started to appreciate life around me.

Eventually, after eight months of struggling, I reached a middle ground with Macrobiotics. My diet constantly changes in subtle ways now, depending on how I feel and my daily condition. I see remarkable changes when I combine my meditations and affirmations with the diet, and I easily spot slight relapses in my skin condition when I create stress for myself. My general appearance has changed dramatically. Lines and wrinkles are fading, my color has changed from grey to brown to rosy,

I stand much taller and, even in cool weather, I stay warm and comfortable. The backs of my legs and insides of my arms still break out periodically, as my cleansing continues, but this comes and goes lasting only one or two days. My physical stamina has greatly increased and I feel better than ever.

Most importantly, I now see that Macrobiotics can best work for me when I use it as a continuous way of life rather than as a symptomatic remedy that I impose on myself. Healing myself has to start from my center, not from something that I impose from the outside. When I started the macrobiotic diet, I used it in much the same way that I used Western medicine and the endless fanatical health food remedies—as separate from the spiritual and emotional aspects of my life. In order to heal, I had to work on changing every area of my life, as the teachings suggested, not just how I ate. Now I enjoy my life more as I continue to learn how to love myself. And I discover the joy of macrobiotic eating and cooking as I learn to cook more appropriately and with a lighter heart, and as I learn to let go of the need to practice with fear and obsession.

Testimonial of Barbara Tschirhart

Several years ago I developed a bladder infection that reoccurred and was not responding to any antibiotics. It was spreading to my kidneys and it was possible that this would lead to kidney failure. Medications just seemed to make things worse. I was so weak that I could barely move and had extremely low blood pressure. The doctors treated me for six months and I just got worse.

Someone who had been healed under Cecile Levin's supervision recommended her. I had been on a standard American diet with plenty of dairy. I became macrobiotic and my boyfriend cooked for me after taking Cecile's classes. Soon afterward, toxins started being released out of my body through my skin. I was told that this was because my kidneys were so weak that they were not eliminating properly. I developed severe psoriasis all over my body, which continued to cleanse in this way for about one year. This discharge process was very difficult, but I could feel my body getting stronger all along. My boyfriend ate the food, too, and became so strong and sensitive that he could no longer tolerate drugs and alcohol, which was a wonderful side-effect for him.

As my body got stronger, my mind became clearer. At first, I felt crazy, confused, and disoriented as the toxins were being released. I could not even read and comprehend. My body, mind, and emotions were clearing up and cleaning up together. I began to feel very balanced and centered. If I ate something too salty or sweet, I could feel the effect immediately and it would make me have cravings. This helped me to understand that food can be used as, and sometimes is, a "drug."

My healing was slow, but very thorough and profound. The macrobiotic diet and way of life under Cecile Levin's guidance has given me my most powerful understanding of life. I now own a jewelry store and am capable of much more than I ever thought possible.

Testimonial of Bonne Tschirhart

In the past I was accustomed to eating a lot of meat, eggs, dairy, especially ice cream and milk, and sugary sweets. As a result, I developed ovarian cysts and amenorrhea, which led to a high secretion of testosterone, causing the development of masculine traits, such as facial hair and a lowered voice. Therefore, I tried the Bieler diet of raw and steamed vegetables, raw milk, high-sodium vegetables, such as celery, zuccini, broccoli, and cauliflower, and took black-nightshade family vegetables, like tomato, potato, and eggplant. I also took lots of green beans. As a result, the testosterone level was lowered. Giving up meat and dairy was a big benefit. I generally ate better. However, menstruation was still irregular and troublesome.

In the meantime, my back was fractured when I was hit by a car while riding my bicycle. In the hospital for two weeks, I was eating very little. The food was so bad that I had relatives bring me steamed vegetables. After getting out of the hospital, I saw a psychic nutritionist who put me on the Bieler diet with steamed vegetables, milk, and boiled eggs. This was unfulfilling and unsatisfying, as well as ineffective.

In the East West Journal, I read about a woman who had cured her female problems with the macrobiotic diet, which I had heard of. At the same time, my sister, Barbara, saw Cecile Levin for macrobiotic instruction. Now I felt confident in my direction and had people to share it with. The timing was perfect. The universe was answering my plea for right food and right guidance. The answer to my prayers came to me without further searching.

I needed to more deeply heal my back and to cure my female problems and regulate my periods. I regret not knowing about Macrobiotics earlier, which would have prevented mistakes in the healing process. I know that my back would have healed faster.

I followed Cecile's recommendations and, over the course of about three months, noticed many big changes. I felt a lot more centered, more focused, clearer thinking, emotionally stable and calm. My judgment regarding food grew dramatically. I could know what was good or bad for me as soon as I put it in my mouth. More important, my periods became regular and my back and muscles became much stronger.

My ability to use my body and move in dancing became more yang, stronger, healthier, with more endurance. I no longer suffered fatigue. My back pain was considerably diminished to the point where I have begun to dance again, which makes me very happy. Dance has taken on new meaning for me. I am very grateful for having found Macrobiotics.

Testimonial of Edmund Spaeth

My problem started with sleeplessness every night between 3 A.M. and 5 A.M. This was accompanied by sudden extreme night sweats, general nervousness, tightness in the jaw, extreme impatience, and feelings of depression. I also suffered weakness in the legs which made me bed-ridden for five months. As a result, I was unable to work for about one year. I was also suffering from low blood sugar and various swellings, pullings, and disturbances in the lymph system.

I tried vitamin injections for low blood sugar and weakness, which helped a little. In Germany I received "fresh-cell" injections from lamb fetuses. This only increased the night sweats and sleeplessness and caused severe tremors, resulting in hospitalization for one week.

I had grown up in Germany and had been accustomed to eating plenty of meat, eggs, cheese and cottage cheese, along with salads and homemade cakes. It was a typical rich German diet. I used to think it was good food.

As my problems increased, I became desperate and felt more and more depressed. I felt very ill. My wife, Karin, read about Macrobiotics in the library and found out about Cecile Levin, from whom she received guidance and instruction.

As soon as I began practicing the macrobiotic way, I began to improve. From almost total sleeplessness and constant sweating, within the first few days, I was able to sleep again. I reoriented my diet to whole grains and vegetables, tailored to my needs, and was also greatly helped by the application of ginger compresses. I found that meridian stretching exercises were also helpful, especially in eliminating night sweats.

I had been to well-known doctors, professors of medicine, and hospitals, both in Los Angeles and Germany, and, though I felt that I was dying, with all their tests, they could not find anything wrong with me. They thought that I was imagining all these symptoms and suggested I see a psychiatrist. I felt that their incompetence was shocking.

I am much better now and feel deeply that Macrobiotics saved my life. As I continue, my health continues to improve. I am so grateful that my wife and I are planning to pursue our studies so that we can begin to help other people, possibly opening an educational center in Germany.

Closing Words

The True Meaning of Macrobiotics

Macrobiotics is the way of Life, it is the way of Creation itself. It is also a way of realizing our oneness with the universe, our oneness with each other, our oneness with God, the Great Spirit. Macrobiotics is neither another medicine nor is it medical practice. It is the fundamental and universal practice of Life.

Food is an essential factor in macrobiotic practice. It is the synthesis of the forces of Heaven and Earth, of the Tai Chi, Prana, Chi or Ki energies, and is a reflection of the Five Transformations of those energies. As such, food is the basic link between health and consciousness. It completes the cycle between Heaven and Earth, Body and Mind. Used with an understanding of the order of the universe to guide our own order of eating and daily life, we can achieve true health, inner peace, and spiritual harmony.

Dietary regulation forms a basic foundation of life, but the roles of diet and healing are only the kindergarten of the macrobiotic way of life. Self-reflection, self-cultivation, and the deepening of understanding of the laws of the universe, the Tao, together with the development of judgment and intuition, form the central core of macrobiotic practice and thinking. Thus, the macrobiotic way of life is the basic foundation of all philosophies, religions, and traditional ways of life, and serves to integrate body, mind, spirit, and humanity. Freed from all conditional contraints, we can more freely follow the Path of Liberation. The goal is Absolute Freedom, Absolute Justice, and Absolute Happiness.

When Fasting (eating only what is essential for life) and Prayer (honest and sincere self-reflection) join hands, can Enlightenment and World Peace be far beyond?

> "Let us hear the conclusion of the whole matter: [know] God, and keep his commandments: for this is the whole duty of man."
>
> —from Ecclesiastes XII: 13
> *Old Testament*

Postscript

With all due respect to the contributions of biochemical and technological medicine, though the occurrence of infectious disease due to lack of hygiene and sanitation has decreased, it is more and more apparent that these remedies are not applicable to the overwhelming incidence of degenerative disease.

It is also quite possible that the weakening of the human organism and the immune system due to the chemicalization of food, water, and air, together with the biochemical inundation of the body with vaccinations, immunizations, antibiotics, medications, and drugs, has led the way to lowered resistance and higher susceptibility to the degenerative process.

Without a profound knowledge of the structure and function of the life-force, "the conception/constitution of the universe," as George Ohsawa expressed, no real healing—on the physiological, psychological, social, or ideological levels—can take place.

It is the time to make use of all the healing wisdom available to us on the planet today. Let us all learn together, share together, grow together, and benefit together.

Wind chimes
Each strung separately in the wind,
Yet together forming a whole.
The wind through each is
the harmony among them all.

Not one
Strives, compares, desires;
Its quality is its only action.
Infinity sounds
according to each tone.

Cecile Tovah Levin

About the Author

Cecile Tovah Levin was born in Brooklyn, New York in 1937, as Cecil Tova Blum. Since childhood she has experienced the world in a state of Light, seeing that it is created in an orderly fashion according to natural laws. Going out of the body in pillars of Light-Fire, the early illuminations revealed to her served as beacons through the difficulties of the ensuing years. During World War II, awakening to her sorrow of the world, she sought for a way to interpret her visions to the people and to help guide them out of their strife into the state of pure joy revealed in the visions.

Discovering Macrobiotics in 1960, she was able to cure her borderline leukemia within the first year. Cecile recognized Macrobiotics immediately as a complete path of self-cultivation, promoting health, emotional stability, long life, healthy children, harmonious relationships, natural ecology, social stability, and world peace. On a personal level, the ultimate goal is enlightenment and liberation. Several years ago, Cecile took Bodhisattva vows, devoting her life to serving others.

Cecile has been a student and teacher of the macrobiotic way of life since 1960. She has studied macrobiotic healing extensively with George and Lima Ohsawa, Michio and Aveline Kushi, Herman and Cornellia Aihara, Hideo Omori, Noboru Muramoto, and other Eastern and Western masters of traditional healing arts.

During an intensive six-year study in Japan, Cecile earned her Teacher's Certificate in Macrobiotic Cooking for Health and Spiritual Development from Mme. Lima Ohsawa. She also studied such health and spiritual disciplines as Palm Healing, Shiatsu, Do-In, Sotai, Katsugen Undo, Taoist Esoteric Yoga, and Meditation.

Cecile holds a B.A. in teaching from the State University of New York and an M.A. degree from New York University. She has studied at the University of Besançon in France, the New School for Social Research in New York, the National University of Metaphysics in Los Angeles, the World University of Ojai, the Acupressure Workshop in Los Angeles, and with the psychic healers in the Philippines. She is presently pursuing studies in Buddhism, Taoism, Chi Kung, and the Kabbalah, and has joined the ranks of Firewalkers.

Cecile is a Neuro-Linguistic Programming therapist, an Early Age and Past Life Regression therapist, and an Ordained Metaphysical Minister and Practitioner, licensed by the State of California to perform weddings and funeral rites. She is also the mother of two daughters, both born by natural childbirth, the second one all alone in less than one hour. They have both grown up macrobiotically without animal food, dairy, sugar, vaccinations, innoculations, or medications of any kind, and are fully enjoying good health.

Cecile is a certified Senior Teacher and Dietary Counselor and Senior Cooking Teacher as qualified by both Michio Kushi and the East West Foundation. She has been a member of the Kushi Institute Teacher Certification Review Boards in Boston and Switzerland as well as a Co-Chairwoman of the yearly North American Macrobiotic Congress. She is also a founding member of, and consultant on, Healing Foods for the Kusa Research Foundation, concerned with research and banking of ancient seeds and healing foods.

As a lifelong student of the universal principles underlying health and spiritual awareness, Cecile has presented Macrobiotic teachings across the United States, in Europe, Hong Kong, India, and Japan, and has taught in universities and wholistic health-training centers. Since 1973, Cecile has been dedicated to integrating the traditional macrobiotic way of life into the modern world through the activities of the West Los Angeles East West Center, now the Los Angeles East West Center.

For further information on East West Centers and certified/qualified teachers and counselors in your area, please contact:

The Kushi Foundation
17 Station Street
Brookline Village, MA 02147
(617) 738–0045

George Ohsawa Macrobiotic Foundation
1511 Robinson Street
Oroville, CA 95965
(916) 533–7702

The following Senior Teachers and Counselors may also be of help:

Marc Van Cauwenberghe
Kushi Foundation
PO Box 1100
Brookline, MA 02147
(617) 738–0045

Edward Esko
Kushi Foundation
PO Box 1100
Brookline, MA 02147
(617) 738–0045

Wendy Esko
Lower Main Street
Becket, MA 01223
(413) 623–5645

Richard France
Kushi Foundation
PO Box 1100
Brookline, MA 02147
(617) 738–0045

Cecile Levin
L.A. East West Center
11215 Hannum Avenue
Culver City, CA 90230
(213) 398–2228

Michael Rossoff
4905 Del Ray Avenue, #400
Bethesda, MD 20814
(301) 656–6545

Bill Spear
Cathole Road
Bantam, CT. 06750
(203) 567–8801

Lino Stanchich
Macrobiotic Foundation of Florida
3291 Franklin Avenue
Coconut Grove, FL 33134
(305) 444–7303

Michael Swain
40 Burroughs Street
Jamaica Plain, MA 02130
(617) 524–7378

William Tara
Star Route, Box 68-A
Hudson, N.Y. 12534
(518) 851–9031

Denny Waxman
1321 Wynnewood Road
Ardmore, PA 19003
(215) 642–4336

Mary Wynn
Center for Traditional Macrobiotics
673 Lincoln Avenue
St. Paul, MN 55105
(612) 224–0638

Murray Snyder
604 E. Joppa Road
Towson, MD 21204
(301) 321–4474

Shizuko Yamamoto
Macrobiotic Center of New York
611 Broadway
New York, N.Y. 11206
(212) 505–1010

Also:

Steve Gagne
RR-8, Box 320 Arrowhead Road
Hopewell Junction, N.Y. 12533
(914) 226–6972

Sandy Pukel
Macrobiotic Foundation of Florida
3291 Franklin Avenue
Coconut Grove, FL 33133
(305) 448–6625

Glossary

aburage Deep-fried tofu.

agar-agar A white gelatin derived from a species of seaweed. Used in making *kanten* and aspic.

age Abbreviation for aburage.

ai knife A Japanese vegetable knife with a pointed tip.

ame A natural grain sweetener made from either rice, barley or wheat, or a combination of grains. Frequently called rice honey or yinnie syrup.

amazake A sweetener or refreshing drink made from fermented sweet rice.

arrowroot A starch flour processed from the root of a native American plant. It is used as a thickening agent, similar to cornstarch or *kuzu*, for making sauces, stews, gravies, or desserts.

azuki beans A small, dark red bean imported from Japan, and also grown in the U.S.A. Especially good for the kidneys.

bancha tea Correctly named Kukicha, bancha consists of the stems and leaves from tea bushes that are at least three years old. It is grown in Japan. Bancha tea aids digestion and is high in calcium. It contains no chemical dyes or caffeine. Bancha makes an excellent after-dinner beverage. Green leaf tea has caffeine.

bok choy A leafy green vegetable.

bonito flakes Fish flakes shaved from dried bonito fish. Used in soup stocks or as a garnish for soups and noodle dishes.

brown rice miso A fermented soybean paste made from brown rice, soybeans, and sea salt.

burdock A wild, hardy plant that grows throughout most of the United States. The long, dark root is highly valued in macrobiotic cooking for its strengthening qualities. The Japanese name is gobo.

chirimen iriko Very small dried fish. High in iron and calcium.

chow mein Chinese-style deep-fried noodle dish served with a vegetable sauce over it.

chuba Small dried sardines, used for seasoning soups, making condiments, in salads, and so on.

couscous Partially refined, cracked wheat.

daikon A long, white radish. Besides making a delicious side dish, daikon is a specific for cutting fat and mucus deposits that have accumulated in our bodies as a result of past animal food intake. Grated daikon aids in the digestion of oily foods.

dentie A black tooth powder made from sea salt and charred eggplant.

dulse A reddish-purple sea vegetable used in soups, salads, and vegetable dishes. Very high in iron.

Foley food mill A special steel food mill, which is operated by a hand crank to make purées, sauces, dips, and so on.

fu Dried wheat gluten cakes or sheets. Very high in protein.

furikake Dried powdered condiment made of a variety of ingredients.

ganmodoki A deep-fried cake made from *tofu* and a variety of different vegetables.

gazpacho Cold chick-pea soup. Usually served in the summer with raw vegetables cut into very small pieces and served on top of the soup.

genmai miso Miso made from brown rice, soybeans, and sea salt.

ginger A spicy, pungent, golden-colored root, used in cooking and for medicinal purposes.

ginger compress Sometimes called a ginger fomentation. A compress made from grated ginger root and water. Applied hot to an affected area of the body, it will stimulate circulation and dissolve stagnation.

gluten The sticky substance that remains after the bran has been kneaded and rinsed from flour. Used to make seitan and fu.

gomashio A condiment made from roasted, ground sesame seeds and sea salt.

Hatcho miso A soybean paste made from soybeans and sea salt and aged for at least three years. Used in making condiments, soup stocks, seasoning for vegetable dishes, and so on.

hijiki A dark brown sea vegetable which, when dried, turns black. It is strong and wiry. Hijiki is native to Japan, but also grows off the coast of Maine.

Hokkaido pumpkin A round, dark green or orange squash, which is very sweet. It is harvested in early fall. Originated in New England, introduced into Japan, and named after the island of Hokkaido.

Irish moss Type of sea vegetable found in the Atlantic Ocean and used for centuries in Europe. Known for its natural gelatinous properties.

ito soba A very thin, short soba noodle.

jinenjo A light brown Japanese mountain potato which grows to be several feet long and two to three inches wide.

jinenjo soba Noodles made in Japan from jinenjo (mountain potato) flour and buckwheat flour.

Julienne Cut in finely slivered pieces.

kanpyo Dried gourd strips. Used to tie cabbage rolls.

kanten A jelled dessert made from agar-agar.

kasha knishes Cakes made from buckwheat wrapped in a pastry dough and baked.

kasha varnitchkes Fried buckwheat, with bow noodles and onions.

kasu-jiru Soup made from vegetables and saké lees. Sometimes contains fish or shellfish. Usually prepared in winter. Known for its warming effect on the body.

kayu Long-cooked grain prepared with approximately five times as much water as grain. Kayu is ready when it is very soft and creamy.

kenchin soup Soup made from left-over vegetable trimmings and fresh or fried tofu.

kinako Roasted soybean flour.

kinpira A sautéed burdock or burdock and carrot dish, which is seasoned with tamari.

kiriboshi daikon Shredded dried daikon.

koi-koku Miso soup made from carp, burdock, bancha leaves, and miso. Known for its medicinal properties.

koji Grain that has been innoculated with *Aspergillus oryzae* mold and used in making such fermented foods and drinks as miso, tamari, amazaké and saké.

kombu A wide, thick, dark green sea vegetable which grows in deep ocean water. Used in making soup stocks, vegetable dishes, condiments, candies, medicinal and many other preparations.

kombu dashi A soup broth made from kombu and water.

kome miso White rice miso made from white rice, soybeans, and sea salt.

kukicha Lower stems and twigs of the bancha tea bush grown in Japan.

kuzu A white starch made from the root of the wild kuzu plant. In this country the plant is called "kudzu." Used in making soups, sauces, gravies, desserts, and for medicinal purposes.

layering method A method of cooking soups, vegetables, beans, and grains, in which ingredients are layered in the cooking pot in ascending order from yin to yang.

lotus root The root of a variety of water lily which is brown-skinned with a hollow, chambered, off-white inside. Especially good for respiratory organs.

mekabu Roots of the wakame. Used in making soups and soup stocks. Has a strong flavor.

mirin A sweet Japanese cooking wine or sherry made from rice.

miso A fermented soybean paste used as a base for soups and sauces.

mochi A rice cake or dumpling made from cooked, pounded sweet rice.

moromi Immature miso. Usually used as a condiment or in preparing condiments.

mugicha A tea made out of roasted, unhulled barley and water.

mugi miso Soybean paste made from barley, soybeans, sea salt, and water.

mugwort A wild plant which can be dried and made into tea, or pounded with sweet rice to make mugwort mochi. Has medicinal properties.

mu tea A tea made from sixteen different herbs. It is very yang and has certain medicinal values.

nabe A one-dish meal, prepared and served in a colorfully decorated earthenware casserole and served with a dipping sauce or broth made of either tamari or miso.

natto Soybeans which have been cooked and mixed with beneficial enzymes and allowed to ferment for 24 hours under a controlled temperature.

natto miso A condiment miso, which is a variation of natto. It is made from soybeans, grain, ginger, and kombu and fermented for a very short time.

nigari Hard, crystallized salt made from the liquid drippings of dampened sea salt. Used in making tofu.

nori Thin sheets of dried sea vegetable. Black or dark purple when dried. Used as a garnish, wrapped around rice balls, in making sushi, or cooked with tamari and used as a condiment.

nori maki Often called sushi. Rice rolled in nori with a combination of ingredients such as vegetables, pickles, fish, shiso leaves, fried tofu. Sliced into small bite-size rounds.

ohagi A rice cake made from cooked, pounded sweet rice and coated with azuki beans, chestnuts, roasted, chopped or ground nuts, sesame seeds, or soybean flour.

ojiya Soft rice and vegetables which have been cooked for a long time. Usually seasoned with sea salt, tamari, or miso. Fish, shellfish, beans, and fried tofu are often used in preparing different kinds of ojiya. Known for its medicinal properties.

okara The coarse soybean pulp left over when making tofu. Cooked with vegetables.

ramen A Chinese-style quick-cooking noodle which has been previously deep-fried and then dried. Made from buckwheat, wheat or rice flour.

red (aka) miso A short-time fermented miso, made from rice koji. soybeans, and sea salt.

saifun A clear noodle made from mung beans. Used in salads, soups, and vegetable dishes. Sometimes called *Beifun*.

saké A Japanese wine made from rice. Usually served warm in small cups.

saké lees Fermented residue left after making saké. Used in soups and in vegetable and pickle dishes.

sashimi Raw, sliced fish.

sea salt Salt obtained from the ocean as opposed to land salt. It is either sun-baked or kiln-baked. High in trace minerals, it contains no chemicals or sugar.

seitan Wheat gluten cooked in tamari, kombu, and water.

sengiri Cut in finely slivered pieces.

shiitake A medicinal, dried mushroom imported from Japan.

shio kombu Pieces of kombu cooked for a long time in tamari and used in small amounts as a condiment.

shio nori Pieces of nori cooked in tamari or tamari and water. Used as a condiment.

shiso Pickled beefsteak plant leaves.

soba Noodles made from buckwheat flour or a combination of buckwheat flour with whole wheat flour or jinenjo flour.

somen Very thin, white or wholewheat Japanese noodles. Often served during the summer.

su Japanese rice or brown rice vinegar.

surikogi A wooden pestle that is used with a *suribachi.*

sukiyaki A one-dish meal prepared in a large cast-iron skillet, containing a variety of vegetables, noodles, sea vegetables, seitan, tofu, fish, and so on.

suribachi A special serrated, glazed clay bowl. Used with a pestle (called a *surikogi*) for grinding and puréeing foods.

sushi Rice rolled with vegetables, fish, or pickles, wrapped in nori and sliced into rounds.

sushi mat A mat made from strips of bamboo tied together with string. Used in making sushi, or as a cover for bowls.

takuan Daikon which is pickled in rice bran and sea salt. Sometimes spelled "takuwan."

taro A potato which has a thick, hairy skin. Often called albi. Used in making taro or albi plasters to draw toxins from the body, or can be eaten as a vegetable.

tamari Name given to traditional, naturally made soy sauce to distinguish it from the commercial, chemically processed variety.

tekka Condiment made from Hatcho miso, sesame oil, burdock, lotus root, carrot, and ginger root. Sautéed on a low flame for several hours.

tempeh A dish made from split soybeans, vinegar, water, and *Rhizopus oligosporus* bacteria, which is allowed to ferment for several hours. Eaten in Indonesia and Ceylon as a staple food. Available prepacked, ready to cook, in some natural food stores.

tempura Sliced vegetables, fish, or patties made of grain, vegetables, fish, tofu, and so on, which are dipped into a batter and deep-fried until golden brown.

tendon A one-dish meal consisting of rice served with tempuraed vegetables with a light tamari broth served over it.

tentsuyu A tempura dip made with soup broth, tamari, saké and ginger.

tofu A cake made from soybeans, nigari, and water.

toshi koshi soba Plain soba and broth. Traditionally served at midnight on New Year's Eve in Japan. Literally means "long-life soba." Is also served often as part of the daily diet.

udon Japanese noodles made from wheat, whole wheat, or whole wheat and unbleached white flour.

umeboshi A salty pickled plum (apricot).

unohana Another name for "okara," which is the soybean pulp left over from making tofu.

wakame A long, thin, green sea vegetable used in making soups, salads, vegetable dishes, and condiments.

wasabi Grated Japanese horseradish.

white (shiro) miso A sweet, short-time fermented miso, made from rice, soybeans, rice koji, and sea salt.

wok A deep, round Chinese skillet.

yannoh A grain coffee made from five different grains and beans which have been roasted and ground into a fine powder.

yellow miso A short-time fermented miso, very mellow in flavor. Made from rice koji, soybeans, rice, and sea salt.

yuba Dried soy milk skin.

zoni A miso soup made from white miso, vegetables, and mochi. Traditionally served in Japan on New Year's Day.

Bibliography

Aihara, Cornellia. *The Calendar Cookbook*. Oroville, Calif.: George Ohsawa Macrobiotic Foundation, 1979.

———. *Chico-San Cookbook*. Chico, Calif.: Chico-San, Inc., 1972.

Aihara, Herman. *Acid and Alkaline*. Oroville, Calif.: George Ohsawa Macrobiotic Foundation, 1980.

———. *Learning from Salmon*. Oroville, Calif.: George Ohsawa Macrobiotic Foundation, 1980.

Carpenter, Edward. *Civilisation: Its Cause and Cure*. Boston, Mass.: TAO Books & Publications, Inc., 1971.

Carrel, Alexis. *Man the Unknown*. New York: Harper and Row; Paris: Plon, 1935.

Chishima, Kikuo. *Revolution of Biology and Medicine*. Japan: Neo-Haematological Society Press, 1972.

De Vries, Arnold. *Primitive Man and His Food*. Chicago, Ill.: Chandler Book Co., 1952.

Dufty, William. *Sugar Blues*. New York: Warner Publications, 1975.

East West Foundation. *Cancer and Diet*. Brookline, Massachusetts, East West Publications, 1980.

———. *A Dietary Approach to Cancer According to the Principles of Macrobiotics*. Brookline, Massachusetts, East West Publications, (from *Macrobiotic Cuisine*, by Lima Ohsawa)

———. *A Nutritional Approach to Cancer*. Brookline, Massachusetts, East West Publications, (from *Macrobiotic Cuisine*, by Lima Ohsawa)

———. *Standard Recommendations for Diet and Way of Life*. Brookline, Mass.: East West Publications, (from *Macrobiotic Cuisine*, by Lima Ohsawa)

Esko, Edward and Wendy. *Macrobiotic Cooking for Everyone*. Tokyo: Japan Publications, Inc., 1980.

Esko, Wendy, *Aveline Kushi's Introducing Macrobiotic Cooking*. Tokyo: Japan Publications, Inc. 1987.

Fukuoka, Masanobu. *The One-Straw Revolution: An Introduction to Natural Farming*. Emmaus, PA: Rodale Press, 1978.

———. *The Natural Way of Farming*. Tokyo: Japan Publications, Inc., 1985.

———. *The Road Back to Nature: Regaining the Paradise Lost*. Tokyo: Japan Publications, Inc., 1987.

Gilbert, Margaret Shea. *Biography of the Unborn*. New York: Hagner Press, 1962.

Hettinger, E. *Springs of Indian Wisdom*. Oakland, Marcel Schurman Co., Inc., not dated.

Hsu, Hong-Yen; Preacher, William G. *Shang Han Lun—The Great Classic of Chinese Medicine*. Los Angeles: Oriental Healing Arts Institute, 1981.

Jacobson and Brewster. *The Changing American Diet*. Washington, D. C.: Center for Science in the Public Interest, (from *Macrobiotic Cuisine*, by Lima Ohsawa)

The Jewish Publication Society of America. *The Torah—The Five Books of Moses*. The Jewish Publication Society of America, Phila., PA, 1962.

Keegan, Marcia. *Pueblo & Navajo Cookery*. Earth Books. Morgan & Morgan, 1977.

Kervran, C. Louis. *Transmutations Biologiques*. Paris: Librarie Maloine S. A., 1963.

Kohler, Jean and Mary Alice. *Healing Miracles from Macrobiotics*. West Nyack, N. Y.: Parker Publishing Co., 1979.

Kushi, Aveline. *How to Cook with Miso*. Tokyo: Japan Publications, Inc., 1978.

Kushi, Michio. *Acupuncture: Ancient and Future Worlds*. TAO Publications, Boston, Mass., 1973.

———. *The Book of Macrobiotics: The Universal Way of Health, Happiness, and Peace* (Revised edition). Tokyo: Japan Publications, Inc., 1987.

———. *The Book of Dō-In: Exercise for Physical and Spiritual Development*. Tokyo: Japan Publications, Inc., 1979.

———. *Cancer and Heart Disease: The Macrobiotic Approach to Degenerative Disorders* (Revised edition). Tokyo: Japan Publications, Inc. 1985.

———. *How to See Your Health: The Book of Diagnosis*. Tokyo: Japan Publications, Inc., 1980.

———. *Macrobiotic Home Remedies*. Tokyo: Japan Publications, Inc., 1985.

———. *The Macrobiotic Way* Wayne. New Jersey: Avery Publishing Group, Inc., 1985.

———. *Natural Healing through Macrobiotics*. Tokyo: Japan Publications, Inc., 1978.

———. *On the Greater View* Wayne. New Jersey: Avery Publishing Group, Inc., 1986.

———. *Oriental Diagnosis*. London: Sunwheel, Ltd., 1978.

———. *The Spiral of Life*. Boston, East West Foundation, 1972.

———. *The Teachings of Michio Kushi, Vol. I*; Boston, East West Foundation, 1971.

———. *The Teachings of Michio Kushi, Vol. II*; Boston, East West Foundation, 1971.

Kushi, Aveline and Wendy Esko. *Changing Seasons Macrobiotic Cookbook*. Wayne, N. J.: Avery Publishing Group, Inc., 1985.

Kushi, Michio and Aveline. *Macrobiotic Child Care and Family Health*. Tokyo: Japan Publications, Inc., 1986.

Kushi, Michio, and Alex Jack. *Cancer Prevention Diet*. New York: St. Martin's Press, 1983.

Mendelsohn, Robert S., M.D. *Confessions of a Medical Heretic*. Chicago, Ill.: Contemporary Books, 1979.

Moon, Yogamundi. *A Macrobiotic Explanation of Pathological Calcification*. San Francisco: George Ohsawa Macrobiotic Foundation, 1974.

Morishita, Kieichi. *The Hidden Truth of Cancer*. Oroville, Calif.: George Ohsawa Macrobiotic Foundation, 1978.

Muramoto, Noboru. *Healing Ourselves*. New York: Avon, London: Michael Dempsey/ Cassell, 1973.

Omori, Hideo. *Macrobiotic Notes*. Tokyo: Intermac, Nippon C. I. Foundation, 1977.

Ohsawa, George. *Acupuncture and the Philosophy of the Far East*. Boston, Mass.: Tao Books, 1973.

———. *Atomic Age and the Philosophy of the Far East*. George Ohsawa Macrobiotic Foundation, 1977.

———. *The Book of Judgment*. Los Angeles: George Ohsawa Macrobiotic Foundation,——.

———. *Cancer and the Philosophy of the Far East*. Binghamton, N. Y.: Swan House, 1971.

———. *Guidebook for Living*. Los Angeles: George Ohsawa Macrobiotic Foundation, 1967.

———. *The Order of the Universe*. Oroville, Calif.: George Ohsawa Macrobiotic Foundation, 1986.

———. *Practical Guide to Far-Eastern Macrobiotic Medicine*. Oroville, Calif.: George Ohsawa Macrobiotic Foundation, 1973.

———. *The Unique Principle*. Oroville, Calif.: George Ohsawa Macrobiotic Foundation, 1973.

———. *Zen Macrobiotics*. Los Angeles: George Ohsawa Macrobiotic Foundation, 1965.

Ohsawa, Lima. *The Art of Just Cooking*. Tokyo. Autumn Press, 1974.

———. *Macrobiotic Cuisine*. Tokyo: Japan Publications, Inc., 1984.

Sacks, Castelli, Donner, and Kass. "Plasma Lipids and Lipoproteins in Vegetarians and Controls." Boston: New England Journal of Medicine. May 29, 1975.

Sacks, Rosner, and Kass. "Blood Pressure in Vegetarians." American Journal of Epidemiology, Vol. 100, No. 5, Baltimore: Johns Hopkins University.

Sakurazawa, Nyoiti. (George Ohsawa), edited by Dufty, William. *Macrobiotics*. London: Tandem Books. Published in the U.S.A. under the title *You are All Sanpaku*. New York: University Books, 1965.

Select Committee on Nutrition and Human Needs, U.S. Senate. *Dietary Goals for the United States*. February 1977.

Soyka, Fred. *The Ion Effect*. New York: E. P. Dutton & Co., Inc., 1977.

Surgeon General's Report on Health Promotion and Disease Prevention. *Healthy People*. Washington, D. C.: September, 1979.

Szekely, Edmond Bordeaux. *The Essene Gospel of Peace*. San Diego, Calif.: Academy Books, 1977.

———. *The Essene Gospel of Peace—Book Two*. San Diego, Calif.: Academy Books, 1975.

Veith, Ilza. *The Yellow Emperor's Classic of Internal Medicine*. London: University Microfilms, Inc., 1949.

Wilhelm and Baynes. *I Ching*. Princeton: Princeton University Press, 1961.

Yamamoto, Shizuko. *Barefoot Shiatsu*. Tokyo: Japan Publications, Inc.; 1979.

Periodicals for Further Reading:

East West Journal. Brookline, Massachusetts.

Le Compas. Paris.

The Macrobiotic Review. Baltimore, Maryland. East West Foundation.

Macrobiotics Today. Oroville, Calif. Vega/George Ohsawa Macrobiotic Foundation.

Macromuse. Rockville, Maryland. Now *Solstice*.

Nutrition Action. Washington, D. C.: Center for Science in the Public Interest.

The Order of the Universe. Brookline, Mass. East West Foundation.

Spiral. Community Health Foundation, London.

American Cancer Society. *Cancer Statistics* **1985**. Ca-A Cancer Journal for Clinicians, Vol. 35, No. 1. New York, Jan/Feb 1985.

Articles by the author:

"Illuminating Macrobiotics," Everyday Life, Fall 1986.

"Fruit," Macrobiotics Today, Sept. 1987.

"The Blue-Green Algae Controversy," Macromuse No. 29, Dec. 1987/Jan. 1988.

"The Art and Science of Macrobiotics." Whole Life Monthly, Jan. 1988.

"The Lifestyle Diet," interview by Carolyn Reuben, L. A. Weekly, Jan. 22–28, 1988.

"Macrobiotic Perspectives on Vitamin C," Whole Life Monthly, Feb. 1988.

"Manifestation of Planetary Peace—The Macrobiotic Way," Conscious Connection, Feb.–March 1988.

"Macrobiotic Perspectives: Miso Soup, Fruit and Time," originally "Evolution of Fruit and Grain," Whole Life Monthly, March 1988.

"Michio Kushi Seminar Report," Macrobiotics Today, March 1988.

"Macrobiotic Perspectives: On Desserts," Published as "The Biological Degeneration of America," Whole Life Times, April 1988.

"Macrobiotic Perspectives: Macrobiotics in the Modern World," Macrobiotics Today, April 1988.

"Macrobiotic Perspectives: The Stages of Practice," published as "Vegetables versus Meat—A Difference between East and West," Whole Life Times, May 1988.

"Macrobiotic Perspective on AIDS," Whole Life Times, June 1988.

"Macrobiotic Perspectives: The Nature of Happiness," Whole Life Times, July 1988.

Index